OTAGO GERMAN STUDIES
Edited by August Obermayer
Vol. 19

Department of Languages and Cultures
German Section, University of Otago
Dunedin, New Zealand

All rights reserved. No part of this publication may be reproduced or transmitted in any way or by any means, except for brief quotation in reviews or criticism, without the express permission of the Copyright holder.

© by the editor of Otago German Studies

Originally published in New Zealand by:

Department of Languages and Cultures
German Studies Section, University of Otago
P O Box 56, Dunedin, New Zealand, 2005

Note: This print-on-demand edition is undertaken by Threshold Publishing, in 2018, on behalf of the Department of Languages and Cultures, German Studies Section, of Otago University, through kind permission of the Editor, Professor August Obermayer.

ISBN:97806481358-2-1

ADRIAN ANDERSON

DRAMATIC ANTHROPOSOPHY

Identification and contextualization of
primary features of Rudolf Steiner's 'anthroposophy',
as expressed in his "Mystery Drama',
Die Pforte der Einweihung (The Portal of Initiation)

University of Otago
Department of Languages and Cultures
German Section
Dunedin
2005

1 INTRODUCTION

Introduction A

1A: The conceptual context of Steiner's worldview

1A1: Steiner's early interest in cognition, spirituality and drama	p.1

1A2: Steiner's spiritual-holistic epistemology	p.8

1A3: Steiner's involvement in Theosophy and esoteric-spiritual drama p.31

1A4: The reception of Steiner's spiritual worldview and his break with the Theosophical Society	p.34

Introduction B

1B: The Romantic context: themes from Goethe and Schiller viewed as formative by Steiner in early years, and viewed as supportive to his 'anthroposophy' in later years

1B1: Schiller's esoteric religiosity (Egyptian Mysteries) and pre-existence	p.46

1B2: Goethe's 'primal skeleton', 'primal plant' and Steiner's 'life-force'	p.66

1B3: Goethe's esoteric religiosity (the Rosicrucians) and a Platonic 'Devachan'	p.79

1B4: Goethe's fairy tale provides the thematic basis of *Die Pforte*	p.91

2 DIE PFORTE, AN OUTLINE OF ITS STRUCTURE AND THEMES

2a: Describing supra-sensible phenomena, metaphor, 'transferring' German into English, including Steiner's neologisms	p.112

2b: An overview of the scenes in *Die Pforte*	p.133

3 THE SCENES OF THE *PFORTE DER EINWEIHUNG*

3a: Prelude: p.154

3b: Scene One p.158

3c: Scene Two p.166

3d: Scene Three p.171

3e: Scene Four p.174

3f: Scene Five p.194

3g: Scene Six p.199

3h: Scene Seven p.200

3i: Interlude p.206

3j: Scene Eight p.208

3k: Scene Nine p.217

3l: Scene Ten p.227

3m: Scene Eleven p.232

4 THE PRIMARY FEATURES OF STEINER'S ANTHROPOSOPHY EXPRESSED IN *DIE PFORTE*

4a: The dramatic elements of Das Märchen provide the template for Die Pforte, but these are adapted for didactic purposes with regard to Steiner's esoteric worldview p.237

4b: Steiner's view of the spirituality portrayed in Die Pforte is quintessentially expressed by his interpretation of Goethe p.258

4c: The concepts of reincarnation and karma are seen as compatible to Christianity, and are understood to have a rational basis p.270

4d: Steiner's earlier holistic epistemology is based on a proto-type of the 'ether-body' postulate p.282

4e: Steiner's holistic epistemological conviction that the limits to knowledge may be extended, is reflected in *Die Pforte*'s portrayal of the efficacy of meditation   p.292

4f: A major element in Steiner's anthroposophy is an esoteric-mystical Christian perspective, in which a connection between conscience and the Second Coming – as understood by Steiner – has a discrete role   p.310

4g: The spiritual development process underlying *Die Pforte* is derived from the view of the human being as an interrelated septenary organism of body, soul, self and spirit   p.316

5   FINAL CONCLUSIONS   p.326

6   BIBLIOGRAPHY   p.329

PREFACE

Rudolf Steiner, 1861-1925, was known until 1901, as a Goethe scholar and author of epistemological texts which argue for the inherent validity of sensory perception, and for ethical individualism. In 1902 he began teaching a spiritual worldview, arguing against the prevailing reductionist attitudes. Steiner's views did not become part of mainstream debate in his lifetime, but his views do have an influence in society today, through the practical application of his ideas. This includes the international Steiner school movement, bio-dynamic agriculture, and his medical therapies. But, as of August 2004, Steiner's esoteric-spiritual worldview had not been academically assessed.

This text is a slightly revised doctoral thesis, undertaken on a scholarship awarded by Monash University, which identifies and contextualizes the primary tenets of Steiner's 'anthroposophical' worldview by an examination of the didactic intentions in his play, "*Die Pforte der Einweihung*" (The Portal of Initiation), written in 1910. This play is Steiner's dramatization of a fairy tale by Goethe, *Das Märchen*. It is substantially modified in Steiner's drama, to reduce the allegorical element, and to allow the process of spiritual development to be portrayed in personalities.

Spiritual themes are examined in Schiller and Goethe which were either formative for his earlier phase, or affirmative for his later phase. In particular, Goethe's notion of an 'Urpflanze' and his 'Proteus', are significant to Steiner. He sees the former as indicative of the Platonic realm of the Idea, and the latter as an 'ether energy', which provides validation of sensory perception. The problem of interpreting Steiner's texts and rendering these into English is also considered. The thematic and rhetorical elements of each scene in *Die Pforte* are examined. Elements in its plot which deviate from the Goethean 'template' reveal significant aspects of Steiner's anthroposophy.

Major elements of Steiner's 'anthroposophical' worldview, expressed in the rhetoric of *Die Pforte*, include reincarnation and karma. These are seen as real dynamics affecting human life, and are viewed as compatible with Christianity. Additionally, human cognitional power can be extended beyond its present boundary, through meditation. The Kantian limits to knowledge are therefore invalid because meditation gives access to higher consciousness states. Further, human life is seen as unfolding on Earth as a microcosmic reflection of a sevenfold macrocosmic evolutionary process.

The attainment of spiritual consciousness is made dependent upon the ethical improvement of the human being. A significant aspect of human spirituality is the conscience. Although the role of religion is minimal in *Die Pforte*, the conscience is subject to enhancement by influences from Christ Jesus. In addition, to Steiner the continuance of unethical activity and attitudes in humanity is harmful to the Earth as a living being, or an organism possessing subtle levels of being.

In the quest for spiritual development, the triune human soul (consisting of thinking, emotion and will) is caught between the influences of not one, but two, fallen spirit beings. However, the soul can bring to expression in itself a triune spiritual quality (of wisdom, purity and goodwill), and attain to the realm of the Idea.

The message of *Die Pforte* is also that the arts offer a valuable method for the instruction in spiritual themes, and artistic experience provides valuable assistance in attaining to spirituality. In so far as this text is an assessment of a written work from Steiner, *The Portal of Initiation*, it is also the first academic critique of one of Steiner's anthroposophical literary texts; the author wishes to thank Assoc. Professor Walter Veit for his invaluable advice in this task.

Finally I would also like to thank Monash University for its generous financial contribution to the University of Otago towards the cost of publishing this work.

1 INTRODUCTION

The conceptual context of Steiner's worldview

INTRODUCTION A
1A1: Steiner's early interest in spirituality, cognition and drama

Rudolf Steiner was born on the Austrian-Hungarian border in 1861, to Catholic Austrian parents, his father worked as a railway employee. During his childhood and youth the family lived in villages in Lower Austria, in the Austria-Hungarian empire, he undertook his tertiary studies in Vienna. Steiner reports in his autobiography that already as a school child he had an interest in attaining to a spiritual worldview, but one which was inherently rational. His school years were spent in small towns in Lower Austria in state schools, namely, Mödling, Pottschach and Neudörfl. He spent much of his free time at home working on mathematical exercises, which exerted a fascination for him.[1]

In his autobiography he writes that he had an awareness that mathematical truths are precise facts, or realities, which have no physical existence and yet they are discovered by the human mind. This realization opened his mind to the idea that other equally precise and objective facts could perhaps be discovered by the enquiring human mind concerning spiritual realities, if appropriately trained.[2] At the age of fourteen, he avidly read a primary epistemological text of Emmanuel Kant (1724-1804), *Kritik der reinen Vernunft (Critique of Pure Reason)*.[3] He applied himself to his schooling and won a

---

[1] Rudolf Steiner, Mein Lebensgang, (Stuttgart: Verlag Freies Geistesleben, 1975), 17.
[2] Steiner, Lebensgang, 23.
[3] Steiner, Lebensgang, 22.

place in tertiary education at Vienna (the "Technische Hochschule").[4] His tertiary studies included mathematics, natural history, chemistry, physics, and additionally he audited botany, mineralogy and geology and also constitutional law.[5]

As a young man his meditative life gave rise to inner experiences, which, he concluded, constituted a basis on which to reject the strengthening scientific-reductionist perspectives of the nineteenth century. Yet there is virtually no report of his involvement in any form of spiritual activity as a young man. A letter of Steiner's from 1881 reveals that at the age of 20, his enquiry into the nature of human consciousness was in fact connected with the acceptance of the existence of spiritual reality, both within the human being, and 'behind' the sense-perceptible world. In this letter he reports that he had been reading texts of Schelling (Friedrich Wilhelm Joseph Schelling, 1775 – 1854),

> I had been occupied until half an hour past midnight with several philosophical problems, and then I threw myself onto my bed. In the previous year I had striven to determine whether it was true, what Schelling said; 'We all possess a secret, wondrous capacity, to draw ourselves out of the changing flow of time, away from all that comes to us externally and into our innermost being, our unveiled self – there we may behold the eternal in us, in an unchanging form.' I believed, and believe still today, that I had discovered this innermost capacity very clearly in myself – which I had intuitively sensed for a long time. The entire idealistic philosophy was now viewed by me as having an entirely different form; what does a sleepless night matter, compared to such a find![6]

---

[4] Lindenberg, Steiner, 42, Lindenberg reports that in the 3rd of high school (in Wiener-Neustadt) Steiner was classified as "an advanced student", and was then exempt from fees.
[5] Lindenberg, Steiner, 67.
[6] Steiner, Briefe 1881-1890, (Dornach: Rudolf Steiner Verlag, (hereafter RSV) 1985) 13, „Ich hatte mich bis 1/2 1 Uhr mitternachts mit einzelnen philosophischen Problemen beschäftigt, und da warf ich mich endlich auf

Consequently, it is indicated that already at this age he was focussed on the pursuit of a spiritual reality in human consciousness. However, this did jeopardize his studies in cognition. It was about this time that he was appointed editor of the text-critical edition of the complete works of the philosopher Arthur Schopenhauer. This work was published in twelve volumes in 1894.[7] Steiner corresponded with notable philosophers in these years, including Eduard von Hartmann (1842-1906) and Friedrich Theodor Vischer (1807-1887),[8] Hartmann had sent Steiner a copy of one of his books, and Vischer had encouraged him in his writing.[9]

Steiner's epistemology was taken seriously by these thinkers, but they were not convinced as to the validity of his conclusions. In 1891 Steiner gained his Doctoral thesis for his study in epistemology. His doctoral thesis, Wahrheit und Wissenschaft (Truth and Knowledge) contains the first systematic outline of his view of human consciousness in terms of cognition; it does not refer to any specifically esoteric or 'spiritual' elements. [10]

He added a subtitle to the published thesis, which describes it as "a preamble to a 'philosophy of freedom'". His thesis attempts to establish an inherent validity and reliability of cognition, in opposition to the general agreement in

---

mein Lager; mein Bestreben war voriges Jahr, zu erforschen, ob es denn wahr sei, was Schelling sagt: 'Uns allen wohnt ein geheimes, wunderbares Vermögen bei, uns aus dem Wechsel der Zeit in unser innerstes, von allem, was von außen hinzukam, entkleidetes Selbst, zurückzuziehen und da unter der Form der Unwandelbarkeit das Ewige in uns anzuschauen.' Ich glaubte und glaube nun noch, jenes innerste Vermögen ganz klar an mir entdeckt zu haben - geahnt habe ich es ja schon längst: die ganze idealistische Philosophie steht nun in einer wesentlich modifizierten Gestalt vor mir; was ist eine schlaflose Nacht gegen solch einen Fund!"

[7] Arthur Schopenhauers Sämtliche Werke in 12 Bänden, herausgegeben von Dr. Rudolf Steiner, (Stuttgart: Cottasche Bibliothek der Welt Literature, 1894)
[8] Steiner, Briefe 1, letter No. 12, 20. June 1882, and No. 124, Autumn 1887.
[9] Lindenberg, Steiner 95, 161.
[10] The term, 'Wissenschaft' in the context of Steiner's epistemological thesis, has more the nuance of 'knowledge' than 'science'.

philosophical works, that this was an invalid, naïve view. Steiner then wrote his principle philosophical text, "The Philosophy of Freedom" which was published in 1894.[11] Steiner's academic work in epistemology in the 1880's and 1890's was to form a philosophical perspective which he viewed as affirmative of the viability of the cognitional dynamics inherent in the experiencing of supra-sensible realities.

Steiner eventually became widely known in central Europe in the late nineteenth century through his epistemological studies and his scholarly interpretation and contextualization of the scientific and literary writings of Johann Wolfgang von Goethe. He also became well known for his various lectures on other scientific topics, including physics, metallurgy, the history of science and psychology. Scientific articles of his in the fields of metallurgy and geology were published in a standard reference work.[12] Through his philosophical writings and scientific articles, Steiner had become a respected academic researcher, and received appointment to the Goethe archives in Weimar, to edit the scientific works of Goethe, published in the prestigious Kürschner National Literature series (1882-1897).

He was recommended for this position by a senior academic in Vienna, Karl Julius Schröer (1825-1900). During this time, Steiner was also appointed editor of the Weimarer Ausgabe of the Complete Works of Goethe. Steiner's ability to contextualize the writings of Goethe made him a leading Goethe commentator, bringing recognition from such notable thinkers as Gideon Spicker (1840-1912).[13] In his later years, from 1900 onwards, Rudolf Steiner often elaborated elements in his spiritual worldview with reference to esoteric or mystical passages in the writings of Johann Wolfgang von Goethe (1769-1832) and to a lesser extent, of Friedrich

---

[11] Rudolf Steiner Wahrheit und Wissenschaft: Vorspiel einer Philosophie der Freiheit, (Dornach: Rudolf Steiner Verlag, 1980).
[12] In Piers Konversationslexikon, 1888, articles by Steiner appeared on Basalt, Alluvium and the Ice Ages.
[13] Rudolf Steiner, Briefe 1, 155.

Schiller (1759-1805). In essence, Steiner's later worldview presupposes the capacity to attain to perception of non-material realities. It elaborates the nature of the human soul, of spiritual beings, and the interaction between these.

However, none of his academic editorial activities, nor his own writings from the early period of his life, (pre-1901), refer to spiritual or metaphysical doctrines. They focus on human cognitive processes and literary themes. Steiner neither lectured on, nor wrote about, spiritual-esoteric themes until he was in his early forties. In addition to his work with Goethe and Schiller, and philosophical interests, Steiner was also active, from his twenties to his late thirties, as a literary essayist, editor and theatre critic in Berlin. During the period from approximately 1884-1902, Steiner was very involved in drama and literature, writing reviews of theatrical productions.

This occurred in his capacity as co-editor of a literary magazine, *Magazin für Literatur* (established in 1832) from 1897 until to 1900, and as editor of another magazine, the Dramaturgische Blätter (Dramaturgical Pages) published in Berlin. In addition, in 1898, Steiner co-produced a play "*Der Ungebetene*" (The Intruder") by Maurice Maeterlinck, a well-known contemporary Flemish spiritual-philosophical author. In an article of that year Steiner writes about Maeterlinck's style,

> He believes in a subtle, mysterious interlinking, on the level of the soul, between all things. When two people are in dialogue, he does not only hear the general content of what they say, he also perceives a deeper connection, an unexpressed relationship. And this unspoken, mysterious element he seeks to incorporate into the things and people whom he portrays. Indeed, he regards all external, visible things as only a means to intimate the deeper, the hidden soul element... Whoever is not able through the things and people which he brings onto the stage, to

feel the intimated, deeper essence, can not understand Maeterlinck.[14]

Steiner's attitude here to Maeterlinck here echoes that of other German literary figures, such as Hermann Bahr.[15] Quite early in the body of Maeterlinck literature, this playwright was enthusiastically thought of as belonging more to German than to French cultural circles, and in one dissertation was referred to as a 'German mystic', as Sondi relates. In addition, Steiner's critique reveals his interest in the portrayal on stage of the inner life of the human being.

The interest which Steiner has shown from his youth onwards in the inner life of the human being, is shown in this positive attitude to Maeterlinck's technique of utilizing events and objects on stage to explore the human soul. In the above essay, Steiner comments further, that it becomes clear that the dramatists who are writing more serious works cannot expect their audience to encompass more than a small circle of devotees,

> Every gesture, each movement, each word on the stage is an expression of the underlying worldview {of the playwright}. Whoever keeps in mind these truths realizes that Goethe, Schiller, Ibsen, Maeterlinck can only have an effect on a definite circle of people; on those who can find their way into the worldview of these poets, who can think and feel

---

[14] Rudolf Steiner, <u>Gesammelte Aufsätze zur Dramaturgie</u>, (Dornach: Verlag der Rudolf Steiner Nachlaßverwaltung, (hereafter, VRSN) 1960) 138, „Er glaubt an feine, seelenartige, geheimnisvolle Zusammenhänge in allen Erscheinungen. Wenn zwei Menschen miteinander sprechen, so hört er nicht nur den gemeinen Inhalt ihrer Reden, sondern er nimmt tiefere Beziehungen, unausgesprochene Verhältnisse wahr. Und dieses Unausgesprochene, Geheimnisvolle sucht er in die Dinge und Menschen, die er darstellt, hineinzuarbeiten. Ja, er betrachtet alles Äußerliche, Sichtbare nur als ein Mittel, um das Tieferliegende, Verborgen-Seelische anzudeuten...Wer nicht imstande ist, aus den Dingen und Menschen, die er auf die Bühne bringt, die angedeuteten, tieferen Wesenheiten durchzufühlen, der kann Maeterlinck nicht verstehen."

[15] Peter Szondi, <u>Das lyrische Drama des Fin de Siècle</u>, (Frankfurt am Main: Suhrkamp Verlag, 1975) 355.

as they do. This is the reason why these artists must have limits {to their appeal}.[16]

Steiner's comments are significant with regard to the intention behind his own dramas, which were never placed in the mainstream cultural sphere, but performed for those in esoteric-religious circles which developed around him in his later, spiritual-esoteric phase. This will be examined in a later section.

---

[16] Rudolf Steiner, <u>Gesammelte Aufsätze</u> 138-139, „Jede Gebärde, jede Bewegung, jedes Wort auf der Bühne ist ein Ausdruck der zugrundeliegenden Weltanschauung. Wer sich diese Wahrheiten gegenwärtig hält, wird einsehen, daß Goethe, Schiller, Ibsen, Maeterlinck nur auf einen bestimmten Kreis von Menschen wirken können, auf diejenigen, welche sich in die Weltanschauung dieser Dichter einleben können, welche denken und empfinden können wie sie. Daher rührt es, daß die Wirkung dieser Künstler Grenzen haben muß."

1A2: Steiner's spiritual-holistic epistemology

Steiner had a strong interest in cognition already in his twenties, as we have noted above. His interest in this is further attested to by a comment in his autobiography, concerning a philosophical text from Friedrich Schiller. The Schiller text referred to here is a collection of letters about aesthetics entitled, "*Briefen über die ästhetische Erziehung des Menschen* (*Letters about the aesthetic education of humanity.*)" This reference to Schiller here is important with regard to the question of Steiner's context. There are two aspects to Steiner's debt to the Romantics, one is that of exerting a formative influence, the other is that of providing an affirmative context to his own worldview.

Steiner, speaking and writing as the teacher of a spiritual worldview, from 1902 onwards, (which he termed, 'anthroposophy' a term which shall be examined later in this in Section), frequently draws on material from Goethe and Schiller. However, these references are used to support and elucidate his anthroposophical postulates, and to demonstrate that his own conclusions on spiritual themes are not incompatible with the great Romantics. This is also the case with the incident quoted in Section 1A1, namely, the letter in which he attests to a prior experiential encounter with a spiritual element of human nature, about which he later read in Fichte.

However, in an autobiographical reference to Schiller, Steiner writes that reading this text, at the age of 22, actively assisted his formulation of ideas on cognition. In these writings, Schiller expounds at length on the state of humanity as being subject to dualistic drives, firstly one which he terms the 'form-impulse', derived from intellectuality, and secondly the 'instinctive impulse', derived from the sensory capabilities of the human being. Of the latter he says, "Mit unzerreißbaren Banden fesselt er den höher strebenden Geist an die Sinneswelt, (with indestructible bonds it chains the spirit, which is seeking to elevate itself, to the sense-world)…"[17] This condition excludes from its subject, all autonomy and freedom. Whilst the former condition, the intellectual state, formulates laws which bind one in an immutable condition, "But when the thought once declares, 'this is how it is', it decides for ever and ever, and the validity of its decision is guaranteed by the personality itself, which defies all change."[18] This condition excludes all dependence and passivity.

However, Schiller concludes that there exists the possibility of a third state, which represents the consummation of the human condition. This third state derives from an interplay of the sensory life and the intellectual life; that is, when the specific, 'formed' intellectual consciousness of a person is efficacious in their feelings, and their sensory, emotive life is efficacious in their understanding. Once this condition is attained, then it becomes, says Schiller, "the state of beauty, in the widest sense of this term, because the soul in gazing at beauty, finds itself in a happy condition, between the law and necessity."[19] This is due in part to its situation of being in the balance between the other two states, and hence beauty "…ought to *temper*, through uniformly exciting the two other natures, and it ought also to *excite* through uniformly moderating them."[20]   (emphasis added).

Steiner further summarizes the Schiller text, recounting Schiller's conclusion that a third, intermediary condition is possible, because from the fact that a human being can develop the aesthetic sense, he can also develop an intermediate state of consciousness. He can develop the

---

[17] Schillers Werke, Nationalausgabe, ed. Fricke et al. (Weimar: Hermann Böhlaus Nachfolger, 1943) (hereafter, SW) Bd. 21, S. 345.
[18] Schiller, SW, Bd. 21, 346, „Aber wenn der Gedanke einmal ausspricht, So ist es, so entscheidet er für immer und ewig…"
[19] Schiller, SW, Bd. 21, 357, „Da sich das Gemüt bei Anschauung des Schönen in einer glücklichen Mitte zwischen dem Gesetz und Bedürfnis befindet. "

[20] Schiller, SW, 361, „…soll auflösen, dadurch daß sie beide Naturen gleichförmig anspannt, und soll anspannen, dadurch daß sie auflöst."

"aesthetic mood" which is not given over one-sidedly to either the compulsion of nature nor the necessity of reason. Now, to the young Steiner, this text meant that in this aesthetic state the soul lives through the senses, but, importantly, it carries a spiritual element into the sensory experience and also into actions determined by the sense world, "One perceives with the senses, but in such a way that it is as if the spiritual has streamed into the senses."[21] Steiner concludes his autobiographical comments on Schiller's 'third state', now viewing it as supportive of his overall holistic epistemological theories in this way,

> Schiller spoke of that consciousness-state which must be there, in order to perceive the beauty of the world. May one not also conceive of such a consciousness state that mediates the truth in the nature of things? If this is a justified concept, then one cannot investigate human consciousness phenomenologically, as it is given in the first instance…in order to ascertain whether this might be able to arrive at the true nature of objects. Rather, one should firstly research that consciousness state through which the human being sets itself into such a relationship to the world, that the objects and realities there do unveil to him their true nature.
>
> And I believed that I knew that such a consciousness state is actually attained, to a certain degree, when the human being not only has such thoughts that depict external things and processes, but thoughts that are experienced as thoughts. This 'living in thinking' revealed itself to me as something entirely different to that which one usually exercises in daily existence and in normal scientific research. If one proceeds further in this 'experiencing of thought' itself, one

---

[21] Steiner, Lebensgang, 50, „Man nimmt mit den Sinnen wahr, aber so, als ob das Geistige in die Sinne eingeströmt wäre. "

finds that one encounters the spiritual reality.[22] (emphasis in the original)

This attitude of Steiner's is reflected in the primary intentions of his main epistemological work, *Die Philosophie der Freiheit* (*The Philosophy of Freedom*). One approach Steiner takes in *Die Philosophie* to establish what he regards as a valid, accurate epistemology to refute the conviction that sense perceptions are inherently invalid, is to examine the underlying logic in the argument which posits subjectivity to these. Steiner is naturally well aware from his extensive involvement professionally in philosophical writings, that the question of just how sense perception can be possible in view of the fact that sensory stimuli become chemical substances in the body is a major conundrum.

In the following extract from *Die Philosophie* he argues with particularly strong conviction against the attitude that sense perception is rendered unreliable by the fact that it is subject to corporeal processes. He comments with regard to epistemological theories in general, that "it would be hard to find another thought structure in the history of human culture upon which a higher level of astuteness has been expended, and yet which, upon closer examination, disintegrates."[23]

---

[22] Steiner, Lebensgang, 50, „Schiller hat von dem Bewußtseinszustand gesprochen, der da sein muß, um die Schönheit der Welt zu erleben. Könnte man nicht auch an einen solchen Bewußtseinszustand denken, der die *Wahrheit* im Wesen der Dinge vermittelt ? Wenn das berechtigt ist, dann kann man nicht...das zunächst gegebene menschliche Bewußtsein betrachend untersuchen, ob dieses an das wahre Wesen der Dinge herankommen könne. Sondern man müßte erst den Bewußtseinszustand erforschen, durch den der Mensch sich in ein solches Verhältnis zur Welt setzt, daß ihm die Dinge und Tatsachen ihr Wesen enthüllen.
Und ich glaubte zu erkennen, daß ein solcher Bewußtseinszustand bis zu einem gewissen Grade erreicht sei, wenn der Mensch nicht nur Gedanken habe, die äußere Dinge und Vorgänge abbilden, sondern solche, die *er als Gedanken selbst erlebt*. Dieses Leben in Gedanken offenbarte sich mir als ein ganz anderes als das ist, in dem man das gewöhnliche Dasein und auch die gewöhnliche wissenschaftliche Forschung verbringt. Geht man immer weiter in dem Gedanken-Erleben, so findet man daß diesem Erleben die geistige Wirklichkeit entgegenkommt."
[23] Rudolf Steiner, Die Philosophie der Freiheit, (Dornach: RSV, 1977) 59, „Es wird schwer sein, ein zweites Gedankengebäude in der Geschichte des menschlichen Geisteslebens zu finden, das mit größerem Scharfsinn

In his line of argument, Steiner writes against the general argument put forward by many philosophers for refuting naïve realism, primarily referring to a contemporary philosopher, Eduard von Hartmann. Naïve realism is the assumption that we do actually perceive what we assume we are perceiving, and hence the reality of the environment is beyond question. As Barry Maund states, "naïve realism …implies that in perception we are directly confronted with the object itself."[24] The conclusions reached by philosophers as a result of their dismantling of naïve realism vary enormously, and need not be considered here. Steiner is concerned solely with invalidating the argument for dismissing the validity of sense impressions. He reviews the argument in general, without referring to a specific philosopher, and then refutes its conclusions,

> One starts with what is given in naïve consciousness, with the thing as perceived. Then one shows that none of the qualities which are found in this thing would exist for us had we no sense organs. No eye, no colour. Therefore the colour is not yet present in that which affects the eye. It arises first through the interaction of the eye and the object. The latter is, therefore, colourless. But neither is the colour in the eye, for in the eye there is only a chemical or physical process which is first conducted by the optic nerve to the brain, and there inaugurates another process. Even this is not yet the colour. That is only produced in the soul by means of the brain process. Even then it does not yet enter my consciousness, but is just transferred by the mind to an object in the external world. There, upon this external body, I finally believe myself to perceive the colour. We have travelled in a complete circle. We became conscious of a coloured object.

---

zusammengetragen ist, und das bei genauerer Prüfung doch in nichts zerfällt."
[24] Barry Maund, <u>Perception</u>, (Chesham: Acumen Publishing, 2003) 8.

That is the first thing. At this point, the thought process starts. If I had no eye, the body would be, for me, colourless. So I cannot locate the colour in the body. I start on the search for it. I look for it in the eye - in vain; in the nerve - in vain; and in the brain - in vain once more. I look in consciousness - here I find it indeed, but not attached to the object. I find the coloured object again only on returning to my starting point. The circle is completed. I believe that I am cognising, as a product of my soul, all that which the naïve man regards as existing outside him, in space.

As long as one stays at this point, then everything is in perfect order. But the matter must once again be examined from the beginning. So far I have only been occupied with one thing, with the external perception, from which, I, as a naïve person, had an entirely false opinion. For I had the opinion: the object has, as I perceive it, an objective status. But now I notice that it disappears with my mental image, that it is only a modification of my own psychological states. Do I have any right at all, in my examination, to start with the perception? Can I say of it that it exerts an influence for my soul? From now on I must treat the table itself, of which yesterday I believed that it did have an influence upon me and thus brought forth in me a mental image, as a mental image. Consequently, my sense organs and the processes within them are merely subjective.[25]

---

[25] Philosophie 59-60, „Man geht zunächst von dem aus, was dem naiven Bewußtsein gegeben ist, von den wahrgenommenen Dinge. Dann zeigt man, daß alles, was an diesem Dinge sich findet, für uns da nicht wäre, wenn wir keine Sinne hätten. Kein Auge: keine Farbe. Also ist die Farbe in dem noch nicht vorhanden, was auf das Auge wirkt. Sie entsteht erst durch die Wechselwirkung des Auges mit dem Gegenstande. Dieser ist also farblos. Aber auch im Auge ist die Farbe nicht vorhanden; denn da ist ein chemischer oder physikalischer Vorgang vorhanden, der erst durch den Nerv zum Gehirn geleitet wird, und da einen andern auslöst. Dieser ist noch immer nicht die Farbe. Sie wird erst durch den Hirnprozess in der Seele hervorgerufen. Da tritt sie mir noch immer nicht ins Bewußtsein, sondern wird erst durch die Seele nach außen an einen Körper verlegt. An diesem glaube ich sie endlich wahrzunehmen. Wir haben einen vollständigen

Steiner then proceeds to argue that the conclusion which this line of thought has to draw, is that all the objects perceived, including one's own nerve and brain substances and processes are mental images, each of which acts upon the other in a non-real continuum, and therefore all these have to be dismissed. The overall attitude of Steiner is one of considerable confidence in his conclusion that sense impressions can not be argued away on the basis of observation of the physiological processes, since observation of these too, is entirely based on sense impressions, "...as soon as it is clear to me that my sense organs and their activity, and also my nerve and soul processes, can only be known through perception, the line of thought described above is revealed in its full absurdity."[26]

Steiner's intention here is to establish the inherent validity of the perceptual process through which we (apparently) register the existence of our environment, (and of our inner life), and secondly to argue that the limits to knowledge are not absolute. With regard to the former, it was especially some

---

Kreisgang durchgemacht. Wir sind uns eines farbigen Körpers bewußt geworden.
Das ist das Erste. Nun hebt die Gedankenoperation an. Wenn ich keine Augen hätte, wäre der Körper für mich farblos. Ich kann also die Farbe nicht in den Körper verlegen. Ich gehe auf die Suche nach ihr. Ich suche sie im Auge: vergebens; im Nerv: vergebens; im Gehirne; ebenso vergebens; in der Seele; hier find ich sie zwar, aber nicht mit dem Körper verbunden. Den farbigen Körper finde ich erst wieder da, wo ich ausgegangen bin. Der Kreis ist geschlossen. Ich glaube das als Erzeugnis meiner Seele zu erkennen, was der naive Mensch sich als draußen im Raume vorhanden denkt.
So lange man dabei stehen bleibt, scheint alles in schönster Ordnung. Aber die Sache muß noch einmal von vorne angefangen werden. Ich habe bis jetzt mit einem Dinge gewirtschaftet: mit der äußeren Wahrnehmung, von dem ich früher, als naiver Mensch, eine ganz falscher Ansicht gehabt habe. Ich war der Meinung: sie hätte so, wie ich sie wahrnehme, einen objektiven Bestand. Nun merke ich, daß sie mit meinem Vorstellen verschwindet, daß sie nur eine Modifikation meiner seelischen Zustände ist. Habe ich nun überhaupt noch ein Recht, in meinen Betrachtungen von ihr auszugehen? Kann ich von ihr sagen, daß sie auf meine Seele wirkt? Ich muß von jetzt ab den Tisch, von dem ich früher geglaubt habe, daß er auf mich wirkt und in mir eine Vorstellung von sich hervorbringt, selbst als Vorstellung behandeln. Konsequenterweise sind dann aber auch meine Sinesorgane und die Vorgänge in ihnen bloß subjektiv."
[26] Steiner, Philosophie 61, „...sobald mir klar ist, daß mir meine Sinnesorgane und deren Tätigkeit, mein Nerven- und Seelen-prozess auch nur durch die Wahrnehmung gegeben werden können, zeigt sich der geschilderte Gedankengang in seiner vollen Unmöglichkeit."

aspects of thinking and volition that Steiner wished to establish as being immediately perceived, and thus not subject to any distorting processes. Steiner was in effect refuting elements of (Kantian influenced) mainstream philosophical attitudes, which argue that a perceived object exists, but its true nature, the thing-in-itself is forever unknowable, and the implied corollary to this statement, that there are the current limits to human cognition are absolute.

As Kant states in his preface to the second edition of his *Critique of Pure Reason*, "From this analysis of our faculty, it is shown that with it, we can never transcend the limits of possible experience….that our rational cognition…has only to do with phenomena, the thing-in-itself possesses a real existence for itself, but is left unrecognized by our cognition."[27] In the main body of this work, his conclusion is elaborated in detail; in the section, *Remarks on Transcendental Ethics*, Kant declares the outcome of the perceptual act, or 'empirical data', to be limited to a surface phenomenon, and thus excludes the thing-in-itself. Taking the example of a rainbow and raindrops, Kant explains that these too are only surface phenomena, and that if one just considers empirical data in general, to see if there is anything in our sense perceptions which represent the thing-in-itself, one will see that nothing of the thing-in-itself can be found,

> …not only are the raindrops mere phenomena, but even their circular form, indeed the space itself through which they fall, is nothing in itself, but both are mere modifications or fundamental dispositions of our sensuous intuition."[28]

---

[27] Immanuel Kants Werke, ed. Albert Görland, *Kritik der reinen Vernunft*, (Berlin: Bruno Cassirer Verlag, 1913) 19-20, „…es ergibt sich aus dieser Deduktion unseres Vermögens…daß wir mit ihm nie über die Grenzen möglicher Erfahrung hinauskonnen können…unsere Vernunfterkenntnis… nur auf Erscheinungen gehe, die Sache an sich selbst dagegen zwar als für sich wirklich, aber von uns unerkannt liegen läßt."

[28] Kants Werke, Kritik 72, „…und nicht allein diese Tropfen sind bloße Erscheinungen, sondern selbst ihre runde Gestalt, ja sogar der Raum, in welchem sie fallen, sind nichts an sich selbst, sondern bloße Modifikationen oder Grundlagen unserer sinnlichen Anschauung…"

Whilst the above extract from Kant encapsulates the conclusions against which Steiner was arguing, Steiner himself does not quote Kant specifically on this issue, and instead he refers to the expression 'the thing-in-itself', and briefly reviews a few philosophers who are supportive of this. In his arguments to establish the validity of the perceived world, Steiner assumes that his readers will be aware that a major trend in epistemological thought for centuries has been to regard perception as not fully disclosing the reality to the observer.

Steiner's epistemological writings reflect his extensive involvement with philosophy, and individual philosophers, including, as noted earlier, his editing of the complete works of Schopenhauer in twelve volumes. However, a detailed critique of Steiner's epistemological dialoguing with the relevant elements of major philosophical writers, such of Kant, Spencer, Berkeley, Hume etc, and the correspondence between himself and von Hartmann and others, which underpins his writings on cognition, cannot be examined here.

In his later anthroposophical teachings, Steiner maintains that the conclusion which declares the impossibility of direct knowledge of physical or spiritual realities is incorrect, because perception is carried by a supra-sensible element in the human organism. Additionally, spiritual realities are accessible by the acolyte on the spiritual path because they undertake a mediative process through which they learn to extend their perceptual capacities, thus there are no limits to perception. However, Steiner admits that spiritual perception is subject to possible distortions (as is sense perception), this theme shall be considered further, in connection with clairvoyant experiences of characters in *Die Pforte*.

Our concern is to ascertain the principal elements of his spiritual worldview, as expressed in his first drama, *Die Pforte der Einweihung (The Portal of Initiation)*. The main characters in *Die Pforte* achieve perception of spirit beings, through a meditative process, incorporating soul exercises. In the drama the inherent validity of such 'spiritual perceiving' in spiritual realms is assumed, analogous to sensory perception in the sense world, (except where a visionary experience is considered to be distorted). Therefore we need to note Steiner's view of cognition, and the relationship of this to his esoteric worldview, for Steiner maintained that his conclusions in his early cognitive texts were compatible with his spiritual research and its consequent conclusions.

The question as to how sensory impressions are cognized is treated in Steiner's works as a decidedly non-reductionist one, although as noted above, his early philosophical works, whilst implying this, do not specify any form of spiritual solution. To Steiner, neither his methodology nor the implications of his anthroposophical teaching were incompatible with his epistemology. In a later section, Steiner's elucidation of his theories in this area to Theosophists will be noted.

In his Doctoral thesis (1892), and later in his *Die Philosophie der Freiheit* (1894), he sought to argue for the inherent validity of perception. In the first chapters of Die Philosophie, Steiner seeks to refute the various ways in which philosophical thought has argued over the centuries that the perceived reality (termed by Steiner, the 'given world-content') is not reliably perceived. The general argument, historically, is that perception is subject to dynamics in the perceiver's mind and body which render such perceptions unreliable in various ways. Steiner wishes to establish that sense perception is inherently reliable and provides accurate impressions of the outer environment.

Steiner establishes firstly the basic ground plan of his approach, namely that the consciousness processes under investigation are not a material reality, but derive from the 'soul', which inhabits the body. The central tenet underlying his epistemological enquiry is that consciousness does not have its origin in the material body, but rather derives from an organism which is suprasensible in nature, namely, the soul. Consciousness, Steiner maintains, is due to the presence of the soul, which animates the body during the lifespan. The attitude which takes the opposite stand to this, and argues that the 'soul' is an outcome of the body, and that thoughts therefore originate in the brain, is termed 'materialistic' by Steiner. A passage from Steiner's *Die Philosophie*, in which he refutes the attitude that thinking is only a by-product of physiological processes, illustrates his approach;

> Materialism can never provide a satisfactory explanation of the world. For every attempt at an explanation must commence in that one formulates *thoughts* about the phenomena of the world. Materialism thus begins with the *thought* of matter, or of material processes. But, in doing so, it is already faced with two different sets of facts: the material world, and the thoughts about it. The materialist seeks to comprehend the latter by regarding them as purely material processes. He believes that thinking takes place in the brain in much the same way that digestion takes place in the animal organs.
>
> Just us he attributes mechanical and organic effects to matter, so he also credits matter, in certain circumstances with the capacity to think. He forgets that, in doing so, he is merely shifting the problem from one place to another. He ascribes the power of thinking to matter instead of to himself {as a soul being}. And he is thereby back again at his starting point. How does matter come to think about its own nature? Why is it not simply satisfied with itself, and accepts its existence? [29] (emphasis in original)

---

[29] Rudolf Steiner, Die Philosophie 25: „Der *Materialismus* kann niemals eine befriedigende Welterklärung liefern. Denn jeder Versuch einer Erklärung muß damit beginnen, daß man sich *Gedanken* über die Welterscheinungen bildet. Der Materialismus macht deshalb den Anfang mit dem Gedanken der Materie oder der materiellen Vorgänge. Damit hat er bereits zwei verschiedene Tatsachengebiete vor sich: die materielle Welt und die Gedanken über sie. Er sucht die letzteren dadurch zu begreifen, daß er sie als einen rein materiellen Prozeß auffaßt. Er glaubt, daß das Denken im

This passage reflects the fact that for Steiner's epistemology, it is critical that he establishes the independence of consciousness from matter. This is an essential basis for his attempts to argue that awareness of independent spiritual realms and beings is possible. There has to be a soul-spirit core pertaining to the human being to enable any encountering of soul-spirit realms to occur, as an organism derived from matter could not perceive spiritual realities.

It is axiomatic in Steiner's worldview that such suprasensible elements as those which figure largely in his teachings, are accurately perceived realities, not theoretical postulates, nor hallucinatory. This element of his worldview emerges from his conclusions in primary Steiner texts, such as, "*Knowledge of Higher Worlds, how is it achieved?*" Published in 1904, this text will be referred to again in a later section.

Therefore, one strand of Steiner's approach to epistemology is to maintain that perception of the inner life (consciousness processes) can also be immediately given. So firstly, in so far as he dealt with cognitional themes, he seeks to establish that sense impressions are genuine; what we see, hear, touch and smell are what we register them to be. And additionally, he wished to establish that elements in the inner life, especially intellectual processes and volitional impulses, are also accurately, that is, immediately, perceived. Thus perception of both the outer environment and the inner life are equally reliably perceived. The corollary to this – that consciousness faculties can be enhanced to encompass supra-sensible realms – is never mentioned in his philosophical writings. However as we noted above, in his later, anthroposophical, period (1901 onwards), Steiner, as inaugurator of a body of spiritual

---

Gehirne etwa so zustande komme, wie die Verdauung in den animalischen Organen. So wie er der Materie mechanische und organische Wirkungen zuschreibt, so legt er ihr auch die Fähigkeit bei, unter bestimmten Bedingungen zu denken. Er vergißt, daß er nun das Problem nur an einen andern Ort verlegt hat. Statt sich selbst, schreibt er die Fähigkeit des Denkens der Materie zu. Und damit ist er wieder an seinem Ausgangspunkte. Wie kommte die Materie dazu, über ihr eigenes Wesen nachzudenken? Warum ist sie nicht einfach mit sich zufrieden und nimmt ihr Dasein hin?"

teachings, argues that such an expansion is possible, and that this mediates equally valid impressions as those accessible by the senses. Steiner's concept of expanding the perceptual horizon will be examined later.

Steiner sees the registering of our environs, whether the external sense world, or the inner life, as the primal cognitive act. He argues that this occurs prior to logical analysis of such perceptions, or any distorting dynamic, and therefore these initial impressions cannot be dismissed as in some manner distorted. Again he makes a general argument, refraining from entering into specific philosophical arguments,

> "... there have of course previously been people who have doubted the possibility of real cognition. One firstly has to become clear as to whether a science of knowledge is possible...This possibility is however a necessary postulate of human reasoning. If one denies the possibility of a science of knowledge then one can do no other than place oneself fully on the standpoint of the sceptic, indicated earlier. But something has to be certain, because something is given; it is only a question of determining what is actually certain.
>
> For if one takes the opposite argument and were to say, nothing is definite; then this sentence, if it is to be generally valid, must, because of its own nature, be applicable to itself; that is, it itself is also not certain. So, it invalidates itself, but only in so far as it is itself valid; it is thus a complete contradiction, and one cannot do anything. Therefore we have to allow the possibility as well as the necessity of a science of knowledge as a postulate of human reason.[30] (my emphases)

---

[30] Beiträge zur Rudolf Steiner Gesamtausgabe Nr. 30, S. 27; ....„es ja schon Leute gegeben hat, die an der Möglichkeit des Wissen gezweifelt haben. Man muß sich nun vorerst klar werden, ob eine Wissenschaftslehre möglich sei....Diese Möglichkeit ist aber ein notwendiges Postulat der menschlichen

Although in *Die Philosophie* Steiner's convictions are argued with logical rigour, he does not continue his argument on to provide evidence of any modus operandi in the human organism by which this postulated reliability of sense perceptions, which have been transformed into physiological components, can be validated. It is enough for him to establish logically to his satisfaction that sensory stimuli, according to his argument, cannot be dismissed as inherently subjective. Indeed in none of his epistemological works does he provide any suggestion as to how sense stimuli can actually be valid if, as he agrees, the sensory data does indeed become physiological substances and electrical impulses in the nerves. The solution which he offers to this conundrum is only provided in the course of his anthroposophical spiritual-esoteric teaching, as this necessitates elements of his spiritual view of the human being. We shall examine the answer later in this thesis.

In regard to various themes proper to epistemological enquiry, an holistic-spiritual attitude towards human nature and consciousness processes prevails in *Die Philosophie*. For example, of thinking Steiner says, "In thinking we have given that element which brings into a unity our particular individuality with the cosmos. In that we feel and sense (and perceive) we are individual specific {beings}, in that we think, we are that All-one Being, which pervades all things."[31] In contrast to the theme of sense perception, where

---

Vernunft. Wenn man nämlich die Möglichkeit einer Wissenschaftslehre leugnet, so kann man nichts anderes tun, als sich völlig auf den oben angedeuteten Standpunkt der Skeptiker stellen. Es muß eben etwas gewiß sein, weil etwas gegeben ist, und es handelt sich nur {darum} auszumachen, was denn eigentlich gewiß ist. Denn man nehme das Gegenteil an und sage: es ist nichts gewiß. So muß der Satz, wenn er allgemein gelten soll, vermöge seiner Natur auf sich selbst anwendbar sein, d. h. er ist selbst nicht gewiß. Er hebt also sich selbst auf, das aber nur insoferne, als er selbst gültig ist, er ist also ein vollkommener Widerspruch, und es ist mit ihm nichts anzufangen. Wir müssen also ebenso die Möglichkeit wie die Notwendigkeit einer Wissenschaftslehre als ein Postulat der Vernunft zugestehen."

[31] Steiner, Philosophie, 72, „In dem Denken haben wir das Element gegeben, das unsere besondere Individualität mit dem Kosmos zu einem Ganzen zusammenschließt. Indem wir empfinden und fühlen, (auch wahrnehmen) sind wir einzelne, indem wir denken, sind wir das all-eine Wesen, das alles durchdringt."

he elucidates his argument in detail, the above substantial remarks are stated, not established.

Looking back briefly to Steiner's doctoral thesis, as a conclusion to his argument, Steiner had maintained that there exists a directly given world-content, that is, the external environs that we register, which we accurately perceive, but in which no trace of cognising as yet exists. Further, he argued that this is one half of the directly perceived given reality in which the human being lives. The other half is the Idea which is intimately linked to the object. Three years later, he now argues this viewpoint in more detail in *Die Philosophie der Freiheit* to this effect. The human being possesses a faculty for intuitive thinking, and from this derives the second part of the immediately given world-reality,

> In the contemplative observation of the world, the union of the two parts of the world content actually occurs: of that which we view as a given on the horizon of our experiences, and that which in the act of cognizing has to be produced, in order to be given. The act of cognition is the synthesis of these two elements.[32]

It becomes obvious that a pivotal strand in his epistemology is that concepts can occur simultaneously with sense perception, namely the Idea from which the perceived object derives its existence. Steiner is arguing here that the term, 'thought' can also refer to the occurrence of insights, and not only to normal, logically formulated thinking. He maintains that the given world-content also consists of those intuitive thoughts that simultaneously occur in us when registering a sense impression. One notes that the underlying attitude here

---

[32] Rudolf Steiner, Wahrheit und Wissenschaft (Dornach: RSV, 1980) 62, „In der denkenden Weltbetrachtung vollzieht sich tatsächlich die Vereinigung der zwei Teile des Weltinhaltes: dessen, den wir als Gegebenes auf dem Horizonte unserer Erlebnisse überblicken, und dessen, der im Erkennntnisakt produziert werden muß, um sich gegeben zu sein. Der Erkenntnisakt ist die Synthese dieser beiden Elemente".

is that the existence of the realm of the Platonic Idea is a reality, as is a spiritual aspect to human nature which has the ability to receive insights from this realm,

> The perception is not something completed, closed off, rather, the one side of the total reality. The other side is the concept. The act of knowledge is the synthesis of perception and concept. But perception and concept of a thing are required to constitute the thing in its entirety.[33]

Hence Steiner regards these 'intuitive concepts' as that which may be given to us, in the moment of perceiving the world-content, and which through their inherent nature leads us beyond the merely given. So to Steiner, 'ideas' are that which may be given to us, in the moment of perceiving the world-content, and which through their inherent nature leads us beyond the merely given. The Idea can lead the observer to an understanding of the full reality of what is perceived, and the other half of reality, the concept which explains it, derives from the archetypal Idea.

That the underlying implication here is that the concept is actually existing in the Platonic realm of the Idea, is indicated in a document written in 1888, a few years before his doctoral thesis. This document, entitled, *Credo*, was found some decades after his death in the Steiner archives in Dornach, Switzerland; it gives the young Steiner's personal creed of life, and commences with the following words,

> The world of Ideas is the primary fountain and principle of all being. In it is never ending harmony and blissful tranquillity. Any existence that was not illumined by the light of the world of Ideas, would be

---

[33] Steiner, Philosophie, 73, „Die Wahrnehmung ist nicht also Fertiges, Abgeschlossenes, sondern die eine Seite der total Wirklichkeit. Die andere Seite ist der Begriff. Der Erkenntnisakt ist die Synthese von Wahrnehmung und Begriff. Wahrnehmung und Begriff eines Dinges machen aber erst das ganze Ding aus."

a dead existence, devoid of essential being, which would have no part of the life of the universe.[34]

The Platonic realm of the Idea, to which Steiner alludes in his *Credo*, is a general concept shared by many writers with a spiritual-esoteric perspective, from the Neo-Platonists through to the Theosophists of Steiner's time. We shall note the acceptance of this general concept in Romantics whose writings were relevant to the formulation of Steiner's worldview. The concept as such is not presented in any one main passage, in Plato's works, in his Phaedrus, he makes some clear statements as to the features of this realm. In particular, here he refers to this realm as a which transcend the paradisaical realms customarily known to those possessing esoteric knowledge, it is "that region beyond the sky {of which} no bard has ever sung."[35]

His philosophical arguments, presented primarily in *Die Philosophie*, remain devoid of esoteric-spiritual content, but his Credo indicates strongly that already in his twenties, Steiner ascribed to esoteric-spiritual ideas. It is not until 1901 that he provides substantiating bases for his holistic conclusions regarding thinking and perception, through his 'anthroposophical' spiritual tenets.

Summing up his spiritual-cognitive orientation so far, in his thesis of 1892, and in *Die Philosophie* of 1894, Steiner maintains that consciousness derives from a soul, which is supra-sensible. Sense impressions and thoughts – that is, intuitive ideas – and volitional impulses are directly, immediately, given to human consciousness. This process, in terms of cognizing the world around one, thus provides valid sense impression, and also it offers the concept which inherently belongs to the perceived object. That is, every

---

[34] Rudolf Steiner, *Credo*, Wahrspruchworte 273, „Die Ideenwelt ist der Urquell and das Prinzip alles Seins. In ihr ist unendliche Harmonie und selige Ruhe. Das Sein, das sie mit ihrem Lichte nicht beleuchtete, wäre ein totes, wesenloses, das keinen Teil hätte an dem Leben des Weltganzen."

[35] Lexikon der Platonischen Begriffe, *Idee*, ed. H. Peris, (Bern: Francke Verlag, 1973) 179; and Plato, *Phaedrus*, Five dialogues of Plato bearing on poetic inspiration, (London: Dutton & Co, 1927) 233.

object has a corresponding Idea from which it derives, and the observer may be able to perceive this.

In *Die Philosophie* Steiner has examined cognition from the perspective of the divide which Kantian philosophical thinking postulates, that is the gap between the perceiving human being and its sense perceptible environment, and the causative Ideas which sustains the created environment. As we have noted above, he maintains that the alienating dichotomous situation of the human being viz-a-viz the world-content, actually already has a solution inherent in it, namely, humanity has the ability to cognize the Idea pertaining to the perceived.

But a few years after *Die Philosophie* appeared, in his editorial remarks on Goethe's scientific writings, he proceeds to take the next step in the elucidation of these ideas, with a more pronounced Platonic and spiritual nuance. His remarks were published as a volume in the Complete Works, in 1987 as, *Goethes Naturwissenschaftliche Schriften Goethe's scientific writings*). In the chapter, 'Goethes Erkenntnis-Art' (The Nature of Goethe's Knowledge) he writes,

> In so far as thinking takes hold of the Idea, it merges with the primal foundation of existence; that which is efficacious from outside, enters into the spirit of the human being. It becomes one with the objective reality at its highest potency. *Becoming aware of the Idea within reality is the true communion of man.*[36] (Italics in the original)

It is relevant to note here that the quasi-religious nuance of this latter sentence needs to be examined. This sentence echoes a primary ethical tenet of his philosophical thoughts.

---

[36] Rudolf Steiner, Goethes Naturwissenschaftliche Schriften (Dornach: RSV, 1973) 126, „Indem sich das Denken der Idee bemächtigt, verschmiltzt es mit dem Urgrund des Weltendaseins; das, was außen wirkt, tritt in den Geist des Menschen ein; er wird mit der objektiven Wirklichkeit auf ihrer höchsten Potenz *eins*. Das Gewahrwerden der Idee in der Wirklichkeit ist die wahre Kommunion des Menschen."

Namely that ethical behaviour is closely connected to the power of insight – at its finest and most empowered. As is implied in the above elucidation of his epistemology, however such thinking unites the mind with the divine archetypal truths, and hence their Creator. All of this requires of course, as a solid fundament, the cognitional-epistemological perspective we have been noting.

The latter half of *Die Philosophie* is devoted to establishing the concept that the human being can also perceive the cognitional power active in the will, not only in thinking or feelings, and active within these volitional forces is the human spirit. The kind of the cognition carried out by the volitional nature is described as 'intuitive', that is, a form of insightfulness, which is not the outcome of a logical process. Steiner maintains in *Die Philosophie* that in the human will are qualities of the highest morality, and perception of them is akin to making them efficacious within one.

By this, Steiner means the human being in this condition – access to which is facilitated by meditation – can attain to an intuitive perception of the inherently moral and then the realization of it in deeds. Acting from such a volitional dynamic is regarded as the primary meaning of the term 'freedom'. So, Steiner's second major postulate in Die Philosophie is that true ethics only arises when it is perceived within one's inner being, from the human spirit, and not drawn from any external source. This second postulate requires the first postulate – the inherent validity of perception – for its validation.

This attitude is also exemplified in a statement which he made as young man, in a university questionnaire from 1892, the year in which his thesis was published. In this document, as a motto, the young Steiner wrote, "An Gottes Stelle den freien Menschen! (In the place of God, the free human being!)[37] The term 'free' (frei in German) also has the

---

[37] Bettle, Erika and Vlerl, Kurt. Eds. Erinnerungen an Rudolf Steiner, (Stuttgart: Verlag Freies Geistesleben,1979) 43, „Motto: An Gottes Stelle

connotation of 'independent' and unrestricted. Steiner's usage here means, as his work Die Philosophie elucidates at length, that the human being who has attained to an intuitive morality, now has an inherent source of ethics.

In his next epistemological book, *'Goethe's Erkenntnistheorie'* (*Goethe's Epistemology*), Steiner now writes from the position of having attained a firm basis for his postulate that the human being has the ability to perceive an immediately given world content. His focus in this volume is the ability of the human being to perceive a spiritual reality, existing in the Platonic realm of Ideas, which itself derives from God,

> When we speak about the nature of a thing, or of the world in general, then we cannot mean anything else than the grasping of reality as *a thought*, *an Idea*. In the Idea we recognize that from which we have to derive everything else: the principle of things. What the philosophers call the absolute, eternal being, the foundation of the world, what religions call God, we call – on the basis of our epistemological elucidations – the *Idea*.[38]

In 1911 an occasion occurred for Steiner to speak to this point philosophically; at that time the president of the fourth International Congress on Philosophy, Prof. Frederico Enriques (Rome), invited him to present a paper about his spiritual-scientific perspectives on epistemology. During this congress he addressed the crucial point of extending the faculties of consciousness, aware that he was now speaking

---

den freien Menschen !"
[38] Steiner, Naturwissenschaftliche Schriften 162, „Wenn wir vom Wesen eines Dinges oder der Welt überhaupt sprechen, so können wir also gar nichts andres meinen, als das Begreifen der Wirklichkeit als *Gedanke*, als *Idee*. In der *Idee* erkennen wir dasjenige, woraus wir alles andere herleiten müssen: das Prinzip der Dinge. Was die Philosophien das Absolute, das ewige Sein, den Weltengrund, was die Religionen Gott nennen, das nennen wir, auf Grund unserer erkenntnistheoretischen Erörterungen: die *Idee*."

academically, but from the social position of a teacher of spiritual matters, an official of the Theosophical Society,[39]

> Anthroposophy believes, on the basis of reliable facts of the soul-life, that it may assert that apprehension is not something completed and closed off, but rather something fluidic, capable of development. Anthroposophy believes it can point out that behind the scope of normal conscious soul-life there is another field of consciousness into which the human being can enter....However this other state of the soul must first be attained by certain soul-exercises, soul experiences.[40]

Steiner's arguments were not experienced as persuasive to philosophical thinkers of his lifetime. Some of the reviewers considered his theory of inner intuitive morality as far fetched, or worse. Critical reviews of his *Die Philosophie* included such conclusions as, "Steiner...goes far beyond Nietzsche, and ends in a theoretical anarchy", or, "...it would be most delightful, if we were so mature that we only needed to reach into our individual {Platonic} Idea-world to create from it captivating motives... for action."[41]

---

[39] The occurrence of the term, 'Anthroposophy' in this text from 1911, where one would expect 'Theosophy' is due to the editors of Steiner's works, who began producing the Complete Edition in 1961. It was not until 1913 that Steiner formed the Anthroposophical Society, and began referring to his worldview as 'anthroposophy', apart from using it in one lecture in 1902, which was his first year as General Secretary of the Theosophical Society.

[40] Rudolf Steiner, "Die psychologischen Grundlagen und die erkenntnistheoretische Stellung der Anthroposophie", Philosophie und Anthroposophie (Dornach: VRSN, 1965) 113; „Anthroposophie...glaubt auf Grund sicherer Tatsachen des Seelenlebens behaupten zu dürfen, daß Erkenntnis nichts Fertiges, Abgeschlossenes, sondern etwas Fließendes, Entwicklungsfähiges ist. Sie glaubt hinweisen zu dürfen darauf, daß es hinter dem Umkreis des normal bewußten Seelenlebens ein anderes gibt, in welches der Mensch eindringen kann....Nur muß diese Seelenverfassung erst durch bestimmte Seelenübungen, Seelenerlebnisse hergestellt werden."

[41] David Marc Hoffmann, ed. Dokumente zur "Philosophie der Freiheit", (Dornach: RSV, 1994) S. 451, 473; quoting from *The Athenaeum, Journal of English and Foreign Literature, Science, the Fine Arts, Music and the Drama*, London No. 3480, p. 17, and *Philosophisches Jahrbuch* 1895, S. 425-428, „...es wäre ja ganz köstlich, wenn wir soweit gereift wären, daß wir nur in

Many other readers would have rejected outright the cognitional theories of Steiner that we have considering above, namely that our sensory perceptions are valid and genuine representations of our physical environment. Such a reader was Eduard von Hartmann, who wrote extensive margin notes in his copy of *Die Philosophie*, rejecting much of Steiner's text on this basis. For example, in response to Steiner's sentence, „Die äußeren Dinge sind wir allerdings nicht, aber wir gehören mit den äußeren Dingen zu ein und derselben Welt (Certainly we are not the external things, but we belong with the external things to one and the same world)" von Hartmann wrote, "This 'we' is inadmissible, it must read, 'I', because the other 'I's' exist only in my consciousness, as something which I mentally represent to myself."[42]

Consequently Steiner's spiritual approach to philosophy did not become part of the ongoing philosophical debate, hence his philosophical writings are widely unknown today.[43] The Kantian perspective prevails widely today, as Strawson notes in his essay in the anthology, *Kant and Contemporary Epistemology*. He examines the major implications in contemporary, Kantian philosophical ideas regarding perception, defining the two possible implications, and then suggests that they are not quite as stark as they may seem,

> And so it may seem that in the critical philosophy we are faced with a choice of interpretations. It seems that either things in space and time, including ourselves and our temporally ordered experiences, are real, and things in themselves are merely those same things considered in abstraction from the conditions

---

unsere individuelle Ideenwelt zu greifen brauchten, um darin hinreißende Motive zum Handeln...zu schöpfen...".

[42] Hoffman, Dokumente 370, „Dieses ‚wir' ist unstatthaft; es muß heißen, Ich, da die anderen Ichs nur in meinem Bewußtsein als von mir vorgestellte existieren."

[43] Thomas Mautner, ed. The Penguin Dictionary of Philosophy, (London: Penguin, 1997) 540, the brief entry for Steiner sums up his epistemology as, "Genuine knowledge, he thought, must always include intuitive and aesthetic elements."

of our knowledge of them – mere cognitive blanks; *or*, a non-temporal, non-spatial supersensible realm of things in themselves (or noumens) is the only reality and there only appears to be anything else. But this is to state the case too starkly. In each case a qualification is called for...[44]

We don't need to consider further arguments of Strawson's, moderating the implications in the Kantian-influenced view, it suffices to note the slight nuance of disquiet about the apparently unreal nature of our environs. This same disquiet existed already in Steiner's lifetime, and in his Doctoral thesis he quotes various dissenting thinkers as support for his own epistemology. However the situation remains that Steiner's conclusions were not incorporated into the ongoing debate, and that as he moved into a new phase of advocating an overtly spiritual worldview the prominence of his philosophical work was eclipsed by his esoteric-spiritual worldview.

Today, he is known for the practical applications of his esoteric-spiritual worldview, for example in education (the Steiner schools) and agriculture (bio-dynamic farming practises). His philosophical writings have been ignored, as the entry in Kindlers Literature Lexikon notes, "So far, an intensive critical engagement with the Philosophie der Freiheit from non-anthroposophists has not occurred".[45] The further implications of Steiner's anthroposophically nuanced epistemology and its consistency or inconsistency to his new spiritual worldview, as expressed in *Die Pforte*, is relevant to the task of identifying the key elements of his anthroposophy. As such it will be considered in the conclusion.

---

[44] Peter. F. Strawson, *The problem of realism and the a priori*, Kant and Contemporary Epistemology, ed. Paolo Parrini, (Dordrecht: Kluwer Academic Publishers, 1994) 172.
[45] Kindlers Literature Lexikon, Bd. 17, S. 7470.

1A3: Steiner's involvement in Theosophy and esoteric-spiritual drama

In 1902, after Steiner had given various lectures on spirituality to the Giordano Bruno Association,[46] he was invited to join the German branch of the Theosophical Society. He accepted and was appointed General Secretary of the German branch, and was also simultaneously appointed head of the Berlin lodge of that organisation. This society had been founded in 1875 in New York, by several people with an interest in esoteric spiritual teachings; Helen P. Blavatsky, Col. Henry S. Olcott and Mr. William W. Judge. The principle goals of the organization are stated to be, "To form a nucleus of a Universal Brotherhood of humanity, without distinction of race, colour, sex or creed, to promote the study of world-religions and sciences. To investigate the hidden mysteries of Nature under every aspect possible and the psychic and spiritual powers of man."[47]

By 1880, the headquarters of this society had been transferred to India, but there was a growing membership in Europe, and by 1902, there were some thousands of members in Europe and England. The Theosophical Society provided probably the largest and most organized platform for teachings of an esoteric-spiritual nature, at that time. Soon an extensive lecturing activity was underway, which eventually included many public talks. This activity continued up to September 1924. Steiner gave some six thousand lectures in that period, of which about 4,000 were recorded stenographically.

In 1907 the international executive of the Theosophical Society, based in Adyar, India, decided that its international conference would be hosted by Germany. Consequently, Steiner, as its General Secretary, was responsible for the program. These conferences were normally devoid of artistic

---

[46] The "Giordano Bruno Bund für einheitliche Weltanschauung" in Berlin; founded by Bruno Wille, 1860-1928, author.
[47] World Theosophy journal, centenary number, (Hollywood) Aug 1931, Vol 1, No. 8, p. 596.

content, and it was Steiner's own decision to introduce for the first time substantial artistic elements into a theosophical conference, including a performance of a drama. Steiner decided upon the performance of *The Sacred Drama of Eleusis*, a drama written by a French theosophist and mystic, Eduard Schuré (1841-1929), in which the Demeter myth of ancient Greece is explored in a mystical, theosophical way.

Steiner directed the production of this play, the German translation of which he had re-cast into blank verse. Steiner commented in his introduction to the performance that, "In *The Sacred Drama of Eleusis* Schuré has re-established, with the intuition of a genius, the sacred drama of Eleusis – that primal drama, which is at once a work of art and of religious cultic activity."[48] This was an attempt at a reconstruction of what he believed occurred in the ancient Greek Mysteries. Dramatic performances were enacted in ancient Greece in places set aside for the worship of various gods, for example at Eleusis and Samothrace, in which various deities and processes of spiritual development were the focus.

In 1909, another Mystery play by Schuré, *The Children of Lucifer*, was translated by Steiner's closest co-worker, Marie von Sivers. It was performed as part of a German Theosophical conference, and again Steiner gave the introduction to the performance. These performances were only for members of the Theosophical Society, and hence there is no record of comments by drama critics to these plays. Steiner commented that Schuré, as an artist and as a researcher of the mystical path of the soul, is able to be a herald of the truth, and concluded that Schuré's entire creative activity shows how deeply permeated he is with the necessity to again unite modern culture with the soul's intimate mystical experience.[49]

---

[48] Rudolf Steiner, May 1904, re-published in Luzifer Gnosis, (Dornach: Rudolf Steiner Nachlaßverwaltung, 1960) 160; „In den Heiligtümern des Orients hat er mit genialischem Sinn das heilige Drama von Eleusis wiederhergestellt, jenes Urdrama, das zugleich Kunstwerk und religöse Kulthandlung war."

[49] Rudolf Steiner, Luzifer, 161, „Denn ihm ist es gegeben, als Künstler ein Künder der Wahrheit und als Forscher ein Enthüller der mystischen

In this sentence, we also have an indication of the attitude of Steiner to such dramatic activity, namely that esoteric spirituality is of necessity restricted to a small circle of adherents, but is nevertheless of great importance of modern times. Schuré's dramas were taken up only one more time, namely in the following year, 1910. By this year Steiner had began to write his own dramas, which he described as 'Mystery dramas', all of which portray the influence of spiritual realities in the inner life of his characters, who are seeking esoteric enlightenment. In doing this, it was obvious that he would be interacting with a very limited circle of people, and thereby greatly limit the circles in which his own activity would be appreciated.

Steiner was very informed as to the dramatic context of his times, from his work as a literary drama critic in the 1880-1890's. In this period he wrote about 270 articles, primarily reviews of plays, including those of Shakespeare, Goethe, Ludwig Tieck, Friedrich Hebbel, Otto Ludwig, Arno Holz, Maurice Donnay, Max Dreyer Heinrich von Kleist, Gunnnar Heiberg, Franz Grillparzer, Theodor Herzl, Hermann Bahr and many others. But in contrast to such playwrights, Steiner's dramas were to be performed specifically to educate those few people interested in understanding his esoteric worldview, namely members of the Theosophical (later, Anthroposophical) Society.

In August of 1910 he wrote, and consequently directed, the performance of *Die Pforte der Einweihung* (*The Portal of Initiation*), at a Society conference. It was the first of four such plays. The performance was part of a European Theosophical conference in Munich. At this conference, Schuré's play, *The Sacred Drama of Eleusis*, was performed for the last time, and there was the inaugural performance of Steiner's first drama, Die Pforte der Einweihung (hereafter,

---

Seelenwege zu sein.... Schurés ganzes Schaffen zeigt, wie tief durchdrungen er ist von der Notwendigkeit, die Zeitkultur wieder zu vereinigen mit dem intimen mystischen Erleben der Seele."

Die Pforte). These theatrical events were not part of the wider social life of Germany, they were 'internal' productions, intended only for participants at the conference. In 1911 he wrote and produced another play, *Die Prüfung der Seele (The Soul's Probation)*, performed in August of that year. In 1912, *Die Hüter der Schwelle (The Guardian of the Threshold)* was written, and performed in August. In 1913, his fourth drama, *Der Seelen Erwachen (The Soul's Awakening)* was written, and performed in the summer of that year, a year in which his to separate his own impetus from association with the Theosophical Society.

1A4: The reception of Steiner's spiritual worldview and his break with the Theosophical Society

Steiner's motivation to write his dramas, especially the first one, *Die Pforte*, is connected historically with the divergence between his view of Christianity, and that of the leaders of the mainstream Theosophical Society. His dramas were written in the decisive years when Steiner's own initiative was emerging as inherently incompatible with the attitudes of the executive of the Adyar branch. The protocols of the meetings of the German branch of the Theosophical Society from 1910 onwards clearly show that as early as 1909 the worldwide Theosophical Society was splitting, along the lines of the German section versus the Adyar-based Besant-Leadbeater faction.[50]

In 1910 Steiner was still the General Secretary for Germany, and enthusiasm for his approach had been growing steadily. The leaders of the International Theosophical Society, Annie Besant and William Leadbeater, then announced that an Indian youth, whom they had discovered, was to become the 'earthly vessel' of the coming World Teacher. Members were

---

[50] Mathilde Scholl, ed. Mitteilungen für die Mitglieder der Deutschen Sektion der Theosophischen Gesellschaft 10 (January 1910). In this, Steiner reports on a lecture by A. Besant on the nature of Christ, commenting that precisely this lecture shows that not disharmony, but harmony is there between East and West if people will only view the subject in the right way.

given to understand that this Teacher was in effect the returned Christ, also referred to as the Maitreya Bodhisattva and various names of high avatar beings, expected in various religious systems.[51] This child had been espied some years earlier, whilst bathing, by Leadbeater in India, and had consequently been subject to a special regimented education and dietetic system in England, under Leadbeater's supervision. Central to Steiner's Christology however, is the view that Jesus will never return in a flesh and blood body, and that the concept of a Second Coming refers to a non-physical event.

The Adyar mainstream founded the Order of the Star of the East in 1910, and held well-attended conferences in India announcing the imminent return of Christ. Early in 1912 they took the young man, known as Krishnamurti, on an European lecture tour, where he made a considerable impact.[52] Alongside this, efforts were made by the leadership of the Theosophical Society to limit the success of Steiner's work by creating doubt about the inherent integrity of his spiritual teachings.[53] This was followed by surreptitious actions, including cancelling without his prior knowledge, an international conference arranged by him.[54]

Steiner's play, *Die Pforte* was written at the same time as the founding of the Star of the East, 1910. The establishing of this Order was an action which was to have major implication for Steiner's involvement with the Theosophical Society. It was in response to the founding of this Order that Steiner

---

[51] Annie Besant, "The Order of the Star of the East", The Herald of the Star (Madras: The Theosophist office, 1912) 80-86.
[52] J. Krishnamurti, "*A Tour*", The herald of the Star (Adyar: July 1912) Vol 1, No. 3, 73-79.
[53] Mathilde Scholl, ed. Mitteilungen für die Mitglieder der Anthroposophischen Gesellschaft (theosophischen Gesellschaft, 2 (June 1913); "Mrs. Besant hat zuerst etwas fabriziert, was gar nlcht in dem Buche steht, wie sie es darstellt, und d a n n w a r n t s i e i h r e L e s e r
d r e i m a l [that is a problem of justification on both sides], m a n müsse vorsichtig sein gegenüber diesen Angaben, in denen Dr. Steiner als okkul t e r F o r s c h e r a l l e i n d a s t e h e u n d n i c h t mit den andern Forschern übereinstimme !!!" 9. (syntax/orthographics in the original)
[54] Mathilde Scholl, ed. Mitteilungen für die Mitglieder der Deutschen Sektion der Theosophischen Gesellschaft, 15 (January 1913) 1-5.

established an independent society, the Anthroposophical Society. The first performance of *Die Pforte* took place only a few months after the founding of the Star of the East. In this play an episode is inserted which specifically identifies the return of Christ as an 'ethereal' process, not a flesh and blood person. A character called Theodora proclaims this in the first scene of Die Pforte. In 1911 and 1912 the political antagonisms intensified, Steiner stood his ground with regard to the Star of the East, and the performance of his second and third dramas, which continued the themes of the first, became a major expression of the independent approach that Steiner was adopting.

The inclusion in the play of the episode with Theodora concerning the Second Coming in the *Die Pforte* is an expression of Steiner's Christology, but in part it was probably also due to Steiner's wish to correct what he saw as an error promulgated by the Star of the East with regards to Christian eschatology. He felt the need to confront the politically inspired machinations of senior personnel in the Theosophical Society, which he felt were threatening to distort the members' understanding of this theme, as comments in a lecture from 1910 reveal,

> Materialism has seized hold of all circles today. It is not only native to the occident; it has also encompassed the orient, except it comes to expression in a different way there. It might happen that the oriental materialism could bring it about that....materialistic thinking transfers the appearance of Christ into a materialistic perspective....Just as little can the Christ-Being be pressed and narrowed by the oriental traditions, just as little can it receive a colouration from the dogmas of oriental dogmatism.[55]

---

[55] Rudolf Steiner, Die Mission der Einzelnen Volkseelen, (Dornach: RSV, 1974) Taschenbuch Ausgabe, 198 and 206, „Der Materialismus hat alle Kreise heute ergriffen. Er ist nicht nur im Okzident heimisch, er hat auch den Orient erfaßt; nur in einer andern Form kommt er da zum Vorschein. Es könnte sein, daß der orientalische Materialismus dahin führen werde, daß....materialistisches Denken das Erscheinen des Christus in eine materialistische Anschauung umsetzen wird. Ebensowenig darf die

This was a signal that Steiner would soon be setting out on his own path, splitting from the Theosophical Society. In December 1912, after continued manoeuvres against him, and the insistence by Adyar that Krishnamurti was the returned Christ, Steiner emphasized that the teachings of the Order of the Star of the East were contrary to esoteric Christian truths and announced his intention to establish the Anthroposophical Society. He informed the Theosophists that membership in this new society was incompatible with membership in the Besant-Leadbeater society. In the next half-year, several thousand Theosophists, mainly in Germany, went with Steiner, thousands more stayed with the Adyar main stream.[56]

The term, 'anthroposophy', chosen by Steiner to differentiate his teachings from those associated with the Theosophical Society, is a Greek neologism, which has the general meaning of 'the wisdom of the human being'. It is not a Steiner neologism, it had been coined separately by various writers over the centuries. The *Historisches Wörterbuch der Philosophie* identifies P.V.Troxler (1780-1866) as the first German writer to use it, in 1828, where it has the meaning of, "A natural philosophy about human cognition (eine Naturlehre des menschlichen Erkennens...)"[57] Prior to this, it was used in the 16th and 17th centuries in Latin in hermetic-alchemical treatises, for example by Eugenius Philalethes and Henry Moore in 1650.[58] Steiner himself regarded his own teachings as quite separate from any formalized theosophical dogmas. This term historically implied in Germany an ennobled form of knowledge; Steiner quotes its use by I.H Fichte;

Christus-Wesenheit gedrückt und beengt werden aus den orientalischen Traditionen heraus, ebensowenig eine Färbung erhalten durch die Dogmen des orientalischen Dogmatismus. "

[56] Harry Collison, "*To the President and members*", Mitteilungen für die Mitglieder der Anthroposophischen Gesellschaft (theosophischen Gesellschaft 1 (April 1913): 23.

[57] Historisches Wörterbuch der Philosophie, Bd. 1 A-C, ed. Joachim Ritter, (Darmstadt: Wissenschaftliche Buchgesellschaft, 1971, 377.

[58] Beiträge zur Rudolf Steiner Gesamtausgabe, Nr. 121, ed. Walter Kugler, (Dornach; Rudolf Steiner Nachlaßverwaltung, 1999) 12-14.

> "...the sense-derived consciousness...together with human sense life in its totality has no other significance than to be that place in which the supra-sensible life of the spirit is accomplished...this fundamental comprehension of human nature henceforth raises 'anthropology' in its end results into 'anthroposophy'." [59]

In 1902 a theosophical conference which was held in Berlin, to formally found the German branch of the Theosophical Society, with Steiner as its General Secretary. Steiner absented himself for a time from the conference, and gave a talk on 'anthroposophy' to members of the Giordano Bruno Bund to whom he had earlier delivered various lectures.[60] Hence his 'theosophical' teachings from the very inception of his new phase of life, were in effect, not restatements of the Adyar-based Society's worldview, but his own esoteric-spiritual conclusions.

Twenty years after the founding of the German branch of the Theosophical Society, in a public lecture from 1923, he described his understanding of this term, giving emphasis to the intention to present his elucidations in a rational manner, in the hope of avoiding his new worldview being dismissed as indefinable (superstitious) 'mysticism',

> Anthroposophy in the first instance, wants to be a knowledge of the spiritual world, a kind of knowledge which can indeed be placed at the side of what we today have in such a magnificent way, as science. It wants to place itself at the side of this science, through scientific conscientiousness, and because it is the case that those who in an earnest manner take up anthroposophy into their heart, don't only want to simply do that, but also want to develop it further –

---

[59] Rudolf Steiner "Menschenseele und Menschenleib in Natur- und Geist-Erkenntnis" 15.Mar. 1917, in Geist und Stoff, Leben und Tod, (Dornach; VRSN, 1961) 169.
[60] Beiträge zur Rudolf Steiner Gesamtausgabe, Nr. 121, „Anthroposophie: Quellentexte zur Wortgeschichte", (Dornach: VRSN, 1999) 52.

and above all, through the situation that such a person must have utilized the strict and earnest methods which natural science today practises.[61]

At this stage the reception of Steiner's work by the early twenties needs to be noted. Despite his success with those Theosophists who made the decision to join the new Anthroposophical Society, his teachings did not make any noticeable impact in the normal cultural life. His intention to present his spiritual conclusions in a manner which evinced a scientific methodology in his research techniques, and hence a rational, coherent quality in his elucidations, did not result in any substantial response from the community.

His philosophical writings and several small books on social and political issues were noted in wider circles in his time, but none of his anthroposophical texts were widely received. In addition to his philosophical and esoteric writings, Steiner was astonishingly creative in art. He made one hundred paintings or drawings, created 1,500 choreographed dance movements for his new dance system called 'eurhythmy', designed several buildings in a new organic style of architecture, and sculpted several sculptures. These artistic activities also remained initiatives that were of limited appeal. Hence the interest in his work was limited for decades to the tiny membership of his Society, although briefly in the years 1919-20 when Steiner lectured on social issues, in the aftermath of World War One, large audiences were drawn to hear him.

---

[61]Rudolf Steiner, Was wollte das Goetheanum und was soll die Anthroposophie? (Dornach: VRSN, 1961) 10, „Anthroposophie will zunächst sein eine Erkenntnis der geistigen Welt, eine solche Erkenntnis der geistigen Welt welche sich durchaus an die Seite stellen kann dem, was wir heute in einer so großartigen Weise als Naturwissenschaft haben. Sie will sich an die Seite stellen dieser Naturwissenschaft sowohl durch wissenschaftliche Gewissenhaftigkeit, wie auch dadurch, daß derjenige, der in ernster Weise nicht bloß Anthroposophie in sein Gemüt aufnehmen, sondern sie aufbauen will, daß der vor allen Dingen durchgegangen sein muß durch alle strengen und ernsten Methoden, welche die Naturwissenschaft heute übt."

There was no critiquing of Steiner's dramas by the wider theatrical public, as they were designed for didactic theosophical-anthroposophical purpose. The dramas had been performed privately in Munich, and a development proposal including architectural plans, was submitted to the city council to construct an international cultural centre for Steiner's initiative. Permission was refused on grounds of architectural incompatibility with the traditional cityscape of that city, and Steiner transferred his activities to Switzerland about 1915.

The proposed centre for his work, the Goetheanum, was constructed there, near the small town of Dornach, in the vicinity of Basel. The construction of this building was not sufficiently advanced to allow it to be used for theatrical purposes until the early 1920's. However, after it was destroyed by an arsonist attack in early January 1923, the dramas were not performed again until 1928, and in a different venue. This is three years after Steiner had died, and before the building had been rebuilt. Although by 1980 the performances of his dramas in Dornach were opened to the public, the preceding history of their performances meant that there were no reviews or articles regarding them, or of Steiner as a dramatist, outside of anthroposophical circles.

Even when prominent persons were drawn to Steiner's ideas, little of this flowed into the mainstream because it was apparently incompatible with current scientific theory. An example of this concerns the decision of several dozen of priests and theologians to join together to form a new church, based on Steiner's anthroposophical Christology. This church, *"Die Christengemeinschaft"* (*The Christian Community*) was founded in 1922 with the help of Steiner. One of these men was a very highly regarded liberal Protestant cleric, Friedrich Rittelmeyer (1872-1938).

Rittelmeyer was a protestant theologian and preacher, well known for his sermons in Nuremberg; he joined the "Neuen Kirche" in Berlin. In his autobiographical work, *"Rudolf*

Steiner enters my life" (1929) he describes how at first, in his search for meaning to his religious life, he lectured in meetings of the Freunde der Christlichen Welt, whom he described as "a body of people who fully recognized the results of modern scientific research, and who were fighting for freedom and truth in the religious life of the future."[62] Shortly afterwards, he encountered Theosophy through a prominent German Theosophist, Michael Bauer, in 1910, and then soon encountered opposition from colleagues, who were sceptical of the attitude of respect for Steiner's teachings.

A year later he met Rudolf Steiner, who made such an impression upon him, that he gradually became convinced of the validity of Steiner's approach to Christology. Rittelmeyer later wrote "Theology and Anthroposophy" in which he attempts to harmonize theological attitudes with the spiritual-esoteric views of Steiner. Later he wrote a book of contemplations on The Lord's Prayer, drawing broadly on Steiner's elucidations of this verse, in which he uses imagery drawn from esoteric Christian traditions elucidated by Steiner. For example, the image of drawing near to the castle of the Holy Grail is used when referring to the process of entering into the inner meaning of the prayer.[63]

When Rittelmeyer left his church to join the new Steiner associated church, and as its first highest ranking clergyman, an article was published in the prominent church journal, *Christliche Welt*, in 1938, expressing its regret at his departure. However the article omits any mention of the name of Rudolf Steiner, even though he was regarded as co-founder of the church. In 1939, in a review of Rittelmeyer's autobiography, wherein Rittelmeyer describes at length why he became an anthroposophist, the editors, in the same church journal, omit to mention Steiner completely.

---

[62] Friedrich Rittelmeyer, "Rudolf Steiner enters my life" (London: The Christian Community Press, 1929) 16.
[63] Rittelmeyer, The Lord's Prayer, (London: The Christian Community Press, 1931) 81.

As Ute Gause comments, writing in a leading German ecclesiastical journal in 1996, Rittelmeyer was described by his ecclesiastical colleagues as "a highly gifted man, around whom at all times was an atmosphere of honour and goodness...a man who knew how to speak to the heart of listeners about Jesus wonderfully." But as Gause concludes, "Apparently, it was required that anthroposophy and its influence on Rittelmeyer be taboo.[64] This, despite the fact a learned scholar and academic, Prof. Dr. Wilhelm Stählin held a seminar on this topic, which was well-attended at the Münster University in the winter of 1934/35. Years later, in 1953, as Gerhard Wehr reports, Stählin wrote an article inviting discussion to Rittelmeyer's book, "Theology and Anthroposophy" in a theological anthology (*Evangelium und Christen-gemeinschaft*), but no responses ever occurred.[65]

The isolation culturally of Steiner's initiatives during his lifetime, and for some decades afterwards, may have been to due the public perception of his movement as sectarian and irrelevant to mainstream concerns. Steiner's attitude to 'Theosophy' and the Theosophical Society was that the tendency to sectarianism was a problem which required monitoring. As noted above, Steiner viewed the term 'Theosophy' itself in the more encompassing manner, invoking the extended meaning which it had prior of the emergence of the Theosophical Society, namely divinely inspired wisdom of any epoch.[66] By the 16th century, 'theosophy' stood for both a knowledge of the divine, as well as magical-hermetic ideas, which in age of rationalism became increasingly. By the end of the 18th century, Romantics such as Schiller and Ch.M. Wieland were able to

---

[64] Ute Gause, „Friedrich Rittelmeyer (1872-1938) Vom Liberalen Protestantismus zur anthroposophischen Christusfrömmigkeit," Zeitschrift für Religions- und Geistesgeschichte, Friedrich-Wilhelm Kantzenbach, Hans-Joachim Klimkeit, Joachim H. Knoll, Julius H. Schoeps, eds, 48th annual edition (Leiden: E.J. Brill, 1966), 153.
[65] Gerhard Wehr, *Theologe und Anthroposoph – In memoriam Friedrich Rittelmeyer*, Mensch und Welt 3, (1968) 101-102.
[66] For example, Friedrich Schiller in his Philosophical Letters, refers to the mystical-spiritual teachings of a character, Julius, as 'theosophy', and the writings of an 18th century mystic, Louis Claude de Saint-Martin (1743-1803) are commonly referred to as 'theosophical'.

see this 'theosophy' with its dual aspects in a positive light – an attitude assimilable and helpful to Steiner's anthroposophy – whilst Kant warned against it, "seeing theology endangered by it", an attitude antagonistic to Steiner's aims.[67]

Hence, Steiner in commenting on Schelling's failure to convince the academy of his spiritual worldview is able to refer to the concepts as theosophical, "Schelling began to teach Theosophy, really Theosophy, in an abstract form certainly, and he had the same result as a person today would have who wanted to teach Theosophy in an university."[68]

Steiner, as General Secretary of the Theosophical Society, taught his listeners that a non-sectarian approach must be striven for,

> In true theosophists, it is not words and concepts which live, rather it is the spirit. And the spirit does not have words and concepts, it is fully alive. All concepts and words are only an external form for this spirit which lives in the human being…then we will perhaps not even speak in terms which were valid in the Theosophical movement, and then we will actually be better theosophists…if we were to differentiate between true-believer and heretics then in that moment we would no longer understand the Theosophical movement.[69]

---

[67] Historisches Wörterbuch der Philosophie, ed. Joachim Ritter and Karlfried Gründer, (Darmstadt: Wissenschaftliche Buchgesellschaft, 1998, 1158.
[68] Rudolf Steiner, Wege und Ziele des geistigen Menschen (Dornach: RSV, 1973) 36 „…Schelling…Er begann Theosophie zu lehren, wirkliche Theosophie, allerdings in abstrakter Form, und er hatte denselben Erfolg, den heute ein Mensch haben würde, welcher Theosophie an einer Universität lehren wollte."
[69] Rudolf Steiner, Spirituelle Seelenlehre und Weltbetrachtung, (Dornach: RSV, 1972) 421-422, „Im wahren Theosophen leben nicht Worte und Begriffe, in ihm lebt der Geist. Und der Geist hat nicht Worte und nicht Begriffe, der hat unmittelbares Leben. Alle Begriffe und Worte sind nur äußere Form für diesen im Menschen lebenden Geist…Dann werden wir vielleicht gar nicht in den Worten spechen, die gültig waren in der theosophischen Bewegung, und wir sind doch bessere Theosophen…Wenn wir Rechtgläubige und Ketzer unterscheiden würden, so würden wir in demselbem Augenblick die theosophische Bewegung nicht mehr begriffen haben."

Nevertheless, despite his attempts to avoid sectarianism, and to propagate his teachings, his activity in this Society, and in the Anthroposophical Society, which he founded in 1913, his activity did not result in a socially significant movement in his lifetime. The inherent distance of modernity from a strongly 'metaphysical' worldview resulted in all such movements – decades before the New Age – being on the fringe of society.

On various occasions Steiner made reference to the ambiguous, and sometimes quite hostile reception of his worldview in various circles. In 1924, he quoted, and then rebutted, a very negative assessment of his writings by Maurice Maeterlinck. The playwright had expressed his view in writing that, in effect, Steiner's teachings may in part be logical and good, but they then deteriorate into virtually insane nonsense,

> One can not read without some irony, what an otherwise so promising a spirit as Maurice Maeterlinck has written about me… just think that in his writings you can find almost verbatim from him; *'in the introductory sections of his writings…Steiner always shows a capacity for discernment, logic, detail; {but} then in his later chapters it appears that Steiner may be insane'*. Well, my dear friends, what consequence can one draw from these words? For that would mean in fact; first chapter, capacity for discernment, logic and detail. Last chapter; insane. Then that book is finished, now another one comes. And again, at first, capacity for discernment, logic and detail, finally: insane. I have written quite a certain number of books {*all of which have this character*}, so therefore I must go through this procedure with a certain virtuosity…[70]

---

[70] Rudolf Steiner, <u>Esoterische Betrachtungen: karmischer Zusammenhänge</u> Bd 5, (Dornach: RSV, 1975) 73-74; „Man kann doch nicht ohne eine gewisse Ironie dasjenige lesen, was ein sonst so hoffnungsvoller Geist wie Maurice

This must have been something of an ironical blow for Steiner, who had, as noted earlier, co-produced a performance of Maurice Maeterlink's drama, "*Der Ungebetene*", in the 1880's. Furthermore, Steiner had written of Maeterlink, as a playwright, "He is one of the most outstanding experiences of the modern soul".[71]

Steiner's approach to spiritual development is a major theme of his drama, *Die Pforte*, and will be explored in Section 3a. Chronologically, the events in *Die Pforte* occur contemporaneous to Steiner's lifetime, and the drama is set in central Europe, in a circle of people cultivating esoteric-religiosity. The context of the drama is evidently meant to embody the dynamics involved with Steiner and his students. I propose to examine the first play, *Die Pforte*, with the aim of identifying its main thematic content, and to then identify the primary elements of his spiritual worldview expressed in it.

In addition I intend to contextualize these elements in terms of Steiner's intellectual roots in the German Romantic tradition, and in terms of their consistency to Steiner's earlier phase, of holistic epistemology, and to his later esoteric worldview. As Steiner's anthroposophical context is clearly an esoteric one, his relationship to mainstream cultural life of his times, such as political, social and literary movements, is not examined in this thesis. Its focus is his holistic epistemology and esoteric-spiritual views.

Maeterlinck über mich selbst...sagt. Denken Sie doch, es findet sich bei ihm fast wörtlich der Satz; *In den Einführungen seiner Bücher, in den ersten Kapiteln, da zeigt Steiner immer einen abwägenden, logischen, weiten Geist; dann in den weitern Kapiteln ist es, als ob er wahnsinnig würde.* Ja, meine lieben Freunde, was hat denn aber das für eine Konsequenz? Das hieße ja: Erstes Kapitel: abwägender, logischer, weiter Geist. Letztes Kapitel: wahnsinnig. Nun ist das Buch fertig, nun kommt ein neues. Wiederum zuerst; abwägender, logischer, weiter Geist, zuletzt: wahnsinnig. Ich habe eine ganze Anzahl von Büchern geschrieben, so daß ich also diese Prozedur mit einer gewissen Virtuosität durchmachen würde..."

[71] Rudolf Steiner Gesammelte Aufsätze zur Literatur, (Dornach: RSV, 1971) 230, „Maurice Maeterlinck ist eines der hervorragendsten Erlebnisse der modernen Seele."

INTRODUCTION B
The Romantic context: themes from Goethe and Schiller viewed as formative by Steiner in early years, and viewed as supportive to his 'anthroposophy' in later years

1B1: Egyptian Mysteries: Schiller's esoteric religiosity and Pre-existence

As we noted earlier, Steiner mentions in his autobiography that Schiller's "Briefe über die ästhetische Erziehung des Menschen (Letters about the aesthetic education of humanity)" were of considerable significance for him as a young man. In his anthroposophical period, Steiner commented of Schiller in lectures to Theosophists that, "His entire way of living, his entire personal striving, was one great self education, and in this sense, he was a practicing Theosophist."[72] Naturally, the term Theosophist here has that broader connotation to Steiner, which we have noted above. In a series of lectures on Schiller, given in 1905, Steiner presents elements of Schiller's spiritual worldview which he found to be affirmative of his own. Such references to Schiller and Goethe by Steiner are consistent with his method of referring to affirmative material from Central European literary figures, in contrast to using material from Indian sources, which were preferred by the leaders of the Adyar-based Theosophical Society.

Commenting on a passage in Schiller's 'Julian Correspondence', Steiner describes that Schiller had developed the view that everything in the world derives from a spiritual primal fundament, and the human being too, has arisen out of this primal fundament.[73] The passage of Schiller's, from which Steiner quotes is,

---

[72] Rudolf Steiner, Ursprung und Ziel des Menschen, (Dornach: RSV, 1981) 403; „Seine ganze Lebensführung, sein ganzes Streben ist nichts anderes als eine große Selbsterziehung, und in diesem Sinne ist Schiller ein praktischer Theosoph".
[73] Rudolf Steiner, Über Philosophie, Geschichte und Literatur, (Dornach: RSV 1983), 243.

> The universe is a thought of God. Once this ideal[74] spiritual image passed over into manifested reality, and the born world has – permit me this human notion – fulfilled its Creator's design, it is the duty of all thinking beings to find again the initial design in this now extant whole; to seek out the principle in the machine, the unity in the compound, the law in the phenomenon, and to transfer retrospectively the edifice back to its {ideal} ground-plan.[75]

The editors of Schiller's Works, in their commentary, point out that quite a number of Schiller's attitudes here can be found in other Romantic writers. The editors characterize Schiller's ideas in his Philosophical Letters as 'theosophical' in the wider sense, and hence in the sphere of 'the esoteric'.[76] Certainly, Schiller expresses here convictions which are closely allied to those which we have considered so far in Steiner's anthroposophy. The capacity in humanity to apprehend the archetypal thoughts, and the conclusion that creation derives from the archetypal Idea is as we have noted, a major element in Steiner's philosophical writings on cognition.

These are elaborated in great detail in his esoteric works, being integral to Steiner's anthroposophical worldview. In his lectures and writings on cosmology, Steiner elaborates a cosmic system in which, in the first instance, Deity – through the efficacy of the nine ranks of hierarchical beings, known to us from medieval theologians – forms the visible created world. These beings use the Idea to bring about an

---

[74] 'Ideal' here is an adjective meaning of, or from, an archetypal Idea, in the Platonic sense.

[75] Schiller, SW, Bd 21, 115, „Das Universum ist ein Gedanke Gottes. Nachdem dieses idealische Geistesbild in die Wirklichkeit hinübertrat und die geborne Welt den Riß ihres Schöpfers erfüllte - erlaube mir diese menschliche Vorstellung - so ist der Beruf aller denkenden Wesen, in diesem vorhandenen Ganzen die erste Zeichnung wiederzufinden, die Regel in der Maschine, die Einheit in dem Zusammenhang, das Gesetz in dem Phänomen aufzusuchen und das Gebäude rückwärts auf seinen Grundriß zu übertragen."

[76] Schiller, SW, Bd. 21, 161.

embodiment of the Idea in the material world. This Idea is condensed into material reality over long periods of time.

Then, moreover, as humanity awakens to its potential in lifetimes upon the Earth, the task devolves upon people to learn to perceive these cosmic archetypal thoughts, and thereby cognize their inherent dynamics, by a sensitive insightful response to the phenomena of the spiritual world. As Steiner explained to his audiences, the acolyte must learn to read 'the hidden script'. The acolyte is to not only attain to images of a psychic nature, but to allow the relationship of these various images to exert an efficacy upon oneself,

> One begins to arrange the lines of force, which move creatively throughout the world, into certain figures and colour formations. One learns to sense an inner connection which is expressed in these figures; this exerts the efficacy of the spiritual tone, of the music of the spheres, for these figures are formed according to the true cosmic relationships.[77]

The implication here is that the esotericist in Steiner's understanding has developed the consciousness state in which the formative lines of force can be perceived. Once perceived, the next step is to sense the connection these have to the archetypal Ideas from the Creator. Schiller's reference to 'seeking out the principle in the machine' does not pose a contradiction for Steiner, rather, it affirms his viewpoint.

To Steiner, the capacity of the human being to conceive ideas is an extension, within the microcosm of humanity, of the creative power of the deity in the macrocosm. When a person creates a concept, whether of a machine or of a virtue or a literary work, there is to be an archetypal idea of these in the 'Devachan', or the Platonic realm of Ideas, "a new thought, a work of art, a new machine, brings something into the world (from Devachan) which was not there before....For the most

---

[77] Rudolf Steiner, <u>Die Theosophie des Rosenkreutzer</u>, (Dornach: RSV, 1979) 162.

insignificant original deeds there are already models in Devachan."[78] Such humanly generated ideas are not considered to be as potent as those of deity, but nevertheless, have an archetypal existence.

In the same lecture on Schiller, Steiner quotes from a remarkable text of Schiller's, namely his theosophical-mystical 'Julian Correspondence', in which two friends discuss esoteric themes. The sentence which Steiner quotes is, "…alles in mir und außer mir ist nur eine Hieroglyph des höchsten Wesens" (everything in me and outside me is only a hieroglyph of the highest being)', commenting that this is an expression of the theosophy of Schiller.[79] Steiner then paraphrases these and the above words of Schiller, in this way, "All things in the world derive from a primal spiritual source of all creation. The human being, too, initially has its origin from this primal source of all creation; it is a confluence of all of the forces of the greater world." [80]

The term, 'a hieroglyph of the highest being' is a prominent metaphor in Steiner's works. In 1920 Steiner gave a course of lectures entitled, "Correspondences between the microcosm and the macrocosm; man as a hieroglyph of the universe." In this lecture cycle he laboured to demonstrate how deeply inherent in the kingdoms of nature is the efficacy of the cosmos, as his introductory words indicate,

> In reality the constitution of the universe can not really be considered unless one continuously makes reference to the human being, unless always tries to

---

[78] Steiner, Rosenkreutzers, 42, „Ein neuer Gedanke, ein Kunstwerk, eine neue Maschine bringt etwas in die Welt, was noch nicht da war…Auch für die unbedeutendsten originellen Handlungen sind schon Vorbilder im Devachan vorhanden."
[79] Steiner, Über Philosophie, 243.
[80] Steiner, Über Philosophie, Geschichte und Literatur (Dornach: RSV, 1983) 242-3, „Alles in der Welt entstammt einem geistigen Urgrunde. Auch der Mensch ist zunächst hervorgegangen aus diesem Urgrund; er ist ein Zusammenfluß aller Kräfte der Welt."

discover in the universe, so to speak, that which is also in one way or another in the human being.[81]

Steiner concludes in his lecture on Schiller from 1905, that to Schiller, the harmony of the world did not appear as something already attained, but as a goal of development. That is, the eternal harmony of nature appeared as something beautiful to him, but also as something which the human being also should strive to attain. This conclusion by Steiner allows Schiller's texts to harmonize very closely with his view of higher spiritual attainment; such an achievement involves a successful striving by the acolyte to attain to an inner harmony. Steiner concluded that this harmony has a perfect expression in the natural world, especially in the movement of the planets in the solar system.[82]

Additionally, the concept of pre-existence, encountered in the Romantics, has a significant role in Steiner's spiritual-esoteric worldview, because, as mentioned earlier, it logically opens the possibility of the concept of more than one life. Repeated earth-lives is a pivotal concept in Steiner's understanding of human existence; he sees a specific purpose to human life, a purpose which can only be fulfilled through more than one life. In effect, Steiner considered that the human being returns to Earth many times, in order to attain ever-higher spirituality and wisdom, through life experience.[83]

With reference to the dramatic works of Schiller, Steiner comments significantly concerning the nature of Schiller's dramas in general, that in these, "Schiller attempted to become clear how a great, transpersonal {law of} destiny exerts an influence within the personality. We have often

---

[81] Rudolf Steiner, <u>Entsprechungen zwischen Mikrokosmos und Makrokosmos, Der Mensch - eine Hieroglyphe des Weltenall</u> (Dornach: RSV, 1987) 53, „In Wirklichkeit kann die Konstitution des Weltenalls gar nicht betrachtet werden, ohne daß man fortwährend auf den Menschen Bezug nimmt, gewissermaßen immer versucht, dasjenige im Weltenall draußen aufzusuchen, was sich auch in irgendeiner Weise im Menschen findet."
[82] Rudolf Steiner, Dec 19, 1904, unpublished archive lecture.
[83] Rudolf Steiner, <u>Theosophie</u>, *Wiederverkörperung des Geistes und Schicksal.*

mentioned this law as the law of karma."[84] That Steiner sees Schiller's dramatic concepts as expressive of the concept of 'karma' is closely connected with his interest in bringing about an acceptance of this concept, (although within a Christian context). Steiner hoped that gradually in Christendom an acceptance of the concept of karma and repeated earth-lives would occur. In Die Pforte, Steiner's view of the concept of karma is presented in detail; it is shown as making understandable, amongst other things, the intense feelings of personal affection or antipathy, between two characters.

Another esoteric-spiritual theme to be found in Schiller's works, and which Steiner experienced as strongly affirmative, concerns esoteric religiosity. Schiller's treatise on the cultural history of the world, *"Die Sendung Moses"* (*The mission of Moses*), emphasizes the existence of the Mystery cults of antiquity, as an important part of history. In this text, Schiller commences by praising the high spirituality attained in the Hebrew people, as expressed in their monotheism, and affirms that the efficacy of this even reaches into his time, "Indeed, in a certain sense it is undeniably true that a great part of the enlightenment which delights us today we have thank to the religion of Moses."[85]

Then, later in this work Schiller focuses on the theme of ancient Egyptian esoteric religiosity, and sees a hidden influence, deriving from the secret Egyptian Mystery teaching of Isis, efficacious in the teachings of the Hebrew prophets. Taking his cue from contemporary writers,[86] Schiller affirms the similarity of Egyptian and later Hebraic religious tenets,

---

[84] Rudolf Steiner, Ursprung und Ziel der Menschen, (Dornach: RSV, 1981) 410, „Er suchte sich klar zu werden, wie in das Persönliche das große Überpersönliche Schicksal hereinspielt. Wir haben oftmals schon dieses Gesetz als das Karma-gesetz erwähnt."
[85] Schiller, SW, Bd 17, 377; „Ja, in einem gewißen Sinne ist es unwiderleglich wahr, daß wir der mosaischen Religion einen großen Teil der Aufklärung danken, deren wir uns heutiges Tages erfreuen."
[86] Schiller SW Bd. 2, S. 263, the editors (Helmut Koopmann and Benno von Wiese), mention in particular, the writings of Karl Leonhard Reinhold as formative for Schiller's views here.

>...the epoptae recognized a single, highest principle of all things, a primal force....the essence of all being....under an ancient statue of Isis were to be read the words, "I am that which is", and upon as pillar at Sais a strange ancient inscription, "I am all that is, that was, that will be; no mortal man has ever lifted my veil.[87]

In his *Die Sendung Moses*, Schiller also describes what scholars believe occurred in the initiation rites of the Egyptian god of Isis and Serapis, which he sees as a precursor to the Grecian Mystery cults of Eleusis and Samothrace. Schiller also wrote a remarkably evocative, long poem on the initiatory process in ancient Egypt, at Sais, which we shall note shortly.

To Steiner, the mystery religions of antiquity were likewise the expression of an awareness of spiritual, supra-sensible realities. This awareness existed to a much higher degree in earlier ages, this was a condition of consciousness naturally present in humanity of earlier ages. Consequently, in his treatment of history, Steiner focused more on cultural developments and the strivings of the Mystery Centres, than on military, political and commercial developments. His lecture cycle entitled, *Die Weltgeschichte in anthroposophischer Beleuchtung and als Grundlage der Erkenntnis des Menschengeistes* (*The History of the World in the Light of Anthroposophy*) treats the development of consciousness of nations, and the primary myths of Mesopotamia as an expression of ancient esoteric religiosity. He devotes lectures to the processes occurring the esoteric life, in the Hibernian and Ephesian Mysteries. Steiner comments in another lecture cycle on the Mystery history of

---

[87] SW Bd 17, S. 385, „Die Epopten erkannten eine einizige höchste Ursache aller Dinge, eine Urkraft der Nature, das Wesen aller Wesen....Unter einer alten Säule der Isis las man die Worte, 'Ich bin, was da ist' und auf einer Pyramide zu Saïs fand man die uralte merkwürdige Inschrift; 'Ich bin alles was ist, was war, und was sein wird, kein sterblicher Mensch hat meinen Schleier aufgehoben'."

humanity, that in more ancient times of human history a more penetrating way of perceiving was retained, and consequently,

> .... one understood something of the permeation of external nature by a soul-element, and because one understood the incorporating of the spirit-soul element into the physical-corporeal, then one understood something of the spirit, as it pulses in wave-like undulations throughout the created world.[88]

To Steiner, the special Mystery sites in which esoteric religiosity was nurtured were places where acolytes had the goal of actively attaining higher spiritual experiences. The earnestness of the spiritual striving that occurred in these Centres was emphasized by Steiner,

> Mystery Centres is what one calls those places where the highest questions of the spiritual life were brought before the students, and answered. And in such Mystery centres the students were not taught in an abstract manner, about such questions. The truths were only made available to them once their soul, their spirit, their entire personality was so constituted that they could see these questions on the right light.

These statements about the esoteric religiosity of antiquity are reminiscent of the Schiller poem, concerning the experiences of an acolyte in the ancient Egyptian cult of Isis, *Das Verschleierte Bild zu Saïs*, (*The Veiled Image of Sais*), ca. 1797. The poem treats the initiatory striving of acolytes in an ancient Egyptian temple community, in which the search for the goddess Isis is the focus. In particular this poem presents the specific dynamics of the spiritual quest, and the

---

[88] Rudolf Steiner, Perspektiven der Menschheitsentwickelung, (Dornach: RSV, 1979) 50-51, „....der Mensch verstand etwas von dem Seelischen Walten auch in der äußeren Natur, und indem er verstand die Einkörperung des Geistig-Seelischen in das Physisch-Leibliche, verstand er etwas von dem die Welt durchwellenden und durchwallenden Geist."

consequences of ignoring these. The setting is a mystery centre of the Isis religion in Sais in ancient Egypt.

The full text of the poem is given here, for this reason and also because its primary theme, not the cult of Isis as such, are seen by Steiner as related closely to that of Die Pforte.

The Veiled Image of Sais

> A young man, whose burning thirst for knowledge
> lead him to Sais in Egypt,
> there to learn the secret wisdom of the priests
> had already hastened through many a degree
> With his quick mind;
> his thirst for research constantly drove him on,
> and scarcely could the Hierophant calm the impatient Seeker.
> "What do I have, if I don't have all?" said the youth,
> "Is there here such a thing as more or less?"
> Is thy Truth, like happiness,
> merely a total sum, of which
> one may possess a greater or lesser amount,
> but always possessing it?
> Is not Truth a single, indivisible thing?
> Take a tone from a harmony,
> take a colour out of the rainbow
> and all that remains to you is nothing, so long as the
> beauteous entirety of tones and colours is missing.
> Once when they were speaking thus,
> they were standing quietly in a solitary rotunda
> wherein a veiled statue of enormous size
> attracted the gaze of the youth.
> Astonished, he looks at his guide and says:
> "What is it that is hiding behind this veil"? –
> "The Truth," is the answer –
> " What ! " called out the other,
> but Truth alone is what I am striving for, and it is
> precisely this which one is hiding from me ?"

"Arrange that with the deity", responded the
Hierophant;
'No mortal", she says, 'will lift this veil until I myself
raise it,
And whoever should raise the holy forbidden thing
with guilty hands, they…', says the deity…"
– "Well?"
– " 'They will see the Truth'."
"A remarkable oracular utterance!
You yourself would never have raised it?" –
"I?" "Certainly not! Nor was I ever tempted to do
so."
"That I don't understand. If only this thin
partition separates me from the Truth –
"And a law", his guide adds interrupting him –
"more important is this thin cloth, my son, than you
realize – light indeed for thy hand,
yet a hundredweight heavier for your conscience."
To his quarters the youth then returned, engrossed in
thought.The burning desire for knowledge robbed him
of sleep, he tossed around on the bed feverishly,
and about midnight he arose.
Unwillingly his diffident steps lead him to the temple,
it was easy for him to climb the wall,
one bold leap brought the daring one
right into the middle of the rotunda.

There he stands now, and dreadfully
does the lifeless stillness envelop the lone seeker,
relieved only by the hollow echoing
of his footsteps among the secret crypts.
From above, the Moon through the cupola's opening,
cast a pale silvery-blue light,
and the figure under its long veil
glows through the darkness of the rotunda
with a terrible light
as if a God were present.

With uncertain step he approached;

already the insolent hand wants to touch the sacred object;
when a burning heat and coldness flashes through his bones and pushes him back with unseen arms.
Unhappy youth, what do you intend ? –
thus did a faithful voice cry out within him.
Do you want to put the Most Holy to the test?
"No mortal", spoke the mouth of the Oracle, "lifts this veil until I myself raise it".
Yet did not the same mouth also say;
Whoever raises this veil shall see Truth?
Be behind it what may, I will lift the veil!"
In a loud voice, he cries out: "I want to behold it"!
.... B e h o l d   i t !

The long shrill echo clangs after him mockingly.
He speaks thus, and has lifted the veil.
"Well", you ask, "and what was revealed to him here?"
That I don't know. Senseless and pale, thus did the priests find him the next day, outstretched by the pedestal of the statue of Isis.
Whatever he there saw and experienced,
his tongue never disclosed it.
Gone forever was his happiness,
a deep sorrow tore him away to an early grave.
"Woe to that person", were his words warning –
"When impetuous interrogators then beset him:
Woe to him who approaches the Truth through guilt!
It will nevermore bring joy to him." "[89]

This poem of Schiller's takes up his fascination with the esoteric cultic life of ancient Egypt implied in his *Die Sendung Moses*. Steiner lectured extensively on the primary theme explored in this poem, namely, the search for Isis,

---

[89]Friedrich Schiller: Gedichte 1789-1805, SW Bd. 1, S. 224-6, ***Das verschleierte Bild zu Sais***
– to avoid a footnote running over several pages, I append the German text to the end of this section.

> This image of Isis, what a lasting impression it makes on us, when we picture it to ourselves, how it stands there in stone, but at the same time the stone is veiled from top to bottom – *the veiled image of Isis*....and it has inscribed on it, 'I am the past, the present and the future...no mortal has ever lifted my veil'.[90]

Steiner's comments on the cognitional tension around the spiritual quest echo those in *The Veiled Image of Sais*; like the great mystic and philosopher Meister Eckart, he emphasizes that what is to be encountered in the journey down into the depths of the human soul is very difficult to describe in human words. Steiner regarded the content of this poem as reflecting an historical instance of a major error which acolytes in the mysteries can make; namely, that of being too hasty in the search for enlightenment, "The young man of Sais wanted to know, unprepared, of the secrets of the spiritual world...he was later reborn..." [91]

In effect, to Steiner, *The Veiled Image of Isis* derived from Schiller's spiritual awareness, which accessed events in a previous age – not necessarily that of Schiller himself – in ancient Egypt. The misstep by the youth of Sais is a potent example of the moral-ethical challenges which the characters in Die Pforte must also encounter.

He maintained that the message of the inscription suggested only that soul who can approach the Mysteries of Isis with reverence may uncover the secrets of Isis. The results of improper questing would be severe,

---

[90] Rudolf Steiner, Innere Entwicklungsimpulse der Menschheit" (Dornach: VRSN, 1964) 166; „Dieses Isis-Bild, was für einen ergreifenden Eindruck macht es uns, wenn wir es vorstellen, wie es dasteht in Stein, aber in dem Stein zugleich der Schleier von oben bis unten: das verschleierte Bild zu Saïs. Und die Inschrift trägt es: Ich bin die Vergangenheit, die Gegenwart, und die Zukunft; meinen Schleier hat noch kein Sterblicher gelüftet."
[91] Rudolf Steiner, unpublished manuscript of a lecture, of unknown date, ca. 1914; „Wissen wollte der Jüngling zu Sais unvorbereitet von den Geheimnissen der geistigen Welt... er wird wiedergeboren...."

> ...in those times in which the ancient wisdom was living, human beings approached this wisdom in the appropriate way, or more precisely, were simply not allowed such access, if they did not approach in the appropriate manner...the priests of the Isis cult "researched the efficacy of the gods in practical life...it was certainly necessary that this temple activity was kept holy, for what mischief could have been undertaken, if had not been kept confidential! [92]

As Steiner was aware, the German poet Novalis has also written on the theme of esoteric spirituality in ancient Egypt, in his work, '*Die Lehrlinge zu Saïs* (*The novitiates of Sais*). In a lecture about the theosophical spirituality prevailing within German Romantics, Steiner comments on this text,

> "In the truly most theosophical manner, Novalis directly voices that which goes like a beautiful theme through the entire period {of the Romantics}, which prevailed in it like a theosophical motto. This contained in the words {of Novalis}; 'One of them was successful, he lifted the veil of the goddess at Sais. But what did he see? – he saw – wonder of wonders – himself.' [93]

These comments from Novalis are not in the text of *Die Lehrlinge zu Saïs*, but are to be found in his notebooks, from

---

[92] Steiner, Innere Entwicklungsimpulse" 167, 192; „...in den Zeiten, in denen uralte Weisheit lebendig war, die Menschen sich dieser Weisheit in der entsprechenden Weise näherten, respektive gar nicht zugelassen wurden, wenn sie sich ihr nicht in der entsprechenden Weise näherten. Das Hereinwirken der Götter in das praktische Leben erforschte man...Es war schon notwendig, daß dieser Tempeldienst heilig gehalten wurde, denn welcher Unfug hätte getrieben werden können, wenn er nicht heilig gehalten worden wäre!"

[93] Rudolf Steiner, Die Welträtsel und die Anthroposophie, (Dornach: VRSN, 1966), 412, In wirklich denkbar theosophischester Weise spricht gerade Novalis das aus, was wie ein schöner Zug durch die ganze Zeit ging, was diese wie ein theosophisches Motto geistig beherrschte. Es ist in den Worten enthalten: "Einem gelang es, er hob den Schleier der Göttin zu Saïs. - Aber was sah er? Er sah - Wunder des Wunders - sich selbst."

May 1798.[94] On various occasions Steiner elaborated the dangers of entering the Mystery Centre's spiritual development process in antiquity. Speaking of the Mesopotamian-Egyptian Mysteries, he describes these as taking the acolyte into the hidden recesses of the soul, including the not yet purified 'lower self'. He maintains that this is the meaning of the expression about the Mysteries, of descending to the door of the underworld, or in Greek Mysteries, of Hades. In his *Das Christentum als Mystische Tatsache* (*Christianity as Mystic Fact*), he writes of the responsibility that is involved when the mystagogue takes on the task of guiding an acolyte to the doorway of the Underworld, echoing the allusions in Schiller's poem,

> "Terrible is the responsibility which one places on oneself … It was the view of the mystagogue that one may not take up involvement in this good fortune {of being initiated} in an impious manner. For what then would be the outcome if the Mystagogue betrayed his secret? …Nothing more than a terrible, life-destroying foreboding would one be then able to impart (to the acolyte). One would have to view that as a crime…everything (the revelation) would be merely an empty noise…yet a deity appears before one! It is either everything or nothing. It is nothing, if you encounter it in the mood in which you encounter everyday objects.[95]

---

[94] <u>Novalis Werke, Tagebücher und Briefe Frierich von Hardenbergs</u>, Bd. 1, ed. Richard Samuel, (München: Carl Hanser Verlag, 1978), *Materialien zu Die Lehrlinge zu Saïs*, 234, „Einem gelang es - er hob den Schleyer der Göttin zu Saïs - Aber was sah er? Er sah - Wunder des Wunders - Sich selbst."

[95] Rudolf Steiner, <u>Das Christentum als Mystische Tatsache</u>, (Dornach: RSV, 1976) 25, „Furchtbar ist doch die Verantwortlichkeit, die man dadurch auf sich lädt. Es war die Meinung der Mysten, daß in dieses Glück nicht frevelhaft eingegriffen werden dürfte. Denn was wäre es zunächst denn gewesen: wenn der Myste sein Geheimnis ‚verraten' hätte? Nicht mehr als eine furchtbare, lebenszerstörende *Ahnung* hätte man ihm geben könnte. Als ein Verbrechen hätte man das auffassen müssen.

In a lecture late in his career (1918), Steiner treats this quest for Isis as a contemporary dynamic, assimilating it to the search for anthroposophical wisdom, "One should not say that the human being can never in any circumstances lift the veil of Isis, but rather, that person can not lift the veil of Isis, who wants to be united only to the mortal {part of their being}, who does want to approach the immortal {part}."[96] Two years later he told an audience, in a lecture on the search for Isis, that "We must rediscover in a certain sense, the Isis legend, the content of the Mystery of Isis, but we must form it from Imagination in a manner suited to our times."[97] The term, 'Imagination' here means the first stage of enhanced spiritual consciousness, not the power of fantasy; Steiner's terms for these visionary states will be examined later in the thesis.

These various references to Schiller's works and to themes adopted by Schiller, by Steiner from his anthroposophical phase (post 1901), indicate a degree of formative influence, and also demonstrate his use of these as providing a respected literary context which is supportive of his spiritual-esoteric worldview. Further, the way in which Steiner interprets such works of Schiller's as *The Veiled Image of Isis*, and his prose work, *The Julian Correspondence*, shows how to Steiner there was a similar 'theosophical' acceptance in Schiller of past lives, of karma, and of esoteric religiosity in general.

Another Schiller text which would have been affirmative to the young Steiner's esoteric views, is a poem, believed to be written in 1781 (his first period), D*as Geheimnis der Reminiszenz: an Laura* (*The Secret of Reminiscence: to*

---

[96] Rudolf Steiner, Mysterienwahrheiten und Weihnachtsimpulse, (Dornach: VRSN,1966) 190.
[97] Rudolf Steiner, Die Brücke zwischen der Weltgeistigkeit und dem Physischen des Menschen, (Dornach: VRSN, 1970) 235, „...wir müssen in einer gewisser Weise die Isislegende, den Inhalt des Isismysteriums wiederfinden, aber wir müssen ihn bilden aus der Imagination heraus gefaßt für unsere Zeit."

Laura), which indicates both pre-existence and the karmic interpretation of personal bonds of love. In reads in part,[98]

Motionlessly clinging to your mouth, eternally –
Who can explain to me this rapturous yearning?
And explain too, the delight to drink in your ambience –
to sink, dying, into your being,
when our eyes beckon to each other…
… …
…have we already been intertwined?
Is this the reason that our hearts so throbbed?
Had we – in the radiance of a sun since extinguished,
in days of bliss, long since buried –
already melted into one?
Yes! – we had! You were intimately united with me
in aeons which have now passed away;
my Muse beheld it written on the dim slate of the Past:
"united with your loving!" [99]

These are subjective verses about personal romantic love, but as the editors of Schiller's poetry make clear, they do incorporate various esoteric-spiritual themes closely allied to those affirmed in Plato's works. These include his doctrine of 'anamnesis', the ability of the soul to remember its prior existence in the World of Ideas. This concept and its corollaries, reincarnation and immortality, were themes present in contemporary discussions in Schiller's life. As

---

[98] The term 'motionlessly' translates 'starr' well, as nuances of rigidity are inappropriate here; and 'rapturous' is appropriate here for 'Wut'; thirdly, 'ambience', appears appropriate for 'Hauch', as the nuance of 'aura' is implied; cf. Muret-Sanders Dict. 1901, "von einem Körper auströmenden Hauch", aura, nerv(e)-aura."

[99] Ewig starr an deinem Mund zu hangen/ wer enthüllt mir dieses Blutverlangen?/ Wer die Wollust, deinen Hauch zu trinken/ in dein Wesen, wenn sich Blicke winken/ sterbend zu versinken ? Waren unsre Wesen schon verflochten?/ War es darum, daß die Herzen pochten?/ Waren wir im Strahl erloschner Sonnen/ in den Tagen verrauschter Wonnen/ schon in Eins zerronnen? Ja, wir waren's ! - Innig mir verbunden/ warst du in Aeonen, die verschwunden;/ Meine Muse sah es auf der trüben/ Tafel der Vergangenheit geschrieben: / Eins mit deinem Lieben !" Schiller SW Bd. 1, Gedichte, 104-5.

Kurscheidt and Oellers point out, reincarnation is present in Vergil's *Aeneid*, a work well known to Schiller.[100]

From a Steiner perspective, Schiller is here affirming a belief in karma, the poem is testifying to the memory of, or at least the conviction of, a young man that in a previous life on Earth he and his beloved were already deeply in love. It is for this reason that now their love has such a potent quality, for, to his delight, his Muse has been able to convey this truth to his searching, ardent mind. Steiner would see as the Muse as the 'guiding angel' of the man. He maintained that these beings specifically hold the memory of the past lifetimes on earth of each individual in their consciousness,

> "For every person we are to presuppose a being who, because it stands one stage above the human being, guides the individuality from one incarnation to another....they preserve the memory of one incarnation until the next so to speak, unless the person man is able to do this of his own accord."[101]

It was however, primarily in Goethe's works that passages are found of an esoteric or mystical nature which were either formative to the young Steiner or elucidated by him in his anthroposophical phase as supportive of his anthroposophy.

---

[100] Schiller SW Bd. 2, Gedichte (Anmerkungen zu Band 1) 98-99.
[101] Rudolf Steiner, Geistige Wesenheiten und ihre Widerspiegelung in der physischen Welt, (Dornach: RSV, 1972) 89-90, „Für jeden Menschen müßen wir voraussetzen eine Wesenheit, welche dadurch, daß sie um eine Stufe höher ist als der Mensch, die Individualität von einer Inkarnation zum andern herleiten...Wesenheiten, die sozusagen das Gedächtnis bewahren von einer Inkarnation zur andern, solange der Mensch selber es nicht tun kann."

Appendix:
The German text of Schiller's poem, *Das Verschleierte Bild zu Sais*

Ein Jüngling, den des Wissens heißer Durst
Nach Sais in Ägypten trieb, der Priester
Geheime Weisheit zu erlernen, hatte
Schon manchen Grad mit schnellem Geist durcheilt,
Stets riß ihn seine Forschbegierde weiter,
Und kaum besänftigte der Hierophant
Den ungeduldig Strebenden. »Was hab ich,
Wenn ich nicht alles habe?« sprach der Jüngling.
»Gibts etwa hier ein Weniger und Mehr?
Ist deine Wahrheit wie der Sinne Glück
Nur eine Summe, die man größer, kleiner
Besitzen kann und immer doch besitzt?
Ist sie nicht eine einzge, ungeteilte?
Nimm einen Ton aus einer Harmonie,
Nimm eine Farbe aus dem Regenbogen,
Und alles, was dir bleibt, ist nichts, solang
Das schöne All der Töne fehlt und Farben.«

Indem sie einst so sprachen, standen sie
In einer einsamen Rotonde still,
Wo ein verschleiert Bild von Riesengröße
Dem Jüngling in die Augen fiel. Verwundert
Blickt er den Führer an und spricht: »Was ists,
Das hinter diesem Schleier sich verbirgt?«
»Die Wahrheit«, ist die Antwort. - »Wie?« ruft jener,
»Nach Wahrheit streb ich ja allein, und diese
Gerade ist es, die man mir verhüllt?«

»Das mache mit der Gottheit aus«, versetzt
Der Hierophant. »Kein Sterblicher, sagt sie,
Rückt diesen Schleier, bis ich selbst ihn hebe.
Und wer mit ungeweihter, schuldger Hand
Den heiligen, verbotnen früher hebt,
Der, spricht die Gottheit -« - »Nun?« - »Der sieht die Wahrheit.«

»Ein seltsamer Orakelspruch! Du selbst,
Du hättest also niemals ihn gehoben?«
»Ich? Wahrlich nicht! Und war auch nie dazu
Versucht.« - »Das fass ich nicht. Wenn von der Wahrheit
Nur diese dünne Scheidewand mich trennte -«
»Und ein Gesetz«, fällt ihm sein Führer ein.
»Gewichtiger, mein Sohn, als du es meinst,
Ist dieser dünne Flor - für deine Hand
Zwar leicht, doch zentnerschwer für dein Gewissen.«

Der Jüngling ging gedankenvoll nach Hause.
Ihm raubt des Wissens brennende Begier
Den Schlaf, er wälzt sich glühend auf dem Lager
Und rafft sich auf um Mitternacht. Zum Tempel
Führt unfreiwillig ihn der scheue Tritt.
Leicht ward es ihm, die Mauer zu ersteigen,
Und mitten in das Innre der Rotonde
Trägt ein beherzter Sprung den Wagenden.

Hier steht er nun, und grauenvoll umfängt
Den Einsamen die lebenlose Stille,
Die nur der Tritte hohler Widerhall
In den geheimen Grüften unterbricht.
Von oben durch der Kuppel Öffnung wirft
Der Mond den bleichen, silberblauen Schein,
Und furchtbar wie ein gegenwärtger Gott
Erglänzt durch des Gewölbes Finsternisse
In ihrem langen Schleier die Gestalt.

Er tritt hinan mit ungewissem Schritt,
Schon will die freche Hand das Heilige berühren,
Da zuckt es heiß und kühl durch sein Gebein
Und stößt ihn weg mit unsichtbarem Arme.
Unglücklicher, was willst du tun? So ruft
In seinem Innern eine treue Stimme.
Versuchen den Allheiligen willst du?
Kein Sterblicher, sprach des Orakels Mund,
Rückt diesen Schleier, bis ich selbst ihn hebe.

Doch setzte nicht derselbe Mund hinzu:
Wer diesen Schleier hebt, soll Wahrheit schauen?
»Sei hinter ihm, was will! Ich heb ihn auf.«
(Er rufts mit lauter Stimm.) »Ich will sie schauen.« Schauen!
Gellt ihm ein langes Echo spottend nach.

Er sprichts und hat den Schleier aufgedeckt.
Nun, fragt ihr, und was zeigte sich ihm hier?
Ich weiß es nicht. Besinnungslos und bleich,
So fanden ihn am andern Tag die Priester
Am Fußgestell der Isis ausgestreckt.
Was er allda gesehen und erfahren,
Hat seine Zunge nie bekannt. Auf ewig
War seines Lebens Heiterkeit dahin,
Ihn riß ein tiefer Gram zum frühen Grabe.
»Weh dem«, dies war sein warnungsvolles Wort,
Wenn ungestüme Frager in ihn drangen,
»Weh dem, der zu der Wahrheit geht durch Schuld,
Sie wird ihm nimmermehr erfreulich sein.«

1B2: Goethe, the primal skeleton, the primal plant, and a 'life-force'

Our concern in this section, and throughout the thesis, is to examine the use of Goethe by Steiner, and the influence of Goethe upon Steiner's thoughts, it is not to examine Goethe himself. The major significance of Goethe for Steiner in his early years was the stimulus he found in Goethe's writings for his own conclusions regarding the cognitional validity of spiritual experiences, or at least of 'intuitive' thoughts. In his later years, Steiner referred to passages in Goethe's writings which he viewed as illustrative of his own anthroposophical teachings. There are three books by Steiner, all written in his earlier years, which critique the worldview of Goethe. One of these comprises the collected editorial comments from Steiner's work on the first publication of Goethe's scientific writings, which we have noted earlier, the other two were specifically written on the implications of Goethe's efforts for epistemology.

In his early years, Steiner had focused on Goethe's efforts to discern the purpose or Idea implicit in the form and qualities of the sense perceptible.[102] Later, in a series of public lectures on philosophy and anthroposophy, Steiner refers to a conversation of Goethe's in which he comments on the words of Albrecht von Haller (1708-1777) that, "No created spirit penetrates into the interior of Nature….blessed is the person to whom she shows only the outer shell." Steiner quotes Goethe reply to this,

> …. 'For sixty years I have heard this repeated. I cursed it, when I heard it, but surreptitiously…Nature has neither kernel nor shell, she is everything at one

---

[102] Rudolf Steiner, <u>Grundlinien einer Erkenntistheorie der Goetheschen Weltanschauung, mit besonderer Rücksicht auf Schiller</u>" 1886 (*Principal features of an epistemological theory of the Goethean worldview, with particular reference to Schiller*) and <u>Goethes Weltanschauung</u> (Goethe's worldview) 1897.

and the same time; test yourself whenever you can, whether for the most part, you be kernel or shell!'

Steiner then comments that on Goethe's response to Haller,

> If a person develops their kernel in the Goethean sense, such a person will reach into the kernel, the essence of nature, but only after infinitely long, earnest and sincere research work. For this essence of nature is manifest in the human being. And what is reflected in the human being is, correctly understood, nothing other than this essence of nature. Spirit is nothing other than the blossom and fruit of nature. Nature is, in a certain respects, the roots of the spirit.[103]

One striking example of Goethe's approach to scientific research is his discovery of the intermaxillary bone in the human skeleton. In his capacity as editor of Goethe's scientific writings, Steiner explains that a significant scientific achievement of Goethe, namely discovering the intermaxillary bone, (a tiny bone in the jaw) was ultimately due to his belief in the archetypal Idea. Steiner writes that Goethe understood that the skeleton of the human being must contain, or at least during its metamorphoses possess for a while, the same foundational bone structures as those present in the animal kingdom. This viewpoint derived from Goethe's intuition that the Earth's ecology provided one primal skeletal form for all animals, from which humanity then developed its own skeleton.

---

[103] Rudolf Steiner, Die Ergänzung heutiger Wissenschaften durch Anthroposophie, (Dornach: RSV, 1973) 150 „ ‚Ins Innre der Natur, dringt kein erschaffner Geist,... Glückselig, wem sie nur die äußre Schale weist'. Goethe sagte dagegen, ‚Das hör ich sechzig Jahre wiederholen. Ich fluchte drauf, aber verstohlen;...Natur hat weder Kern noch Schale, alles ist sie mit einenmale, Dich prüfe du nur allermeist, Ob du Kern oder Schale seist!, Entwickelt in dieser Goetheschen Gesinnung der Mensch seinen Kern, dann dringt er auch vor, wenn auch nur in unendlich langer, ernster und aufrichtiger Forschungsarbeit - in den Kern, in das Wesen der Natur. Denn dieses Wesen der Natur, es prägt sich aus im Menschen. Und was sich im Menschen spiegelt ist, richtig verstanden, nichts anderes als der Natur Blüte und Frucht. Natur ist in gewisser Beziehung des Geistes Wurzel".

However, although it was an accepted fact in Goethe's time that indeed the human skeleton did have virtually all bone formations of the animal kingdom in it, there was the one exception, that is the intermaxillary bone. It was understood that this does not exist in the human skeleton. Goethe's discovery was received with much interest by prominent zoologists; two prominent zoologists, Johann Heinrich Merck (1741-1791) and Samuel Thomas Sömmerring (1755-1830) at first rejected the discovery, but eventually acknowledged that Goethe had made a major discovery.[104]

Steiner emphasises that in his research, Goethe was inspired by a postulate directly linked to the Platonic Idea, namely that the *idea* of the human body is attained by metamorphosis from the *idea* underlying the skeletal structures of the animal kingdom. The implication of this is that therefore in the skeleton of humans, all the primary animal bone formations must occur, even if only early in the development of the skeleton. As supportive evidence for this, Steiner refers to a letter Goethe wrote to Knebel in 1784, accompanying his treatise on zoology. In this letter Goethe writes,

> ...one can not find anything that differentiates at all between a human being and an animal. Rather, the human being is most closely related to the animals. The inherent correspondence of the entirety makes each creature what it is.... and so again is every creature but a tone, a nuance, in a great harmony, which one also has to study in its full entirety, otherwise each separate thing is a dead letter."[105]

As this letter indicates, Goethe, following the implications of the archetypal Idea, pursued his research, and eventually

---

[104] Steiner, Naturwissenschaftliche Schriften, 60-72
[105] Goethes Briefe, HA Bd 1, 459, "...man nämlich den Unterschied des Menschen vom Thier in nichts einzelnem finden finden könne. Vielmehr ist der Mensch aufs nächste mit den Thieren verwandt. Die Übereinstimmung des Ganzen macht ein jedes Geschöpf zu dem was es ist...Und so ist wieder jede Creatur nur ein Ton eine Schattierung einer grossen Harmonie, die man auch im ganzen und grossen studieren muß sonst ist jedes einzelne eine todter Buchstabe."

through some attentive observation of skeletons, perceived in a part of the human skeleton, during a phase of its growth, the transient existence of this bone. He was consequently able to establish scientifically, that indeed there is such a bone in the human being. In addition, Goethe's research discovered that all specialized bones in the animal were metamorphoses of the basic vertebrae. Today the existence of the intermaxillary bone is a clearly recognized fact.[106]

To Steiner this achievement of Goethe embodied his concept that the meditative contemplation of the sense world, phenomenologically, can lead one to perception of the Idea. Steiner comments' as editor of the Kürschner edition of Goethe's scientific works, indicate how, already in his thirties, he saw this achievement of Goethe in terms of the Platonic idea and in terms of subtle life-energies in nature,

> This was a discovery of the most wide ranging significance, for it was thereby shown that all members of an organic entirety are identical, according to the Idea; and that 'inwardly metamorphosed' organic substances open up externally in differing ways. Also that it is one and the same thing, which, on the lower level as spinal column nerve substance, and on a higher level as sense organ nerves, opens itself up in different ways to the external world. The latter open themselves as receptive, registering, comprehending sense-organs. Every living thing is thereby shown to be embedded in a power that forms and moulds it outwards from within; a living thing was now for the first time comprehended as truly living. [107]

---

[106] "Goethe's activities in the scientific field; studies on the metamorphosis of plants and animals, his discoveries of the intermaxillary bone in man and his ...", Website: Google, Goethe Museum, Düsseldorf, 6ᵗʰ July 2004.

[107] Steiner, <u>Naturwissenschaftliche Schriften</u> 67, „Dies war eine Entdeckung von der weittragendsten Bedeutung, es war damit bewiesen, daß alle Glieder eines organischen Ganzen der Idee nach identisch sind und daß «innerlich ungeformte» organische Massen sich nach außen in *verschiedener* Weise aufschließen, daß es ein und dasselbe ist, was auf niederer Stufe als Rückenmarknerv, auf höherer als Sinnesnerv sich zu dem die Außenwelt aufnehmenden, ergreifenden, erfassenden Sinnesorgane aufschließt. Jedes

In addition to skeletal metamorphosis, Goethe's work on plant metamorphosis was also of great significance to Steiner in terms of the archetypal Idea. Goethe's research on plant metamorphosis lead him to the concept of the Urpflanze, a suprasensible primal plant from which all plants derive, in all their various forms. To Goethe the individual forms of the flora are expressions of the primal plant, which in itself has the capacity to assume numerous forms, and which in a specific case assumes that form which is most appropriate for the external environmental conditions. These external conditions are simply inducements to cause the inner powers of metamorphosis to be expressed in a special way. These latter alone are the constitutive principle, the creative power in the plant.

Steiner quotes from a letter Goethe wrote (Naples, 17 May 1787) to Herder about the *Urpflanze*, which he refers to as a 'Proteus',

> Actually, I had realized that in the organ of the plant, which we normally refer to as leaf, lies hidden the true Proteus, which can conceal itself and manifest itself in all forms {of the plant}. Retrospectively and in its further life, the plant is always only leaf, so indivisibly united with the future seed, that a person cannot conceive of the one without the other.[108]

Lebendige war damit in einer von innen heraus sich formenden, gestaltenbildenden Kraft aufgezeigt; es war als *wahrhaft Lebendiges* jetzt erst begriffen."

[108] Rudolf Steiner, Goethes Naturwissenschaftliche Schriften (Dornach; RSV, 1973) 35: originally published in J.W. Goethe, Sämtliche Werke, Briefe, Tagebücher und Gespräche, 40 Bände, eds. Friedmar Apel et al. 1. Abtlg. 15-2, *Italienische Reise* ed. Christoph Michel und Hans-Georg Dewitz 2 Bde. (Frankfurt: Deutscher Klassiker Verlag, 1993), Bd.1. S. 344, „Es war mir nämlich aufgegangen, daß in demjenigen Organ (der Pflanze), welches wir gewöhnlich als Blatt ansprechen, der wahre Proteus verborgen liege, der sich in allen Gestaltungen verstecken und offenbaren könne. Rückwärts und vorwärts ist die Pflanze immer nur Blatt, mit dem künftigen Keime so unzertrennlich vereint, daß man sich eins ohne das andere nicht denken darf."

Goethe has drawn the term, 'Proteus' from Greek mythology, where it is a minor sea god, a shape shifter. Goethe incorporates Proteus as a character in *Faust*, (Part Two, Act 2, Classical Walpurgis Night, lines 8225-8460), where, as Trunz explains (HA Bd. 3, S. 570), he is virtually equated with eternally metamorphosing matter. For these reasons, Goethe also called it a hen kai pan (One and All) of the plant world (letter of 6th September 1787).[109] Goethe also had here the support of the great philosopher Georg Wilhelm Friedrich Hegel (1770-1831), who wrote to him in 1821,

> …to have detected the Simple and Abstract, which you so appropriately call the ur-phenomenon… and to separate it from other ambient factors that are accidental to it – to comprehend it in abstracto, as we call this process… this I regard as a matter of great spiritual understanding of nature and that process itself I regard as the truly scientific aspect of knowledge in this field…[110]

Steiner regarded this as a major discovery, for he considered that Goethe, through his phenomenological approach, had perceived another manifestation of the prevailing Idea, the archetypal Idea of the plant. That is, to Steiner, Goethe had apprehended the concept which belongs to the percept 'plant', the archetype of the plant form, extant in the realm of Ideas.

---

[109] Steiner Naturwissenschaftliche Schriften, 34, „Bei Goethe sind die einzelnen Veränderungen verschiedene Äußerungen des Urorganismus, der in sich selbst die Fähigkeit hat, mannigfache Gestalten anzunehmen und in einem bestimmten Falle jene annimmt, welche den ihn umgebenden Verhältnissen der Außenwelt am angemessensten ist. Diese äußeren Verhaltnisse sind bloß Veranlassung, daß die inneren Gestaltungskräfte in einer besonderen Weise zur Erscheinung kommen. Diese letzteren allein sind das konstitutive Prinzip, das Schöpferische in der Pflanze. Daher nennt es Goethe am 6. September 1787 auch ein hen kai pan (Ein und Alles) der Pflanzenwelt." The letter to Herder is published in Goethe, Sämtliche Werke, Bd. 1, S. 423.

[110] Steiner Naturwissenschaftliche Schriften 226, „…das Einfache und Abstrakte, das Sie sehr treffend das Urphänomen nennen …auszuspüren, es von den andern ihm selbst zufälligen Umgebungen zu befreien, - es abstract, wie wir dies heißen, aufzufassen, dies halte ich für eine Sache des großen geistigen Natursinns, sowie jenen Gang überhaupt für das wahrhaft Wissenschaftliche der Erkenntnis in diesem Felde…"

In a conversation with Schiller, Goethe discussed his perception of the Urpflanze, and wrote a report of the discussion, in a brief autobiographical text, called *Glückliches Ereignis* (*Happy Event*). Goethe reported that he through his plant observations, he had experienced the Urpflanze, and could confirm that it was a reality. Schiller declares that it was not possible to have an actual experience of such a thing, because it is an idea, to which Goethe then retorts, "It could be very pleasing for me, if without knowing it, I have Ideas and indeed can see them with my eyes.[111] The comments by Steiner on this discussion show that he considers the substantiation of his own epistemology is to be found in Goethe's approach,

> "For Goethe there is one source of knowledge only, the world of experience, in which the world of ideas in included. For him it is impossible to speak of experience and idea, because to him, the idea is there before the eyes as a result of the spiritual experience, just as the sense world lies before the physical eyes.[112]

Steiner then comments further, consolidating the basis for his interpretation of Goethe, that the question, "what is the relationship – outside of the human being – between Idea and the sense world?" is an unsound one for the Goethean worldview …. because for it there exists outside the human being no sense world (nature) which is apart from the Idea.[113] But this conclusion of Steiner's, whilst invoking the Platonic

---

[111] Goethes Werke, HA Bd 10, 540-41, „Das kann mir sehr lieb sein, wenn ich Ideen habe, ohne es zu wissen, und sie sogar mit Augen sehe."
[112] Steiner, Goethes Weltanschauung, (Dornach: RSV, 1979) 23, „Für Goethe gibt es nur eine Quelle der Erkenntnis, die Erfahrungswelt, in welcher die Ideenwelt eingeschlossen ist. Für ihn ist es unmöglich, zu sagen: Erfahrung *und* Idee, weil ihm die Idee durch die geistige Erfahrung so vor dem geistigen Auge liegt, wie die sinnliche Welt vor dem physischen."
[113] Steiner, Weltanschauung, 29, „Deshalb kann man sagen, für die Goethesche Weltanschauung ist die Frage, 'welches Verhältnis besteht *außerhalb des Menschen* zwischen Idee und Sinneswelt?' eine ungesunde, weil es für sie keine Sinneswelt (Natur) ohne Idee *außerhalb des Menschen* gibt."

Idea, also contains within it an implication which invalidates an aspect of Platonism. It refutes a central tenet of the worldview which gradually developed from the Platonic writings, namely that there is an unbridgeable gap between the Idea and the observer.

Steiner's book, *Goethes Weltanschauung,* written towards the end of his time in the Goethe archives (1897), deals with this. He refers to Plato's famous account of the cave, and comments that, "The Platonic worldview tears the mental image of the universe apart, into two pieces, into the mental image of an illusory world and into another, of the Idea world, which alone is meant to correspond to the true, eternal reality.[114] Plato's myth of the cave is given in Book Seven of The Republic and teaches that the perceived images of objects in the physical world has the same relationship to the reality of those objects, as does the shadows of people thrown up onto a wall, to the actual people.[115]

Steiner proceeds to explain his disagreement with Platonists who separate the archetypal Idea from the perceived object, by assuming an insurmountable gap between them,

> The difference between Idea and perception has a validity only when one is discussing the way in which human knowledge arises. The human being must allow the {material} things to speak to him in a twofold manner. Of one part of their being, they speak voluntarily. He only needs to listen carefully. But the other part he has to illicit from them. He must make his thinking active, then his inner life fills itself with the Idea of the things. The scene of action is within the personality, which is also where the things unveil

---

[114] Steiner, Weltanschauung, 26, „In zwei Teile reißt die platonische Anschauung die Vorstellung des Weltganzen auseinander, in die Vorstellung einer Scheinwelt und eine andere der Ideenwelt, der allein wahre, ewige Wirklichkeit entsprechen soll."
[115] Plato, The Republic, trans. Paul Shorey (London: Heinemann, 1963) 125.

their Ideal inner nature. They declare that which remains hidden forever to external experience.[116]

Steiner concludes that Platonists, in separating out the Idea from the sense world, has given to western intellectual development a completely superfluous question, with which it has been preoccupied or centuries. Steiner, as editor of Goethe's scientific writings, comments here,

> Whoever acknowledges in his thinking a perceptual capacity which exceeds the sense-perceptible, that person must also by necessity acknowledge objects which exist beyond the sense perceptible reality. The objects of thinking however are the Ideas; for in the process of thinking taking hold of the Idea it merges into the primal foundations of cosmic existence; that which is efficacious from without {thus} enters into the spirit of the human being; it becomes one with the objective reality in its highest potency. The becoming aware of the Idea in its {full} reality is the true communion of the human being. The Idea is the content of subjective thinking, rather the result of research…to cognize means; to supplement the half reality of the sense perception with the perceiving of thinking, so that the representation becomes complete.[117]

---

[116]Steiner, Weltanschauung, 27, „Die Unterscheidung von Idee und Wahrnehmung hat nur eine Berechtigung, wenn von der Art gesprochen wird, wie die menschliche Erkenntnis zustande kommt. Der Mensch muß die Dinge auf zweifache Art zu sich sprechen lassen. Einen Teil ihrer Wesenheit sagen sie freiwillig. Er braucht nur hinzuhorchen. Dies ist der ideenfreie Teil der Wirklichkeit. Den anderen aber muß er ihnen entlocken. Er muß sein Denken in Bewegung setzen, dann erfüllt sich sein Inneres mit den Ideen der Dinge. Im Inneren der Persönlichkeit ist der Schauplatz, auf dem auch die Dinge ihr ideelles Innere enthüllen. Das sprechen sie aus, was der äußeren Anschauung ewig verborgen bleibt."

[117] Steiner Naturwissenschaftliche Schriften 125, 150, „Wer dem Denken seine über die Sinnesauffassung hinausgehende Wahrnehmungsfähigkeit zuerkennt, der muß ihm notgedrungen auch Objekte zuerkennen, die über die bloße sinnenfällige Wirklichkeit hinaus liegen. Die Objekte des Denkens sind aber die Ideen, Indem sich das Denken der Idee bemächtigt, verschmilzt es mit dem Urgrunde des Weltendaseins; das, was außen wirkt, tritt in den Geist des Menschen ein : er wird mit der objektiven Wirklichkeit

Returning to Goethe's "Proteus", Steiner sees this to be the invisible factor in the plant world, which is the underlying, directing force in the plant. In Steiner's view, this discovery also means that perception of the physical object, and the conclusion that it is complete in itself, was now shown to no longer be valid. Instead, the plant is now to be seen as a unified reality which requires perception of the Idea behind it, and this perceptual process can be applied to any other created object,

> Physical perceiving was no longer sufficient, we must conceptually understand the unity, if we want to explain the phenomenal. Through this {discovery of Goethe} however, perceiving and concept become separated from each other {with regard to the plant world}. Now the concept hovers above that which is perceived, the connection between the two is difficult to see. Whereas with the inorganic world, concept and reality are one, but now {through Goethe} they appear to diverge {in regard to plants}, and to belong to two different worlds. What one sees with the senses in this situation does not appear to have its validity, its real nature in itself. The object no longer appears to be explainable from itself, because its concept is not taken from itself {as molecular reality}, but from something else.[118]

---

auf ihrer höchsten Potenz eins. Das Gewahrwerden der Idee in der Wirklichkeit ist die wahre Kommunion des Menschen. ...Die Idee ist nicht Inhalt des subjektiven Denkens, sondern Forschungs resultate! ...erkennen heißt : zu der halben Wirklichkeit der Sinnenerfahrung die Wahrnehmung des Denkens hinzufügen, auf daß ihr Bild vollständig werde..."

[118] Steiner <u>Naturwissenschaftliche Schriften</u> 74, „Es genügt die Anschauung nicht mehr, wir müssen die Einheit begrifflich erfassen, wenn wir die Erscheinungen erklären wollen. Dadurch aber tritt eine Entfernung von Anschauung und Begriff ein; sie scheinen sich nicht mehr zu decken; der Begriff schwebt über der Anschauung. Es wird schwer, den Zusammenhang beider einzusehen. Während in der unorganischen Natur Begriff und Wirklichkeit eins waren, scheinen sie hier auseinanderzugeben und eigentlich zwei verschiedenen Welten anzugehören. Die Anschauung, welche sich den Sinnen unmittelbar darbietet, scheint ihre Begründung, ihre Wesenheit nicht in sich selbst zu tragen. Das Objekt scheint aus sich selbst nicht erklärbar, weil sein Begriff nicht von ihm selbst, sondern von etwas anderem entnommen ist."

Steiner's point here is that whilst even the mineral kingdom cannot be fully perceived without access to the archetypal idea, it can at least appear to be a cognized without such access. But once the element of life-processes is allowed in a material object, Steiner maintains that a gap opens between the object and the concept, the object can no longer be honestly regarded as understandable, for its behaviour breaks the laws of inorganic matter. The reason Steiner saw a gap existing between the plant world and the concept which we normally have of a plant, is that he ascribes to the plant the additional element, namely a subtle life force.

That is, to Steiner the life-processes that differentiate minerals from plants are due to the efficacy of an invisible life force. In other words, Steiner concluded that Goethe's Urpflanze and Proteus demonstrated that he had perception not only of the archetypal Idea of 'a plant' as such, but also as a result of this enhanced consciousness, an intuitive perception of a subtle, non-molecular factor in a plant which makes such life processes possible.

The above comments of Steiner's demonstrate his conviction that living organisms require the efficacy of an energy field, or life force organism in order to function. Goethe had perceived, according to Steiner, that the growth process, through which the archetypal form was being brought into reality, was itself derived from a non-molecular reality, a subtle life-force. Specifically this happens with the metamorphoses that occur in vegetation (and other living organism). These life-energies have power over molecular processes. Hence he maintains that Goethe, in considering the phenomenon of plant metamorphosis, is in effect drawing attention to a sphere beyond molecular substance, beyond matter.

That is, Steiner concludes that in the chemicals of the plant's organism there is no explanation for this apparently intelligent and complex phenomenon of metamorphosis. To Steiner, this Proteus is what could be termed a life force organism, efficacious within the biochemistry of any living body. It is very likely that Steiner would today maintain that the genetic substances now regarded as causing the metamorphosing of plant forms, are themselves in turn responding to this life-force of the plant.

He refers to this life force as the plant's 'ether-body'. Steiner maintains that the human being also has such an energy field around the physical body. In his *Theosophie*, he comments that around every physical body is an invisible energy form, called an 'ether-body' or a 'formative force body'. It is "a real, independent entity which first calls forth...physical materials and forces into life....The ether-body is an organism which preserves the physical-body every moment during life from dissolution."[119]

In his anthroposophical works, Steiner strives to demonstrate that such an energy-field is not a theoretical construct which he has projected onto the given world reality, but is an actuality. However he is fully aware of the discredited 'ether postulate' of post-Renaissance thinkers, and emphasizes that his life-force concept or ether energies is not to be equated with this,

> It is not of some imaginary phantasm what anthroposophical spiritual science identifies as a supra-sensible ether-body or life-body. It is not the hypothetical ether-body, which science has rightly relinquished; it is something which results from a thoroughly factual perceiving, and which for the *strengthened* process of forming mental images

---

[119] Rudolf Steiner, Theosophie, Deutsch-Englisch Ausgabe (London: Rudolf Steiner Press, 1975) 50, „...eine selbständige, wirkliche Wesenheit, welche die genannten physischen Stoffe und Kräfte erst zum Leben ruft....Der Lebensleib ist eine Wesenheit durch welche in jedem Augenblicke während des Lebens der physische Leib von dem Zerfalle bewahrt wird. "

> becomes a reality, once it has been developed – just as the external sense-world is a reality.[120]

The above extract builds upon his earlier epistemological conclusions as to the validity of perceiving, including in spheres beyond the sense-world, and his argument that the limits to knowledge are not absolute. He maintains that life-processes in the organic world and cell division, such as occurs in healing and in reproduction, are maintained by these life energies. In these life forces there is an imprint of the template (itself from the realm of Ideas) of the physical object, for example, the shape of a flower, and its primary characteristics. In effect, Steiner understands this composite entity to be Goethe's Proteus.

However, Steiner also found much else, of a directly esoteric-religious nature, in Goethe which resonated with his own spiritual convictions, some of which is implicit in Die Pforte.

---

[120] Rudolf Steiner, Die Wirklichkeit der höheren Welten (Dornach; VRSN, 1962) lect. of 25 Nov.1921; 21, „Es ist nichts phantastisch Ersonnenes, was die anthroposophische Geisteswissenschaft als übersinnlichen Äther- oder Lebensleib anspricht. Es ist nicht die hypothetische alte Lebenskraft, die mit recht von der Wissenschaft verlassen worden ist, es ist etwas,was sich in ganz realer Anschauung ergibt, was eine Wirklichkeit wird für das verstärkte Vorstellungsleben, das entwickelt worden ist, wie die äußere Sinneswelt eine Wirklichkeit ist."

1B3: Goethe, esoteric religiosity (the Rosicrucians) and a Platonic 'Devachan'

Apart from the Goethean approach to cognitive processes and the plant kingdom, there are many other elements in the works of Goethe which Rudolf Steiner referred to as supportive of his own worldview. In a letter written to a friend when he was 28, Steiner comments that to him, Goethe was an esotericist in the best meaning of the word. He then quotes what he sees as a significant phrase used by Goethe from 1812, which was not yet published, namely a brief enigmatic note-book entry which simply states, "The exoteric and the esoteric".[121]

Here Steiner is obviously regarding the two words as referring to privileged initiatory information, and the lack of same, and this may be the case in this Goethean note-book entry. Goethe also used these words in their alternative meaning, namely specialist knowledge and popular, commonly known ideas, for example in his Maxims and Reflections (no. 474) he writes, "Only through an enhanced procedure can the sciences exert an influence on the external world; for actually they are all esoteric and they can only become exoteric through the improvement of an activity of some kind. All other participation leads to nothing."[122]

However, Steiner's interpretation here is reasonable in view of the well known interest of Goethe in esoteric-mystical themes, this is illustrated for example in his long poem "The Secrets" which shall be considered in this section. To Steiner, the esotericist is that person who – after assiduous study of spiritual ideas – is capable of acquiring an understanding of lofty esoteric-spiritual truths, because through meditation he

---

[121] Steiner, Briefe 2, 54, „...Goethe...ein Esoteriker in des Wortes bestes Bedeutung...", to F. Eckstein, Nov. 1890.
[122] Goethes Werke, HA Bd 12, „Nur durch eine erhöhte Praxis sollten die Wissenschaften auf die äußere Welt wirken; denn eigentlich sind sie alle esoterisch und können nur durch Verbessern irgendeines Tuns exoterisch werden. Alle übrige Teilnahme führt zu nichts."

has developed the capacity to directly experience spiritual realms.[123] His book on meditation and initiation, "Knowledge of the higher worlds, how is it attained?", is intended to help his students, after an assiduous study of his research, and the adoption of a more meditative life style, to become esotericists.

A major theme in Steiner's anthroposophy is that of esoteric religious groups of earlier ages, or the Mystery-history of earlier ages, as we have seen. Goethe wrote a long poem called *"Die Geheimnisse"* (*The Secrets*) in which he expounds at length on the nature of a secretive, esoteric group in medieval Europe. This poem, like Schiller's The Veiled Image at Sais, is concerned with esoteric spiritual activity in earlier epoch. The poem itself, though long, is a fragment, never completed by Goethe, which recounts the journey of a pilgrim in medieval Europe to a monastic building which was home to a mystic Christian Order. There are twelve knights in the order, and the symbol of the Order is a cross with roses entwined around it. It is clear that this poem does specifically incorporate themes found in esoteric literature about the Rosicrucians, especially as found in the writings of the mystical alchemist, Johan Valentin Andreae.[124]

Steiner viewed the poem as affirming the existence of an actual, historical Rosicrucian movement in earlier centuries, and he uses this poem on a number of occasions to affirm his understanding of the principles and ideas of the Rosicrucians. He does not regard any so-called 'Rosicrucian' organisation of today as part of this earlier movement. He told an audience in 1906 that the poem presents the spiritual ideals of the Rosicrucians to unite, and then renew, all the major spiritual-esoteric wisdom of humanity. He refers here to Goethe's

---

[123] Rudolf Steiner, Die geistigen Wesenheiten in den Himmelskörpern und Naturreichen, (Dornach: RSV, 1974) 19, „Die Esoterik beginnt nicht erst mit der okkulten Entwickelung. In dem Augenblicke, wo wir uns mit irgendeiner geisteswissenschaftlichen Vereinigung verbinden und mit unserem ganzen Herzen dabei sind und fühlen, was uns in den Lehren der Geisteswissenschaft liegt, da schon beginnt die Esoterik, da beginnt unsere Seele sich umzuwandeln..." (syntax in original)
[124] Erich Trunz, Goethes Werke, HA, Bd 2, 588.

comments that each of the twelve knights of the Order which has the rose-cross as its symbol represent a religious stream.[125] The pilgrim's encounter with the brotherhood dwelling in this place is replete with allusions to esoteric spiritual activity. Our interest here is to see how Steiner relates to, and uses, Goethean texts, rather than the circumstances of such Goethean material. Several verses from this epic will be given here, these are among the verses which were quoted by Steiner in a lecture on this poem,

And as at length he has attained the summit,
Below a softly sloping valley lies;
his quiet look with inward pleasure brightens,
Before the forest full of joy he spies
a stately building in a greening field,
which the departing sun with lustre dyed.
Ere long he nears through meadows dewy damp
a monastery lit with gleaming lamp…

The poem continues, the narrator informing us that the pilgrim espies a cross, intertwined with roses, affixed to the wall of the remote chapel, before which the pilgrim stands in reverence,

"…on the arch of the closed door
he sees a mysterious image.
He stands and contemplates and lightly whispers words
of worship, which well up from his heart….
The cross here is densely entwined with roses.
Who has added the roses to the cross?"

Some verses later, the pilgrim has been welcomed in, and is told of the mysterious knowledge and remarkable significance of this Order,

Miraculous were the paths which lead thee here,

---

[125] Rudolf Steiner, Kosmogonie (Dornach: RSV, 1979), 69, „Nach einer Erklärung des Dichters, die Goethe selbst jungen Leuten gegeben hat, repäsentiert jeder der zwölf Ritter des Rosenkreuzes eine religiöse Strömung." Goethe's comments are published by Trunz, in HA Bd. 2, S. 587.

The aged brother says in friendly tone to his guest:
Oh, let these symbols bid thee stay until
Thou hast learnt of many heroic deeds;
For what is here concealed can never be guessed'
Until we will confide to thee,
Indeed thou dost divine much of what
here has been endured, experienced,
lost and disputed…[126]

To Steiner, Goethe here is affirming the reality of the Rosicrucians, as an Order which was an historical reality, discretely functioning behind the external flow of history. He maintained that through the writings of Valentin Andreae, Europe was being deliberately informed as to the existence of the Order, and furthermore this brotherhood "had the mission of letting some esoteric influences flow in spiritual ways into the culture of central Europe".[127] Since Steiner refers to his drama, Die Pforte, as a "Rosicrucian mystery drama", it may be deduced that this drama is also intended to disseminate some esoteric influences into modern European culture, although overtly, and not, as previously, covertly.

In mainstream historical circles, the historicity of the Rosicrucian brotherhood is disputed, but generally it is not regarded as an historical reality. The historian Frances Yates, noted for her study of the esoteric-religious movements of Renaissance Europe, concluded that Andreae's mystical

---

[126] Werke, HA, Bd. 2, S. 271-281, „Und wie er nun den Gipfel ganz erstiegen,/ Sieht er ein nahes, sanft geschwungnes Tal,/ Sein stilles Auge leuchtet von Vergnügen;/Denn vor dem Walde sieht er auf einmal/ in Grüner Au ein schön Gebäude liegen,/ Soeben trifft's der letzte Sonnenstrahl: Er eilt durch Wiesen, die der tau befeuchtet,/Dem Kloster zu, das ihm entgegenleuchtet….. "Du kommst hierher auf wunderbaren Pfaden",/ spricht ihn der Alte wieder freundlich an; „Laß diese Bilder dich zu bleiben laden, Bis du erfährst, was mancher Held getan;/Was hier verborgen, ist nicht zu erraten/ Man zeige denn es dir vertraulich an;/Du ahnest wohl, wie manches hier gelitten, Gelebt, verloren ward, und was erstritten./

[127] Rudolf Steiner, Die Theosophie des Rosenkreutzers, (Dornach: RSV, 1979) 12, „Im achtzehnten Jahrhundert hatte diese Bruderschaft die Mission auf einem spirituellen Wege etwas Esoterisches einfließen zu lassen in die Kultur Mitteleuropas…"

Order had no actual historical existence, but was a fantasy inspired by esoteric interests of an hermetic and alchemical nature.[128] Similarly, Marie Roberts, in her detailed study of Rosicrucian influences in English literature, concluded that there was no historical basis to the Rosicrucian Order announced by Andreae. However, Roberts writes that the question is not closed, as "scholars still debate whether this clandestine brotherhood ever existed, or whether it was an elaborate hoax."[129] Roberts also hints at the inherent difficulty in establishing the existence of a secretive organisation, when she writes that "It may seem curious to embark upon a study of a society reputed to be so secret that it was even believed to be {constituted of} invisible {persons}."[130]

In May 1907, Steiner held a series of lectures entitled, '*Die Theosophie des Rosenkreutzers*' (*The Theosophy of the Rosicrucians)* in which his anthroposophical approach to theosophical themes was expounded, and in which he, in effect, simultaneously defined anthroposophy as a modern expression of the Rosicrucian movement. In this lecture cycle he described the Rosicrucian Order of earlier centuries as offering a path to spiritual development, consisting of seven distinct stages. The first stage of which was study of spiritual-esoteric themes, other stages encompassed insight into the correspondence of the microcosm (the human being) to the macrocosm (the cosmos); the seventh stages was union with God.[131] Since the "Theosophy' being taught in this lecture cycle was Steiner's own worldview, it is clear that Steiner regarded the Rosicrucian Order not only as an historical fact, but viewed his own anthroposophical worldview as an expression of this same stream, in modern times. This conclusion is confirmed in a series of lectures he held one month later, in June 1907,

---

[128] Frances A. Yates, The Rosicrucian Enlightenment, (London: Routledge, 1972) 32, 44. Yates' earlier work was *Giordano Bruno and the Hermetic tradition*.
[129] Marie Roberts, Gothic Immortals, (London: Routledge, 1990) 2.
[130] Roberts, Immortals 2.
[131] Steiner, Rosenkreutzers, 158.

> What does this Rosicrucian theosophy want to bring us? Knowledge of the higher worlds, that means, those realms to which the human being will still belong, when this, our physical body, has disintegrated. Knowledge of life, knowledge of the nature of death and of human development; in this way it will bring to people a re-strengthening in regard to religious truths and religious life.[132]

It is significant in this regard, that one of Steiner's earliest 'theosophical' books was *Knowledge of the Higher Worlds, how is it attained?* (1904). Another predominant element in Steiner's earlier writings, is, as we noted earlier, the Platonic 'Realm of the Idea'. We have also noted that it exists as an element of Goethe's scientific works, and won the acclaim of Steiner in his editorial work in the Goethe archives. As we have seen when examining Steiner's view of cognition, he sees consciousness of this realm as an especially important achievement. In his later anthroposophical phase, this realm figures largely, indeed attainment of direct perception of it is an especial goal of Johannes, the primary character in Die Pforte. This realm is regarded by Steiner as a cognate with a spiritual realm known in Theosophical literature as "Devachan", a Sanskrit term. In Theosophical texts, it is in this realm that the higher ego, or triune human spirit is said to exist between incarnations on the Earth.[133]

Steiner finds evidence of this realm in the literary works of Goethe, namely in his drama, *Faust*. The passage in question occurs in Part Two, where Faust is seeking to find Helen

---

[132] Rudolf Steiner, Menschheitsentwickelung und Christus-Erkenntnis, (Dornach: VRSN, 1967) 18, Was will uns nun diese Rosenkreuzer-theosophie bringen? Erkenntnis höherer Welten, das heißt derjenigen Welten, denen der Mensch noch angehören wird, wenn dieser und der physischer Leib schon zerfallen sein wird; Erkenntnis des Lebens, Erkenntnis des Wesens des Todes und der menschlichen Entwickelung. So wird sie den Menschen eine Wiederbefestigung bringen in bezug auf religiöse Wahrheiten und religiöses Leben.
[133] The Theosophical Glossary, Devachan, eds. H.P. Blavatsky and G.R.S. Mead, (London: Theosophical Publishing House, 1892) p. 91, "A state intermediate between two earth-lives, into which the Ego (Atma-Buddhi-Manas, or the Trinity made One) enters..."

(Part 2, Act 1, lines 6239 – 6248 & 6275 – 6278). To Steiner, this passage presents Goethe's view of a lofty archetypal realm. Hence Steiner interprets this passage as an indication that Goethe was one of those rare persons who knows something of this realm, "…we can regard his description here…as an approximate description of this realm".[134] Goethe places the mysterious figures, *The Mothers*, in this realm. Reference to The Mothers occurs as an esoteric theme from the ancient Greek Mysteries, about which little knowledge has been handed down from antiquity.[135]

That Goethe does intend the realm of The Mothers to represent some kind of spiritual supra-sensible realm, is agreed to by various Faust critics, not only Steiner.[136] Faust is seeking to find the ideal archetypal self – personified as Helena. Mephistopheles tells Faust that he must venture forth into a realm which is not perceptible (initially) – and which transcends space and time,

> And if you had swum through the ocean,
> and there beheld boundless space,
> You would nevertheless see wave upon wave coming,
> even though you might be afraid of going under,
> You would at least see something!
> Perhaps dolphins streaking by in the greenness of stilled seas,
> see perhaps also clouds floating past, see sun, moon and stars –
> Nothing shall you see in the eternally empty distance,
> Neither hear your own footstep, nor find
> any solid thing, whereupon you may rest!
> Descend then! I could also say – arise! …..

---

[134] Rudolf Steiner, Über die astrale Welt und das Devachan, (Dornach: RSV, 1999) 93, „Goethe hat dieses Land mehr äußerlich durch seinen Mephistopheles beschreiben lassen. wir können dies….als eine annähernde Schilderung dieses Reiches ansehen."
[135] The primary reference to this theme occurs in Plutarch's Lives, (New York: Random House, undated) in the section, *Marcellus*, where these beings are mentioned in connection with a political crisis, p. 381.
[136] Goethe, HA, Bd. 3, In the Anmerkungen, Trunz quotes various critics to this effect, 545-6.

> Flee from the Created to the realm freed of structured forms!
> Be delighted amidst what long since has ceased to be!
> [137]

Steiner concludes that here the expression, "what long since has ceased to be" means that all created things – or rather, the Ideas thereof – are to still be found in Devachan. In Steiner's anthroposophical viewpoint, it is in this realm that the Ideas of the divine-spiritual beings who have brought forth creation exist, and these Ideas are supra-temporal. To Steiner, the Faustian phrase "the realm freed of shaped forms" refers to the dynamic which is operative in the Idea realm, because forms shaped from material substance or even from an energetic reality have no existence there, rather the <u>concept</u> of such forms only is to be found.[138]

In lectures delivered to Theosophists in 1904, Steiner described this realm as having seven distinct stages to it. He gave descriptions of the 'contents' of this realm of Ideas, in a manner which is evidently derived from what he considered to be personal perception,

> In the second realm of {the archetypal Spiritual Worlds} the Universal Life, which in physical life is bound up with the forms of human, animal and plant kingdoms, and in which each being is delimited, flows like the waters of the sea. One sees this universal life flowing there...reddish-lilac in colour,

---

[137] From Faust, Part Two, ls. 6240-6245, 6275-78; „Und hättest du den Ozean durchschwommen, das Grenzenlose dort geschaut, So sähst du dort doch Well' auf Welle kommen, Selbst wenn es dir vorm Untergange graut. Du sähst doch etwas. Sähst wohl in der Grüne gestillter Meere streichende Delphine; sähst Wolken ziehen, Sonne, Mond und Sterne - Nichts wirst du sehn in ewig leerer Ferne, Den Schritt nicht hören, den du tust, Nichts Festes finden, wo du ruhst....Versinke denn! Ich könnt' auch sagen: steige! 's ist einerlie. Entfliehe dem Entstandnen in der Gebilde losgebundne Reiche! Ergetze dich am längst nicht mehr Vorhandnen;..."
[138] Rudolf Steiner, <u>Wo und wie findet man den Geist</u>? (Dornach: VRSN, 1961) 336.

from plant form to plant form, from animal form to animal form, as if embraced in the unity of life.[139]

A further element in Steiner's worldview which is found in Goethe is the pre-existence of the soul. As a logical concomitant to rejecting the concept that the soul (that is, human consciousness) comes into being with, and as a corollary by-product of, the substances and nerve processes in the embryo, Steiner also strongly affirms acceptance of the idea of the pre-existence of the human soul. Although there are no similarly detailed and complex elucidations of the concept of pre-existence in Goethe as those of Steiner, in Goethe's works are various brief indications that he held that the soul pre-existed, and reincarnates. His letter about his beloved Charlotte von Stein to Christoph Martin Wieland (Weimar, April 1776) is an example. In his musing on Charlotte, Goethe indicates he felt that he had been able to remember or at least sense something of this past life;

> I can only explain the significance – the power, which this woman has over me – through the {concept of} transmigration of souls – yes, we were once man and wife! Now we know of each other – veiled in the fragrance of the spirit. I have no name for us – the past – the future – the All."[140]

In addition, Goethe indicated this conviction in a well known poem, sent to Charlotte, where he forthrightly declares, like

---

[139] Rudolf Steiner, <u>Vor dem Tore der Theosophie</u>, (Dornach: RSV, 1978) 44, „In der zweiten Region flutet das allgemeine Leben, das im physischen Leben an die Menschen-, Tier- und Pflanzenform gebunden, in jeder Wesenheit abgegrenzt ist, wie die Meereswässer dahin. Man sieht es dahinfluten, das allgemeine Leben...rötlich-lilafarben flutet von Pflanzenform zu Pflanzenform, von Tierform zu Tierform, als in der Einheit des Lebens begriffen."

[140] <u>Goethes Briefe</u>, Hamburg, ed. Erich Trunz, Vol 1, (Hamburg: Christian Wegner verlag, 1962) 212, „Ich kann mir die Bedeutsamkeit - die Macht, die diese Frau über mich hat, anders nicht erklären als durch die Seelenwanderung.- Ja, wir waren einst Mann und Weib! - Nun wissen wir von uns -verhüllt in Geisterduft. - Ich habe keine Namen für uns - die Vergangenheit - die Zukunft - das All."

Schiller, that the reason for the special bonds of love he feels between them derives from a past life,

> "Say, what does destiny intend for us? Say, just how did we become so finely bonded? Oh, in times now past, you were my sister or my wife, you know every element of my nature, you espy how the finest nerve of mine resounds..."[141]

In 1906, Steiner referred to these comments of Goethe about Charlotte, as indicative of Goethe's acceptance of reincarnation and karma, and then comments that Goethe had written another poem which specifically refers to reincarnation,

> But the deepest which he had to say, that he said in images, among others, in the beautiful poem where he compares the soul of the human being with the water and the destiny of the human being with the wind, the soul as that which flows on its way from incarnation to incarnation in the stream of life and destiny with the wind, which lets this soul surge up and down in the continuous waves... "The soul of the human being, how like the water you are! Fate of man, how like the wind!" This is what he says at the end of the poem, where he directly portrays the reincarnation into earthly life. "The soul of the human being is like water: it comes from heaven, it rises to heaven and must return back to the earth, eternally alternating". Goethe represents the soul in this way. It comes from the spiritual world, descends to the earth, returns back to heave and comes again in a new incarnation..."[142]

---

[141] Goethes Werke, HA Bd 1, S. 123, „Sag, was will das Schicksal uns bereiten?/Sag, wie band es uns so rein genau?/ Ach, du warst in abgelebten Zeiten/ Meine Schwester oder meine Frau; Kanntest jeden Zug in meinem Wesen, Spähtest, wie die reinste Nerve klingt..."

[142] Rudolf Steiner Die Welträsel und die Anthroposophie, (Dornach:VRSN, 1966) 305, „Aber das Tiefste, was er zu sagen hatte, das sagte er im Bilde, unter anderm in dem schönen Gedicht, wo er die Seele des Menschen vergleicht mit dem Wasser und das Schicksal des Menschen mit dem Winde, das diese Seele auf und ab wogen läßt in immerwährenden Wellen.... 'Seele des Menschen, wie gleichst du dem Wasser, Schicksal des Menschen wie

Goethe's habit of utilizing his literary artistic skills to represent his perspective on life was admired by Steiner, who described his own approach to representing the anthroposophical worldview as similar to this method of Goethe. In 1923, in a public lecture, Steiner referred to the holistic conclusions of Goethe's ideas as a basis for anthroposophy. He refers firstly to Goethe's scientific writings, wherein the entirety is considered, rather than a compartmentalized approach, as affirmative of his anthroposophy, and then proceeds to the artistic attitude of Goethe,

> Anthroposophy takes hold of the entire human being. In this way, in yet another way, it is an expression of the Goethean worldview. It is an expression of the Goethean worldview in the first instance, in that it is stimulated by the manner and way in which Goethe observed the life of plants and animal life, in their metamorphoses, in their transformations....But Goethe was also that personality who has built the bridge from knowledge across to art. Indeed, Goethe from his artistic convictions, has spoken the beautiful expression, 'art is a revelation of secret laws of nature, which, without this art would never become manifest'....Such knowledge which has its roots in the life of the spirit in this way, like that of anthroposophy, streams quite naturally into artistic creativity..."[143]

---

gleichst du dem Wind', so sagt er am Schlusse des Gedichtes, wo er geradezu die Wiederverkörperung im Erdenleben darstellt. 'Des Menschen Seele gleicht dem Wasser, vom Himmel kommt es, zum Himmel steigt es, und wieder nieder zur Erde muß es, ewig wechselnd'. So stellt Goethe die Seele dar. Sie kommt aus der geistigen Welt, steigt zur Erde nieder, geht zurück zum Himmel und kommt wieder in neuer Verkörperung..."

[143] Steiner, Was wollte, 39, „Anthroposophie ergreift eben den ganzen Menschen. Dadurch wird sie noch in einer anderen Beziehung ein Ausdruck der Goetheschen Weltanschauung. Sie ist zunächst ein Ausdruck der Goetheschen Weltanschauung, indem sie angeregt worden ist durch die Art und Weise, wie Goethe das Pflanzenleben, das Tierleben betrachete in seinen Metamorphosen, in seinen Verwandlungen....Aber Goethe war auch diejenige Persönlichkeit, welche die Brücke hinübergebaut hat von dem

Steiner sees a vastly more significant and profound expression of esoteric concepts than the above 'eternal romantic love' theme in one of Goethe's fairy tales, which has a very significant relationship to Steiner's drama, Die Pforte. This text is the fairy tale which Goethe simply called "Das Märchen" (The Fairy Tale). This tale is referred to by Steiner as The Green Snake and the Beautiful Lily, a term which emphasizes the two main characters in it.

To Steiner, the realm in which the fair Lily dwells, and to which the other characters are striving to ascend, is the Platonic realm of the Idea. This title of Steiner's also distinguishes the tale from other fairy tales of Goethe, such as *Melusine* and *Der neue Paris*. In this tale, Steiner sees numerous and potent allusions to the Platonic realm of the Idea, or Devachan, as well as to the pathway to conscious perception of the divine.

Erkennen zur Kunst. Goethe hat ja aus seiner künstlerischen Überzeugung heraus das schöne Wort gesprochen, Die Kunst ist eine Offenbarung geheimer Naturgesetze, die ohne diese Kunst niemals offenbar würden....Solche Erkenntnis, die so im Leben des Geistes wurzelt, wie die Anthroposophie, die strömt von selbst auch in das künstlerische Schaffen ein."

1B4: Goethe's fairy tale provides the thematic basis of Die Pforte

"Das Märchen" was written in 1795, it was incorporated into a longer work, a collection of tales, Unterhaltungen Deutscher Ausgewanderten (Conversations between German emigrants). The tale gripped the imagination of people throughout Europe, as Mommsen testifies.[144] People clamoured for Goethe to write an explanation, but this never happened. Readers felt that he had drawn on the mystical perspectives which fascinated him throughout his life. Steiner regards the overall imaginative perspective underlying Goethe's *"Das Märchen"* as very closely linked to that given in his own anthroposophical (theosophical) texts. Indeed Steiner regards Goethe as, in effect, a theosophist,

> You just cannot understand entire areas of Goethe's writings, if you don't have some idea of Theosophy. In a broader sense, Goethe's achievements in regard to the plant world can only be understood by those who have a feeling for what Goethe called the life-processes or the metamorphoses of plants.[145]

In a public lecture Steiner describes this Goethean tale as an especially theosophical, artistic presentation of the processes involved in spiritual development,

> That Goethe was a Theosophist is clear from his 'hidden' writing, which is indeed included in every edition of his works, but which is the least read – from his fairy tale of The Green Snake and the Beautiful Lily. This contains all of Theosophy, but in

---

[144] Katharina Mommsen, Goethe Märchen, (Frankfurt: Insel Verlag, 1984) 195, „...die erste Reaktion des Publikums war eine Mischung von echter Bewunderung, respektvoller Ratlosigkeit und – Neugier."

[145] Rudolf Steiner, Ursprung, 62, „Sie können schon ganze bestimmte Gebiete bei Goethe nicht verstehen, wenn Sie nicht eine Ahnung haben von Theosophie. Goethes Ausführungen über die Pflanzenwelt versteht nur derjenige, welcher eine Ahnung davon hat, was Goethe die Lebensvorgänge oder die Metamorphose der Pflanzen nennt."

the way in which theosophical truths have been communicated, since time immemorial. Only since the founding of the Theosophical Society have these truths been communicated; earlier they could only be presented in a pictorial form. The Fairy Tale is one such pictorial expression of theosophical truths.[146]

Steiner maintains in his comments on this fairy tale, that it speaks to its readers of the path to esoteric spiritual development, using images drawn from the spiritual heritage of Europe. In his commentary on Goethe's *Unterhaltungen Deutscher Ausgewanderten*, Trunz quotes Rudolf Steiner for his interpretation of *"Das Märchen"*; cf. *HA6*, 613, among a range of other interpretations.[147] Steiner understands this fairy tale to depict the process of esoteric-spiritual development, or initiation, in remarkably insightful and accurate detail. It is this same process which he depicts in his drama, Die Pforte, and which we shall consider in detail in the following sections. In *Die Pforte*, Steiner attempts to depict the spiritual development process in human terms, and hence the characters are almost entirely personalities, not allegorical figures.

By contrast, Mommsen for example, views the tale as a Utopian description of the yearning of the artist to change the world for the better, because of the 'happy ending' – wherein the Youth and the Lily unite to each other. She reaches this conclusion that it has to be a Utopian ideal, because nowhere could such a blissful reality exist on Earth.[148] While

---

[146] Rudolf Steiner, Ursprung, 62, „Daß Goethe Theosoph war, geht aus einer „verborgenen" Schrift hervor, die zwar in jeder Ausgabe vorhanden ist, jedoch von den wenigsten gelesen wird; aus dem „Märchen von der grünen Schlange und der schönen Lilie". Das enthält die ganze Theosophie, aber so, wie von jeher die theosophischen Wahrheiten mitgeteilt worden sind. Erst seit der Begründung der Thesophischen Gesellschaft sind dies äußerlich zum Ausdruck gekommen; früher konnten sie nur bildlich dargestellt werden."

[147] Trunz, HA, Bd. 6, *Anmerkungen,* 613.
[148] Mommsen, Goethe, 201, „Auf diese Happy-End-Lösung hin ist das gesamte *Märchen* angelegt....Da Zustände dieser Art in Wirklichkeit niemals existieren können...Was Dichter und Philosophen so oft erträumten, eine utopische Veränderung der Welt..."

Mommsens's view has some merits, it appears to ignore, among other things, the specific placement by Goethe of *Das Märchen* in the *Unterhaltungen*, a collection of mainly supernatural tales. Steiner's view is to the contrary, he places it firmly in Goethe's esoteric context. He may have been influenced also by a letter of Goethe's in which Goethe's interest in esoteric material (alchemical, Rosicrucian) is evinced. Written on 28. June 1876, to Charlotte von Stein, Goethe states that he has read the central Rosicrucian source text, "*The Chymical Wedding of Christian Rosenkreutz*", and that "there is a lovely Märchen in it, once it is re-born" in a new form. This letter is not included in the Hamburger edition of Goethe's works, but it is included in the Weimarer edition of Goethe's works.[149]

Certainly to Steiner, the 'Utopian' element in this tale is not Utopian, but realistic, in so far as it portrays the blessed state able to be experienced by the successful attainment of high spiritual development, "the fair Lily, the ideal of perfect knowledge and perfect life and creativity....In the fairy tale, Goethe depicts in the Youth, the person striving for the highest bride, and that with which he should be united, is called the 'fair Lily'."[150]

Steiner's drama, *Die Pforte*, is specifically written as a parallel work to Goethe's *Märchen*. In the preliminary drafts of *Die Pforte*, published posthumously by the administration of the Steiner archives, the characters in this drama – in the first scene – actually bear the names of the characters in the fairy tale.[151] Because of the close parallel of *Das Märchen* to

---

[149] Goethes Werke, Weimarer Ausgabe, Bd. 7, Goethes Briefe, (Weimar: Hermann Böhlau Verlag, 1891) 233, „Christian Rosenkreutz Hochzeit habe ich hinausgelesen, es giebt ein schön Mährgen zur Stunde zu erzählen, wenn es wiedergebohren wird..."

[150] Rudolf Steiner, Wo und wie findet man den Geist? 73, „...die schöne Lilie, das ideal vollkommener Erkenntnis und vollkommenen Lebens und Schaffens" and, 83, „Goethe zeigt in dem Märchen den nach der höchsten Braut strebenden Menschen in seinem Jüngling, und das, womit er vereingt werden soll, nennt er die schöne Lilie."

[151] Steiner, Entwürfe, Fragmente, und Paralipomena zu den vier Mysteriendramen, (Dornach: VRSN, 1969) 63.

Steiner's first drama, an additional supplementary volume to Steiner's Complete Works was published, containing his twelve lectures on the tale. Some of the characteristics of characters of *Die Pforte,* and the events which befall them, can only be meaningfully interpreted through knowledge of the fact that there is a direct parallel between this drama and the Goethean fairy tale. We will now consider briefly the major dynamics of the Goethean fairytale.

The opening scene of the fairytale is a little hut on the bank of a mysterious river that effectively divides two realms. In the hut dwells the Ferryman, who alone is empowered to ferry various beings across the waters. Then two strange creatures, Will-o'-the-Wisps, appear and importune the Ferryman to row them across the river immediately. This he does, and demands that his fare be paid not with pieces of gold which the Will-o'-the-Wisps so easily shake from themselves, but with *the fruits of the Earth.* Their gold pieces are to him most unwelcome, indeed he says they would enrage the river should they fall into it.

The Will-o'-the-Wisps are completely disinterested in all his concerns, and set off from him, but the Ferryman holds them fast with magical power until they agree to meet his demands at some later time. He takes the gold and throws it into a cleft in the rocks. The gold pieces tumble down into a cave, where we see the green snake slumbering; she is awakened by their clinking noise, and immediately begins to greedily eat them. As she does so, she begins to develop a luminous glow. She sets forth to discover the source of gold, and re-encounters the Will-o'-the-Wisps.

A dialogue ensues, and the Will-o'-the-Wisps reveal they are in search of the renowned beautiful Lily. The Lily is beautiful beyond compare, and loved by all who know her, and yet she is lonely, and to some extent, despondent. The way to the Lily is an arduous path, and her touch is death to all living creatures. The Green Snake informs the Will-o'-the-Wisps that her realm is remote, and that it is situated on *other side* of the river; she dwells there, wistfully yearning for the fulfilment of a mysterious event. The Will-o'-the-Wisps are told that the Ferryman cannot take anyone back across the river, he can only bring them to this side. However the Green Snake reveals there are two ways in which one can cross back to the other realm; one is via the snake, but only at midday when she forms an arch across the river. The second way is via an ominous giant, this opportunity opens only at twilight an dusk, when the sun is either just setting or just rising; on the back of his moving shadow one can be carried across the river.

The group part company and we follow the green snake back into her cave, where she intends to explore a mysterious grotto, with the help of the luminosity now emanating from her inner being. She had previously sensed the presence of four mysterious statues there, but now, radiant, she beholds a great underground temple where statues of four enthroned kings are clearly visible. Three of these are noble in appearance and are made from precious metals, but the fourth king has a malignant, disharmonious appearance. This encounter has startling consequences, the statues come to life and the kings, like hierophants in an ancient mystery ritual, begin a gripping dialogue with the green snake.

Though brief, the dialogue is immensely tantalising through its mystical cryptic allusions. The entire scene is raised to dramatic heights when we witness the Man with the Lamp emerging from the solid rock walls and joining in the dialogue, bringing it to an end with a loud cry, 'The time is at hand!'. After this powerful musical tones reverberate through the temple, followed by the exiting of the Green Snake and the Man with the Lamp through the solid rock walls.

The scene now moves to the cottage of the Old Man and his wife, who is in great distress. Will-o'-the-Wisps, she recounts, had visited her and consumed all the pure gold veneer used in the cottage. Furthermore she had to promise the Wisps that she would repay the debt to the Ferryman. The scene then changes to the journey of the Old Woman, setting out for the hut of the Ferryman on the bank of the river, with fruits of the Earth (three cabbages, three onions, three artichokes). But on the way she stumbles across the giant who steals one third of her precious cargo; so the Ferryman does not accept it now, but requires her to make a pledge to the river.

At this point another passenger disembarks from the boat of the Ferry man, the forlorn Youth, consumed with a yearning to encounter his beloved, the beautiful Lily. He meets the Old Woman with the cargo and sets out together with her to find the Lily. At midday they see the arch of the green snake crossing the river, and they hurry across, together with the Wisps. In the meantime a hawk, belonging to the Prince, has killed a canary belonging to the Lily; whom we now see singing a plaintive song, full of sadness, waiting for the time when a great temple shall rise up from inside the Earth, and when she shall meet her true love. She has three maids-in-waiting attending her. The Youth, seeing her, rushes forward knowing full well the consequences, and touching her, falls at her feet, apparently dead. At this point the Green Snake forms a magic circle around the Youth, whilst the Old Man with the Lamp is invoked by the Lily.

The Green Snake prepares to sacrifice herself, for she seems to know that she holds the key to redeem the situation. Then a remarkable procession scene begins, in which all the characters in the fairytale move into the subterranean temple of kings. A dramatic scene follows in which the temple shudders and then begins to ascend up through the crust of the Earth to its surface. The fourth king now collapses and the three great kings carry out a ritual for the Youth, who comes partly to life, and who then is lead by the Old Man with The Lamp to the waiting fair Lily. Now that he is spiritually reborn, these two may unite, and in so doing the Youth is restored to his full faculties and these two now commence to reign over their kingdom. In the meantime a bridge over the river has been formed from exquisite gemstones which is what is all that is left of the green snake. The Giant briefly appears on the bridge but is soon turned into a harmless lifeless object. The Green Snake has provided a permanent and wholesome way for all people to cross over the barrier between the two realms. Steiner's drama, Die Pforte, is a dramatization of the Goethean tale, keeping a close parallelism with the tale, except where notable exceptions are made. Steiner views this fairy tale as an allegorical portrayal of the quest for higher consciousness. The correspondence between the list of characters in both works, as noted by Steiner, is as follows,[152]

Lilie (Lily) - Maria
Mensch (Youth) - Johannes Thomasius
1. Irrlicht (Will-o'-the-Wisp) - Capesius
2. Irrlicht (Will-o'-the-Wisp) - Strader
Der Mann mit der Lampe (the Old Man with lamp) - Felix Balde
König des Willens (king: the will) - Romanus
König des Gefühls (king: the emotions) - Theodosius
König des Denkens (king: the intelligence) - Benedictus
1. Mädchen (1st maiden) - Philia
2. Mädchen (2nd maiden) - Astrid
3. Mädchen (3rd maiden) - Luna
Riese (Giant) - German (Gairman)
Kanarienvogel (Canary) - Kind (child)
Fährmann (Ferryman) - Der Geist der Elemente
                     (Spirit of the Elements)
Gemischter König (the mixed king) - Retardus
Die grüne Schlange (the Green Snake) - Die andere Maria
                                       (the Other Maria)
Die Alte Frau (the Old Woman) - Felicia Balde
Der Habicht (the Hawk) - Theodora

With regard to the names of the characters in *Die Pforte*, Steiner commented in a lecture delivered two months after the first performance of *Die Pforte*, "With all the names it is the case, that they are coined for the individual beings

---

[152] Steiner, Entwürfe, 12.

specifically according to their nature."[153] In addition, in the list of characters for *Die Pforte* Steiner gives a key as to what each of them represents.

The allegorical meaning embedded in the name of each character will be considered in Section 2b, where a brief overview of each scene is made. The following synopsis of Steiner's view of *Das Märchen* is drawn from *Goethes geheime Offenbarung*, the volume of collected Steiner lectures on this tale, mentioned above.[154] The River is seen to be the barrier which divides the mundane world from the realm of the spirit (the Lily). Although a river is often used poetically to symbolize time and change and constancy, Steiner's view of the river as the boundary between the physical reality and the Other World – where the Unborn, and also the Dead exist – is consistent with his interpretation of the Goethean tale, and bears strong similarities to ancient Greek mythology.

In this mythology, a river is also the boundary between the living and the Dead, and the aged ferryman, Charon, plies his boat between the two realms.[155] The river is a kind of elemental realm, an intermediary realm between the material world and spiritual realms, in which the human being is to be found, prior to birth, or more correctly, prior to conception. The main intentions of the Youth, the Will-o'-the-Wisps and the Old Woman, is to cross the barrier between this physical world and enter a higher, spiritual state.

To Steiner, therefore, the initial scene of this tale is in the realm of the soul, where souls, in the pre-conception stage, are waiting to incarnate. The two Will-o'-the-Wisps are urgently importuning a type of Charon, an aged ferryman, to

---

[153]Rudolf Steiner, 17th Sept 1910, *Über Selbsterkenntnis, anknüpfend an das Rosenkreuzermysterium „Die Pforte der Einweihung"*, in Wege und Ziele des geistigen Menschen, (Dornach: RSV, 1973) 114, „Alle Namen sind so, daß sie für die einzelnen Wesenheiten ganz wesenhaft geprägt sind."

[154] Rudolf Steiner, Goethes geheime Offenbarung, (Dornach: RSV, 1982).
[155] The Oxford Classical Dictionary, ed. N. G. L. Hammond, 2nd edit. (Oxford: Clarendon Press, 1970) 228.

take them across the river, in this sense the ferryman is the reverse of Charon, who takes the soul up into the other worlds, as he only takes souls down into the earthly world. The Will-o'-the-Wisps represent in Steiner's model the egocentric, earthwards-bound impulses in human souls, driving them to enter into earthly life.

Steiner refers to the realm of the unborn as the 'soul world' or 'astral world', a realm, which is intermediary to that of the 'spiritual realm'. In his lectures to Theosophists, he maintained that the true spiritual realm referred to in Theosophical literature as 'Devachan' is cognate with the Christian 'Heaven', and also with the realm of the 'Idea'. His conclusions derive in this instance from his 'spiritual research'. When Goethe's tale is viewed in this way, a key Steiner concept, pre-existence of the soul, is affirmed.

As we have noted earlier, in the higher realm, beyond the soul world, exist the Ideas which govern and create the physical world and its objects. An element in Steiner's view of reincarnation is that as the soul returns to a new life, and is firmly clothed in a physical body at birth, it nevertheless retains a semi conscious awareness of its original spiritual condition. The result of this faint memory is the yearning to re-achieve this primal condition. This perspective of Steiner's is even to be found in his *Credo*, which he wrote as a 27 year old,

> The human being however feels and knows itself to be a separate individual, when it awakens to its full consciousness {entering adulthood}. But at the same time, he has implanted with himself, the yearning for the Idea. This yearning drives him on, to overcome the separateness, and to allow the spirit in himself to come to life, to be like unto the spirit….the human being must will to do that which the spirit, the Idea in him wills.[156]

---

[156] Rudolf Steiner, Wahrspruchworte 273, „Der Mensch aber fühlt und erkennt als Einzelnes sich, wenn er zu seinem vollen Bewußtsein erwacht.

This same concept is elaborated in various of his lectures, and he presented meditative verses to his students, encapsulating this concept. The first of the following examples was inscribed into a student's copy of his book, "*Knowledge of Higher Worlds; how is it attained?*",

> Why does the seeking soul of the human being strive for knowledge of the higher worlds? Because every look into the sense-world, born of the soul, becomes a question, full of yearning for the being of the spirit. Why does the human soul, following a dim yearning, strive towards self-knowledge? Because the Being of the world is not comprehensible through glitter of Ideas and not in the entanglement of concepts. It lies within the human self, once this unveiled, then evolving being of the cosmos is unveiled.[157]

To Steiner therefore, what could be characterized as ego-centric, earthwards bound, instinctive impulses in human souls, driving people to enter into incarnation, is not the sole impulse in the incarnating person. There are also the higher impulses, in which this memory of the divine is preserved – these exist in the realm of the Idea. It is these memories which impel the soul, once it is incarnate, to seek for spiritual development. The search for the realm of the beautiful Lily by various characters in Goethe's tale therefore is seen by Steiner as depicting the urge of various aspects of the human

---

„Dabei aber hat er die Sehnsucht nach der Idee eingepflanzt. Diese Sehnsucht treibt ihn an, die Einzelheit zu überwinden und den Geist in sich aufleben zu lassen, dem Geiste gemäß zu leben...der Mensch muß...was wollen, was der Geist, die Idee in ihm will."

[157] Rudolf Steiner, Wahrspruch 231 and 235, „Warum strebt des Menschen suchende Seele nach Erkenntnis der höheren Welten? Weil jeder seeleentsprossene Blick in die Sinneswelt zur sehnsuchtvollen Frage wird nach dem Geistesein." (orthographics/syntax in original)
„Warum strebt, dunkler Sehnssucht folgend: nach Selbst-Erkenntnis des Menschen Seele? Weil nicht im Ideen-Schein und nicht in Begriff-Gewebe der Welten Wesen faßbar. Es liegt im Menschen-Selbst; enthüllt sich dieses: so enthüllt sich der Welten Werdewesen."

consciousness for perception of the realm of Ideas, a process which implies spiritual development.

An early episode in the Goethean tale is that of the two Will-o'-the-Wisps being encountered by the Green Snake, who has been eating pieces of gold which come these two strange beings. They are disconcerted at the fact that the Ferryman insists that they must repay a debt to him, and to do this they are in search of the fair Lily. To Steiner, this dynamic indicates that the everyday imperfect 'self' does produce the gold of enlightenment, but does not know how to use it, and is not able to find the way to spirituality.

The quality in the personality, however which selflessly engages with life, and learns from life experiences can become illumined through this. These two beings are unsatisfied with the guidance provided by the Green Snake and proceed on their way without her. The tale recounts that they then enter into the house of the Old Woman (the core values of the soul) and eat the gold that lines the hearth, leaving her distraught. But the tale's narrator recounts that before they leave her home, the Old Woman has promised her two strange visitors that she shall repay their debt.

In Steiner's model, the two negative aspects of the soul, the Will-o'-the-Wisps, the unedified emotive and intellectual tendencies, are as yet unaware that they need to journey with selflessness, and hence they shall indeed incur a debt to the spiritual powers who created humanity. They bring about a loss by causing attrition of the residual wisdom and religious impulses from earlier times, through their modern, humanistic materialism. The Old Woman sets out to do repair the damage or repay the debt, taking the demanded three fruits of the Earth, but she encounters the Giant, who robs her of some of these. To Steiner, this episode means that the soul's core values attempt to repair the damage of the materialistic mental qualities, by 'harvesting' some valuable outcomes of life experience, but cannot avoid losing some of this to retrograde atavistic impulses, which undermine the self's integrity.

In the meanwhile, the Green Snake, now somewhat luminescent, encounters the three kings. Steiner views the three kings as representatives of specific triune spiritual faculties dormant within the human being. In this interpretation of the three kings episode by Steiner, the reason that the Green Snake, once she has consumed some gold, can see them, is that there is now sufficient insightfulness in the personality, the everyday ego, to enable it to more directly sense the existence of the triune spiritual potential, even if these are still immersed under layers of un-illumined soul qualities. Thus the dialogue of the Green Snake with the three Kings becomes a dialogue between the self, in which the urge for spirituality is developing, and the higher self.

The rest of the tale, from Steiner's viewpoint, recounts the processes wherein the self undergoes initiatory spiritual renewal, learning how to dialogue with the triune spiritual potential, and harmonize its will with its triune soul qualities (the three maidens). Further, the self must learn to not cause harm to its own higher possibilities by premature and ego-centric spiritual questing (the hawk frightening the Lily's canary). Eventually the Youth shall succeed in his quest, and restore harmony to the human being overall, and the spiritual realms which interface with it. But all of this only occurs because the Green Snake provides a selfless, humble element, offering advice, seeking to become illumined, etc.

Her actions culminate towards the end of the tale, in a crucial episode, which enables the Youth and the Lily to unite; she sacrifices herself by forming herself into a ring, by taking her tail into her mouth, and this results in the creation of a resplendent, bejewelled bridge across the river. Prior to this, the snake forms itself into a ring by grasping its tail, is a common symbol in esoteric Hellenistic literature, where it is known as a symbol of eternity or eternal consciousness.[158] Steiner's interpretation of the specific incident where she forms a ring, will be considered in Section 3 of this thesis.

After this event the Green Snake's actions culminate in the process of forming a link between the spiritual and the earthly realities, which is in effect, the jewel-like fundament of the new personality, which can cross the barrier, the river, between the mundane and the spiritual realms, as Goethe describes it, "a broad and stately bridge stretching with many arches across the river". To Steiner, therefore the Green Snake represents the inherent tendency towards selflessness, a potential that becomes actual when the crucial moment calls for this, "The snake, the selfless life-experience – developed in love of wisdom, through experiential wisdom – surrenders its existence, to build a bridge between the sensuality and spirituality."[159] To Steiner, the character of the Green Snake is Goethe's way of representing the fact that selflessness and humility are to become a firm reality in the personality seeking spiritual development.

An alternative interpretation of the Green Snake forming a bridge, is given by Mommsen, who interprets the entire tale as a work alluding to the role of art in culture, and the influence of Schiller in Goethe's inner life. She does not consider that the snake represents the above Hellenistic esoteric motif, because of a passage about the snake symbol in a letter written by Goethe, in which he declares he sees the symbol differently. Goethe wrote as follows on 5th January 1814,

> One uses the snake which made itself into a circle, as a symbol of eternity; I however gladly regard it as an allegory of a happy temporality. What more can a

---

[158] Charles William King, The Gnostics and their remains, reprint of the 1887 2nd ed. (San Diego: Wizards bookshelf, 1982) 437.
[159] Rudolf Steiner, Goethes Geistesart (Dornach: VRSN, 1956) 77, „Die Schlange, die selbstlose, in Liebe zur Weisheit, in erlebter Weisheit entwickelte Lebenserfahrung, gibt ihre Existenz auf, um eine Brücke zu bilden zwischen der Sinnlichkeit und der Geistigkeit."

person wish for than it be granted him, to connect the end to the beginning, so in what other way can this occur, than through the lasting nature of affection, of trust, of love, of friendship."[160]

Mommsen concludes that "this shows how the snake symbol is to be interpreted in the Märchen also; as a symbol of friendship...it was his friendship with Schiller which Goethe portrayed in the form of an enigmatic image."[161] However, Goethe here is referring to the Gnostic image of a snake with its tail in its mouth, only, not a snake in general. However, the Green Snake acts as a crucial catalyst to the rising action of the tale in various ways, whilst in its normal state, the forming of itself into ring is not required for these.

For example, when it whispers to the Old Man with the Lamp during the dialogue with the three Kings, a very dramatic event ensues, which we noted earlier, namely the Old Man declares that 'the time is at hand', and the characters hurtle away through the earth. Further, the dialogue itself only arises because the Green Snake consumes the gold pieces cast off by the Will-o'-the-Wisps. Hence Mommsen's conclusion ignores various other, important actions of the Green Snake, she has no comments on how to assimilate these episodes into her model.

These episodes could be seen as susceptible to Steiner's perspective, in which they to correlate to specific initiatory processes; we have just noted that the becoming luminous of the Green Snake is seen as the soul developing wisdom. Whereas, the expression, 'the time is at hand', in the Steiner model, refers to the incipient preparedness of the self to

---

[160] Mommsen, Goethe, 222, „Man bedient sich als Symbol der Ewigkeit der Schlange, die sich in einen Reif abschließt, ich betrachte dies hingegen gern als ein Gleichnis einer glücklichen Zeitlichkeit. Was kann der Mensch mehr wünschen, als daß ihm erlaubt sei, das Ende an den Anfang anzuschließen, und wodurch kann dies geschehen, als durch die Dauer der Zuneigung, des Vertrauens, der Liebe, der Freundschaft."
[161] Mommsens, Goethe, 222, „Es ergibt sich, wie auch im *Märchen* das Schlangengleichnis zu deuten ist: als Freundschaftssymbol...es war seine Freundschaft mit Schiller, die Goethe in Form eines Bilderrätsels darstellte."

jettison the lower egocentric tendencies. Without this preparedness, the union of the Youth to the fair Lily is impossible. In a public lecture from 1908 Steiner describes the nature of the Green Snake in terms of his earlier philosophical writings, including the ethical nuance mentioned above, but now extending it to integrate his epistemological conclusions. He refers back to the Goethean Urpflanze,

> Think about what Goethe does with the concept of the primal plant...he takes the concept, proceeds to the plant and sees how it shapes itself into this or that form, how it assumes entirely different forms in lower or higher regions and so on. Then step by step, he follows how the spiritual reality creeps into every shape existing in the sense world. He himself creeps around like the Green Snake in the crevasses of the earth. Thus for Goethe the concept world is nothing else than that which lets itself be woven into the fabric of objective reality. The snake is to him a representative of that soul-power which does not strive egoistically upwards into higher realms of existence, wanting to be raised above everything, rather it is that soul-power which patiently lets the concept be shown to be correct through observation, which patiently goes from experience to experience, from event to event.[162]

---

[162] Rudolf Steiner, <u>Wo und wie findet man</u>, 71, „Denken sie sich aber, was Goethe mit dem Begriff der Urpflanze tut....Er nimmt den Begriff, geht von ihm aus zur Pflanze über und sieht, wie sie sich in dieser oder jener Form ausgestaltet, wie sie ganz andere Formen annimmt in niederer oder höherer Gegend und so weiter. Nun verfolgt er von Stufe zu Stufe, wie die geistige Realität oder Gestalt in jede sinnliche Gestalt hineinkriecht. Er selbst kriecht da herum wie die (grüne) Schlange in den Klüften der Erde. So ist für Goethe die Begriffswelt nichts anderes als das, was sich in die objektive Wirklichkeit hineinspinnen läßt. Die Schlange ist ihm der Repräsentant der Seelenkraft, die nicht in egoistischer Weise hinaufstrebt zu den höheren Gebieten des Daseins und sich über alles zu erheben versucht, sondern die geduldig den Begriff durch die Beobachtung fortwährend bewahrheiten läßt, die geduldig von Erfahrung zu Erfahrung, von Erlebnis zu Erlebnis geht."

The above remarks of Steiner demonstrate his view of Das Märchen as an esoteric text, in which also the primal and quintessential epistemological act – in Steiner's view – uniting the perceived with the Idea thereof – is embodied in the figure of the Green Snake. Thus this fairy tale of the Green Snake and the Beautiful Lily becomes, in Steiner's eyes, an exposition of esoteric spiritual development in the wider European theosophical tradition. This kinship of Goethe's Märchen with Steiner's anthroposophical phase is remarkably relevant to Steiner's own life.

In particular it is relevant to his taking up a new career path as a teacher of spiritual subjects, and leaving behind the academic, philosophical work. We noted in the Introduction (1a) that the opportunity for Steiner's new career path of elucidating spiritual themes came in 1902, when he tentatively started lecturing, and was consequently approached by theosophists. That is, he was invited to join the Theosophical Society as a General Secretary, after giving lectures to a Giordano Bruno Association in Berlin.

Steiner reports in his autobiography that it was in fact his lecture elucidating the esoteric meaning Goethe's Märchen, which he terms, the The fairy tale of The Green Snake and the Beautiful Lily, which resulted in the invitation from the theosophists. As he comments in his autobiography,

> "It was an important experience for me to be able to speak in words which were moulded from out of the spiritual world, whereas previously I was compelled, owing to the circumstances in my time in Berlin, to only allow the spiritual to shine through my presentations."[163]

---

[163] Steiner, Lebensgang, 276; „Es war ein wichtiges Erlebnis für mich, in Worten, die aus der Geistwelt heraus geprägt waren, sprechen zu können, nachdem ich bisher in meiner Berliner Zeit durch die Verhältnisse gezwungen war, das Geistige nur durch meine Darstellungen durchleuchten zu lassen."

In Section 1B4, we noted the parallelism between the *Die Pforte* and *Das Märchen,* it became clear that the characters of Steiner's drama are representative of those in the fairy tale. We noted then, to Steiner the primary intention of Goethe's fairy tale is to communicate the process by which the barrier between earthly consciousness and the spiritualized state is overcome and spirituality is attained. As Steiner explains on lectures on his drama, in *Die Pforte* he utilizes the dynamics and allegorical elements of Das Märchen to describe the processes and challenges which a contemporary acolyte on the spiritual path has to encounter, in order to achieve initiation or esoteric spirituality in his sense of the phrase. Most of the characters in Die Pforte are representatives of those in Goethe's tale.

The three women in *Die Pforte* Philia, Astrid and Luna, represent the three maidens serving the fair Lily; as such, they are understood by Steiner to portray the thinking (Astrid), emotion (Philia) and will (Luna). The other set of characters in the Goethean tale, portraying triune dynamics are the three Kings – the gold, silver and brass kings. These are represented in *Die Pforte* by the three hierophants, Benedictus, Theodosius and Romanus. In his list of characters, Steiner notes that these three characters represent the higher self, he views the higher self as a triune entity. There is also a fourth, negative, king that falls away in the course of the fairy tale, just as does the fourth hierophant, Retardus in *Die Pforte*, this character is a negative hierophant. The Youth is seen striving somewhat blindly toward the goal (the fair Lily); he can thus be seen as representing the normal self, and this is represented by Johannes Thomasius in *Die Pforte*.

The Old Man with the Lamp, is Felix Balde in *Die Pforte*, he is an aspect of the human spirit, active as a spiritual advisor to the soul. His wife, Felicia, the 'Old Woman' of the Goethean tale, represents the attitudes and feelings which are normal and decent in 'everyman'. The two Will-o'-the-Wisps are represented by the historian Capesius and the technician,

Strader. It is clear from Steiner's commentaries on the Goethean tale, and his description of the characters in *Die Pforte*, that he views many of the characters are aspects of the one entity, the normal human being. Similarly, in *The Portal* many of the characters are aspects of Johannes, or embody specific qualities which are of particularly relevant to Johannes's quest.

In terms of the goal of the spiritual quest, this is portrayed by the fair Lily in Goethe's tale; she is represented by the character, Maria, in *Die Pforte*. Steiner's comments on the nature of the Lily reveal his view of the goal of spiritual initiation and hence his intention in creating the personality traits in the character, Maria. With regard to the quest for spiritual development in *Das Märchen*, in one of his lectures on this tale, Steiner comments,

> The highest {condition} towards which the human being can strive, the highest into which the human being is able to transform, was denoted by Goethe with the symbol of the Lily. This is cognate with what we call the highest wisdom…"[164]

This view of Steiner's can be assimilated to some extent to the recognized meanings of the lily symbol in so far as it is usually understood to refer to purity, peace, a virgin goddess, virginity, the blessed Virgin Mary. Steiner is evidently associating the highest wisdom with the classical 'divine feminine', and this in turn is equates with the various symbolic usages of the lily.

Steiner continues, commenting that the term, 'lily' was used in the Mysteries to denote "that highest condition of consciousness where the human being is permitted to be free, because he will never misuse his freedom…because the

---

[164] Steiner, Goethe's Geheime, 152, „Das Höchste, was der Mensch anstreben kann, das Höchste, in was sich der Mensch verwandeln sollte, das bezeichnet Goethe mit dem Symbolum der Lilie. Es ist gleichbedeutend mit dem, was wir die höchste Weisheit nennen."

human being has been purified, transformed". That Steiner does see the lily in these terms, and hence the 'fair Lily' of the Goethean tale, is clear from a lecture on *Das Märchen*, in which he refers to the 'Chorus Mysticus' in Faust, Part Two,

> "So we see that Goethe expresses his deepest profession of life's meaning precisely there...where he brings his great professional poem to a conclusion...after he has made his way through to union with the fair Lily, to that condition which finds its expression in the passage mentioned in the Chorus Mysticus, which expresses the same as what Goethe's philosophy and Spiritual Science and Das Märchen says, "...Das Ewig-Weibliche zieht uns hinan! (The eternal-feminine draws us onwards!)".[165]

As we have noted earlier, to Steiner the fundamental message of the Goethean tale is that there is a way to achieve union with the divine, by crossing over a barrier to this spiritualized state, for there exists a yearning to cross over this barrier. In *Die Pforte* Steiner explores the processes and challenges which a contemporary acolyte on the spiritual path has to encounter, in order to achieve initiation or esoteric spirituality in his sense of the phrase. Before proceeding to consider the scenes of *The Portal of Initiation*, it is necessary here to consider what Steiner meant by the term *Initiation*.

His term for Initiation in German is 'Einweihung', which means in effect, to be inducted into a state of consecration (Weihe), an action which is traditionally associated with religious practise. In Christian usage, consecration traditionally means to be set apart from the mundane in order to be a vessel for a source of holiness, which is understood to

---

[165] Rudolf Steiner, Goethe's Geheime, 77, „So sehen wir, daß Goethe geradezu sein tiefstes Bekenntnis...da ausspricht, wo er sein großes Bekennntnisgedicht zum Abschluß bringt, nachdem er....emporgedrungen ist bis zur Vereinigung mit der schönen Lilie, bis zu dem Zustande, der seinen Ausdruck findet in der erwähnten Stelle des Chorus mysticus, die dasselbe ausdrückt, was Goethes Philosophie und Geisteswissenschaft und was auch das „Märchen" sagt:....'Das Ewig-Weibliche zieht uns hinan'!"

derive from God or Christ.[166] In distinction, the term, "initiation", which is also used in German, refers more generally to the ceremony of admission into society, such as a "religious ceremony in a tribe or clan to signify the coming of age or puberty of its members."[167]

From Steiner's comments on this subject is it clear that he regards the term 'initiation' as very closely allied to the term 'consecration', although he does give some extended nuances to its meaning. Passages in his teachings about the meaning of initiation often include an exposition based on the famous maxim in the ancient Grecian mystery centre at Delphi, "Know thyself!" to which Steiner repeatedly drew attention in his lectures. Steiner understands this maxim to mean that after initiation a person is now able to have a conscious interaction with the divine, in effect, he gains 'knowledge'. The divine constitutes another part, a second part, of human nature to which initiation grants access, as he maintained in a lecture on the Gospel of St. John,

> ...and so it becomes a reality for those who follow the indications of the spiritual researcher and say to themselves, the ego of which I had known up to now, shares in the entire external world, it is transient like the external world. But in me there slumbers a second ego, of which people are not aware, but of which they can become aware, and which is united with the non-transitory, just as the first ego is united with the transient and temporal. And with {spiritual} re-birth, this higher ego can look into a spiritual world, just as the lower ego can look into the sense world through the senses – eyes, ears and so on.[168]

In these words, Steiner affirms his belief that there are two parts to the human being, 'the other part', which is referred to

---

[166] J.D. Douglas, ed. The New International Dictionary of the Christian Church, "Consecration", (Exeter: The Paternoster Press, 1974) 254.
[167] Macquarie Dict. 1988, p. 899.
[168] Rudolf Steiner, Das Johannes Evangelium im Verhältnis zu den drei anderen Evangelien, (Dornach: RSV, 1975) 15.

in this text, means the divine or higher self. To Steiner the process of becoming initiated requires the development of the potential for spirituality, and this involves the encounter with one's unethical qualities and then eventually an encounter, a merging, with the divine. This activity should then result in the spirit – in Goethean terms, the fair Lily – becoming united to one's being.

The characters present speeches – which are often quite long – in which their inner life, and supra-sensible experiences are portrayed. The audience only find this drama 'dramatic' if they empathize with the experiences and subsequent inner questioning of the characters. Additionally, there is the further barrier to making *Die Pforte* a drama in the customary sense, and that is the difficulty which Steiner has in expressing his understanding of the initiatory process which of necessity requires elucidation of supra-sensible experiences. The 'covert' dramatic element in *Die Pforte* is only sustainable to the extent that the language of the speeches succeed in conveying this supra-sensible element. In the following section, Steiner's struggle with this aspect shall be considered.

Steiner's exposition of the Goethe tale, that is, of the theosophical wisdom which sees inherent in it – and which had been formative for him – was in effect, the launching pad for his new career as a teacher on spirituality. The formative influence of *Das Märchen* in Steiner's life is reflected in his decision to write a dramatized version to this tale, namely, *Die Pforte der Einweihung*.

2 THE BACKGROUND TO DIE PFORTE

2a: Describing supra-sensible phenomena, metaphor, 'transferring' German into English, and Steiner's neologisms

As we noted earlier, (Section 1A1) the emphasis on artistic activity – including poetry and dramatic productions – forms a noticeable element in Steiner's worldview. We also noted (Section 1A3), that Steiner introduced the performance of dramas into Theosophical Society conferences, in 1907, when he also required the conference schedule to include recitation of poetry, performance of music, and had the venue decorated with works of art. He viewed artistic consciousness as similar in its dynamics to the enhanced consciousness which the person attains through spiritual development.

Steiner was especially keen to integrate the artistic element into German theosophical activity. As he stated in the program for the 1907 conference in Munich,

> The artistic presentations should be so selected, in the area of sculptural, as well as musical and poetic art, that these items should, together with what is presented from the theosophical view of the world, form an harmonious entirety. For this reason, in one of the sessions, the attempt will also be made to present a Mystery in a dramatic form.[169]

The drama performed at the 1907 conference was written by Edouard Schuré, *The Sacred Drama of Eleusis*. Steiner's drama, Die Pforte, was specifically termed "a Rosicrucian

---

[169] Rudolf Steiner, Der Münchner Kongress Pfingsten 1907, und seine Auswirkungen, (Dornach: RSV, 1977) 25, „Die künstlerischen Darbietungen sollen sowohl auf dem Gebiete der bildenden, wie der musikalischen und poetischen Kunst so ausgewählt werden, daß das Einzelne sich mit dem aus der theosophischen Weltauffassung Vorgebrachten zu einem harmonischen Ganzen zusammenfügt. Deshalb soll in einer der Veranstaltungen auch der Versuch gemacht werden, im Dramatischen die Vorstellung eines Mysteriums zu geben."

Mystery Drama", indicating that Steiner considered his drama to be of the same genre as the ancient Greek dramas, but deriving its inspiration from his understanding of the Rosicrucians. Die Pforte consists of a Prelude, an Interlude and one Act which has eleven scenes. As the title suggests, the intention of the drama is to portray the challenges encountered by modern individuals, in their striving on the path towards the initial stages of esoteric spiritual development, as taught by Steiner. In his lectures on the art of speech and drama, Steiner emphasised his conclusion that dramas originated as part of the celebration of the sacred Mysteries in ancient Greece, and only later became secular entertainment,

> For in the final analysis however, the development which has lead to our contemporary theatre, had its beginning, its germinal form, with all that which was regarded as a Mystery. And one only attains the appropriate understanding of the dramatic art, if one goes back to the art of the Mysteries. In the Mysteries, the concern of art was to trace the primal form of all dramatic portrayals back into those impulses which penetrated into human beings from the spiritual world.[170]

Steiner understood these ancient dramas as performances that were designed to depict for esoteric-pedagogical purpose, the spiritual dynamics occurring in the path to initiation. That is, the dramas were to assist in the training of the acolytes in the temple communities, and also to communicate elements of the mystery-religion to the community at large. Although the precise origin of Greek theatre is unclear, many authorities share the viewpoint held by Schuré and Steiner that the

---

[170] Rudolf Steiner, Sprachgestaltung und Dramatische Kunst, (Dornach: VRSN, 1969) 226, „Denn letzten Endes liegt die Entwickelung zu unserem Schauspiel hin dennoch in ihrem Anfang, in ihrem Keime bei alledem, was als Mysterium empfunden wird. Und man bekommt nicht eine würdige Auffassung von der Schauspielkunst, wenn man nicht zurückgehen kann zur Mysterienkunst. Mysterienkunst aber war... darauf aus, alle Darstellung zu verfolgen bis zu jenen Impulsen, die aus der geistigen Welt in den Menschen eindringen."

celebration of the esoteric religious cults of ancient Greece was the origin of theatre.[171] In any event, it is clear that dramatic performances about the various deities and their significance for human beings were the focal point of rituals in such places.[172]

To Steiner the Mystery dramas of antiquity were designed as didactic artistic presentations of the path to initiation. For example, writing of Eleusis, he states, "The festivals which were celebrated twice yearly offered the great cosmic drama of the destiny of the divine in the world and of the human soul.....with these festivals initiations were connected. The symbolic representation of cosmic and human dramas formed the final act of the consecration of the mystics, which were undertaken here."[173]

In a lecture on the Mysteries of antiquity Steiner describes those of ancient Greece as specifically designed to lead the acolyte to encounter divine beings in two spheres, namely in the cosmos, and in the human soul. He termed the former endeavour the way to the upper gods, and the latter path, which lead to an encounter of deities in the depths of human consciousness, he termed, the way to the gods below.[174] Steiner's language here is an adoption of the terminology found in the second century initiatory novel, The Golden Ass, by Apuleius, concerning the purposes of the initation process in the Mysteries of Isis, "...I entered the presence of the gods

---

[171] Ronald W. Vince, Ancient and Medieval Theatre, (London: Greenwood Press, 1984). Vince provides a clear historical overview of the various theories put forward concerning the link between the Greek Mysteries and the birth of secular theatre.

[172] Michael B. Cosmopoulos, Greek mysteries: the archaeology and ritual of Greek sacred cults, (London: Routledge, 2003), and S. Angus, The Mystery Religions, (New York: Dover, 1975).

[173] Rudolf Steiner, Das Christentum als mystische Tatsache und die Mysterien des Altertums, (Dornach: RSV, 1976) 94, „Die Feste, die zweimal im Jahre gefeiert wurden, boten das große Weltdrama vom Schicksal des Göttlichen in der Welt und dem der Menschenseele...Mit den Festen waren Einweihungen verbunden. Die symbolische Darstellung des Welt- und Menschen-dramas bildete den Schlußakt der Mystenweihen, die hier vorgenommen wurden."

[174] Lecture of 27th August 1909, in Rudolf Steiner, Der Orient im Lichte des Okzidents, (Dornach: VRSN, 1960) 92-109.

of the under-world and the gods of the upper-world, stood near them and worshipped them."[175]

Hence, the task of *Die Pforte* is not only that of communicating various elements of the supra-sensible, it also has to convey a sense of a reaching towards a sacred reality. In this task, Steiner used poetics, especially the metaphor and neologisms, as a tool for the task of communicating his spiritual worldview. He wrote some 300 poems expressing his anthroposophical perspective, as well as his four mystery dramas. In the latter, he made use of metaphorical language to assist overcoming the limitations of purely rational discourse, in the task of presenting the dynamics invoked as a person encounters the spirit.

Steiner's method of using a poetic approach to themes usually treated in rational discourse, rather than the accepted Aristotelian derived logical approach, was typically criticised in the brief notice of his basic text, "*Die Geheimwissenschaft im Umriß*", in Kindlers Literature Lexikon,

> The book is impaired through the situation that the method of describing spiritual existence is limited to metaphors, which are taken from the sensual world, and that the interface of the categorial connections is very thin, so that the spirit is not grasped 'as a realm with its own laws' (Max Dessoir).[176]

Steiner's view here has affinity to those who advocate the value of metaphor in philosophical (and spiritual) debate, such as Ernesto Grassi, to whom metaphor is fundamental to

---

[175] Apuleius, The Golden Ass, trans. Robert Graves, (Harmondsworth: Penguin, 1956) 286.
[176] Kindlers Literature Lexikon im dtv, ed. Gert Woerner, Rolf Geisler and Rudolf Radler, 1978, Bd. 9, ed. Valentino Bompiani, *Die Geheimwissenschaft im Umriß*, S. 3816, „Das Werk ist dadurch beeinträchtigt, daß die Methode der Beschreibung des geistigen Seins sich auf Metaphern beschränkt, die der Sinnenwelt entnommen sind, und daß das Geflecht der kategorialen Beziehungen sehr dünn, das Geistige also nicht *als ein Reich eigener Gesetzmäßigkeit* (Max Dessoir) erfaßt ist."

the process of learned discourse usually reserved for philosophical rationalism,

> Furthermore Aristotle makes the decisive statement that rhetoric and philosophy arise from a common presupposition, 'In philosophy too, it is characteristic of the one who accurately aims (eustochos) to see the similarity between things (to homoion...theorein) that are most distant from each other'.[177]

As Veit writes, supporting Grassi, "Knowledge of the phenomena has been subsumed under the categories of logic and the non-rational is dismissed, thus suppressing any awareness of the older function of metaphor as something which expresses 'archaic' analogies."[178] A Steiner poem dedicated to the poet Fercher von Steinwand embodies both his attitude to artistic presentation of spiritual themes and his own use of metaphorical language to express spiritual themes,

Im Chor der Urträume zu ergreifen Ideen,
To understand Ideas within the chorus of primeval dreams
die zur Offenbarung werden Des Kräftewesens,
which become revelation of that empowered Beingness
das im Urgetriebe dem Weltensein die Seele ist:
which in the primal impelling urges of cosmic existence
Is the soul itself –
Das wollte dieser Dichter;
Thus was this poet's will,
Und schön ist's, ihm zu folgen
And it is beautiful to follow him through primeval dreams
Durch Urträume hindurch In das Reich der Urtriebe.
on into the realm of the primordial urges.[179]

---

[177] Ernesto Grassi, Rhetoric as Philosophy, (University Park: Pennsylvania State University Press, 1908) 95.
[178] Walter Veit, *The Potency of Imagery – the Impotence of Rational Language: Ernesto Grassi's Contributions to Modern Epistemology,* Philosophy and Rhetoric, ed. Donald Philip Verene, Vol 17, No. 4. 233.
[179] Rudolf Steiner, "Fercher von Steinwand", Wahrspruchworte (Dornach: VRSN, 1969) 233.

The complex issues raised with regard to primordial or archaic metaphors cannot be examined here; before this is attempted, there is a prior task of assessing Steiner's texts in terms of metaphorical usage, for what appear to be metaphors, in the accepted sense of the term, in his view, are non-metaphorical, 'spiritual-scientific' descriptions. He views his experiences of spiritual realities as a supra-sensible equivalent of sense perception. It is clear from the way in which Steiner refers to a form of- light in supra-sensible realms, that this usage is not intended to be metaphorical, but rather a parallel to the sensory images, as he comments,

> So the occultist differentiates the radiant self-luminosity of the spirit, from the remarkable glistening quality of the light which is reflected back from the realm of forms, as soul-light. 'Soul' means, reflected spiritual light, 'spirit' means radiant, creative light.

This challenging attitude is clearly cognizable at times, for example in Scene Three of *Die Pforte*, the spiritual leader of Johannes, Benedictus, invokes a spiritual blessing for Johannes saying, "Let be radiant in his inner being, that which can illumine his soul with spiritual light / Let resound in his inner being, what can awaken for him the self to the spirit's joy of coming into existence."[180]

These poetic expressions are not considered by Steiner as metaphorical, but as referring to specific spiritual agencies. When a person attains to the Platonic realm of the Idea, this realm imbues him with a power that creates radiance in the soul, and which also creates a non-physical, audible element. That is, the soul body of the meditant becomes radiant, and they also become aware of a type of speaking emanating from spiritual realities. These concepts which are associated

---

[180] Pforte, 74, "...Im Innern lasset ihm erstrahlen, was ihm durchleuchten kann die Seele mit dem Geistenlicht. Im Innern lasset ihm ertönen, was ihm erwecken kann das Selbst zu Geistes Werdelust."

with Steiner's view of enhanced consciousness capabilities, are examined further in Section 4f.

There is a further technique used by Steiner in this regard, which seeks to convey that the non-metaphorical quality of his perceiving in the supra-sensible. Indeed Steiner seek to indicate that such a perception is inherently valid, even when the mental picture of the perceived thing is incorrect. Such a situation therefore shows merely the unskilled cognizing of the perceived, and thereby subtly confirms the accuracy of the perceiving itself. This intention forms a parallel to the conviction Steiner expresses in his early epistemological works (examined in Section 1A2), that when an optical illusion interferes with sense perception, resulting in an incorrect conclusion (mental image), this merely demonstrates the accuracy of the sense organs.

An example of this non-metaphorical imagery occurs in Scene Two; whilst Johannes is in a meditative state he leaves his body and perceives his deceased girl friend. He says to himself, "I see my bodily shell. It is an alien entity outside me; it is remote from me. There hovers towards me another body. I have to speak with its mouth: 'He has brought me bitter distress; I had trusted him completely, he left me in my grief alone'..." The reference here to seeing another body is decidedly strange, and will be examined in the next paragraph. Steiner clearly means to convey that the self of Johannes is literally outside his body – but still capable of perceiving – and that he beholds his deceased girl friend, and actually experiences her grief and stress.

At this point, the experience is described as if it were a factual not a metaphorical thing. It bears similarity in terms of its perceived objective, factual nature, to descriptions of out-of-the body experiences found in New Age literature. But Johannes describes what he sees as "another {physical} body", which in the entire context of Steiner's worldview is seriously inconsistent. Her body no longer exists; it can only be a soul-body which moves around in that continuum, so what Johannes is seeing must be something else. But neither this mysterious thing in question, nor Johannes' experiencing of it, is intended to be metaphorical, for he soon has a direct experience her grief, which he later acknowledges as fully objectively valid. So, here Steiner is intending to convey that both the girlfriend and her emotive state are specific realities, and objectively perceived. However, with regard to Johannes' perception of the form of his girlfriend, he has made an erroneous mental picture as to its true nature.

Thus instead of this passage having metaphorical elements, the audience is learning that, in Steiner's view, perception in the spiritual realm is valid and indeed – in terms of the conclusions made from the perceptions – is subject to the same kind of distortions as the sense world. Furthermore, analogous to the sense perceptions distortions associated with a line of trees disappearing into the distance, any such distortions in the supra-sensible sphere which lead to erroneous conclusions, simply validate the inherent accuracy of the perceiving organs, but highlight the unskilful analysis of the perceptions.

Furthermore, in considering Steiner's approach to metaphor, in terms of interpreting his texts, and of rendering them into English, there is also the problem of Steiner's use of language in general. In *Die Pforte* Steiner includes poetic passages, which are often burdened by neologisms. The purpose of his method is to facilitate his presentation of dynamics, which are alien to mundane reality, but particular to spiritual realms and spiritual beings. Content of this kind in *Die Pforte* is often used to express strikingly unusual supra-sensible postulates, and these would be very unwieldy to elucidate in prose. If cast into a prose form, or a non-metaphorical form, such a speech would stultify the dramatic element considerably, but his use of the poetics often results in enigmatic passage. For example in Scene Five, Benedictus, the great spiritual teacher, wants to know what another character, called Felix Balde, can say about the needs of the Earth for human spirituality; the Earth is considered to be a living being. Felix replies, "The light, which shines forth in the human being as the fruit of knowledge – it is to become the nourishment of those powers who, in the earthly darkness, serve the cosmic course" [181]

In the process of assessing the scenes in *Die Pforte*, to ascertain the primary elements of Steiner's anthroposophy, one encounters several problems. Firstly, in the context of an English language appraisal of his texts, there is the translation problem as the original is in German, but in addition, Steiner's German has several characteristics that cause particular difficulties. Firstly, in the poetic passages, or in prose texts, there are phrases which refer to a spiritual reality, which is never clearly explained. Secondly, there is the use of remarkable neologisms, which can be grammatically ambiguous, creating a barrier to assessing the syntax.

These factors enhance the normal difficulty of rendering Steiner's scholarly German into English, rendered more problematic through the situation that applies to mystical texts in general. Namely, Steiner is communicating conclusions about supra-sensible matters in 'earthly' language. In the course of endeavouring to communicate his ideas, Steiner also makes specific use of metaphors. These can be quite useful where the thematic is in effect, 'mundane', and the lateral link between the metaphorical image and that which it is intended to represent both belong to this sensible word or to common human experience.

But where in metaphorical usage, a mundane image is invoked into use to represent a supra-sensible factor, then the link is harder to discern. In this situation, the reader, or the audience in a theatre hall, has to attempt to link the sensible image to a reality quite alien to their experience. In this sense, the criticism in *Kindlers Literatur Lexikon* of Steiner's presentation of spiritual processes effective in humanity's

---

[181] Pforte, 94, „Das Licht, das in den Menschen als Frucht des Wissens leuchtet, es soll zur Nahrung werden den Mächten, die im Erdendunkel dem Weltengange dienen."

evolution, is understandable, but of limited validity, in that the metaphor itself can provide some assistance to the imagination to grasp aspects of the supra-sensible which are not assimilable into a logical description.

The above Steiner verse, dedicated to von Steinwand, already indicates the overall problem. In using the German term 'Kräftewesens' he wishes to refer to something like a 'forces-quiddity', which is understood to be within the primordial urges (Urgetriebe) that are inherent to 'cosmic reality'. He then concludes that this 'forces-quiddity' *is* the human soul. My rendering, 'empowered Being-ness' for a more literal 'forces-quiddity', and 'primal impelling urges' for primordial urges, attempts to firstly bring these unusual German metaphors into a readable English form.

At the same time the result has to assist the English reader to formulate two metaphorical images which approximate to the German images. This in turn, should facilitate the process of relating these metaphors to each other and then to comprehend the elusive conceptual conclusion presented in the original text, namely "that empowered Being-ness in the primal impelling urges of cosmic existence".

These difficulties inherent in understanding Steiner's texts, including *Die Pforte,* and in translating his material into English, are exemplified in a variety of published Steiner texts, which contain passages that strikingly exhibit the problems that interpreters of Steiner's worldview encounter. However, the problems in these published texts do not derive entirely from the use of metaphor, there is also the question of the level of skill in textual criticism and of expertise in Steiner's worldview. A number of Steiner's verses have been in print for decades in such books as *Verses and Meditations.*[182]

This volume includes a verse concerning planetary influences, 'The Mysteries of Ephesus'. Its last two lines are,

---

[182] <u>Verses and Meditations</u>, First published by Rudolf Press, London, in 1961.

"Daß Saturns Weltenalte Geist-Innigkeit / Dich dem Raumessein und Zeitenwerden weihe!" The published translation renders this as, "that ghostly Saturn's old-world-memoried-devoutness unto the world of space and time thee hallow."[183] The problem here, for an assessment of Steiner through the English language, is similar to that of the above poem to von Steinwand. The above text is quite false to the surface meaning of the German text, and indeed is false to the actual intended meaning, so far as this can be ascertained. The task has to be to express supra-sensible realities from Steiner's worldview in English, but without specialist knowledge of his works, it is difficult to ascertain precisely the underlying concept, which he wishes to convey.

In this instance, the phrase includes one German term, Innigkeit, which in Steiner's usage, is quite resistant to being translated into English, because its referent is not associated with human relations of any kind. This term is usually rendered as intimacy, affection, warmth, sincerity or closeness. With regard to the above Steiner phrase, Saturns Weltenalte Geist-Innigkeit, it is clear that generally he is ascribing to Saturn a link to spiritual realms which is potent, ancient and which also is directly efficacious in humanity with regard to bringing about an orientation towards spirituality.

This is already a very dense statement, but without extensive knowledge of Steiner's cosmology, the verse remains very obscure. In Steiner's cosmology, evolutionary phases are presented, in which the efficacy of planetary and zodiac influences are elucidated, in a succession of aeons; from knowledge of this perspective, the verse can become more readily comprehended. In anthroposophical cosmology, the planet Saturn is understood to have an association with the primal spiritual influences active at the dawn of creation of humanity. [184] He maintained, that these spiritual influences

---

[183] ibid, p. 77.
[184] Steiner's cosmology is presented in many volumes of his Complete Works, commencing with lectures from 1903; his main written text which

commenced several aeons ago, and are they understood to have created the foundation of the human will, or volition; on another level, they also created the rudiments for the metabolic process and also the limb system in the human body.

It is these aspects of the human corporeality which are understood to be the vessel for the human will. These ancient Saturn forces are regarded as still efficacious today, within the sub-conscious volition of the human being, where their activity manifests very subtly, in a variety of ways. These include in the sensing of one's destiny, and in maintaining a feeling for the existence of the spirit, in particular of God. The details of these elements, and all their dense ramifications, are not our focus here, but in the event that a person had acquired such knowledge of Steiner's works that these ideas were clearly grasped, then – and this is one of the difficulties inherent in comprehending Steiner's poetic presentations of his anthroposophy – the above verse could be more clearly understood. It could then be rendered so as to clarify Steiner's view that in the pre-existence phase (pre-incarnate stage) of the human soul, these spiritual forces are accessed. The line may then read, "that Saturn's primeval attunement to the Spirit may consecrate you to the world of space and the flow of time."

These difficulties inherent in understanding Steiner's texts are a common feature to his verses; this is exemplified in "Der Seelenkalendar" (The Soul Calendar). This is a work comprising 52 verses, to be used as a contemplative guide to help the student of Steiner's teachings feel the spiritual element active within the seasonal processes. It is a type of pericope, but designed to accompany the natural cycle of the year, not the ecclesiastical year. Like the speeches in *Die Pforte,* the verses of *Der Seelenkalendar* often contain neologisms, in the attempt to present complex spiritual dynamics, which however, are often not specifically defined.

---

gives a brief description of the spiritual forces associated with Saturn, is in Die Geheimwissenschaft im Umriß, written in 1910.

Verse 34 is a good example of *Der Seelenkalendar* text; it occurs each year in late autumn,

Geheimnisvoll das Alt-Bewahrte
mit neuerstandenem Eigensein
Im Innern sich belebend fühlen:
Es soll erweckend Weltenkräfte
In meines Lebens Außenwerk ergießen
Und werdend mich ins Dasein prägen.

A published version in English renders the verse in the following form,

Mysteriously to feel within,
The quickening of the treasur'd past,
With Selfhood, newly risen;
This shall, arousing forces of the world,
Pour itself into my life's outer work
and growing root me in existence.[185]

Due consideration has to be given to the fact that this verse comes from a specialized context, and also that understanding of it is dependent upon some of its antecedent verses. However, even so, the above English text remains obscure. There are also some awkward English phrases, but the main factor is the obvious difficulty to the translator in understanding the German original. The same awkward phraseology, and too narrow interpretation of the German text, is to be found in various passages in the published translation of the *Die Pforte*, and these shall be examined shortly.

For example, in the first line of verse 34 of *Der Seelenkalendar*, the expression, 'das Alt-Bewahrte' occurs; this is a German idiom which refers to something found to be of value over the generations (or decades, or years) and hence

---
[185] The Calendar of the Soul, transl. William and Liselotte Mann, (Stroud: Hawthorn Press, 1990).

carefully kept as a treasured thing. However, a careful appraisal of the entire book reveals that here this expression is used in an unusual manner, the time frame being just a little over three months. It is referring to a seasonal process connected with the late summertime. An examination of the Soul Calendar reveals that this text has several mirror image patterns built into it, wherein particular sets of verses reflect each other, as in a polarity. The mirror image pattern of interest to us here, is one in which the first two lines of a verse are the reverse of those in its opposite verse. Verse 1 starts as follows,

"Wenn aus den Weltenweiten
(When from the wide expanses of space)
Die Sonne spricht zum Menschensinn"
(The sun speaks to human sense)

It is the mirror image of the last verse, number 52,
"Wenn aus den Seelentiefen
(When from the depths of the soul)
Der Geist sich wendet zu dem Weltensein"
(The spirit turns towards cosmic being)

Similarly, verse 2, commences as follows,
"Ins Äußere des Sinnesalls
(In the outer world of the senses)
Verliert Gedankenmacht ihr Eigensein"
(The power of thought lose its own being)

It stands in contrast to the penultimate verse, number 51,
"Ins Innre des Menschenwesens
(Into the inner-being of the human being)
Ergießt der Sinne Reichtum sich".
(The senses' richness pours itself)

The mirror-image verse for verse 34 is number 19; it commences with,
"Geheimnisvoll das Neu-Empfang'ne
 (Mysteriously, the Newly-conceived)

Mit der Erinnerung zu umschließen".
(to encompass with the memory)

And this compares with verse 34, in a published translation,
as given above,
Geheimnisvoll das Alt-Bewahrte
(Mysteriously the treasur'd past
mit neuerstandenem Eigensein
(With Selfhood, newly risen)

So, verse 34 has reference to a process that verse 19 specifically expresses, and which occurred some three months earlier. An examination of Steiner's lectures on the subject of the seasonal cycle, reveals that he sees the human soul as absorbing 'spiritual forces' from the summer sun; these are preserved in the Earth's spiritual aspect, and become absorbed by the human soul.[186] This is the 'Neu-Empfang'ne' (newly conceived) of verse 19.

By the late autumn this spiritual element has now become the 'treasured something' from the (recent) past, the summer. It has been preserved within the human soul, and in the autumn may become efficacious in the soul. The beginning of this process is alluded to in verse 19. To ascertain Steiner's understanding of the yearly cycle with sufficient clarity, to be able to select the correct nuance of a German expression in all of the 52 verses when rendering them into English is a very substantial task, given the size of his literary estate. Verse 34 would perhaps then be rendered along these lines,

1 To feel mysteriously the Treasure,
2 from some time ago,
3 With its own being newly arisen,

---

[186] The sources for the remarks concerning Steiner's spiritual ecology in these paragraphs derive from the many references and elucidations in his Complete Works, in particular, GA vols. 219, (Das Verhältnis der Sternenwelt zum Menschen und des Menschen zur Sternenwelt), 223 (Der Jahreskreislauf als Atmungsvorgang der Erde und die vier großen Festezeiten), 224 (Die menschliche Seele in ihrem Zusammenhang mit göttlich-geistigen Individualitäten), 229 (Das Miterleben des Jahreslaufes in vier kosmischen Imaginationen).

4 quickening itself within me:
5 It shall pour awakened cosmic forces
6 Into my life's external deeds
7 And, evolving on, imprint me into existence.

This entirely different nuance arises when the text is considered on the basis of Steiner's spiritual ecology. With regard to line 1 and 2, the treasure, being something received in the summer derives from a *recent* past, and it is *this* (unidentified) treasure which is quickening, not the past itself. Further, with regard to lines 3 and 4, in Steiner's worldview, the neologism, "eigensein' (own, specific being-ness), can be an attribute of many kinds of self aware beings.

But it especially applies to something existing in a lesser, 'elemental' condition of consciousness, which is devoid of self awareness. An example of such as an organism would be one composed of Steiner's ether forces. The term 'selfhood', in contrast to 'eigensein', cannot be applied to a class of entities or organisms which have no soul, but only ether energies. Hence the text can be understood to mean that the *treasure* is what is undergoing a vivification in the student, resulting in the treasure having an enhanced existence, but *not* attaining selfhood.

In addition, in the context of Steiner's extensive elucidations of this subject, with regard to lines 5 and 6, from the ambiguous syntax, quite a different conclusion can be made respecting the treasure, which the translator above described as 'arousing forces of the world', and tends to imply earthly influences. Namely, since this treasure is described by Steiner, in various lectures, as deriving from cosmic origins, the phrase may become, it 'shall pour awakened <u>cosmic</u> forces' into the soul. Further, with regard to the term 'Welt', which is normally used to refer to the Earth or the universe in German, there are several possible referents in Steiner's use, namely, the planet Earth, or it may be cognate with 'cosmos' (which is not only the universe but the spiritual reams as well) or the term can be applied to what he describes as 'our zodiac-solar system'.

In any event, the forces imbued by the planet in summer are understood to be from beyond the Earth. Additionally, the ambiguous nature and position of 'erweckend' (awakened/awakening) allows another interpretation, that the treasure is <u>not arousing</u> the forces in question, but rather, the treasure <u>is</u> the cosmic forces, and these forces become awakened (or efficacious) naturally, as the autumn proceeds. Again, as with the line from the 'astrological' verse, one experiences that the interpretation of a Steiner poetic text faces very substantial obstacles. Additionally, it seems clear that this cannot have escaped the notice of Steiner – a point to which we shall return later in this section.

A final example of textual difficulties, outside of *Die Pforte*, is a very striking example of the confusion which these difficulties incur for those who wish to engage with Steiner's texts. It concerns a neologism in his central meditative verse, the Die Grundstein Meditation (The Foundation Stone Meditation). This is a large verse, given in late December 1923, on the occasion of the re-founding of the Anthroposophical Society. 1923 had been a difficult year for this Society for a variety of reasons, in particular the burning down of the building, the Goetheanum. Steiner wished to give a stronger impetus, enthusiasm and dedication to his movement. As part of his renewal attempts, he provided this large verse, as a quintessential expression of the anthroposophical worldview. In the last section of it, he refers to the Christian truth that as a result of the life of Christ, divine reality entered the Earthly reality, "In der Zeiten-Wende /Trat das Welten-Geistes-Licht in den irdischen Wesenstrom…" [187]

The verse goes on to say, in a direct allusion to the Christmas festival, that this light streamed into human hearts, warmed

---

[187] Rudolf Steiner, „Die Weihnachtstagung zur Begründung der Allgemeinen Anthroposophischen Gesellschaft, 1924-1224", (Dornach: VRSN, 1963), 59.

the simple shepherds' hearts, illumined the wise head of kings, and so on. The neologism here, a triple noun, "Welten-Geistes-Licht" has been understood in such a way as to be translated, "At the turning-point of time the Spirit-Light of the World entered the earthly stream of being". However, the noun is ambiguous (the referent or referents of the genitive cases are unclear), hence it may also be translated as, "the Light of the Spirit of the Cosmos".

Whereas the former rendering is vague and tends to imply a source of spiritual light from within the world, the earthly realm, especially our planet, the latter rendering enables a specific element in Steiner's worldview to be identified. Research into Steiner's nomenclature for divine beings, provides reasons to query the accepted version, and to approve the latter version. The term, 'the Spirit of the Cosmos', appears to be the more correct, as it is used to refer to three specific divine beings; all three of which are reasonably applicable in this instance.

The decision has then to be made as to which of these three beings is meant in this verse. One of these appears to be particularly applicable, namely the primal, uncaused God. However, for this one of the three usages of this neologism, the only clear evidence as to its meaning, is a note in the Steiner archives, namely an entry in one of Steiner's private note-books. This note identified the 'Weltengeist' as 'the creative primal Power of the cosmos', in effect God. [188]

This again confirms the barrier to comprehension of Steiner's anthroposophical texts through the use of dense neologisms and elusive metaphors in a context where clarifying elucidations of key terms are rare. The point here is that, without specialist knowledge of Steiner's corpus, The problem is increased by the various, unexpected range of nuances of meaning in his texts. Hence the possibility to

---

[188] Rudolf Steiner, Seelenübungen mit Wort- und Sinnbild Meditationen, (Dornach: RSV, 1997) 496, „{'Er' ist das Kraftwort} für den Weltenwillen, den Weltengeist …Dieser…ist die schaffende Urkraft der Welt."

absorb and respond to the subtle the dramatic tension of Die Pforte is likewise restricted, especially if the audience has not undertaken prior study of the text.

Whereas the above examples indicate more a problem of style, there are other examples of the multiple difficulties involved in assessing passages from Steiner's drama. For example, at the end of in Scene Three, the scene ends with a spirit-voice that sums up the essence of Johannes' newly developing spiritual consciousness. The rhetoric in this passage alludes to the Platonic Idea-realm, which plays a major role in Steiner's worldview. The German text was published with a syntactical error. A reading of Steiner's draft notes for *Die Pforte* reveals that this passage in the final edition, as published in German, is syntactically wrong.

In the published German version of this speech, there is a full stop after Urweltgründe, in the phrase, 'Es steigen seine Gedanken in Urweltgründe. Was als Schatten…' However in the draft version, the final word is not followed by a full stop, but by an 'em' dash. Restoring this original syntax alters the passage, giving it a clearer meaning. It is, correctly,

> Es steigen seine Gedanken in Urweltgründe – Was als Schatten er gedacht, was als Schemen er erlebt, entschwebet der Gestaltenwelt, von deren Fülle die Menschen denkend in Schatten träumen, von deren Fülle die Menschen sehend in Schemen leben.

This difficult passage is used as a specific dramatic device, namely as the voice of an unseen spiritual being, providing a summary of the primary dynamics of the entire scene, and indeed to some extent, of the preceding scenes. Therefore, it has to express clearly the essential purpose of Steiner's view of spiritual development. It is translated in the published Pusch text as follows;

Thoughts now guide him to depths of world-beginnings;
what as shadows he has thought,

what as phantoms he has felt,
soars out, beyond the world of forms,–
world of whose fullness men,
when thinking, dream in shadows;
world, from whose fullness men,
when seeing, live within phantoms.

The passage as rendered here by the translator appears to be erroneous, because it is inconsistent in its meaning. In this English rendering, the speech appears to say that Johannes's own mental productions were mere phantasms, but now soar out beyond this realm of formed things to a realm associated with the beginnings of Creation; however, notwithstanding that, the world of Form is, in its fullness, only vaguely encountered by human beings.

As we shall see, from a consideration of the scenes in *Die Pforte*, the purpose of Johannes' strivings is to point out to the audience that the acolyte who does begin to achieve higher consciousness, enters the formless, archetypal Platonic 'realm of Ideas'. This realm is beyond the 'world of Forms', wherein created, hence formed (structured and materialized) objects exist. From a consideration of Steiner's view of this 'world of Ideas', and of spiritual development in general, it is clear that this passage has been misunderstood. By taking cognizance of the 'Em' dash at the end of line one, it is clear that the subject of the initial phrase is the subject also of the descriptive clauses, which make up the bulk of the passage.

On this basis, and in light of the above, it is therefore correctly rendered in English as,

His thoughts are descending into
the foundations of the primeval world –
what he thought as shadows,
what he experiences as apparitions,
now soars above the World of Forms,
into a realm of whose fullness, people,
in thinking, are merely dreaming in shadows,

of whose fullness people, in seeing,
are merely living in apparitions.

Its meaning is even more clearly revealed by achieving a more English style in the syntax of the translation,

> His thoughts descend into the foundations of the primeval world – a realm of whose fullness, people, in thinking, are merely dreaming in shadows, of whose fullness, people, in seeing, are merely living in apparitions. What he thought as shadows, what he experiences as apparitions, now soars above the world of Forms.

In other words, in this rendering, the passage shows that spiritual development is viewed by Steiner as quintessentially developing the capacity to attain to consciousness of the archetypal spiritual realm of the Platonic Idea. However, as we have noted earlier in this section, clarity of meaning of poetic passages in Steiner's texts, calls for study of the extensive body of his works. We also noted that this dynamic would have been quite clear to Steiner; so it becomes evident that his verses in his drama, *Die Pforte*, are not designed for ease of assimilation by large numbers of people. *Die Pforte* is not intended to be a popular drama.

On the contrary, it presents challenges, if not obstacles, to the person seeking to engage with it. In this connection, it is known that in the ancient Mysteries of various cultures entry was barred to the acolyte until a time of probation had been successfully passed. It seems clear that Steiner's poetic-meditative verses, (not his specifically elucidatory texts) and thus to some extent *Die Pforte* itself, were designed to embody that 'Mystery' dynamic. Now that these conclusions have clarified the dynamics in Steiner's literary works, an overview of the individual scenes in Die Pforte can be undertaken, followed by a detailed consideration of their qualities.

2b: An overview of the scenes in Die Pforte

The Prelude

Die Pforte commences with the Prelude, in which two women discuss their lives in respect of attitudes to cultural matters and spirituality. From the dialogue between these two, the audience learns that the two women friends cannot go out together that night because they are going to see two different plays. We noted earlier that the name of each character in *Die Pforte* has a specific allegorical meaning. However, in the printed text of the drama, where a 'key' to this allegorical element is provided, two characters, Sophia and Estella, are not included as having an allegorical meaning. Nevertheless, it does appear to apply to them; the name "Sophia" derives from ancient Greek, and means 'wisdom'.[189] In his exegetical lectures on the New Testament, Steiner describes this name as a designation in esoteric circles of antiquity for the soul who has achieved spiritualisation.[190]

The name "Estella" is generally thought to derive from the phrase 'a star'.[191] In this connection, however, the name of one of the three women who represent the three consciousness strands in the soul, Astrid, needs to be noted. This name also means a 'star' or star-like, but whereas Estella derives from the Latin term, 'stella', the name 'Astrid', comes from the Greek term, 'astron', even though it has been transmitted into English via Latin literature, deriving from 'astrum', meaning 'a star'.[192] Thus in *Die Pforte* there is the representative of thinking – Astrid – with a nuance of classical Greek culture, and the representative of a way of thinking which rejects the esoteric-spiritual, Estella, derived

---

[189] Oxford Dictionary of Christian Names, ed. E.G. Withycombe 259.
[190] Rudolf Steiner Das Johannes Evangelium (Dornach: RSV, 1981) 203.
[191] Oxford Dictionary of Christian Names, ed, E.G. Withycombe 101, "Estella" appears to have been coined in French dramatic circles in the nineteenth century.
[192] A Latin-English Dictionary, eds. Rev. John. T. White and Rev. J.E. Riddle, (London: Longman, 1862) p. 171, "*Astrum*", "*Stella*" p. 1848. The Oxford Dictionary of English Etymology, ed. C.T. Onions, (Oxford: OUP, 1966), p. 57 "*astral*", p. 867 "*stellar*".

from Latin. Stella remains a character who, though intellectually gifted, rejects esoteric-spiritual concepts, and is linked to the Roman world.

The allegorical element here reflects Steiner's view of Roman culture as one which was 'earth-bound' and antagonistic to the spiritual, in which the transition from priestly wisdom to human wisdom took place.[193] Whereas Astrid is a character who responds well to the request of Maria to spiritualize herself, and has a Greek aspect, thus the implication – of an intellectuality which can absorb spiritual concepts – reflects Steiner's view of classical Greek culture which accepted the spiritual, indeed it nurtured the source of esoteric wisdom, the Mysteries. Hence Astrid has a place in the initiatory processes of the drama, whilst Estella remains outside of this, she only appears on stage in her home.

The Society of which Sophia is a member (it is in effect, the Theosophical-Anthroposophical Society) is producing a drama, whereas Estella is booked to see another play, entitled, *"The Disinherited of Body and Soul"*. In using this device of 'a play within the play' (or least an allusion to another play), to commence the exposition of the dramatic plot, Steiner is establishing the social context for Die Pforte in relation to mainstream culture. Estella is sceptical of the belief system of her friend Sophia, and thus has no interest in the esoteric play which Sophia is going to see.

In using this technique, Steiner can juxtapose the attitude typical of many educated people, which he views as primarily sceptical of spiritual-esoteric themes, to the underlying thematic material of Die Pforte. Estella is very forthright regarding the personality problems to be found amongst followers of this spiritual Society;

> **Estella**: …those of your fellow-thinkers are who swear by your ideas and manifest the worst sort of spiritual conceit, even though the emptiness and

---

[193] Rudolf Steiner, Theosophie des Rosenkreutzers, 134.

banality of their minds is expressed in every word they say, and in their entire behaviour. And I don't want to point out how indifferent and unfeeling some of your adherents show themselves to be towards their fellow human beings.[194]

Sophia responds that people in her movement make every effort to not overestimate an individual, merely because they are part of the movement. However, in that Estella also points out that many of Sophia's associates are not 'spiritual' people, this allows affirmation of the criticism of individuals in spiritual movements, whilst also indicating that this does not invalidate the movement inaugurated by Steiner as such. The dialogue between Estella and Sophia permits acknowledgement of the personality problems found in such societies, as well as the inherent divergence between anthroposophical and mainstream attitudes to deeper life questions. This theme is developed further in the Prelude, and will be examined again later.

Scene One

Scene One is primarily concerned with the exposition of the plot. The main human characters are introduced, and they speak of their responses to a lecture that has just been delivered by their teacher, Benedictus. This name means "blessed" in Latin, to correspond to his position as the great teacher. One of the characters is Maria, whose role in assisting her friend Johannes, to find his way to spirituality is very significant, and it is likely that the name 'Maria' is indicative of the virtue which is ascribed in Christianity to Mary, the woman who had the sanctity necessary to enable her to be the mother of the Redeemer. The major character is Johannes, his efforts at developing spirituality is a primary

---

[194] Pforte; 17, „...diejenigen deiner Gesinnungsgenossen, die auf eure Ideen schwören und den geistigen Hochmut in schlimmer Art zur Schau tragen, trotzdem die Leerheit und Banalität ihrer Seele aus jedem ihrer Worte und aus ihrem ganzen Verhalten spricht. Und auch darauf will ich dich nicht weisen, wie stumpf und gefühlslos gegen ihre Mitmenschen gerade manche eurer Anhänger sich zeigen."

theme in the drama.[195] It is likely that Johannes refers to St. John the Divine, 'the beloved disciple' of Christ. That St. John is a very significant entity to Steiner, is shown in the fact that the Goetheanum was originally called '*das Johannesbau*', 'the Johannes building', in honour of St. John.[196]

The setting of this scene is an ante-room where the audience is discussing the lecture that Benedictus has given. The first speech is that of Maria, who notes how depressed is her friend Johannes, who is an artist,

> It concerns me deeply, my friend, to see you withering in soul and spirit...once when I saw your eyes there was reflected in them only joy at all they saw.....now it is as though within you every power is extinguished, creative joy is dead in you...[197]

Johannes agrees that he is despondent, but does not volunteer any reason for this despondency, until Maria reveals that she perceives it is her presence in his life that has created this. Johannes affirms that this despondency was brought to the surface at first by the effect of his unrequited feelings for Maria; "What carries your soul into the clear heights of heaven, if I share it with you, casts me down, into murky realms of death."[198] Significantly, Johannes, who has all this doubt and despair, is given a surname, 'Thomasius', a name that, like Johannes, also has a strong New Testament allusion. St. Thomas, like St. John, was a disciple of Christ, and he

---

[195] The actual meaning of the name, 'Mary' is probably not under consideration here, as its meaning is disputed and hence unlikely to be used for symbolic purpose by Steiner. For example, The Oxford Dictionary of Christian Names, ed, E.G. Withycombe, London: OUP, 1950, lists "wished-for-child"; whereas J.T. Shipley lists "bitter", Dictionary of Word Origins, (Totowa: Littlefield Adams, 1967).
[196] Lindenberg, Steiner, 535.
[197] Pforte, 21 „So nahe geht es mir, mein Freund, dass ich dich welken seh' an Geist und Seele....Ich sah in deine Auge einst: Sie spiegelten Freude nur an aller Dinge Wesenheit.....und nun ist wie erloschen in deinem Innern alle Kraft, wie tot ist deine Schaffensfreude..."
[198] Pforte, 24 „Was deine Seele trägt in lichte Himmelshöhen, will stürzen mich, erleb ich es mir dir, in finstre Todesgründe."

became known as the 'doubting disciple' after the episode reported in John's Gospel (20:24) where Thomas doubted the reports of the resurrected Saviour.

His friend Maria expresses regret that she has this effect on him, for it is distressing and enigmatic to her, in as much as various people, in close proximity to her, often lose their happiness. This dynamic is continued in Scene Two, and will be the subject of more detailed consideration in Section 3c.

After this initial discussion between Maria and Johannes, the rest of the cast – excluding spirit beings – are introduced, the various spirit beings appear in later scene. The people are all members of the anthroposophical audience, and they are discussing the impact of the lecture, that they have just heard. Two further characters are Felix and Felicia Balde, a couple who live in nature, up in the mountains, their names denote happiness in Latin and they represent spiritual wisdom and the treasures of past spiritual-religious traditions. In so far as their surname, Balde, appears to derived from the German term "bald" which means soon, it may be that these two have a role of conferring or presaging imminent happiness for the Youth, and others.

It is also the case that 'Balde'may be a refernce to '"Baldur", the Druidic (Edda) god representing the power to perceive the spiritual in nature. These other characters make only small speeches; these include the three women, who represent elements of the soul, Philia whose name is probably derived from Greek, since she represents the emotions and sensitivity, and Philia can be derived from 'phileo', the Greek verb for affection.[199] So Philia feels the differing opinions being expressed in the ante-room, and to her they are "as a chorus, which unites everyone".

---

[199] A Greek-English Lexicon of the New Testament, ed. Walter Bauer, 2nd revised ed., eds. F. W. Gingrich and F. W. Danker, (Chicago: Univ. Chicago press, 1979) 859, fil~w.

The second person, Luna, represents volition, and her name is the Latin term for 'moon-like', and she speaks of "the purpose and goal of life". Why Steiner correlates the moon to the will is a feature of his 'Mystery' rhetoric. It is not meant to be understood until extensive knowledge of the details of his worldview is acquired. This is one of numerous elements in *Die Pforte* of this nature, which gives the drama, to a limited extent, a similar enigmatic quality to Goethe's allegorical fairy tale. However, an investigation into Steiner's view of the will reveals that he concludes that it has a spiritual link to dynamics active in sleeping and dreaming, and the moon can symbolize the night-time, with its dreams.[200]

In addition, later in this scene, Astrid, (thinking) speaks, showing her spiritually inclined intellectuality by supporting the esoteric-spiritual perspective of the lecturer, against the doubts expressed by two well educated men, Capesius (an historian) and Strader (a technician), "Oh, if two could only tread the ground which your thinking wants to avoid!"[201] Capesius reveals an aversion in intelligence to the spiritual, but in his feelings he is more open to it than Strader. The name Capesius may have been coined from two Latin terms, 'caput' which means 'the head' and 'capesso' which means 'to catch at something with zeal'.[202]

In any event he does show an eagerness to hear fairy stories from Felicia Balde, to enrich his mind, "And Felicia tells many a tale, in fabulous pictures...I do not ask the sources of her words, I think then on just one thing with clarity, how new life flows forth into my soul..."[203]

---

[200] Rudolf Steiner, Die Ergänzung heutiger Wissenschaft durch Anthroposophie, (Dornach: RSV, 1973), 73.
[201] Pforte, 38, „Ach könntet ihr den Boden doch betreten, den euer Denken meiden will!"

[202] A Latin-English Dictionary, 254, 258.
[203] Pforte, 41-42, „...Und Frau Felicia erzählt in Bildern wunderbar...Ich frage nicht, woher sie ihres Worte hat. Ich denke dann an eines nur mit Klarheit, wie meiner Seele neues Leben fließt..."

On the other hand, the name Strader may be coined from the German verb, 'strahlen' which means to shine, but is also it is used to mean releasing radioactive energy – a pivotal new interest for science a century ago. Strader, as a materialist scientist, rejects any spiritual concept, but is yet attracted to the lectures. In addition there is Theodora (a psychic woman), her name means 'God's gift', and through her psychic powers she helps the characters in various ways.

Benedictus himself makes a short speech indicating how much he treasures the participation of these two country folk. Another character, named 'the Other Maria', who represents the Green Snake, makes a long speech which affirms the value of esoteric wisdom, as it gives her solace and inner support for her social work,

> On many missions I could certainly feel my own will's powerlessness; I had to continually seek new strength from the abundance, which flows here from sources of the spirit. The warm and magical power of the words to which I listen here, streams down into my hands and flows through them on like balsam, when they touch people laden with sorrow.[204]

The nuance here of a selfless surrendering to the spirit is a keynote of this character, she shall be considered further in Section 3. Two further characters are Theodosius and Romanus, these are described by Steiner as representing love and initiative, respectively. Theodosius means in Latin, 'divinely given', and the term, Romanus implies a person of Rome – as we noted earlier, to Steiner, Rome is associated with the more earthly element, but it is also associated with strong individualism, as indicated by their formulation of a system of jurisprudence to define the rights of each citizen.[205]

---

[204] Pforte, 46 „Ich fühlte wohl auf vielen Wegen die Ohnmacht meines Willens; Ich muß stets neue Kraft mir holen aus dem Reichtum, der hier aus Geistesquellen fließt. Die warme Zauberkraft der Worte, die hier ich höre, ergießt in meine Hände sich und fließt wie Balsam weiter, berührt die Hand den Leidbeladnen."
[205] Rudolf Steiner, Geisteswissenschaftliche Menschenkunde, (Dornach: RSV, 1973), 48; and Das Johannes Evangelium, (Dornach: RSV, 1981) lect. 3.

There is also an allegorical character called German in the original, (and translated as 'Gairman' in the published English versions), who is described as representing "the Earth-brain", an explanation which itself calls for some elucidation, but which is left unexplained. Gairman represents the Giant of Goethe's tale, he is viewed by Steiner as representing atavistic psychic tendencies with their notoriously unreliable and often psychologically unwholesome qualities.[206] By contrast, the Youth in Goethe's tale, or Johannes in *Die Pforte* is seen by Steiner as striving towards a modern, wholesome form of extended consciousness. Hence the name 'German', which probably refers to the ancient, past name for the German people, namely, the Germanen, as distinct from the current term, the Deutsch; as such its best English rendering is probably, Teuton.

The seeress Theodora has a major role in this scene, as she has an experience of the Second Coming of Christ. This experience of Theodora provides one of the few moments of the drama in which some dramatic tension occurs. This episode involves an involuntary clairvoyant experience in which she is transported directly into a spiritual vision in which the Second Coming of Christ is experienced as a reality, which is in the process of descending to manifestation on the physical level. This episode is examined in more detail in Section 3b, here it shall just be noted that, already in Scene One of *Die Pforte,* through this Theodora episode, Jesus Christ is brought into association with the process of spiritualisation, albeit indirectly. Although this Theodora episode belongs to the expository phase of the plot, and has a major role in the exposition both in terms of dramatic impact and religious-spiritual nuance, it not (overtly) present in the rest of the drama. As shall be noted later, there is however, a subtle integration of this element of the exposition into the rising action.

---

[206] Steiner, Goethes Geheime, 218-219.

Towards the end of Scene One, Maria is alarmed when Johannes becomes especially despondent, and asks him for an explanation. He replies that he had become painfully aware of an unethical act he had committed in earlier years. He had deserted a woman who was in love with him; "I had no sense of guilt remaining from the days when I had torn apart the bonds which for the other soul meant life itself..... in that room our teacher said ...earnest words, {these} woke knowledge of the heaviest guilt."

Maria is unable to help him at this stage, and Scene One closes with a dialogue between Johannes and another character, Helena, who proceeds to castigate him for his depressive state. To her, this is a poor response to such a noble quest. Helena insists that only blissful joy can result from an earnest involvement with the path to spiritual development,

> (Johannes) "And has this light only brought you joy?" (Helena) "Not only joy of the kind with which I was already acquainted. But that joy which grows in these words through which the spirit proclaims itself." (Johannes), "Yet I say to you that that which works creatively can also crush." (Helena) "Then an error must be creeping with craftiness into your soul, if that is possible."[207]

In this last brief dialogue two features of the process of spiritual development, as understood by Steiner, are presented. Firstly that it is naïve to consider that the dynamics involved in spiritual development do not at some time draw a person into painful and challenging inner confrontations. Further, Helena is described by Steiner in the list of characters, as a representative of influences from "Lucifer", a

---

[207] Pforte, 55, Johannes, „Und dir hat Freude nur dies Licht gebracht?" Helena; „Nicht Freude nur von jener Art die früher mir bekannt. Doch jene Freude, die in den Worten keimt, durch die der Geist sich selbst verkündet." Johannes; Ich sage dir jedoch, das auch zermalmen kann, was schaffend wirkt. Es muss ein Irrtum sich mit List in deine Seele schleichen, wenn dies möglich ist."

being which in Steiner's worldview is seen as a fallen spirit, but not one which is evil in the full sense. Hence, this type of intellectual immaturity is typical of what Steiner refers to as a "Luciferic" state of mind. The role of manifesting fully evil intentions is assigned to another fallen spirit called "Ahriman".

In Steiner's teachings, Lucifer is a being responsible for the existence of naïve and self-centred tendencies in human beings. Lucifer appears on stage in Scene Four; the role of this being in the dramas, and hence in Steiner's worldview, is examined in the section 3f. Here we need to only briefly note that the speech of Helena here implies the view that spiritual beings effect changes in, or at least, influence, human consciousness.

Scene Two

The content of Scene Two occurs for Johannes whilst he is meditation, and completes the exposition phase of the plot. The leitmotif used for this scene is the maxim inscribed above a Delphic temple, "Know yourself". This maxim, to which Steiner often referred, was one of seven carved into the vestibule of the temple of Apollo at Delphi.[208] This phrase is used repeatedly throughout the drama, as the primary admonishing maxim for Johannes. Numerous events portrayed in *The Portal* concern non-physical places and beings, which are in fact witnessed by Johannes in his meditations.

The didactic nature of the rhetoric in this regard is striking; of the eleven scenes in *Die Pforte* the events in scenes two, four, six, nine and ten are entirely the contents of Johannes' meditating, whilst Scene Three is set within a 'meditation room'. Many of the scenes depict events and meetings between the characters in transcendent realms, of which Johannes has knowledge solely as a direct result of his

---

[208] Evi Melas, ed. Temples and Sanctuaries of Ancient Greece (London: Thames and Hudson, 1973) 67.

meditating. No specific details are provided in the stage directions or speeches, concerning the meditative practise which Johannes is undertaking.

Johannes, through his meditating upon this maxim, now experiences an episode reminiscent of the so-called 'dark night of the soul' of mystics. He has his first experience of 'self-knowledge', namely of his lower qualities. He becomes aware of a malignant being, which is also an aspect of his own personality. In effect, Johannes encounters his own potential for evil, or his "lower self" as Steiner describes this. This is the culmination of a period of Johannes' life which has been characterized by despondency.

Scene Three

At the beginning of this scene, a character is briefly introduced, a child which has been adopted by Maria. This is the representative of the canary in Das Märchen; the child's name is not given, and it only has this minor role in *Die Pforte*. It does not appear again in the drama, although a very brief reference to it is made in Scene Seven. It is in this scene that the rising action of the drama commences, as Johannes undergoes further experiences concerning the nature of the spiritual realities and the efficacy of spiritual beings. Johannes experiences his close friend Maria leaving her body, to enter higher worlds, but in this process, Maria has her body temporarily taken over by a malignant being. Johannes is thus introduced to the reality of malignant beings, and learns that their intention is to undermine the work of their great teacher, Benedictus. In experiencing this event, and in being able to maintain his mental clarity by overcoming his doubts about the integrity of Benedictus and the overall process of esoteric development, Johannes has now gained the right to progress further. The scene ends with a speech made by a 'spirit-voice', affirming that Johannes is attaining towards higher consciousness.

Scene Four

In this scene, the rising action of the plot continues, with however, the action being more concerned with the nature of spiritual experince, rather than external actions. This is another scene which is to be understood as the content of Johannes' experiences during meditation, in which the two 'fallen' spiritual beings, whom we briefly noted earlier, 'Lucifer' and 'Ahriman', appear. The step towards further knowledge or enlightenment concerning spiritual development concerns the subtle influence of Lucifer and Ahriman on human beings.

After these two beings appear, Strader and Capesius come on stage, discovering that they have been transported into a spiritual realm by a mysterious being, the Spirit of the Elements. They discover that the realm where they find themselves, which is possessed of a certain elemental life, vehemently rejects their modern humanistic way of thinking.

They are confronted by the regent of this realm, the Spirit of the Elements, and in the ensuing dialogue every statement by this being is misunderstood by them. The two men realize that their inner life has a direct impact on this elemental realm. These two men are identified in the list of characters as representations of the two "Will-o'-the-Wisps" of the Goethean tale. These are the two characters who, like the Youth, also seek the truth (the Fair Lily), but who, similarly, are intrinsically alien to the realm of the Lily. The list of characters in the published text of the drama informs us that Capesius reflects the qualities assigned to Lucifer, and those of Strader reflects those assigned to Ahriman.

The qualities of these fallen beings will be considered later, in Section 3f. Then an unusual entity makes its appearance, 'the Other Maria' of Scene One; but she is now costumed as a green snake-like woman. This character represents the Green Snake of the Goethean tale, who confronts the two Will-o'-the-Wisps. The Other Maria tells the two men about the two pathways to enlightenment, just as the Green Snake in Das Märchen tells of two pathways which the Will-o'-the-Wisps could take to enter the realm of the Fair Lily.

It is obvious from this brief view of the scene, that it contains substantial content. It develops the theme of the two different spiritual sources of ethical imperfections in humans, and it also presents an esoteric ecological perspective in which there is a spiritual milieu linking humans to another realm. Additionally, this scene introduces the pivotal Green Snake theme. We shall note in later scenes, that there is a numerical factor to the thematic element of *Die Pforte*, in particular the number seven is conspicuous. The fourth episode is the pivotal, central episode in any series of seven, and Scene Four in terms of content and introduction of substantial new thematic elements is a pivotal scene.

Scene Five

In Scene Five, the action continues to build – in the sense of Johannes acquiring further experiential spiritual knowledge. A dialogue between four sage-like characters, the Hierophants, is underway, affirming the need in modern times for some people to undertake spiritual development, and with specific reference to the quest by Johannes for initiation. These four sages have a parallel in the Goethean tale, namely, the four kings who carry out various conversations with the Green Snake, once her luminosity has her given the ability to see them.

Steiner views three of these kings as an allegorical depiction of the mind's capacity for spirituality, whilst the fourth relates to the negative potential in human nature. In his 'Theosophie', Steiner maintains that the soul consists of three specific dynamics, the power of thought, of emotion and of volition. Similarly, he maintains there that the human spirit has a triune nature, and that the spiritualization of the soul is a process wherein the soul qualities become permeated by one of the three spiritual potentials of the human being. Accordingly, with the term, 'the human spirit', and hence spirituality, Steiner makes a distinction from 'soul'; maintaining that our spirit derives from the realm of the Platonic Idea or Devachan, whilst the soul derives its being from what he terms the 'soul world'.

To Steiner, the golden king is the representative of initiation in respect of the capacity for spiritual thought, the silver king is representative of initiation in respect of the capacity for purifying the feelings or objective emotionality, and the brass[209] king is the representative of initiation regarding the will's capacity for knowledge.[210]

Thus in this scene of *Die Pforte*, Johannes' spirituality is considered with specific reference to his triune mental capacity. This figuring of human consciousness as triune features strongly in Steiner's view of human nature, it was elaborated already as a basic factor of human nature in his first Theosophical text from 1904, "Theosophie. Einführung in übersinnliche Welterkenntnis und Menschenbestimmung (Theosophy: an introduction to suprasensible knowledge of the world and the destination of humanity)".

In Scene Five, Benedictus, (the golden king), who represents higher spiritual wisdom, declares that Johannes "has passed through the trials of suffering and has in bitter distress laid the foundation for consecration, which is to bring him {spiritual} knowledge."[211] Theodosius, (the silver king), who represents the power of love, declares that warmth is now flowing into Johannes' heart, and that "He shall realize how he draws near to the cosmic spirit, by giving up the illusion of

---

[209] Goethe uses the term, "Erz" for the third king, which is an ambiguous term, but the copper alloy, brass, is probably intended, however it could be 'iron', if the classical Ages human history of antiquity were being referred to; these were known as the gold, silver and iron Ages.

[210] Rudolf Steiner, Wo und wie findet man den Geist? (Dornach: VRSN, 1961) 64, „Der goldene König ist Repräsentant der Einweihung für das Vorstellungsvermögen, der silberne König ist der Repräsentant für die Einweihung mit dem Erkenntnisvermögen des objektiven Gefühls, der eherne König ist der Repräsentant der Einweihung für das Erkenntnisvermögen des Willens."

[211] Pforte, 89, „Er ist geschritten durch die Leidensproben und hat in bittrer Seelennot den Grund gelegt zur Weihe, die ihm Erkenntnis geben soll."

his self-bound life." The third of the sage-kings, Romanus (the brass king), who represents the will (volition) speaks, declaring that, "thus shall this power lead him through the boundaries of space and the ends of time..." [212]

The fourth king, Retardus, is a negative figure, as his name indicates, he seeks to hold up the process of Johannes' initiation. He dialogues with the other three, pointing out that he shall endeavour to prevent them bringing illumination to Johannes. Retardus declares that he is so permitted, "As long as yet no mortals have come unto this place, who uninitiated, can set the spirit free from sense reality, then so long am I permitted to curb your eagerness."[213] Retardus is thus seen to have a justified position in the cosmic order of things, a role similar to that of Mephistopheles in Goethe's *Faust*, who appears before the Lord, and dialogues about the moral condition of humanity, and in particular, Dr. Faust.

Scene Six

Scene Six is another scene which is to be understood as the content of Johannes' experiences during meditation. It is a very brief scene, contributing further to the rising action, bringing in the factor of the interrelatedness of humanity with the surrounding spiritual realms. It concerns the indebtedness of humanity to the realms of the elemental powers behind nature. Felicia Balde is required by the ruler of the nature spirits, the Spirit of the Elements, to tell a fairy story to the living, elemental realm in general. This same theme occurs in the Goethean tale, where the Old Woman has to pay the Ferryman a debt. Felicia does this because, as this spirit-being explains, a debt is owed by humanity to the hosts of elemental beings who maintain the life-forces which sustain the natural world.

---

[212] Pforte: 89-90, „Theodosius: Er soll begreifen wie er dem Weltengeist sich naht durch Opferung des Wahnes seiner Eigenheit. Romanus: So soll die Kraft ihn führen durch Raumesgrenzen und Zeitenende."
[213] Pforte: 92, „So lange nicht betreten haben den Raum, in welchem wir beraten, die Wesen, die noch ungeweiht den Geist entbinden können aus Sinnes-Wirklichkeiten, so lange bleibt mir's unbenommen, zu hemmen euren Eifer."

Felicia accordingly tells a story which is evidently heard by them. It is about the presence of love and hate in human life, and that these are observed by spiritual beings. But in particular, it is about the act of selfless compassion by such an observing spirit being, to assist an elderly human. As such, Felicia's fairy tale is a polar opposite of the fairy tales which, relating the adventures of strange fairy folk, delight human children; the perspective taken here is that of spirits observing the basic psychological dynamics of human existence as a strange and puzzling reality.

Scene Seven

The setting of this scene is described as "the realm of the spirit", it is a long scene which forms the climax of the drama, and its focus is substantial. The focus is on the three powers at work in the spiritualizing of Johannes' triune soul, who is now gaining 'karmic insight', that is, knowledge of his and Maria's past life. The former theme is paralleled in Goethe's tale by the activity of the three handmaidens of the Fair Lily, who generally assist her as maids-in-waiting. In *Die Pforte* these three characters are called Philia, Astrid and Luna.

They have spoken only briefly in earlier scenes, but in the seventh scene, the focus is on their role in helping to metamorphose a particular strand of Johannes' consciousness into a higher mode of existence. Their speeches will be examined later, in Section 3i. The second theme, reincarnation, is presented by another character from Scene One, Theodora, the psychic woman. It involves a remarkable vision of hers, in which she sees the form of Maria's past incarnation appear from her brow in a vision,

> "I am impelled to speak. Out of your brow Maria springs forth a shining light...I look into long vanished times. The holy man, whose form ascended from your head – from his eyes there streams forth the

> purest soul peace, and a depth of feeling shines forth from his noble features…"[214]

This event evidently occurs in the realm of the Platonic Ideas, as Steiner views these past life thought-forms, perceptible only to the seer, as existing in this realm.[215] Maria encourages Johannes to keep in mind all that he has learnt, and Benedictus closes the scene by invoking a blessing for Johannes' further progress.

The Interlude

In the Interlude, which forms a transition from the climax to the falling action, Sophia and Estella meet again and discuss the merits of artistic performances, in this instance, that of dramatic productions. We are now informed that the foregoing scenes of *Die Pforte* are the play which Sophia has been attending, while her friend Estella, has attended the performance of *"The Disinherited of Body and Soul"*. Estella's play is described by her as a gripping, emotional portrayal of the tragic circumstances of an artist, who deserts his girl-friend, to pursue his art,

> "this caused him to neglect, more and more, a poor girl who had been faithfully devoted to him… and who finally, dies of grief….in such a life situation the young woman he had forsaken began to haunt his memory….without a single ray of hope, he ended in utter despair."[216]

---

[214] Pforte, 113, „Es drängt zum sprechen (sic!) mich. Aus deiner Stirn, Maria, entsteigt ein Lichtesschein….Ich schau in lang entschwundne Zeit. Und jener fromme Mann, der deinem Haupt entstiegen ist, er strahlt aus seinen Augen die reinste Seelenruhe, und Innigkeit erglimmt aus seinen edlen Zügen."

[215] Rudolf Steiner, Vor dem Tore der Theosophie, (Dornach: RSV, 1978) lecture 4.

[216] Pforte, 121, „Dadurch vernachläßigte er immer mehr ein armes Geschöpf, das ihm in Treue ergeben war und das schließlich aus Gram starb…in solcher Lebenslage kam ihm auch wieder seine arme Verlassene in den Sinn…Ohne Aussicht auf irgendeinen Lichtpunkt siechte er dahin."

It is obvious to the audience of *Die Pforte*, that the artist in the play seen by Estella is placed in the same life circumstances as those of Johannes in *Die Pforte*. But the play, *"The Disinherited of Body and Soul"*, stops at the purely human dilemma, and has no inclusion of spiritual dynamics. The two friends then engage in a discussion, in which Estella disagrees with Sophia's perspective that art can only be satisfactory if it attempts to portray the spiritual reality 'behind' the human dilemma and the sense perceptible.

Scene Eight

Scene Eight returns to the setting of Scene One, some three years on, wherein Johannes is painting at an easel, in the presence of Capesius and Strader. Here the falling or consolidating action of the plot includes the tentative steps towards the spiritual path, (on which Johannes has made such progress), by these two men. Thus in addition to the falling action of this scene there is also a rising action (suitable for elaboration in a subsequent drama by Steiner), in which the further efforts of these two men in the area of spirituality could be explored. Johannes has regained his equilibrium, and is making real headway with his artwork. As Capesius notes, "This picture truly is for me a wonder, and yet a greater one is its creator. The change which occurred in you is unlike anything which men like me have until now held possible."[217] This improved situation of Johannes represents a paradigm central to Steiner's cosmology, wherein the evolution of human beings occurs in a specific rhythm of time, a point which will be considered further in Section 3k.

Capesius speaks further, revealing that Johannes has recovered from his depressive state, through attaining to higher consciousness on the pathway established by

---

[217] Pforte, 126, „Dies Bild ist mir ein Wunder wahrlich. Und noch größ'res ist mir sein Schöpfer. Die Wandlung, die in euch geschehn, es kann ihr nichts verglichen werden, was Menschen meiner Art bisher für möglich hielten."

Benedictus, "I have often heard you say that you owe your artistic ability to that gift of perceiving consciously in other worlds".[218] Capesius and Strader then discuss Johannes' paintings, with differing responses to its spiritual ambience. Each man's response subtly manifests influences from one of the two 'fallen' spiritual beings who appeared in Scene Four. Capesius' feelings are full of admiration, whilst Strader's mind is disturbed by its spiritual power. In effect, their conversation highlights the achievements of Johannes, who through his inner development has distanced himself from such problems.

Scene Nine

Scene Nine further consolidates the thematic aspects of the plot, and again the number seven has a role; for just as seven scenes earlier, Johannes is again in meditation, where he had first heard the Delphic maxim resound. Johannes now hears the Delphic maxim, "Know yourself", again, but it no longer admonishes, for now uplifts and affirms him, it resonates again and again from the living elemental environment itself. It brings about an inspiring experience, which manifests to him his real spiritual potential. His time of catharsis now results in an enhanced moral-ethical nature, his conscience is again strengthened, leading him to resolve to make amends to his earlier partner, for the tragic circumstances she endured. The implication of this numerological cycle of seven will be considered in a Section 3k.

Soon thereafter, he has a glimpse of his true spiritual self, and senses how his consciousness is ascending into spiritual heights, "I feel now how my thinking penetrates deep hidden grounds of worlds, and how its radiant light illumines them. Such is the germinating power of these words, "O man, know yourself."[219] In the expression 'deep hidden grounds of

---

[218] Pforte, 128 „…Ich höre oft euch wiederholen, daß ihr die Künstlerschaft allein der Gabe dankt, bewußt in andren Welten zu empfinden…"
[219] Pforte, 137, „Ich fühle wie mein Denken dringt in tief verborgne Weltengründe; und wie es leuchtend sie durchstrahlt. So wirkt die Keimkraft dieses Wortes: O Mench, erlebe dich!"

worlds' the allusion here is to the Platonic realm of Ideas, a major theme in Steiner's commentary on Goethe, and in Die Pforte.

Scene Ten

Scene Ten shows Johannes once again in meditation, and in preparation for the final phase of Johannes' spiritual development. This scene incorporates an element essential to the exposition of the difficulties within the initiatory process, namely, Johannes' imperfections and merely nascent capacity for reliable spiritual observation. In his meditative state, Johannes encounters approvingly, a tempting and flattering spiritual being, soon thereafter he seems to sense, with dread, the approach of an evil being, but in fact it is his great teacher, Benedictus, whom he then encounters. Soon after this, both Lucifer and Ahriman appear and address him. These actions all demonstrate the continued presence in Johannes of unwise and self-centred influences. The implications of this scene are considered further in Section 31. Finally, the scene ends with a 'spirit-voice' indicating future success of Johannes, heralding the ascent of his consciousness to the Platonic realm of the Ideas.

Scene Eleven

In Scene Eleven the denouement of the initiatory process is presented, but yet in this scene, too, the future possibilities of Capesius and Strader are incorporated, giving scene eleven the character of an expository scene, with regard to the sub-plot, namely the future quest for spirituality by Capesius and Strader. Most of the characters of Scene One are gathered in a sacred temple, where the spiritual achievement of Johannes is confirmed by Maria. This parallels the final episode in the Goethean tale, wherein the Fair Lily embraces the now empowered and jubilant Prince, in a temple. However, in the final minutes of the scene the future potential of Capesius and Strader are the focus, Benedictus declares that Capesius shall find the way forwards, and Theodora prophesises that Strader shall win through to the light. In Section 3m the details of this scene are considered.

In summary, although *Die Pforte* is conceived as a mystery drama, in the ancient sense of depicting the interaction between the human and divine realities, there is a major sociological difference between Steiner's dramatic efforts and the ancient Mysteries. In ancient times, rituals carried out in Eleusis and elsewhere, took place in seclusion, the acolytes gathered in secluded Mystery centres, separated from the general community. Whereas Steiner's drama seeks to depict a path of esoteric-spiritual development in the contemporary world, for people whose life circumstances are placed within the technological-industrialized world, and who remain actively living and working within this social context.

It is also presupposed that the audience has considerable knowledge of Steiner's anthroposophical views, as without this, much that occurs in the drama is especially dense. As the drama takes about seven hours to perform, not all of its minor themes and their parallel in Goethe's tale, can be considered in this thesis, however each scene shall now be considered in some detail.

3: THE SCENES IN DIE PFORTE DER EINWEIHUNG

3a: The Prelude

As we noted in Section 2b, the title of Stella's play, *"The Disinherited of Body and Soul"* is highly suggestive, because this play, as the intellectual nourishment of a person who rejects the esoteric wisdom Steiner is offering, is in effect an epithet intended to describe the condition of such people. The title can be seen as a direct description of the soul-state of modern humanity – that portion of humanity that has no interest in holistic spirituality, as seen by Steiner. Indeed this title is virtually Steiner's definition of the modern human predicament, hence of the soul-state of Estella herself and of the community in general. The condition of modern consciousness is characterized by Steiner as particularly materialistic, hence as embracing of scientific-technological goals – not a bad feature in itself – but to the exclusion of broader spiritual and religious values. [220]

Another negative feature Steiner sees in modern culture is the rejection of sources of spiritual renewal, including traditional religious heritages. Steiner maintained that humanity in earlier times possessed a vibrant, holistic consciousness, and retained a natural awareness of spiritual reality. Hence it was natural for earlier humanity to have an active religious cultic-life and also esoteric striving carried out systematically in Mystery centres. Therefore our new human condition is seen as 'materialistic', and urgently requires a spiritual renewal. Steiner explained in a lecture from 1913, four months prior to the performance of *Die Pforte* in that year, that, according to his spiritual research, people of the ancient Egyptian-Mesopotamian cultures felt a sense of unity with spiritual forces in the cosmos, but by the Greek epoch this had faded,

---

[220] Rudolf Steiner, *Die Änderung der Seelenverfassung der Menschheit seit dem 15. Jahrhundert*, in Die neue Geistigekit und das Christus-Erlebnis des zwanzigsten Jahrhunderts, (Dornach: VRSN, 1970).

Thus, in the old Egyptian-Chaldean epoch, to human sentience, the soul and the cosmos were one. In the Greek era, the human soul and human body became one, but through the body, the human being was still united with its view of the cosmos. But, the spirit-soul element {of the human being} has more and more been released, entirely released from that which it views as valid content of its worldview. Alone, closed off to itself is the human soul {now}….What the human being is striving for, in our epoch, in contrast to the earlier Greek epoch is above all, to attain a scientific worldview which is disconnected from his soul-element….In recent times the worldview is there for itself, separated from the soul experiences of the human being.

And nevertheless we have to say: in modern times, as the human soul hurled itself out of the objective worldview, where it longer finds anything of the soul in that which moves outside mechanically-objectively, because it has broken the connection with external cosmic existence, in this condition it wants to acquire for itself the capacity for knowledge, for the worldview, for its entire existence. Still for the Greek person it would have been unbelievable, if someone had said to him: Be daring, use your intellect![221]

---

[221] Rudolf Steiner, Ergebnissse der Geistesforschung, (Dornach: VRSN, 1960) 470-71, „So waren in der alten ägyptisch-chaldäischen Zeit für das Empfinden des Menschen Seele und Welt eins. In der griechischen Zeit waren Menschenseele und Menschenleib eins, aber durch den Menschenleib war der Mensch noch verbunden mit seinem Weltbilde. Nun hat sich das Geistig-Seelische immer mehr und mehr gelöst von dem, was es für den berechtigten Inhalt des Weltenbildes hält. Einsam, in sich geschlossen ist die Menschenseele. Was der Mench gegenüber der früheren griechischen Epoche in unserer Epoche vor allen Dingen erstrebt, das ist, ein von seinem Seelischen unabhängiges naturwissenschaftliches Weltbild zu gewinnen….In der neueren (sic!) Zeit steht das Weltbild für sich da, abgetrennt von dem seelischen Erleben des Menschen….Und dennoch müssen wir sagen: In der neueren Zeit, als die Menschenseele sich aus dem objektiven Weltbilde herausgeworfen hat, wo sie sich nicht mehr seelisch in dem findet, was draußen mechanisch-objektiv verfließt, als sie den Zusammenhang mit dem äußeren Weltendasein unterbrochen hat, da will sie in sich doch die Kraft für die Erkenntnis, als Weltbild, für ihr ganzes Sein gewinnen. Dem Griechen

These words clarify the significance of the title of the play which Estella is seeing, which is in effect is, the modern condition of humanity, in Steiner's view. This perspective on history, in which humanity moves from a previously holistic-psychic state, in which the cosmos is the projection into matter of a spiritual reality, to one which is mechanical-materialistic, thus isolating the human being, which finds itself living an alien environment, is a predominant feature of Steiner's anthroposophy.

Estella, as the disinterested materialistic humanist, declares quite abruptly what she thinks of the esoterically inspired ideas,

> **Estella**: "It makes me shudder when I think, dear Sophia, that instead of being interested in living Art, you prefer something which seems to be nothing but outdated didactic, allegorical style, gazing at hollow abstractions, instead of living people, and admiring symbolic actions which are quite remote from everything in ordinary life which appeals to our compassion and our active concern." [222]

To Estella, the esoteric worldview is somehow artificial and remote from contemporary life issues. We are not informed here, as to the nature of Sophia's worldview, except it does take seriously esoteric-symbolic depictions of spiritual themes. Sophia attempts to convince Estella of the value of her worldview,

> **Sophia**: "My dear Estella… like so many people, the only kind of spirit you know about is the bearer of knowledge; you are only aware of the *intellectual* side

---

noch wäre es unglaublich gewesen, wenn jemand ihm gesagt hätte: Erkühne dich, dich deiner Vernunft zu bedienen!"

[222] Pforte, 17, „Und mir graut, wenn ich nun denken soll: Du meine liebe Sophie, ziehst diesem Interesse an lebensvoller Kunst etwas vor, was mir doch nichts anderes zu sein scheint als die abgetane lehrhaft-allegorische Art, welche puppenhafte Schemen statt lebendiger Menschen betrachtet und sinnbildliche Vorgänge bewundert, die fernstehen allem, was im Leben täglich an unser Mitleid, an unsere tätige Anteilnahme sich wendet."

of spirituality…you believe that one can only form *ideas* about a human character; hence that it has to mould itself. You don't want to see how thought dives into the creative spirit, reaches to the primal source of all existence, and then proves to be itself the creative seed. As little as the forces of the seed have to *teach* the plant how to grow, but prove themselves to be the living reality within – so little do our ideas teach; they stream into us, enkindling and bestowing life…." [223]

The Prelude then, implies that the social milieu into which *Die Pforte* is being placed, is one of being *Disinherited of Body and Soul*, and this amplifies the comments of Steiner considered earlier, that playwrights such as Maeterlinck can not expect to have their productions appreciated by more than a tiny portion of humanity. Scene One ushers the audience into a rarefied, unusual setting; a circle of people committed – in varying degree – to an esoteric-spiritual worldview.

---

[223] Pforte, 18, „Meine Liebe Estella…du kennst, wie so viele, von dem, was Geist genannt wird, nur das, was Träger des Wissens ist; du hast nur ein Bewußtsein von der Gedankenseite des Geistes.…Du glaubst, man könne sich nur Gedanken über einen menschlichen Charakter machen: dieser aber müsse sich gleichsam von selbst formen. Du *willst* nicht einsehen, wie der Gedanke in den schaffenden Geist taucht, an des Daseins Urquell rührt und sich entpuppt als der schöpferische Keim selbst. So wenig die Samenkräfte die Pflanze erst lehren, wie sie wachsen soll, sondern sich als lebendig (sic!) Wesen in ihr erweisen, so lehren unsere Ideen nicht; sie ergießen sich, Leben entzündend, Leben spendend in unser Wesen."

3b: Scene One

Scene One opens onto an ante-room leading from a lecture hall, where people are discussing an anthroposophical lecture which has just finished. Maria is addressing her friend, Johannes. She is disturbed at his despondent state of mind, "…and now it is as if within you all your strength is extinguished, your joy in being creative as if dead, and the arm which, a few years ago was young and fresh, powerfully guiding the brush, is lamed."[224]

In Section 2b, we saw that Johannes is representative of the distressed Youth and was complaining of suffering from a despondent condition. In his lectures on the tale of Das Märchen, Steiner refers to the stage on the path to higher spirituality in which the person is too impatient, this is what the Youth (Johannes) portrays. It is the stage similar to that of the hasty acolyte in Schiller's *Das Verschleierte Bild zu Saïs*, an impatience to unite with the spirit, "…if he yearns immaturely to take hold of the highest that can be achieved in consciousness, then this knowledge is something which can kill, something which can confuse and lame the soul."[225]

The attitude that the acolyte must refrain from too rapid a transformation of his or her current consciousness into one that enables perception of a divine reality, is an important topic in Steiner's texts on spiritual development. As such it constitutes a primary theme throughout *Die Pforte*. It was also the theme of a writer whose works were known to, and recommended by Steiner, namely, the English esotericist, Bulwer-Lytton (1803-1873). Lord Edward George Bulwer-Lytton wrote several esoteric works in Steiner's lifetime, including a novel of initiation, *Zanoni*. This novel explores

---

[224] Pforte, 22, „Und nun ist wie erloschen in deinem Innern alle Kraft, wie tot ist deine Schaffensfreude, gelähmt fast scheint der Arm, der jugendfrisch vor Jahren den Pinsel kräftig führte."

[225] Rudolf Steiner, Goethes Geheime, 223, „…wenn er unreif erfassen will das Höchste, was an Erkenntnis errungen werden kann, dann ist diese Erkenntnis etwas für ihn, was töten, was die Seele verwirren, lähmen kann."

the impact on an acolyte of a premature encounter of the spiritual reality beyond the threshold between the physical and the spiritual worlds. His main character is called, Glyndon, and he is tempted to cross the threshold prematurely, in the absence of his Master. This results in a premature exposure to his own 'lower self'.

Steiner commented only briefly on this English author, concluding that Bulwer-Lytton, through his "especial {psychological} constitution was indeed able to penetrate into certain mysteries,[226] and that "One who understands what is said in Zanoni, will read it with much profit."[227] Bulwer-Lytton's novels were deeply connected with esoteric-spiritual themes, and he was himself attracted to Rosicrucian literature, although the question of his membership of any contemporary so-called Rosicrucian order remains unresolved.[228] Steiner commented in 1906 that the various esoteric depictions in the novel *Zanoni* were especially important, and in 1922, he asked his secretary, Günther Wachsmuth to translate it into German, and arranged for its publication that year.[229] The encounter by Johannes of his lower self is left for Scene Two.

It becomes clear that an additional reason for Johannes' despondency is a strange tension which he is now experiencing. Johannes complains that his despondency intensifies on each occasion that he is exposed to the spiritual teachings that form the central element of his spiritual life, not only to Maria. Furthermore, this phenomenon occurs not only when he is listening to a lecture, but also when people discuss associated themes, "first came our leader's words,

---

[226] Rudolf Steiner, Anthroposophie als Kosmosophie, (Dornach: RSV, 1972) 17, „...durch seine besondere individuelle Konstitution fähig war, schon in gewisse Mysterien einzudringen.."
[227] Rudolf Steiner's words are quoted – without any source – by Paul M. Allen in his preface to Bulwer-Lytton's Zanoni (Blauvelt: Rudolf Steiner Publications, 1971) 4.
[228] Marie Roberts, Gothic Immortals, (London: Routledge, 1990) 156-168.
[229] Hella Wieberger, ed. Rudolf Steiner und die Tempellegende, (Dornach: RSV, 1979) 352.

and then the various comments of these people – now I feel shattered to the core."[230]

Further dialogue shows that Johannes has been too hastily striving, ignoring his true human condition. Johannes reports that his depressive state has become intensified through an very conscious realization of his guilt with regard to a shameful episode in his life. He had broken off a relationship with a young woman, in order to pursue his spiritual interests. In response to his neglect of her, this woman had taken her own life. Recently after hearing a lecture on spiritual matters, he suddenly becomes very aware of his guilt, "In me however, it {the lecture} woke the knowledge of the heaviest guilt. Through it I learnt how erroneously I have striven."[231] These words indicate an awakened power of conscience in Johannes, and this theme is taken up in the next scene. The way in which other passages in the drama present the role of the conscience will be explored in relation to Scene Two.

Further, it is also clear that there are still other causative elements to this condition. For Johannes also complains of a growing feeling of inner emptiness, which is triggered only partially by this feeling of remorse about the fate of his ex-partner; "…I started boldly along the path taught here. And it has turned me into a nothingness!"[232] Maria expresses understanding of this, but nevertheless in Scene One no explanation is forthcoming for this disturbing condition. This characteristic is a strong feature of *Die Pforte*; events and attitudinal dynamics are presented, and occasionally even a character, without any explanation. This situation necessitates that the interested member of the audience undertakes to research Steiner's indications about the particular topic, to find an explanation.

---

[230] Pforte, 51, „Erst unsres Führers Worte, dann dieser Menschen bunte Reden! Erschüttert bis ins Mark erschein ich mir. "
[231] Pforte, 54, „In mir jedoch erzeugte sie Bewusstsein schwerster Schuld. Ich kann durch sie erkennen, wie irrend ich gestrebt."
[232] Pforte, 52, „Betrat ich kühn den Weg, der hier gewiesen ist. Er hat ein Nichts aus mir gemacht. "

The dynamic expressed in Johannes' speech is an allusion to Steiner's perspective on the effect, on the soul of the turbulent initial phases of the pathway. The following extract from a lecture by Steiner on ancient Mysteries presents this,

> Only when, in a certain respect, one has enthusiasm for the {esoteric} knowledge, when one regards knowledge as a life-question, does one feel what is said {*earlier in this lecture about the spiritual realities, as revealed by anthroposophy*} to be precisely the first great trial of the soul. This trial occurs if from such knowledge, one has to say something like the following: in this is resounding to us from remote Ages the great words of wisdom, 'Know yourself!'" Self-knowledge shines before us, as a lofty ideal, as the crux of all other true knowledge. That is, in so far as we have in any sense the wish to gain knowledge, we are attempting firstly to aspire to know our own selves, to know that what we are. [233]

With regard to Steiner's view of the processes which occur in the soul, that is, psychological dynamics, derives from his spiritual observation of what occurs in the soul-body. His view of these are an integral part of the majority of his anthroposophical elucidations. He rejected, for the most part, contemporary psychological theories developed by others, although he acknowledges some of their work as of value. Steiner's psychological conclusions cannot be examined here, it is characteristic that Steiner places psychological processes

---

[233] Rudolf Steiner, Weltenwunder, Seelenprüfungen und Geistesoffenbarungen, (Dornach: RSV, 1977) 143, „Erst dann, wenn man in gewisser Weise enthusiasmiert ist für die Erkenntnis, wenn man Erkenntnis als Lebensfrage betrachtet, dann fühlt man das, was gesagt werden soll, eben doch als erste große Seelenprüfung. Sie tritt dann ein, wenn man sich aus einer solchen Erkenntnis heraus etwa das Folgende sagen muß: Da tönt uns herüber aus uralten Zeiten das große Weisheitswort: „Erkenne dich selbst!" Selbsterkenntnis als Angelpunkt aller anderen wahren Erkenntnis leuchtet uns als ein hohes Ideal vor, das heißt, wir versuchen anzustreben, indem wir überhaupt zu einer Erkenntnis kommen wollen, zuerst uns selbst zu erkennen, das zu erkennen, was wir sind."

in a spiritual context, involving spiritual beings, and dynamics in the ether-body and soul-body.

Johannes has entered the first great trial, and this is because he has been assiduously reading and listening to lectures, with an earnest and enthusiastic approach. In effect Scene One is demonstrating that a modern acolyte is already facing a trial in attempting to really comprehend the radical perspective on spiritual questions that are expressed in Steiner's teachings. According to Steiner's viewpoint, the trial arises because of the effect of the privileged esoteric knowledge. It creates an awareness indeed of the divine, higher realities, and hence of the 'spiritual self' of the acolyte, but in so doing it also creates two feelings in response. Firstly, a sense of one's current unworthiness or lack of spirituality, and secondly a sense of having merely an illusory personality, illusory because it has not made any effort to merge with a truly great or spiritual core. The following Steiner verse indicates the seriousness with which he approaches the subject of attaining self-knowledge,

In seeking, know yourself,
Im Suchen erkenne dich,
And to you, you shall become
Und wesend wirst du dir.
ever more yourself.
Entzieht das Suchen sich dir:
But if seeking should cease in you,
Du hast dich zwar im Sein,
You indeed still have yourself in Being,
Doch Sein entreißet dir
But Being removes from you
Des eignen Wesens Wahrheit.
The truth of your own being.[234]

The implication here appears to be ascertainable by examining the use of the word 'self'. In line 1, the self is the current personality, but in line 3, it is probably the higher

---
[234] Steiner, Wahrspruchworte, 170.

self. This is indicated by the following lines, which imply that the spiritual quest, if stopped, will bring about an inner distancing from the higher self, but does not, cannot, actually remove the current personality or normal self. Johannes in this scene is positioned uncomfortably in the transition between the two selves, so to speak.

Another element of the plot in this scene concerns the Theodora episode, which announces the imminence of the Second Coming of Christ. This is a striking deviation from the parallelism with the Goethean tale; there is no parallel event in *Das Märchen* to the Theodora episode. It appears that Steiner has done this in response to his conviction as to the importance of this event, and its relevance to the plot of Die Pforte. Theodora proceeds to announce that the resurrected Jesus Christ is soon to appear to humanity,

> "I am impelled to speak. Before my spirit stands a form in shining light, and from him there come words. I feel myself in future times and human beings I can see who are not yet in life. They too behold the form, they too can hear the words…"[235]

This seeress in effect also proceeds to in effect manifest that event for the characters gathered around her, by proclaiming its imminence, which to her is an immediate, actual reality, from within her visionary condition wherein she beholds Jesus.

The Theodora episode specifically introduces the imminence of a mystical Christian event, of central importance in Christian eschatology, the Second Coming of Christ. The inclusion of the Christian element could have been effected by Steiner without any reference to an imminent Second Coming. Hence this episode is expressive of a major element

---

[235] Pforte, 36, „Es drängt zu sprechen mich: Vor meinem Geiste steht ein Bild im Lichtesschein, und Worte tönen aus ihm; In Zukunftszeiten fühl' ich mich und Menschen kann ich schauen, die jetzt noch nicht im Leben sind. Sie schauen auch das Bild, sie hören auch die Worte..."

in Steiner's Christology. In fact, it was Steiner's view that this event was only a few decades away from occurring, and that only because of this fact, could such an enhanced spirituality occur for Johannes, as is portrayed in Die Pforte. Steiner's view of this theme will be examined in the Conclusion, in Section 4f.

In this connection, it is relevant to note that Steiner does not directly present apologetics for Christianity in any other way in *Die Pforte*. For after Theodora has spoken, this theme is not taken up again by anyone, the response of the characters is limited to brief discussions as to whether any psychic experience is inherently possible or reliable. Steiner saw the Second Coming in non-apocalyptic terms, it is to be a discrete spiritual experience, this subject is examined further in Section 4.

No further mention of Christ or of Biblical characters is made anywhere else in the drama. This episode is in effect a device which implies the subtle presence of Christ in the dynamics which are to unfold in Die Pforte. We noted earlier the feature in Steiner's worldview, that humanity is placed between two kinds of evil, the hosts of Lucifer and of Ahriman. These two beings are also portrayed in *Die Pforte* as exerting an influence on the characters in their experiences.

The instructions for Scene One direct that a statue of the evil being, Ahriman, is to be present on the stage, as part of the furnishings of the room. In addition, there is the brief speech by Helena, (noted in Section 2b), who is identified as a representative of Lucifer. Thus, the influence upon humanity of the two kinds of evil, and of the redeeming Being (Christ) is subtly indicated. These devices imply the actual efficacy of these beings, within the consciousness of the characters. But consequently, another triune group of characters is created, too, namely Lucifer, Ahriman and Christ; the efficacy of Christ against the other two beings is to be understood as a factor, albeit subtly in the events that follow.

As a consequence of this perspective, and to further illustrate the nature of this event to the audience, Theodora also experiences that a person in the host around the Saviour separates out and approaches her, in order to inform her, as one human being to another, that she should spread word of a coming imminent event, through which a new higher consciousness shall be stimulated and nurtured.

> You should announce to all, who wish to listen to you, that you are now beholding what people will soon experience.....for near is the future wherein the human being is to be gifted with the new seeing. What once the senses beheld at the time of Christ, will be seen by souls {in a form of vision}, as soon as the time is fulfilled. [236]

Here Theodora attests to the concept that a form of spiritual perception is needed for a person to behold the Christian Saviour. Scene One ends with the dialogue between Johannes and Helena which we discussed in Section 2b; Johannes rejects her glib admonishing assurance that genuine spiritual development brings only happiness.

---

[236] Pforte, 36, „Du sollst verkünden allen, die auf dich hören wollen, dass du geschaut, was Menschen noch erleben werden. Doch nahe ist die Zukunft, Da mit dem neuen Sehen begabt soll sein der Erdenmensch. Was einst die Sinne schauten zu Christi Erdenzeit, es wird geschaut von Seelen werden, wenn bald die Zeit erfüllt wird sein. "

3c: Scene Two

As we saw in Section 2b, Scene One set the general context of the people and their attitudes, whilst Scene Two begins the actual theme of spiritual initiation, with Johannes in meditation and undergoing challenging experiences. In this scene, the dynamics afflicting Johannes in Scene One grow stronger. Steiner emphasizes in a lecture on *Die Pforte*, held a few month after its first performance, that in this scene, the Delphic expression, "Know yourself!" resounds from all sides of the stage, as if the entire environs of this spiritual realm is alive and thereby presents self-knowledge to Johannes,

> The words…of the Delphic oracle …take on a new life for people {entering esoteric development}, but first it is a life of alienation from oneself. Johannes, as someone who wants to know himself, is immersed in all external existence. He lives in air and water, in rocks and springs, but not in himself. All the words – which one can only have resounding from the outside – are actually words of the meditation… Then the person who wants to know himself is immersed in the various other beings; in this way he learns to know the things into which he submerges himself.[237]

Johannes become stronger as he enters into meditation and then finds himself in a spiritual realm. During this experience, there resounds repeatedly from the environs, which have an elemental life of their own, the call to self-knowledge – "O Mensch, erkenne dich selbst" (O man, know yourself). This ancient maxim resounds from the environs to

---

[237] Rudolf Steiner, Wege und Ziele des geistigen Menschen, (Dornach: RSV, 1973) 106, „...die Worte...des Delphinischen Orakels...gewinnen ein neues Leben für den Menschen, aber zunächst ein Leben der Entfremdung von sich selbst. Johannes geht als Sich-selbst-Erkennender in allen äußeren Wesen unter. Er lebt in Luft und Wasser, in Felsen und Quellen, aber nicht in sich selber. Alle die Worte, die man nur von außen tönen lassen kann, sind eigentlich Worte der Meditation...Dann taucht der Selbsterkennende unter in die verschiedenen anderen Wesen; dadurch lernt er die Dinge kennen, in die er untertaucht."

Johannes as the curtain opens, and throughout his soliloquy, and again as the curtain falls at the end of the scene.

Regarding this process of attaining to 'self-knowledge', Steiner maintained that the acolyte has to cross a kind of threshold, has to attain a decisive, specific state of consciousness, in order to become enlightened. This is not achieved without a struggle against one's own 'lower self'. In this context, he reminds his audience of the well-known fact that in ancient times, there was a definite time of probation, in which various quite severe trials had to be withstood by the candidate. As Steiner emphasizes in his comments on the search for Isis at Sais, these trials were designed to help the acolyte achieve the integrity, the purification needed.[238]

However, in the modern era, the dynamics have changed, according to his *Knowledge of Higher Worlds, how is it attained*. Although this same higher integrity is needed, the preparatory testing must now occur within the person's own struggle with their ethical challenges. The focus is on the integrity of the heart, and the capacity to think intuitively, or spiritually. But at some point the acolyte will nevertheless vividly perceive his or her own impure, lower impulses, and thus gain a real, unveiled knowledge of what qualities still need to be transformed in them.

The trial now commences in earnest for Johannes, as his conscience becomes ever more intense, and he now actually perceives, as a vision, the young woman whom he deserted. He sense her pain, he feels that he is alive within her disembodied soul, and thus within her suffering, "the one whom I deserted, the poor thing, I was actually her. I had to experience her suffering. Knowledge has given me the strength to pour myself into another self." [239]

---

[238] Mozart presented a similar view of initiation in his opera, *The Magic Flute*.
[239] Pforte, 54, „Kein Schuldgefühl verblieb in mir aus jenen Tagen, da ich zerriss ein Band, das Leben war der andern Seele….bedeutsam sprach in jenem Saale vorhin der Führer nun, mir jedoch erzeugte sie Bewusstsein schwerster Schuld."

When Johannes expresses repugnance at his own callousness in deserting his partner, this is due to the efficacy of his conscience. The efficacy of this spiritual element of the human being serves as a counter balance to the solemn dynamic of encountering the lower self. Conscience has a prominent role in Steiner's worldview, he regards it as having a sacred spiritual source. The conscience is here differentiated from inculcated moral-ethical values, received by the growing child from parents, church and so on, "…the human conscience, this valuable asset of the human soul, which calls out like a voice of God with regard to the good and the evil in each individual person…"[240]

Hence when Johannes experiences these pangs of conscience he is in fact experiencing the results of a spiritually supportive and even transformative influence. In various lectures Steiner links the efficacy of the conscience in the human being to an influence proceeding from Christ.[241] This theme shall be explored further in Section 3f, where Johannes' enhanced conscience is once again significant in the rhetoric.

In Scene Two Johannes undergoes a kind of Dark Night of the Soul, in which he now perceives his own lower self, alive and animated, with a frightening potential. There is the implication that his conscience has become so strong as to result in him no longer just sensing, but directly seeing (psychically) the unredeemed qualities in himself,

> There from the dark abyss, what creature glares at me? I feel the bonds which hold me chained to you. Prometheus was not bound so firmly to the rocks of

---

[240] Rudolf Steiner, Die Christus-Impuls und die Entwickelung des Ich-Bewu˜tsein (Dornach: VRSN, 1961) 121, „…das menschliche Gewissen, dieses teure Gut der Menschenseele, welches wie eine Gottesstimme ruft gegenüber dem Guten und gegenüber dem Bösen in jedem individuellen Menschen…"
[241] Rudolf Steiner, Der Christus-Impuls und die Entwickelung des Ich-Bewußtseins, lect. 6, (Dornach: RSV, 1982)

Caucasus as l am bound to you. Who can you be, dreadful creature? O, I know you, it is myself.[242]

This dramatic theme, the encountering of this 'lower self', as it is called by Steiner, can be seen as a major cause of the despondent attitude developing in Johannes. This lower-self, the dawning of awareness of which is causing despondency in Johannes, is a term used to designate the immoral and antisocial feelings, thoughts and intentions in the human being. To Steiner, these three malignant tendencies are imbued with a certain elemental power that creates the tendency for them to be the predominant dynamic in the human being. Furthermore, this urge is intensified by forces external to the human soul, which derive from malignant spiritual beings. Steiner maintains that these negative elements need to be removed in order to allow a genuine and full spiritual transformation to occur, because a spiritualised person cannot retain such dynamics in themselves.

The spiritually questing soul will therefore become increasingly aware of a stumbling-block to spiritual development within itself, of which it was previously unaware. Part of this experience of encountering the tainted qualities, includes perceiving these influences of these two fallen beings; this theme will be noted further in regard to Scene Four. Scene Two ends with a dialogue between Maria and Johannes, the latter lamenting that he is not in the blessed state of Maria, but must continue intensely to wrestle with his own problems, with his feeling of inner hollowness. In this speech, Steiner uses alliteration, 'führen, Furcht, Finsternis', and also 'Wort, Weisheit, Wesen', (creating a difficult neologism: Wesenswort'), these are not preserved in the translation. He regards alliteration as an effective way to create the mood of experiencing visionary impressions, as exemplified in the Edda, where this is very common and

---

[242] Pforte, 59, „Da, aus dem finstern Abgrund, welch Wesen glotzt mich an? Ich fühle Fesseln, die mich an dich gefesselt halten. So fest war nicht Prometheus geschmiedet an des Kaukasus Felsen, wie ich an dich geschmiedet bin. Wer bist du, schauervolles Wesen ? O, ich erkenne dich. Ich bin es selbst."

which regards as deriving from clairvoyant experiences.[243] In Johannes's speech alliteration serves to emphasize that he has just recently been plunged into a spirit realm,

> Johannes: "In light, in darkness, you {Maria} will affirm yourself....but every moment can deprive me of myself....from fear they lead me into the darkness, and hunt me through the darkness with fear, these words imbued with wisdom: O Man, know yourself!"[244]

His friend, Maria, discusses the experience with him, and speaks to him of the illusory perspective that the normal self encounters,

> I have often reminded myself of the lofty wisdom that, across all of our life is spread mere semblance and illusion, as long as our thinking grasps its surface only. And ever again it said, you must be clear that an illusion is shrouding you, though it may often seem the truth to you'....[245]

Johannes replies in a despondent mood, still feeling his inner emptiness, "I would have to believe that the origin of being is nothingness, if I were to cherish the hope that from the nothingness in me a human being could ever develop."[246] As the curtain falls, the Delphic maxim once more resounds.

---

[243] Rudolf Steiner, Die Mission der neuen Geistesoffenbarung, (Dornach: RSV, 1975), 213-215.

[244] Pforte, 63, „Du wirst in Licht und Finsternis dich selbst bewahren...mir aber kann ein jeder Augenblick mich selber rauben. Mich führt aus Furcht in Finsternis und jagt durch Finsternis in Furcht der Weisheit Wesenswort: O Mensch, erkenne dich! "

[245] Pforte, 62, „Die hohe Weisheit, dass stets über alles Leben nur Schein und Trug sich breitet,wenn unser Denken seine Oberfläche bloss ergreift, ich habe sie recht oft mir vorgehalten. Und immer wieder sprach sie: Du musst erkennen, wie dich Wahn umfängt, so oft es dir auch Wahrheit dünkt...."

[246] Pforte, 63, „Ich müßte glauben können, daß aus dem Nichts der Wesen Ursprung sei, wenn ich die Hoffnung hegen sollte, daß aus dem Nichts in mir ein Mensch je werden könnte."

3d: Scene Three

Scene Three opens with a dialogue between Benedictus and Maria about a foster child of hers; it has become disaffected of Maria because of a fright it had when experiencing the clairvoyance of Theodora. As we noted in Section 2b, the child is a representation of the canary in Goethe's tale, which forms a minor sub-theme in Das Märchen. Steiner mentions the canary only briefly; he understands it to represent the ongoing awareness (or memory) of the physical world within the consciousness of the Higher Self. In Goethe's tale, the Youth's hawk, which Steiner regards as the incipient development of the higher faculties in the Youth, swoops down upon the court of the fair Lily, and harms her canary.[247] So, as read by Steiner, the harm caused to the canary by the hawk, represents stresses imposed upon the Higher Self, by the too eager yearnings of the normal self for a higher state; in effect, the condition of the young man expressed in Schiller's Das Verschleierte Bild zu Saïs.

As we noted earlier (Sect.2), the main focus of the speeches in this scene is Johannes' further experiences in which Johannes has to learn that a human being is not his or her body, and further, the essential element of the human being is a spiritual reality, which is not directly expressed in earthly human nature. Subsequently, Johannes witnesses an episode in which Maria leaves her body, and malignant powers speak through her lips. Benedictus soothes his distress by informing him that evil powers do seek to have access to human souls. He also explains to Johannes that the spiritual reality of Maria is a model of that higher human being to which he is to aspire, and that the soul of this spiritually awakened person "hovers in those spiritual heights where the human beings find the archetype of their own being, which has its origin within itself".[248] This is a reference to the realm of Ideas,

---

[247] HA Bd. 6, S. 223.
[248] Pforte 72, „Es schwebet ihre Seele in die Geisteshöhen, wo Menschen ihres Wesens Urform finden, die in sich selbst sich gründet."

and presents Steiner's view of the spiritual place from whence the human spirit derives.

Consistent with his understanding of the Platonic realm of Ideas, in connection with primeval 'depths' or 'foundations', Steiner uses the verb, 'steigen', which usually means 'to arise' or ascend'. However, in older German, this verb can also mean 'to descend', which correlates to his view of the realm. Steiner equates the 'realm of Ideas' with Devachan, which he asserted was neither above nor below, but transcendent of spatial qualities, in effect, all around us. In Section 1B3 we noted Steiner's perspective on the passage in Faust Two, where Faust is about to enter a transcendent realm, in which the 'uncreated' exists, in apposition to the physical realm, filled with the 'created'. But in addition, Steiner notes with approval Goethe's attitude, expressed through Mephistopheles, that to enter this archetypal realm, one can either ascend or descend. To Steiner the realm of Ideas is beyond spatial considerations.[249]

At the end of this scene, the realm of the Platonic idea is again the focus. This occurs in the speech of the Spirit-voice, which we examined in Section 2a, and noted in Section 2b,

> His thoughts descend into the foundations of the primeval world – a realm of whose fullness, people, in thinking, are merely dreaming in shadows, of whose fullness, people, in seeing, are merely living in apparitions. What he thought as shadows, what he experiences as apparitions, now soars above the world of Forms.

This speech is not only alludes to the illusory nature of normal consciousness, as compared with the goal of esoteric development, this speech also appears to allude to the Platonic myth of the Cave, which we discussed in Section

---

[249] Rudolf Steiner, Über die astrale, 94, „...Mephisto: *Versinke denn! Ich könnt auch sagen: steige!* Also, nicht oben und nicht unten, sondern überall ist Devachan." ("...Mephisto; *so sink down now! I could also say, arise!* So, not above and not below, rather Devachan is around about us.")

1B1. There we noted that Steiner, without denying the greater reality of the Idea realm, strongly disagrees with the implication that the gap between this true reality and the human condition is unbridgeable. He maintains that precisely through spiritual development, human consciousness can attain to this realm. Here in Scene Three the implication is that precisely this attainment is underway in Johannes.

3e: Scene Four

We noted in Section 2b, that this scene has a pivotal role in the development of the plot, as it is the central scene in the first segment of the drama, a group of seven scenes. In *Die Pforte*, the first seven scenes form a unity, and are followed by the Interlude, before Scene Eight opens. In Steiner's cosmology, the flow of evolution occurs in seven phases, both vast periods and subdivisions thereof into smaller phases, each of these consists of seven units.

He maintains that during the large evolutionary cycles, in the fourth cycle, a new element enters into the dynamics and it is this which is the impetus to the dynamics of the preceding three becoming manifested in the last 3 cycle on a higher level. Through this process, a new factor enters into manifestation by the seventh phase.[250] The introduction of substantial new thematic material into Scene Four is a response to this principle of the evolutionary dynamic having its reflection in humanity. That these dynamics are interwoven into the structure of *Die Pforte* reflects Steiner's conclusion that the cosmic septenary process is echoed on a much smaller scale within each human life. The underlying perspective here is that the human being is a microcosm of the macrocosm.[251]

This scene opens with Johannes again in meditation, as in Scene Two; this time he does not encounter his own lower self, rather – as the element which introduces the next evolutionary 'leaven' for Johannes – he becomes aware of the presence of two beings, Lucifer and Ahriman. How Johannes responds to the 'trials' posed by these two beings is crucial to his quest for spirituality. We noted briefly in Section 2b, that to Steiner the unethical qualities in human consciousness are

---

[250] This concept is outlined in a fragmentary manuscript, *Entwurf zur Darstellung der geisteswissenschaftlichen Kosmologie* in Bewußtsein, Leben Form, (Dornach: RSV, 2001) and is then presented in detail in his Geheimwissenschaft im Umriß, for each of the four great aeons which have so far elapsed.
[251] Steiner, Geheimwissenschaft.

exacerbated by malignant beings, in fact, two hosts of such beings, each of which has a leader, these leaders are Lucifer and Ahriman. Steiner maintains that in the Bible the above two forms of evil are referred to, even if subtly. References to 'the Devil' are in effect, to Lucifer, whereas references to 'Satan' are to the much more evil being, Ahriman.

Whereas 'Lucifer' is term known to the Christian religious tradition, as an alternative name for the Devil, the term, Ahriman, is less well known. It is a Persian term, the name for the primary evil being in Zarathustrian religious texts, in particular, the Zend-Avesta. The term,' Ahriman', is a later variant of the original name for the primary evil being known to the Zoroastrian religion of the ancient Persians, Angra Mainyu. The nature of Angra Mainyu/Ahriman is elucidated in the sacred texts of Zoroastrianism, he is principally as being who directly opposes the will of the true God, Ahura Mazdao. He is lord of a host of demons created by him "to destroy the world of the good principle", he is described as being "…full of death, the worst-lying of all Daevas..." [252]

Scene Four commences with Lucifer directly on stage, revealing through his words his significance for human beings. Yet he is not directly addressing Johannes; this technique seems to imply that any meditant who attains to such a consciousness as Johannes has attained, will have this experience. Through Lucifer's soliloquy, Johannes becomes more aware of this entity's existence, and gains an understanding of the nature of the influences imparted by him.

Lucifer adapts the Delphic temple maxim by declaring, "O man, know yourself, O man, feel me", and then proceeds to declare that the human being on the earth has wrestled its way out of the clutches of divine beings. He explains to the audience that humanity has been seeking to find their own real self, and here on the Earth succeeded in gaining freedom,

---

[252] The Zend-Avesta, part 2, The Sirozahs, Yasts und Nyayis; trans. James Darmesteter, (Delhi: Motilal Banarsidass, 1884, repr. 1981) 45, 227.

which occurred as they fled from existence in spiritual realms. He then goes further to declare that we thereby encountered him – and this our reward and indeed our destiny. Lucifer seeks to convince humanity that their sense of selfhood and its mental and emotional freedom (independence from godly injunctions) derives from him

> "You have wrenched yourself away from spirit guidance, and you have fled into free earthly realms. You've sought your own being in Earth's confusion; to find yourself proved your reward, and proved your fate. You found me."[253]

The nuance of an independent or rebellious spirit being, whose influence in humankind is to stimulate a similar dislike of the correct, selfless, ethical attitude is clearly present in this speech. In this scene, Lucifer declares that he gave to humanity an independence of volition, whereas the other deities (that is, hierarchies who serve God) sought only to ensure that humanity followed their will, but then Lucifer proceeds to condemn the true divinities, and claim to have given to humanity its real individual will, "Spirits wanted to cast a veil over the sense. I tore the veil apart. Spirits desired in you to follow only their own will. I gave you your own will."[254]

The esoteric implication here is that the normal self, or the lower self of the human being, is to some extent, a manifestation of 'Luciferic' qualities. In this connection, an intriguing passage in Isaiah (14:12) has relevance; it castigates a malignant being for becoming a fallen being. He is reprimanded for wanting to excel over his associates, and make himself "like the most High". Isaiah refers to him as the morning star. Although in modern translations this being is

---

[253] Pforte 76, „Du hast dich entrungen der Geistesführung und bist geflohn in freie Erdenreiche. Du suchtest eignes Wesen in Erdenwirrnis; dich selbst zu finden, es ward dir Lohn, es ward dein Los. Du fandest mich."

[254] Pforte; 76, „Es wollten Geister dir Schleier vor die Sinne legen. Ich riss entzwei die Schleier. Es wollten Geister in dir nur ihrem Willen folgen. Ich gab dir Eigenwollen."

considered to be an oppressor of Israel, traditionally this passage is understood to refer to Lucifer, and also identifies him as the star of the twilight or Venus.[255] Hence Lucifer is associated with an attractive radiance, which is not however, the true solar light. Steiner describes Lucifer as a source of egotistic, self-centred yearnings, and in terms of consciousness dynamics, this may be represented metaphorically as an attractive, but false light.

These speeches of Lucifer enable the audience to clarify retrospectively the significance of Helena's speech in Scene One. Her protestations to Johannes that spiritual development brings only blissful experiences are intended to be 'Luciferic'; this is alluded to through Steiner's choice for her name, "Helena". The term Helena derives from ancient Greek and implies a brightly shining light.[256] So, she is a radiant light, but perhaps not the true (solar) light; this has allusions to the name, 'Lucifer', which means 'light-bringer', yet obviously this can not mean the true light, where light is a metaphor for consciousness or perhaps influences affecting humanity. So, Helena likewise appears to suggest an ethically dubious, even if possibly quite attractive, light, and as such it alludes to the term, 'Lucifer', which originally meant the 'Light-bearer'.

Then Ahriman speaks, again adapting the Delphic maxim, but in the opposite direction to Lucifer, "O man, know me. O man, feel yourself". This speech thereby implies that the human being in encountering Ahriman, will sense his own true reality. Ahriman then proceeds to speak about the human reality,

> You have fled from spiritual darkness. You have found the light of Earth. So suck the power of truth

---

[255] More recent translations (such as the NIV) tend not to support the age-old interpretation that this passage refers to Lucifer, as exemplified in the Vulgate, and in the King James version, but the allusion to Lucifer in Helena has reference to this ancient tradition.

[256] The Oxford Dictionary of English Christian Names, ed. E.G. Withycombe, (Oxford: Clarendon Press, 1950), 2nd edit, 141.

from my solidity. I harden secure ground. Spirits wanted to rip you away from the senses' beauty. I bring about this beauty in dense light. I lead you into true being. Spirits wanted to tear you away from the senses' beauty. I make effective this beauty in solid light. I lead you into true being.[257]

There are various key implications here in the rhetoric for the audience. In this speech Ahriman accentuates the ontological integrity of the state of human consciousness that derives from life in physical reality; in comparison with it, existence in higher realms is existence in "spiritual darkness". In Steiner's anthroposophy the consciousness state of the human being in the physical world is one in which awareness of the spiritual realm (the Idea realm) is usually minimal, we are on this side of the river, looking across to the realm of Lily. Hence the consciousness state that accretes from coming into life in physical reality is the antithesis of the 'right' state, or the state which spiritual development bestows. Hence in Steiner's terms, Ahriman's speech is especially untruthful. He identifies Ahriman as the being who is 'the father of lies'. The following extract from a lecture of Steiner's expresses his perspective on this,

> In this world of the senses and of the deductive mind, in normal consciousness, we perceive in sturdy density, material objects and material processes, which fill the space around us. When on the one hand, through our senses and the deductive mind, we have for our experiencing, the coarse material things and processes of the material world, then there are present on the other hand, the unreal thoughts and unreal sensations, about which in every age, philosophising

---

[257] Pforte, 77, „Du bist entflohen aus Geistesfinsternis. Du hast gefunden der Erde Licht. So sauge Kraft der Wahrheit aus meiner Festigkeit. Ich härte sichern Boden. Es wollten Geister der Sinne Schönheit dir entreißen. Ich wirke diese Schönheit in dichtem Licht. Ich führe dich in wahre Wesenheit."

> people have argued as to how these are related to reality.[258]

The lesson here is that to Steiner 'true being' is not found – in normal consciousness – on the Earth, and that the 'power of truth' cannot be found in the sphere of dense material substance (except by transcending this and accessing the realm of the Idea). Further, in the expression, "you have found the light of Earth", an additional false attitude, in Steiner's terms, can be seen. This phrase can be viewed as affirming that the "un-enlightened" state of the earthly ego is a condition which is 'illumined'. As such, it stands in stark opposition to Steiner's viewpoint that only when spirituality is attained, thereby transcending normal Earth consciousness, does the person enter into an 'enlightened' condition.

He maintains that this is literally so, because this wisdom possesses a potent radiance. Steiner strongly emphasizes this concept, describing the supernal radiance inherent in spiritual wisdom, which he terms, 'cosmic thoughts' and how this illumines the soul of the developed person. By inference, therefore, the non-initiated, sense-bound consciousness is dark, so to speak,

> ...the experience of the spiritual world consists precisely in this, that one knows oneself to be living within it. One knows that oneself is living within the weaving of {cosmic} thoughts. It is precisely when this frame of mind commences, that one knows oneself to be consciously within the weaving of thoughts, that this passes over into knowing oneself to

---

[258] Rudolf Steiner, <u>Was wollte das Goetheanum und was soll die Anthroposophie</u>? (Dornach: VRSN, 1961) 115, „In dieser Welt der Sinne und des kombinierenden Verstandes im gewöhnlichen Bewußtsein nehmen wir in derber Dichtigkeit die stofflichen Dinge and stofflichen Vorgänge wahr, welche den Raum erfüllen....Wenn wir auf der einen Seite stehen, haben für unser Erleben durch die Sinne und durch den kombinierenden Verstand die derb stofflichen Dinge und Vorgänge der Außenwelt, dann stehen auf der anderen Seite die unwirklichen Gedanken, die unwirklichen Empfindungen, über die zu allen Zeiten philosophierende Menschen gestritten haben, wie sie sich zu der Wirklichkeit verhalten."

be in radiantly shining light. For thoughts proceeds from the light. The thought weaves in light.[259]

Here the rhetoric, with its reference to 'light' and to 'weaving' could appear to be entirely metaphorical, but the points we discussed in Section 2a are relevant here, to the effect that these are not intended to be metaphorical.[260]

The complex question of how a perception in a supra-sensible context – can be related to the validity or otherwise of perception, and how this in turn can be understood in terms of metaphorical tendencies in language, cannot be examined in this thesis. We can note that to Steiner it is axiomatic that perceptions in supra-sensible realms are inherently valid, provided that the rigorous inner preparation is carried out before hand. His use of the participle, 'weaving' appears to be metaphorical, that is, he regards thought as actively permeating the milieu of the spiritual realm, which is light-filled.

Hence to Steiner, 'weaving' describes an experienced, that is, spiritually perceived, process of permeation, even though he may have adopted the term from Goethean texts, where 'weaving' is specifically metaphorical, as in Faust Past One, *Faust's Study* 1922-1927; here the 'fabric of thought' is 'like a weaver's masterpiece'. Indeed Goethe specifically refers to using a metaphorical approach because of the difficulty of uniting the Idea with experience (perception), "The intelligence cannot think of as unified, what sense experience

---

[259] Rudolf Steiner, Menschenschicksale und Völkerschicksale, (Dornach: VRSN, 1981) 178, „...darin besteht gerade das Erleben in der geistigen Welt, daß man sich darinnen lebendig weiß. Man weiß sich lebendig im Weben der Gedanken. Gerade wenn dieser Zustand anfängt, daß man sich bewußt im Weben der Gedanken darinnen weiß, dann geht das unmittelbar über in ein Sich-Wissen im hellstrahlenden Licht. Denn der Gedanke ist aus dem Licht. Der Gedanke webt im Licht."

[260] Steiner, Spirituelle Seelenlehre, 348, „So unterscheidet der Okkultist das strahlende Selbstleuchten des Geistes von dem eigentümlichen Glimmern des Lichtes, welches zurückgestrahlt wird von der Welt der Gestalten, als seelische Flamme. Seele heißt, zurückstrahlendes Geisteslicht, Geist heißt, ausstrahlendes schöpferisches Licht."

presents to it as separate…therefore we justly take refuge for some satisfaction into the sphere of poesy…"[261] Nevertheless, despite these Goethean origins, Steiner's usage is understood by him to be primarily non-metaphorical.

The significance for human beings of these two beings in Steiner's worldview is twofold, one is an influence which results in specific, and traditional identifiable unethical activity, the other is a more subtle, and often unrecognized, generic unethical tendency. The influence of these two beings as represented in their speeches here is of the subtle, generic nature, rather than what one could refer to as more traditionally unethical nature. The influence of 'Lucifer' is seen as manifesting in two ways. Its more traditionally unethical form is as egocentric desires, as well as un-grounded, immature attitudes, from which many immature misdeeds originate, as well as crimes of passion. In a more general sense, it manifests as an inherent part of every person's soul, it is identified as one which does not intend to cause evil, but rather, results in self-centred inflamed yearnings and immature ideals. With regard to the influence of Satan or "Ahriman" Steiner sees the more traditionally unethical aspect, as activities where 'hardening of the heart' are carried out, that is, in actions which lead to cold, callous premeditated actions or crimes.

Whereas the overall nature of the Ahrimanic influence, as an inherent part of every person's soul, causes thinking to become what Steiner sees as spirit-denying intellectuality. An example of this to Steiner was the emerging atheistic scientific thinking. In today's world, an extension of that would be the re-defining of the human being's essential nature, such as allows a gradual movement towards seeing the ideal human state as that of the android human being.
That these two beings appear to Johannes in this scene indicates that any person who is seeking to develop a

---

[261] HA, Bd. 13, *Bedenken und Ergebung*", S. 30, „Der Verstand kann nicht vereinigt denken, was die Sinnlichkeit ihm gesondert überlieferte..Deshalb wir uns billig zu einer Befriedigung in die Sphäre der Dichtkunst flüchten..."

heightened spirituality must encounter the influences of these two ranks of fallen beings, active within one's lower self. They are not considered by Steiner as metaphors which allow a placing of polar opposite ethical dynamics before the acolyte. He considers them to be realities, as actual beings, perceived by the enhanced consciousness faculties, and who manifest in opposite fields of activity. In line with his conviction that perception of the sense world or of the spiritual realms is inherently valid (under healthy circumstances) Lucifer and Ahriman are specific beings, with a historically traceable field of influence.

After these two fallen spirits have spoken, they remain on stage, and two friends of Johannes, Strader and Capesius appear. They are accompanied by another being called, the 'Spirit of the Elements'. We noted in Section 2b that these two men are individuals, not allegorical characters, but that Strader has a tendency towards 'ahrimanic' thinking, and Capesius has a tendency towards 'luciferic' attitudes. Since Ahriman and Lucifer remain onstage, the speeches of these two men will embody and attempt to typify the influence of these fallen spirits in fully human terms.

The unawareness of esoteric-spiritual realities prevailing in Capesius and Strader is indicated already in the deep bewilderment shown by them towards 'Spirit of the Elements'. The Ferryman is understood by Steiner to represent a spiritual being who incorporates 'incarnating' souls into the earthly world. He explains that indeed he is normally quite unknown to mortals, "Mich schaut die Menschenseele, erst wenn zu Ende ist der Dienst, den ich ihr leiste (the human soul beholds me only when services which I render to him are at their end)." In the first draft of the *Die Pforte* the 'Spirit of the Elements' (the Goethean Ferryman) was designated by Steiner as "Macrocosmos".[262]

As such, this being is a regent over hosts of nature spirits whose task as 'Nature's craftsmen' is to work at fashioning

---

[262] Entwürfe, Fragmente, 12.

the forms of corporeal bodies (of plants, animals and humans), and maintaining the life-energies which sustain earthly existence. This activity fashions the interconnecting link between the cosmos and humanity, a concept reflected in the stage directions for this scene. Every speech by the two men arouses intense anger amongst these beings, who remain unseen off stage, but after every speech by either of the two men a vehement display of lighting and thunder is required.

The two perplexed men, Capesius and Strader, whose intellectuality and haughty attitudes are so vehemently rejected by the nature of the elemental realm, are told by the Spirit of the Elements, in a slightly unusual, archaic syntax, "If you defeat me not, with your stunted weapons of thought, nothing are you more than a fleeting imaginary figment of your own delusion."[263] The phrase, 'a fleeting imaginary figment of your own delusion' here is a strong allusion to Steiner's concept of the everyday self as illusory, in a sense, in contrast to the truly real, higher self.

The admonitions of the Spirit of the Elements offer a potent stimulus to this developmental process, and would normally only be perceptible to the person who is achieving higher consciousness, "Myself the human soul beholds, only when to an end has come the service, which I do for it. And yet through all the cycles of time it obeys my powers."[264]

Thus in *Die Pforte* it is Johannes who indicates some comprehension of the words of The Spirit of the Elements, as he leaves his meditative state, the two men have not understood the dynamics in the spiritual realm at all. These two characters are representative of the Will-o-the Wisps, and the experiences they have with the Spirit of the Elements are representative of the episode in Das Märchen, where the Will-o'-the-Wisps treat the ferryman with contempt.

---

[263] Pforte, 81, „Bezwingst du mich mit deinen stumpfen Denkerwaffen nicht, bist mehr du nicht als flüchtig Truggebild des eignen Wahnes nur. "
[264] Pforte, 79, „Mich schaut die Menschenseele, erst wenn zu Ende ist der Dienst, den ich ihr leiste. Doch folgt sie meinen Mächten durch all Zeitenläufe. "

Similarly, to Capesius and Strader, as representatives of the everyday, non-illumined self-awareness, his words are meaningless, and eventually he vanishes from their perception, as it becomes clear that they will not respond to his advice.

The Wisps were astonished to be told by the Ferryman that they must render a service to the ferryman, if they wanted to achieve the goal of finding the Fair Lily. The Ferryman then extracts a promise from the Will-o'-the-Wisps that the Old Woman is to pay their debt, by bringing him 'three fruits of the Earth'. Then he leaves them to their further journeying, it is clear that they cannot comprehend his admonitions.

In *Die Pforte*, the Ferryman – as the Spirit of the Elements – does not demand the three specific tributes of the Goethean tale, but rather, he makes it clear that some form of compensation is required, "The world is ordered so, that work undertaken demands a service in return. I have given you your self, you owe me due reward." [265] To the two men, unable to understand the dynamic involved, the concept is totally foreign; they point to their intellectual powers as something which justifies their existence, and hence should satisfy the Ferryman. As representative of the abstract, non-holistic view of life, their attitudes are antagonistic to the spiritual realms. Similarly, the gold pieces of the Will-o'-the-Wisps are most unwelcome to the Ferryman, indeed, he says the gold pieces would enrage the river should they fall into it. In *Die Pforte* this episode is paralleled by the anger aroused in the elemental sphere, which manifests as thunder and lightning.

This scene has a challenging feature to it, in that the two men declare their noblest aspirations and ideals, only to have them vehemently rejected. Strader says, "I have stood amidst the storms of life for many years. People believe what I entrust to

---

[265] Pforte, 82, „Es ist die Welt geordnet so, Daß Leistung stets verlangt die Gegenleistung. Ich habe euch das Selbst gegeben; Ihr schuldet mir den Lohn."

them from my deepest sense of truth." Then Capesius declares that "I will create out of my soul the spiritual counterpart of things. And when nature, to ideals transfigured, arises in human deeds, then is nature sufficiently rewarded in being truly mirrored." [266]

After both of these speeches, the elements break out in angry thunder and lightning – the living elemental realm rejects their words. This is a puzzling episode, as their sentiments appear to be quite ethical, however, its didactic purpose is indicated in the next speech by Capesius. The Spirit of the Elements points out to Capesius and Strader just how antagonized the elemental forces are by their words, "You could behold how little your bold words are worth within my realm. For they unfetter storms and rouse the elements in wrath to rage against all order."[267] To this Capesius responds, unconcerned, saying that for humans the creative activity itself is reward enough, "The bird's song pouring from its throat is in itself enough. And likewise it is reward for man when he, creating, finds bliss in his activity." [268]

The first sentence in the above passage is in fact a quote from Goethe, a verse sung by an old man in *Wilhelm Meisters Lehrjahre*. Whereas we would normally think of such a sentiment as truly poetic, to Steiner it is a passage in Goethe's writings where he finds an antithetical perspective to his own. It is placed in Capesius' speech, to represent an abstract, theoretical attitude, directly opposed to the spiritual view which Steiner sought to communicate. The Goethean

---

[266] Pforte, 80, 82, Strader: „Ich habe viele Jahre lang im Lebenssturm gestanden. Man glaubt mir, was aus tiefsten (sic!) Wahrheitssinn ich Menschen anvertraut.
Capesius: Ich will aus meiner Seele schaffen der Dinge geistig Ebenbild. Und wenn Natur, zu Idealen verklärt, ersteht in Menschenwerken, ist sie belohnt genug durch ihre echte Spiegelung."

[267] Pforte, 82, „Ihr könntet sehen, wie wenig eure kühnen Worte in meinem Reiche gelten. Den Sturm entfesseln sie, und Elemente rufen sie zu aller Ordnung Gegnern auf."

[268] Pforte, 83, „Es ist des Vogels Lied, das aus der Kehle dringt, sich selbst genug. Und so ist Lohn dem Menschen auch, wenn schaffend er im Wirken Seligkeit erlebt.

verse which Capesius is quoting is, "I sing, like the bird which dwells in the branches. The song which pours from the throat, is a reward, which richly rewards..."[269] Thirteen years after the composition of *The Portal*, Steiner comments on this concept in a lecture on spiritual ecology, concerning the inner dynamics of the season of summer.

It is quite striking to find this Goethe quote inserted here, in a Steiner text which itself is inspired by Goethe's greatness, as an example of a luciferic-ahrimanic attitude. But in fact, it is the case that in this scene, it is not only this Goethean verse which is rejected by the spirits, but also those fine idealistic words of the two men, quoted above. The reason such beautiful poetry is so strongly rejected is embedded in the esoteric aspects of Steiner's anthroposophical worldview. Steiner rejects the passage about the birds' song emphatically, even though it is a Goethean passage, saying,

> The bird would never say, 'The song which pours from its throat is a reward, which richly rewards'. And just as little would the students of the ancient Mysteries have said it. For when in a certain season the larks, the nightingales sing, then what is formed in this activity pushes out into the cosmos, not through the air, but through the etheric element, up to a specific boundary. Then it vibrates back to the Earth, and then the animal world receives this which has vibrated back. But now it has united itself with the being-ness of the divine-spiritual element of the cosmos....The larks send their song out into the world. Then the divine-spiritual element, which participates in the forming, in the overall moulding, of the animal kingdom, again streams back to the Earth on the waves of that which flows back from the out-flowing songs of the larks and nightingales.[270]

---

[269] HA Bd. 7, 130, „ Ich singe, wie der Vogel singt, der in den Zweigen wohnet. Das Lied, das aus der Kehle dringt, ist Lohn, der reichlich lohnet..."
[270] Rudolf Steiner, Der Jahreskreislauf als Atmungsvorgang der Erde und die vier großen Festezeiten, (Dornach: RSV, 1980) 61-62, „Der Vogel selber würde es nämlich niemals sagen: „Das Lied, das aus der Kehle dringt, ist

It appears from this passage that to Steiner, his research into the spiritual aspect of the birds and their behaviour, reveals that in Goethe's image here is a projection of human attitudes onto the bird life. The birds are in Steiner's worldview, placed in a vital interaction with the elemental realm. In a very similar manner, when the two men speak of their ideals, they are rejected because in effect, their wisdom and ethics is only illusory; they may say the right thing, but their inner being is not at all able to fully embody it. As the list of characters makes clear, Capesius has a hidden luciferic quality, as his emotional life is not spiritualized, whilst Strader's intellectual life contains a hidden ahrimanic quality.

When the two men offer their rationalistic intellectuality, and when this is rejected, Capesius and Strader, like the Will-o'-the-Wisps, ignore the demand for compensation. The Spirit of the Elements sternly declares that this is not right, and that Felicia Balde must pay the debt. This woman is the parallel to the Old Woman, the wife of the Man with the Lamp, in Goethe's tale, where she is the foil to the actions of the two Will-o'-the-Wisps, their deeds directly affect her.

Steiner sees her as the memory of all that has been learnt and experienced in life, from which wisdom could possibly arise. In addition, she represents the memory of edifying religious principles. As Felicia Balde in *Die Pforte*, she represents core elements of the soul-life, specifically of Johannes. In the Goethean tale, three fruits of the Earth are demanded from

---

Lohn, der reichlich lohnet." Und ebensowenig hätten es die alten Mysterienschüler gesagt. Denn wenn in einer bestimmten Jahreszeit die Lerchen, die Nachtigallen singen, dann dringt das, was da gestaltet wird, nicht durch die Luft, aber durch das ätherische Element in den Kosmos hinaus, vibriert im Kosmos hinaus bis zu einer gewissen Grenze; dann vibriert es zurück auf die Erde, und dann empfängt die Tierwelt dieses, was da zurück-vibriert, nur hat sich dann mit ihm das Wesen des Göttlichen-Geistigen des Kosmos verbunden...Die Lerchen senden ihre Stimme hinaus in die Welt, und das Göttlich-Geistige, das an der Formung, an der ganzen Gestaltung des Tierischen teilnimmt, das strömt auf die Erde wiederum herein auf den Wellen dessen, was zurückströmt von den hinausströmenden Liedern der Lerchen und Nachtigallen."

the Will-o'-the-Wisps, whereas in *Die Pforte*, Felicia has to tell a fairy tale to the living milieu of the elemental realm.

This omission in *Die Pforte* of the triune element in Goethe's tale is significant, as normally Steiner seeks to emphasize this triune factor. However, this triune element is represented in Die Pforte in another way. The three women, Philia, Luna and Astrid are deeply involved in assisting the struggle of Johannes to attain to spiritual development. They have to make a specific effort, under the guidance of Maria, to help Johannes. The three hand-maidens to the fair Lily, and the three women, Philia, Astrid and Luna, represent the triune elements in the soul-life. These three are required to bring influences of a spiritual nature to bear upon the soul of Johannes, so that he may become fully spiritualized. The demands placed upon these three will be discussed later. Steiner sees the soul or consciousness as consisting of three specific elements, thinking, emotion and will. This is described in detail in his 'Theosophie', and is elaborated in many of his lectures.

In the Goethean tale, the Ferryman demands that his fare be paid not with pieces of gold which the Will-o'-the-Wisps so easily shake from themselves, but with *the fruits of the Earth*, namely, three cabbages, three artichokes and three large onions. The obvious interpretation of this demand is that the human being must offer the results of its earthly life to those powers which have given it life upon the Earth.

In his commentaries on the Goethean tale, Steiner points out that these three vegetables are in fact angiocarpous plants, that is, their edible portion is not part of the calyx. The calyx is in effect enveloped in several layers. Furthermore, one of these plants (the onion) is a root vegetable, another (the artichoke) is a flower vegetable, whilst the third (the cabbage) is a leaf vegetable. To Steiner this unusual stipulation by the Ferryman in the Goethe's tale corresponds very closely to his view of the human being, and of the goals of spiritual development.

In his *Theosophie*, the three faculties which require to be spiritualized, namely thinking, emotion and will, are viewed by Steiner as three sheaths or integuments surrounding the self, or ego. Hence the three angiocarpous vegetables stipulated by the Ferryman are thus a simile for the three consciousness strands around the ego of the human being. Furthermore, there is a correlation in Steiner's works of parts of the plant to aspects of human consciousness. Namely the roots have a symbiotic association with the thinking capacity, whereas leaves of the plant with the heart and lungs, and the flower with human volition. Steiner concludes that the dense mineral nature of the brain's composition stands in a symbiotic relationship with the root system of plant. Consequently any root vegetable has an association with the brain and with thinking. The onion, the root vegetable of the three plants stipulated by the Ferryman, is symbolic of the thinking capacity of the human being.

Whereas the leaves, which constitute the breathing organ of the plant, and which demonstrate a rhythmical quality in their form and in the pattern of emergence from the branch of the plant, have a similar connection to the lung and heart system in the human being. Consequently, the leafy vegetables become a symbol of the emotive life of the human being, since he views the emotions as interconnected with the heart and lungs. Finally, the flower of a vegetable is an integral part of its reproductive system, and this is an expression of the volition of the plant organism, namely the impulse to survival through propagation.[271] Therefore to Steiner the artichoke, as an edible vegetable flower, represents the will capacities of the human being.

Hence in Steiner's interpretation, the Ferryman, as the representative of the powers responsible for giving human beings access to life on Earth, as a conscious personality endowed with life-energies, is demanding compensation for

---

[271] Rudolf Steiner, Meditative Betrachtungen und Anleitungen zur Vertiefung der Heilkunst, (Dornach: VRSN,1967) 75-87.

providing this function. The compensation required is the spiritualizing of humanity's triune faculties of consciousness, thinking, emotion and will.

In Goethe's tale, the Will-o'-the-Wisps leave the Ferryman behind and set off to find the fair Lily, and soon encounter the Green Snake, who eagerly devours the gold which the Will-o'-the-Wisps dispense so freely. When she eats it, it causes her to become radiant. This radiance in turn allows her to see for the first time the four mysterious kings, deep in a hidden cavern. While she is there, a dialogue ensues between her and the kings. This is paralleled in two stages in *Die Pforte;* firstly in Scene Four of *Die Pforte*, in that Capesius and Strader, after their conversation with the Spirit of the Elements, encounter the Other Maria, who represents the Green Snake. Later, in Scene Five of *Die Pforte*, four hierophants who work in the Mysteries commence a discussion which parallels that of the four kings. This dialogue concerns the spiritualizing of the triune soul, enabling the triune spirit to become efficacious in Johannes.

In addition, there are other parallels between Goethe's Märchen and this scene in *Die Pforte*. After the discussion with the Spirit of the Elements, the two men are left briefly on their own, alienated from their environment. It is in this state that they encounter the Other Maria, who appears, "as if the rock itself had given birth to her", in like manner, the Green Snake dwells in the clefts amidst the rocks. Capesius and Strader, like the Green Snake, are also bewildered by her, asking themselves, "…welch sonderbares Wesen! …aus welchem Weltengrund erstehen solche Wesen? (What a strange being!…from what cosmic foundation do such beings arise?")

The name for this representative of the Green Snake in Steiner's drama, the 'Other Maria' is, as with the names of all the other characters, indicative of the dynamic she portrays. The dynamic which Johannes' close friend Maria embodies, is that of a soul which has developed spirituality, which is permeated by its empowered spiritual potential, hence the person has attained to wisdom, loving compassion and higher faculties. The Other Maria is in effect those qualities, but not yet individualized, not yet empowered, as she herself says, "You see in me only the humbler sister of that high being who dwells in that realm from which you have just come."[272]

The Other Maria's introduction of herself to the two men presents more clearly Steiner's understanding of those qualities which the Green Snake represents, and which as we noted earlier, he defined as 'a love for wisdom, and the ability to selflessly engage in life'. The Other Maria describes herself,

> I wrestle my way through rocky depths, and seek to clothe the rocks' own will in human words; I can detect the scent of earthly being-ness and I want to think the Earth's own thoughts in human heads. I sip pure living-air and transform powers of air into human feeling.[273]

The force of this speech is to ontologically equate the Other Maria with the Earth itself, since 'the will of the rocks' appears to designate the intention behind the creation of the physical Earth. So the Other Maria seeks to have consciousness of the Earth living in human consciousness. The reason for this can be more readily grasped by Steiner's elucidation of the meaning of the Green Snake. In the twelve lectures on the Goethean tale, Steiner refers to the Green Snake five times. Steiner sees this character as a deeply spiritual element residing within every human being, but more as a latent potential than an actuality. He says,

---

[272] Pforte, 86, „Ihr seht in mir die niedre Schwester nur des hohen Geisteswesens, das jenes Reich bewohnt, aus dem ihr eben kommt."
[273] Pforte, 85, „Ich ringe mich durch Felsengründe und will der Felsen eignen Willen in Menschenworte kleiden; ich wittre Erdenwesenheit und will der Erde eignes Denken im Menschenkopfe denken. Ich schlürfe reine Lebenslüfte und bilde Luftgewalten in Menschenfühlen um".

"The human soul-life encompasses a force by which is borne the development of the soul through to the state of the free personality. This force has its task on the way to this state. Once this is achieved, it loses its significance. It brings the soul into relation with the experiences of life. That which life and science manifest, it transforms into inner wisdom of life. It makes the soul ever more ripe for the spiritual goal towards which one is longing. Once this is achieved, it loses its significance as it represents the relationship of the human being to the external world. There this power has to undergo self-sacrifice, then in the transformed human being it has to continue to exist, within the other aspects of the soul-life, as a permeating ferment, without its own individual existence."[274]

Steiner saw Goethe's achievement of creating the *Das Märchen* as an exceptionally insightful stroke of genius. In five of his twelve lectures on this tale, Steiner quotes a Goethe aphorism which is closely allied to the character of the *Green Snake,* namely, "And so long as you don't have it, this dying and becoming, you are but a dreary guest upon the dark earth".[275] A clearer understanding of Steiner's view of the Green Snake is afforded in another of his commentaries on the Goethean tale, "The snake has always been the symbol of the self which does not remain in itself, but rather can

---

[274] Steiner, Goethes Geheime, 16, „Im Umfange des menschlichen Seelenlebens gibt es eine Kraft, von welcher die Entwickelung der Seele getragen wird zu dem Zustande der freien Persönlichkeit. Diese Kraft hat ihre Aufgabe auf dem *Wege* zu diesem Zustand. Wäre dieser erreicht, so verlöre sie ihre Bedeutung. Sie bringt die Menschenseele mit den Lebenserfahrungen in Zusammenhang. Sie verwandelt, was Wissenschaft und Leben offenbaren, in innere Lebensweisheit. Sie macht die Seele immer reifer für das ersehnte Geistesziel. An diesem verliert sie ihre Bedeutung, denn sie stellt das Verhältnis des Menschen zur Außenwelt her....Da muß diese Kraft sich aufopfern...sie muß als das übrige Seelenleben durchsetzendes Ferment ohne Eigenleben im verwandelten Menschen weiter leben."
[275] HA Bd. 2, 19, *West-östlicher Divan, Buch des Sängers,* „Und so lang du das nicht hast, diese Stirb und Werde, bis du nur ein trüber Gast auf der dunklen Erde." Steiner also quotes this in lectures on the Apocalypse of St. John.

selflessly take up into itself the divine; can sacrifice itself; humbly, selflessly, it gathers earthly wisdom, in that it crawls around in 'the chasms of the Earth'..."[276]

Since the Other Maria is the representative of the Green Snake, when she declares in the above speech that she "seeks to clothe the rocks' own will in human words" then it may also be the case that she endeavours to distil human understanding from the experiences of earthly life. She is the antithesis of the disdainful, proud intellectuality which is strewn all around, just as the two Will-o'-the-Wisps cast off their gold. This interpretation of the above speech by the Other Maria is strongly affirmed by his preliminary draft version of her speech, later discarded. In this she declares, "I am the rocks' own voice...and I ponder the thoughts of the Earth...and I form myself from its existence."[277] This draft version indicates that the 'will of the rocks' is the purpose of life within physical existence.

In Johannes this forming of oneself from earthly life, towards wisdom, is his challenge, so he has to examine his personality and life experiences in such a way that he grows wiser and thus nearer to the realm of the Idea. This perspective of engaging more meaningfully with life experiences, and thereby attaining to wisdom, is also inherent in the Other Maria's statement to Capesius and Strader that if she absorbs their words (intellectual attitudes) and then allows them to resound from her, then these bring her insights into life, "The way you speak is incomprehensible to me, but if I first allow your words to resound from my being, they spread out over all things which fill my environment and interpret their riddles." [278]

---

[276] Rudolf Steiner, Goethes Geheime, 96, „Die Schlange ist immer das Symbol gewesen für das Selbst, das nicht in sich bleibt, sondern in Selbstlosigkeit das Göttliche in sich aufnehmen kann, sich hinopfern kann; das demütig, selbstlos Erdenweisheit sammelt, indem es in den „Klüften der Erde" umherkriecht..."
[277] Steiner, Entwürfe 108, „...und bin der Felsen eigne Stimme...und sinne der Erde eignen Sinn...und bilde mich aus ihrem Sein."
[278] Pforte, 86, „So wie ihr selber sprecht, ist unverständlich meinem Ohr. Doch lasse ich erst eure Worte aus meinem Wesen anders tönen, verbreiten sie sich über alle Dinge, die meinen Umkreis füllen, und deuten ihre Rätsel."

The Other Maria's words here, that understanding of life speaks to her, once she lets the words of the two men resonate from within her, alludes strongly to the episode in Goethe's tale, where the Green Snake becomes luminous and can thereby see and understand her environment better, after eating the gold of the Will-o'-the-Wisps.

Steiner continues his elucidation in the lecture quoted above, concluding significantly that the capacity of the Green Snake to become radiant (after consuming the gold) is a metaphor of the capacity in the human being, to <u>become</u> the higher Self. From the above considerations, it emerges that this process happens only as the human being actually does absorb life experience, through humility and the commitment to the quest for spirituality. The action of the Green Snake, in building a bridge across the river, is the quintessence of this process.

Capesius and Strader ask for her advice as to how they can find a way to the source of wisdom, but find her answer unsatisfactory. Like the Will-o'-the-Wisps, Capesius and Strader feel themselves alien to her reality, Strader rejects her advice, "Das ist kein Weg für uns. Es heißt in unsrer Sprache Schwärmerei. (That is not a path for us. It is called 'fantasy' in our language.)" This dynamic affirms a primary theme in this scene, that normal everyday consciousness is incapable of finding a way to incorporate spiritual reality. Scene Four ends with Johannes expressing understanding of the preceding activity, which has been revealed to him in his meditating.

3f: Scene Five

Again, Johannes is in meditation, experiencing the content of the scene. The setting for this scene is a subterranean temple in which the hierophants of the Mysteries meet to carry out their spiritual work, and discuss their concerns with Felix Balde. In Goethe's tale, a parallel episode occurs, when the Green Snake decides, since she has now become luminous, to descend into a cavern wherein she had previously detected several statues – but only by the sense of touch. She can now see that these statues depict four kings, who presently become animated and dialogue with her; during this process the Old Man with the Lamp appears and facilitates the conversation.

Steiner sees the dialogue of the four kings as illustrative of the triune human spirit; we noted above (Section 2b) that to Steiner the human spirit is separate from the 'soul'. This triune spiritual element consists of the archetypal Idea from which thinking, emotion and will – as soul qualities – derive. In his teachings on personal development, Steiner emphasizes that the acolyte is to refine their emotive responses, overcoming tendencies towards instinctive, base desires and yearnings. To Steiner, the spiritualizing of the emotive responses, resulting in a person in whom personal desires are overcome, enables selfless dedication to greater purposes of life to be achieved. Secondly, the thinking life has to overcome what Steiner refers to as 'materialistic' or 'abstract' thinking, which rejects spiritual realities. These attitudes will regard thinking as derived from the body (brain) processes, and hence such spiritual concepts as pre-existence and repeated earth-lives as quite unfounded. In effect, to Steiner the spiritualizing of thinking – when undertaken in conjunction with the refinement of the emotive life – results in wisdom, a gradual attainment of understanding of deep spiritual truths.

Thirdly Steiner maintains that the volitional life needs to be refined, this results in releasing the will-forces from self-centred aims and personal ambitions, and aligning the volition to the greater good of the community. Hence in Steiner's model, the golden king is an image of the potential for wisdom, the silver king of compassion and purity of heart, whereas the brass king represents the attainment of selflessness in the will, thus allowing the intuitive cognitive faculty inhering therein to be accessed. In Goethe's tale, the dialogue between the Green Snake and the Gold King proceeds as follows,

Gold King: "Where do you come from?"
Green Snake: "From the crevices where the gold dwells."
Gold King: "What is more glorious than gold?"
Green Snake: "Light."
Gold King: "What is more animating than light?"
Green Snake: "Conversation."

In terms of Steiner's model, the above dialogue has the following interpretation. The gold king represents the spiritualized intellectual capacity that results in wisdom, as distinct from cleverness. The Green Snake has begun to be radiant with a golden light, and therefore has now some wisdom, and consequently a communion between the personality and its spiritual potential can commence. The acolyte is now aware that it is in a realm or state of darkness, but, vitally, in this earthly realm the impetus to wisdom can be found.

Similarly, the Green Snake is also aware that the wisdom does not have its locus in the earthly sphere; it is really within the spiritual light. The third question, "What is more animating than light?" has also been rendered simply as "What is more refreshing than light?"[279] But in terms of Steiner's interpretative model, the term 'animating' (or 'quickening' in older English) is more appropriate. This is because in his commentary on this tale, he argues that the 'conversation' referred to here is that which occurs between divine beings in realms of light.[280] The model is then internally consistent, as the communion of the creator beings generates and sustains the light, which in turn becomes wisdom in human beings.

---

[279] „Was ist erquicklicher als Licht? fragte jener. "Das Gespräch," antwortete sie." The Fairy Tale of the Green Snake and the Beautiful Lily, transl. Thomas Carlyle, (New York: Steiner Books, 1979) 16, "What is more refreshing than light"? inquired the king. "Speech," answered she. Goethe HA, Bd. 6, S. 215.
[280] Rudolf Steiner, Lecture 28th Dec 1905; unpublished, archive manuscript.

At this point in the Goethean tale, the Old Man with the Lamp appears and facilitates the dialogue on behalf of the snake. Steiner maintains that he represents a wise person who gives guidance to the questing acolyte, and is represented in *The Portal* by Felix Balde. A very important episode now unfolds, when the Green Snake announces that she knows the "manifest secret"; it becomes clear later that this means that she has realized her need to undertake an act of self-sacrifice. As we noted earlier, in Steiner's model, it is precisely this dynamic of selflessly absorbing the higher spiritual qualities, by letting go of egocentric tendencies, that makes the spiritualizing process possible.

In parallel to this, in *Die Pforte,* four hierophants are gathered to discuss the spiritual progress of Johannes, and Benedictus makes it clear that Johannes has undergone the painful trials which are inevitable if the initiation is to be successful, "He has passed through the trials of suffering and in bitter pain of soul, he has prepared the ground for consecration, which shall grant him knowledge."[281]

Then the hierophant of love, the equivalent to the silver king, declares that, "Let warmth flow into his heart. He shall realize how he draws near to the Spirit of the Cosmos through sacrificing the illusion of his self-bound life…this love will give him the power to feel himself as spirit..."[282] Then Romanus, described in the list of characters as 'the spirit of initiative', declares that, in the name of cosmic Will, the power which Johannes now has, through the efficacy of the preceding hierophants, shall indeed serve to ensure that he can transcend space and time and enter into the spheres of the divine-spiritual creator gods. After this speech Retardus speaks, he is obviously a representative of the negative

---

[281] Pforte, 89, „Er ist geschritten durch die Leidensproben und hat in bittrer Seelennot den Grund gelegt zur Weihe, die ihm Erkenntnis geben soll." Again here are similarities to Mozart's opera, The Magic Flute.

[282] Pforte, 90, „Es fließe Wärme in sein Herz. Er soll begreifen, wie er dem Weltengeist sich naht durch Opferung des Wahnes seiner Eigenheit….Die Liebe wird die Kraft ihm geben, sich selbst als Geist zu fühlen."

powers (Lucifer and Ahriman) who seek to hinder such a spiritual development.

He declares that there has been no sign given by the Earth that such a consecration is needed, and therefore he may continue his appointed task of preventing this happening, "I am holding back therefore your spiritual light in this temple, so that it does not cause harm instead of healing through unprepared souls encountering it."[283] However the others insist that his attitude is wrong, and that Johannes can indeed take a further step on the quest for the spirit. Retardus is the equivalent of the Mixed King in Goethe's tale, who objects to the declaration from the Old Man with the Lamp that his power over the Youth will soon be lost.

The dynamic expressed in these speeches concerning Retardus illustrates Steiner's view, noted earlier, that the evil powers – Lucifer and Ahriman – have a certain cosmic justification. Steiner defines the mixed king (Retardus) as, "The capacity of thought, which is still clouded by the sense impressions, the fire of the soul which is not unfolded in love, but lives in desires and instinctive urges, and the chaotic will of the human being…"[284]

The scene ends as Johannes emerges from his meditation and confirms the events in this scene.

---

[283] Pforte, 92, „Ich halte euer Geisteslicht deshalb zurück in diesem Tempel, auf dass nicht Schaden statt Heil es bringe, wenn es die Seelen unreif trifft."
[284] Steiner, Ursprung 98, „Die Denkkraft die noch von den Sinneseindrücken getrübt ist, das Feuer der Seele, die nicht Liebe entfaltet, sondern in Begierden und im Trüben lebt, der ungeordnete Wille des Menschen..."

3g: Scene Six

Scene Six is a brief scene which concerns the debt to the Spirit of the Elements that Felicia Balde has had to take up on behalf of Capesius and Strader. This had been introduced as a demand on Felicia in Scene Four; we have noted above in connection with Scene Five that the debt in its fuller implication concerns the triune consciousness dynamics (or 'soul') of the human being. These need to be transformed into the spiritual equivalent. However, in terms of parallelism to the Goethean tale, Felicia is that character whom, as the representative of The Old Woman, has to carry out some form of remuneration.

Further, just as in Goethe's tale, the repayment of the debt by the Old Woman is unexpectedly impaired by the malignant Giant, so too in *Die Pforte* Gairman, unexpectedly impairs, in terms of social etiquette, Felicia's act, by mocking it. As the representation of the Giant, he represents unwholesome psychic tendencies and generally atavistic tendencies. This scene ends with Johannes noting that Gairman "was that man who said that spirit light had entered as if of its own decision into his brain."[285] The didactic direction of the rhetoric here is clear, this sentence expresses succinctly Steiner's view of spiritualism, and other atavistic psychic powers, namely that they are not the product of conscious effort by the human self, and hence are an 'unfree' condition.[286]

If spiritual insights occur spontaneously, and not as the result of strenuous inner development, then in Steiner's system of spiritual development, this is an unwholesome atavism. Secondly, such insights are only cognized when they are registered by the brain, hence they are by Steiner's definition, not transcendent, since they are not perceived directly in the life-force organism.

---

[285] Pforte, 104, „Dies war der Mann, der von sich sagte, das Geisteslicht sei wie von selber in sein Gehirn gedrungen. "
[286] Rudolf Steiner, <u>Goethes Geheime</u>, 113.

3h: Scene Seven

Scene Seven commences with a speech by Maria calling upon Philia, Astrid and Luna to contribute to the task which she has undertaken. It is in this scene that these three have to undertake their work to spiritualize Johannes' soul; so in terms of Das Märchen, they must bring forth the three fruits of the Earth. Their task is to quicken Johannes' consciousness, so that he does really attain to spiritual enlightenment. The following episode involves the ether energies that we noted earlier, in connection with Goethe's Proteus. Steiner describes the realm of the ethers as being composed of four distinct kinds of energies.[287] These four distinct modes of ether energy are referred to here, without any elucidatory comments.

In this scene, Maria affirms that the three soul forces have so often been her helpers, and are needed again now to help her effect changes in these ethers, and that these in turn may influence the soul of Johannes,

> Be this for me in this hour too, in which I may make the cosmic-ether resound within itself. It shall resound harmoniously, and resounding, permeate a soul with cognition…Johannes, in his striving, shall be raised through our creativity to true existence.[288]

Maria requires that Astrid carries out an action for her, these actions are to assist in the development of higher, spiritual consciousness. As we saw in Section 2a, Astrid is to "create the power of darkness in the flowing light, so that it may shine in colours, and member tonal being-ness so that cosmic substance, weaving, may live, resonating." At first, this appears to be entirely metaphorical, a poetic dialogue

---

[287] Rudolf Steiner, Das Evangelium Lukas, lect. 7, (Dornach: RSV, 1985)
[288] Pforte,106, „Seid mir es auch in dieser Stunde, dass ich den Weltenäther in sich erbeben lasse. Er soll harmonisch klingen und klingend eine Seele durchdringen mit Erkenntnis…Johannes der Strebende, er soll durch unser Schaffen zum wahren Sein erhoben werden."

between the self and an aspect of the soul. But instead, Steiner is intending to communicate that the soul's own intelligence is able to exert an efficacy in the realm of the ethers, or subtle life-forces.[289]

One such action is to bring about the emergence of colour from light, by exerting an influence upon what Steiner refers to as the 'light-ether', one of the four ethers. It is from this ether that light-phenomena arise. He regards colour as emerging from the light in response to subtle influences, that is, an etheric force.[290] Secondly, he views sound as emerging from a specific ether energy-field also, which he designates as the tone-ether.[291] Hence Astrid is to exert an efficacy upon this specific energy-field to bring about the desired 'membering', or integrating, of cosmic ether into this ether, so it may live within it, and bring forth ethereal sounds.

The implication here appears to be when higher consciousness unfolds, the person sees spiritual visions or inwardly hears subtle spiritual truths resonating, but for this to occur, the ether energies have to be prepared in advance for these phenomena to occur. In these words, Steiner is expressing an important element in his view of consciousness, namely the soul (hence its three stands, thinking, emotion and will) can exert an influence upon the realm of the ethers. Furthermore, these in turn, can have an influence upon the individual's ether-body.[292] Accordingly, in this scene, Maria requests Philia to "breathe in the light's lucid nature from far-extending space", and Astrid to "engender the power of darkness in the flowing light, that colours may glow". Through these processes, Maria says that she will be able "to entrust feeling of the spiritual to seeking human senses". Maria then asks Luna representing the third element, volition, to "unite the copy of your own individual

---

[289] Rudolf Steiner, Die Geheimnisse der Biblischen Schöpfungsgeschichte, (Dornach: RSV, 1976)
[290] Rudolf Steiner, Welche Bedeutung hat die okkulte Entwickelung des Menschen für seine Hüllen, (Dornach: RSV, 1986)
[291] Rudolf Steiner, Das Lukas Evangelium, (Dornach: RSV, 1985)
[292] Rudolf Steiner, Lukas Evangelium, Lect. 7

being to the gifts of her sisters, so that certainty of knowledge may be granted to the soul-seeker."

When further dialogue between these three soul-forces and Maria concerning the details of their working together, is over, Maria declares herself satisfied that the special intention of this focussed activity will enable Johannes' consciousness to properly function in the realm of archetypal realities, and that this event is about to happen; "With you, my sisters, united for this noble work, I shall succeed in what I yearn to do. The call of the severely tested man penetrates into our realm of light."[293] This entire section of Scene Seven represents the episode in Goethe's tale, where the three handmaidens are called in to actively assist in the process of helping the Youth with his difficulties in uniting with the fair Lily.

Johannes then appears and confirms to Maria, that he has indeed attained to the exalted state wherein his consciousness functions in the archetypal realm, "I felt myself released from fetters of sense. My gaze was freed from those limits imposed upon it by the present…and clarifying light of discernment shone forth in my new world."[294] Soon after this the seeress Theodora appears, and makes another revelation. She speaks of seeing Johannes and Maria, as different individuals, in a past life. This episode forms the second main theme in Scene Seven, namely, that of repeated lives on Earth. Theodora proceeds to describe the reason for the feeling of attachment which Johannes feels for Maria. Maria at that time was a missionary, who sought to convert the tribes in the forests of central Europe from their worship of the gods of the Edda, to Christianity.

---

[293] Pforte, 107, „Du meine Philia, so sauge des Lichtes klares Wesen aus Raumes-weiten…und auch du, Astrid, erzeuge Dunkelkraft im fließend Licht, daß es in Farben scheine….So kann ich Geistesfühlen vertrauen suchendem Menschensinn….Und du, o starke Luna, vereine mit der Schwestern Gaben das Abbild deiner Eigenheit, daß Wissens Sicherheit dem Seelensucher werde."
[294] Pforte, 111, „Ich fühlte mich entronnen den Sinnesfesseln. Befreit ward mein Blick von jenen Schranken, die ihm die Gegenwart umschließen, und klärend Urteilslicht erstrahlte in meiner neuen Welt."

Johannes, she reveals, was at that earlier time a woman, in medieval Europe, and had encountered Maria – who was at that time a man. Johannes then formed a romantic attachment to this person, "The woman standing there before him falls at his feet. She feels herself transformed. A soul is praying to the human-god; a heart is given in love to the messenger of God." [295] Maria then urges Johannes to become fully conscious of this past dynamic. It is this encroachment of personal affection upon impersonal spiritual-religious issues which has created the problem in Johannes in this life, as he deals with the stress of Maria not reciprocating his yearnings.

Here Steiner adds a new element to Goethe's tale of the Green Snake, which emphasizes the concept of reincarnation, and the attendant concept of karma. The concept of reincarnation is very closely connected with the concept of a formative interlinking between lifetimes or karma, as the preceding life will have an influence upon the succeeding lifetime. In Europe in Steiner's context, the concept of repeated incarnations was part of Theosophical beliefs, and was inextricably intertwined with that of 'karma', which teaches that a person's abilities, and major experiences, are the outcome of his or her previous life on the Earth. This Society's teachings are not nihilistic or fatalistic, it place emphasis upon the individual's need to evolve ever further as a result of these life experiences, rather than seeking to escape from the Earth into Nirvana.[296]

The Theosophical Society was a major vessel for the popularisation of this concept in Europe and elsewhere. Steiner, as the General Secretary of its German branch, held views on the general definition of karma which were

---

[295] Pfort,; 114, „Das Weib, das vor dem Manne steht, es fällt zu dessen Füßen; verwandelt fühlt es sich. Es betet eine Seele zu dem Menschengotte; es liebt ein Herz den Gottesboten."

[296] Helena Petrovna Blavatsky, Theosophical Glossary, "*Karma*" (London: Theosophical Publishing Co, 1892) 161-162, "Karma, the law of Ethical Causation...when Buddhism teaches that ....the moral kernel alone survives death and continues in transmigration, it simply means that.... only that which is immortal in its very nature and divine in essence, namely the ego, can exist forever."

generally compatible with this Society. This view of karma advocated an active striving with the negative qualities in the soul-life, inherited from a past life, in order to move further ahead in one's spiritual status. Steiner's approach is to maintain that acceptance of karma is conducive to a positive attitude to life,

> Karma is a law without which life is not comprehensible to human beings. The law of karma is not simply a theoretical law or something which simply comforts our desire for knowledge. No, at every step it is something which gives energy to actions and confidence in our life, and which makes all that which is not comprehensible, comprehensible.[297] It is a great, mighty thought to also know that nothing is futile that one does, that everything has its efficacy on into the future. Thus this law does not have a depressive effect, rather it fills us with the most beautiful hope."[298]

However, on one major point, he was at odds with his Society. He integrated his esoteric viewpoint on Christianity into the concept of karma. As we have seen above, the past lives of Maria and Johannes were linked in medieval Europe, but the milieu in which their lives unfolded, and the link between them was forged, was one in which Christianity plays a major role. One of the characters was a Christian teacher.

Scene Seven concludes with powerful affirmative words from the spiritual teacher, Benedictus, who confirms that Johannes

---

[297] Rudolf Steiner, Vor dem Tore der Theosophie, (Dornach: RSV, 1978), „Karma...ist ein Gesetz, das dem Menschen das Leben eigentlich erst verständlich macht. Das Karma-gesetz ist nicht bloß ein theoretisches Gesetz oder etwas, was bloß unsere Wißbegierde befriedigt. Nein, auf Schritt und Tritt ist es für das Leben etwas, was Kraft zum Handeln und Sicherheit gibt, was alles Unverständliche verständlich macht."

[298] Rudolf Steiner, Die Theosophie des Rosenkreutzers, (Dornach: RSV, 1979) 78, „Es ist ein großer, gewaltiger Gedanke, zu wissen, daß, was man auch tut, nichts vergeblich ist, daß alles seine Wirkung, in die Zukunft hinein hat. So wirkt das Gesetz nicht bedrückend, sondern es erfüllt uns mit schönster Hoffnung."

has now attained, at least in a preliminary form, the ability to function within the realm of spirit, (the Platonic realm of Ideas). His success is due to his ability to now work in soul-unison, with Maria,

> ...Destiny has united you, to unfold together the forces which are to serve good creative activity. And as you walk on the soul's path, Wisdom itself will teach you that the highest things can be achieved when souls...unite to work in faithfulness for the well-being of the world.[299]

This scene overall proceeds in close parallel with the episode in Goethe's tale, where the beginning of the redemption of the Youth occurs. Through the intervention of the Old Man with the Lamp, with the help of the Hawk (represented by Theodora in *Die Pforte*), who summons him to help, the Prince is being prepared for his rebirth out of the coma into which he fell, after prematurely touching the Fair Lily. The three handmaidens of the Lily rally to help her, and they set off to enter the temple, wherein the Prince shall be restored to full consciousness, and in fact, he shall attain to union with the Lily. Similarly in Scene Seven, the three friends of Maria, Philia, Astrid and Luna specifically assist her, Theodora provides the illuminating the revelation of the past lives, and directly thereafter, Benedictus appears to counsel Johannes.

The above words of Benedictus parallel in Goethe's tale, the words of the Old Man, "We have come together at an auspicious hour; let each one perform his task, let each one do his duty, and a common happiness will dissolve within itself the grief of individuals, just as a common misfortune consumes individual joys." So the seventh scene – the final in the seven phases of evolutionary development – affirms that Johannes is on the verge of achieving the goal of his quest.

---

[299] Pforte, 119, „Es hat das Schicksal euch verbunden, vereint die Kräfte zu entfalten, die gutem Schaffen dienen müssen. Und wandelnd auf dem Seelenpfade, wird euch die Weisheit selber lehren, daß Höchstes kann geleistet werden, wenn Seelen...in Treue sich zum Weltenheile binden."

3i: The Interlude

In Section 3f, we noted that Steiner maintains that evolution proceeds within a process of seven vast evolutionary 'aeons', and each of these contain seven smaller phases or 'cycles'. Additionally, in Steiner's cosmology, each one of these seven great periods of evolution, and also each of the seven smaller phases, are followed by an interlude, a time of consolidation of what has been achieved before. Steiner designates this time of introverted non-manifestation in which the past achievements are consolidated, as a 'time of rest' (Ruhepause) [300] or by a theosophical term drawn from Sanskrit, and introduced into the Theosophical Society's terminus technic by Blavatsky, namely, a 'pralaya'.

After Scene Seven, the interlude, the introspective cosmic pause, a 'pralaya' period occurs, in which the past events are assimilated and gradually give rise to a new potential. Estella is enthusiastic about the exoteric drama, "*The disinherited of Body and Soul*", and the play-within-the-play is brought further to expression. The drama, which Estella has seen, has a plot that closely follows that of Johannes, up to a point. It follows the life of a young, idealistic artist, who ignores the pleading of his girl friend, because he has an infatuation with another woman, who was a patroness to him. When he hears the news of the death of this young woman, he is not particularly moved. As he finally realizes that his patroness will never enter into a relationship with him, he lives on as a broken, disillusioned man.

Sophie recounts the plot of the theosophical-anthroposophical play, which is in fact that of *Die Pforte* itself. Since in *Die Pforte* by contrast, Johannes has been able to overcome his conscience stricken state through the influence of his esoteric knowledge, the plot of Stella's play reflects the tragic implications of human endeavour, occurring outside an esoteric-spiritual social milieu. This extension of the technique of 'a play-within-the-play', demonstrates that the

---

[300] Steiner, Geheimwissenschaft.

difficult life circumstances of Johannes are alleviated through the possibility of an encounter with the spiritual, through the existence of anthroposophy. This fact reinforces the message that the esoteric life brings a welcome, indeed, essential, further element into human life. For in *Die Pforte,* the artist, Johannes, instead of stopping at a tragic event, is shown in later scenes as progressing on with the task of redeeming his actions by ennobling his personality.

Gradually as the difference in the two dramas become apparent, the two women argue about the virtue of art. In particular, Estella believes that art should follow precisely the fullness of human life, in the humanistic sense, she declares that art can only reach to its heights if it remains faithful to the whole of life. As we know from the Prelude, Estella's outlook is humanist in a general sense, so she is in effect excluding the efficacy of a spiritual element in human life. Sophie argues that this is precisely not the full validity of art, and uses as an example the art of painting, saying that the painter needs to instil in the artwork an element which transcends the given sensory appearance. The implication is that likewise, a drama should portray the spiritual context encompassing human interaction, and not take the humanist view. She argues, "To look at an imperfect rendering of the reality accessible to the senses must cause discomfort, whereas the imperfect portrayal of that which is hidden behind external observation can be a revelation." [301]

In these remarks of Sophie, and in the Interlude overall, two major and distinctive elements of Steiner's view of art – including dramatic art – is communicated. One is the underlying inference of the importance of art for his students; this inference becomes quite tangible in the next scene, where Johannes' painting becomes the topic of discussion. Secondly, there is the concept that it is inherent in artistic

---

[301] Pforte, 124, „Das Gewahrwerden einer unvollkommenen Wiedergabe der sinnenfälligen Wirklichkeit muss Unbehagen hervorrufen, während die unvollkommenste Darstellung dessen, was sich hinter der äußeren Beobachtung verbirgt, eine Offenbarung sein kann."

activity to reach beyond the sensory, and art is only fully successful when it achieves this.

There is an additional element in this dialogue, in so far as Sophia has been referring to paintings during her discussion to press home her point. Estella objects to her statement that 'An imperfect rendering of the reality accessible to the senses must cause discomfort', by saying that no (naturalist) artist would seek to merely duplicate a nature scene, but always try to instil an additional element to it. Stella has not perceived that Sophie's argument, whilst using paintings as illustrative, is equally applicable to drama. Sophie, in replying, does not try to enlighten her as to this applicability to drama. Instead, Sophie, in her response to Estella's objection speaks as if the referent of her response is restricted to paintings, saying, "This is just the weakness of many works of art – that the creative activity through itself leads beyond nature, and the artist does not know the appearance of that which the senses do not observe."[302]

3j: Scene Eight

The stage directions specify that the setting for this scene is the same as that of Scene One; the initial locus is repeated. This provides confirmation that the Interlude marks the division between the first seven scenes, which constitute a completed evolutionary cycle in cosmological perspective developed by Steiner – played out in miniature in human life – and the rest of the drama. A cycle has been completed and now the actors on 'the stage of life' step out again, now one cycle higher in their achievements – or at least Johannes has developed further. The characters in this scene are Johannes, Maria, Capesius and Strader, and the focus is on the now revived skills and enthusiasm of Johannes as an artist. Importantly, the audience is informed by Capesius that some

---

[302]Pforte, 125, „Darin liegt gerade die Unvollkommenheit vieler Kunstwerke, daß die schöpferische Betätigung durch sich selber über die Natur hinausführt, und daß der Künstler nicht weiß, wie das aussieht, was nicht in die sinnliche Beobachtung fällt."

three years have elapsed between scene seven and scene eight,

> This picture is truly a wonder to me, and yet a greater wonder to me is its creator. I can't compare the transformation which has occurred in you with anything, which men like me have until now considered possible....I first saw you three years ago, when I was privileged to come in contact with the group, in which you raised yourself to such heights....you were a deeply troubled man at that time.[303]

So, accordingly, in Scene Eight, Johannes has completed an important microcosmic cycle of development, and in his time of non-appearance or being secluded from the audience, he has assimilated the lessons from his experiences in the earlier scenes, and consequently has moved a step forward, and appears once more on the stage. This dynamic is directly paralleled in Steiner's cosmology, which maintains that the great evolutionary epochs are separated by times of rest, in which the primeval, developing human beings are <u>further consolidated</u>, ready to take the next step.

For example, with regard to the result of the first of these aeons (which he designates as the Saturn aeon), he writes that "as a result of the Saturn development it is shown that the germinal human being had developed itself up to certain level....Thus the germinal human being rests in the womb of the cosmos.....the germinal human being emerges from its hidden, secluded condition and begins through its own ability

---

[303] Pforte, 126, „Dies Bild ist mir ein Wunder wahrlich. Und ein noch größ'res ist mir sein Schöpfer. Die Wandlung, die in euch geschehn, es kann ihr nichts verglichen werden, was Menschen meiner Art bisher für möglich hielten....Ich sah zuerst euch für drei Jahren. Ich durfte damals jenen Kreis betreten, in welchem ihr zu eurer Höhe euch erhobet. Ein sorgvoller Mensch wart ihr zu jener Zeit."

to develop itself, from the forces which had been placed into it in Saturn."[304]

This same dynamic is to be found in theosophical cosmology. It is presented in an ancient poetic text published by Blavatsky in her Secret Doctrine, referred to as the stanzas of *The Dyzan*, which were viewed positively by Steiner.[305] The following few phrases from this text, which starts with the most recent pralaya, indicate its nature,

> "....Time was not, for it lay asleep in the infinite bosom of duration. Universal mind was not, for there were no 'Ah-hi' {hierarchies} to contain it. The seven ways to bliss were not...the seven sublime lords and the seven truths had ceased to be, and the universe, the son of necessity was immersed in paranispanna {complete absorption into non-manifested being}, to be out-breathed by that which is and yet is not....the seven sons were not yet born from the web of light..."[306]

This dynamic, of Johannes being on the verge of a new personal development, was inferred at the end of Scene Seven in the words of blessing by Benedictus, as we noted above. Now a new phase begins for Johannes, and, significantly, in another departure from the Goethean tale, it is in his <u>artwork</u> that Johannes' newly attained spiritual enlightenment is manifested to others. So the Interlude between these two scenes constitutes an incubating 'pralaya'.

The subject of the conversation between Estella and Sophie in the Interlude was in fact, the significance of art. It was

---

[304] <u>Geheimwissenschaft</u> 170,173, „Als Ergebnis der Saturnentwickelung erscheint, daß sich der Menschenkeim bis zu einer gewisse Stufe herangebildet hat. So ruht der Menschenkeim zu neuem Erwachen im Schoß der Welt....Der Menschenkeim tritt aus seiner Verborgenheit hervor und beginnt aus eigenem Vermögen heraus durch die Kräfte, die ihm auf dem Saturn eingeimpft worden sind, sich zu entwickeln."
[305] Rudolf Steiner, <u>Ursprungsimpuls der Geisteswissenschaft</u>, (Dornach: RSV, 1989) 52.
[306] H.P. Blavatsky, <u>The Secret Doctrine</u>, (Los Angeles, The Theosophy Company, 1925) 27-28.

Sophie's attitude that in artistic activity, one can give to the world what has not yet been set before the senses. It is where the powers of creation have left the world of matter unfinished that man can apply his creative striving. That this theme in the Interlude is dealt with in this way fulfils the parallelism between human and spiritual development in the cosmic evolutionary process. In the 'time of rest', the consolidation of the essential evolutionary ferment occurs, so that it can re-emerge and take a step further. Likewise, in that Estella and Sophie are discussing art, the artistic element is being brooded (in Johannes), and consequently emerges on a higher level.

Johannes has just completed a portrait of Capesius, who finds the image very stimulating, and affirms that his newfound ability derives from his higher spiritual consciousness,

> I often hear you say that you owe your power in art solely to the gift of consciously perceiving in other worlds, and that you can put nothing in your art which you have not first beheld in spirit. I see in your works, how the spirit efficaciously manifests itself.[307]

In a dialogue which then ensues between Capesius and Strader the precise sense of this 'spiritual inspiration' is given further definition, clarifying Steiner's teaching here. Strader objects that he has always understood that in every artist the spirit livingly expresses itself. To this, Capesius answers,

> I have never doubted that spirit shows itself as efficacious in the human being; but the person is usually unconscious of the spirit's being; he creates from the spirit, but does not understand it. Thomasius

---

[307] Pforte, 128, „Ich höre oft euch wiederholen, daß ihr die Künstlerschaft allein der Gabe dankt, bewußt in andren Welten zu empfinden, daß ihr nichts in eure Werke legen könnt, was ihr nicht erst im Geist erschaut. Ich seh' an euren Werken, wie der Geist sich wirksam offenbart."

however creates within the world of sense, that which he can consciously observe.[308]

In Scene One, there is a departure from the dynamics in the Goethean tale, by the insertion of Theodora's visionary experience, from which she announces the imminent Second Coming. As we noted earlier, this departure reflects the significance of this event in Steiner's worldview. In the above dialogue about Johannes' painting, there is another instance of a major departure from the dynamics of Goethe's tale. The motivation for this derives from the significance which Steiner places on art as such.

As we noted earlier, when the international Theosophical Society, decided to hold its conference in Munich in 1907, Steiner as General Secretary, was responsible for planning it. Steiner incorporated an extensive program of artistic events, and consequently wrote a text for the program sheet, explaining the significance of art, from his point of view. Part of this program text reads,

> Yet, it would nevertheless be desirable, if even in only a humble way, if it could be shown for once how the theosophical worldview is in a condition to quicken the artistic life. The important thing with all of these conferences will be, to bring to expression the fact that Theosophy does not have to remain only a sum of theoretical viewpoints, but is able to experience the transformation {of itself} into the something clearly perceptible to the senses and which speaks to the feelings. In these ways, it should have a fructifying influence on the rest of the culture.[309]

---

[308] Pforte, 128, „Ich habe nie bezweifelt, daß Geist im Menschen wirksam sich erzeigt; doch bleibt ihm sonst des Geistes Wesen unbewußt. Er schafft aus einem Geiste, doch er versteht ihn nicht. Thomasius jedoch erschafft im Sinnensein was er bewußt im Geiste schauen kann."

[309] Rudolf Steiner, Der Münchner Kongreß Pfingsten 1907 (Dornach: RSV, 1977) Das Kongreß-Programm, 25, „Doch wäre es immerhin wünschenswert, daß, wenn auch nur in bescheidenem Rahmen, einmal gezeigt werden könnte, wie die theosophische Weltauffassung das Künstlerische zu beleben imstande ist. Das Maßgebende bei allen diesen Veranstaltungen wird sein, zum Ausdruck zu bringen, daß die Theosophie nicht nur eine Summe von

In addition to this, Steiner placed great value on art because he saw it as an experience which, involving as it does, the sensory organs, it had direct influence upon the ether-body. As we have noted, the ether-body is regarded by him as the vessel to sense stimuli. This in turn has a direct relevance to his attitude that spiritual development should not be limited to consciousness, defined only as the three strands of thinking, emotion and will. The spiritualizing of the ether-body or life-forces is also important to him. According to Steiner, when the triune soul is spiritualized, attaining to compassionate wisdom, this is not yet the end of the quest for spirituality. Although spirituality is the quintessence of what is generally regarded as the definition of high ethical development, Steiner includes a second element.[310] He sees this as represented by the Silver King in Goethe's tale, and by Theodosius in *Die Porte*.

This second element, attainable fully only after the first has been developed, derives from the spiritualizing of the life-force organism, or ether-body. Whereas he refers to the spiritualized soul-body as "Spirit-Self", he refers to the spiritualized ether-body as "Life-Spirit". Once this faculty is developed, then compassion is endowed with an additional capability, its inherently passive nature attains to a capacity for potent activity, wherein healing powers and 'miraculous' capabilities emerge. He describes this second element of the triune human spirit as a transformed ether-body, which is the power behind procreation, cell-regeneration, and also sensory and spiritual perception, "If you think of the usual creative power in the customary sense-life, united to love, but not a receiving love, but to an utterly giving love; this is Buddhi {Life-Spirit}."[311]

---

theoretischen Anschauungen bleiben muß, sondern die Umwandlung in das Sinnlich-Anschauliche und stimmungsgemäß Wahrnehmbare erfahren kann. Auf diesem Wege muß sie ja befruchtend auf die übrige Kultur wirken."

[310] Steiner, Theosophie, *Der Geistige Wesen des Menschen.*
[311] Rudolf Steiner, Die Welträsel und die Anthroposophie, (Dornach: VRSN, 1966) 289, „Wenn Sie die gewöhnliche produktive Kraft im gewöhnlichen sinnlichen Leben vorstellen, gepaart mit Liebe, aber nicht als empfangende Liebe, sondern als eine ganze und gar gebende Liebe: das ist Buddhi."

In essence, Steiner is conveying his conclusion here that this (second) aspect of the human spirit enables a spiritualized soul, who has achieved active selfless compassion, and artistic sensitivity, to become empowered in their creative intentions with the full potential of the ether-body. This bestows a remarkable creative power upon the person, because they can now access the creative force implicit in the ethers. We noted this element of Steiner's philosophy in Section 1B2 in connection with Goethe's "idea" of a primal plant; this idea being to Steiner a reality in the realm of Ideas. We also considered there the Goethean 'Proteus'. To Steiner this refers to the ether-forces which are the invisible forces responsible for the metamorphosis of plants.

The term 'Buddhi' is a Theosophical word which he equated with his own term, 'life-spirit'. The life-spirit as a part of the extended Steiner view of the human spirit, also needs to be developed by Johannes. In various lectures, Steiner explained to his audiences that it is precisely artistic creativity that encourages the development of the life-spirit,

> "But we can raise ourselves to another condition of consciousness than simply that which reproduces the experiences of our intelligence...There are certain conditions of a creative activity, where the human spirit becomes a creator, and can create something new, something never seen before. Such an instance is that of the soul-condition of the sculptor in the moment of conception, where he sees before his spirit in a sudden flash, the form of a statue, the like of which he has never seen before, but which he creates. Of such kind is also the soul-condition of a poet, whom in one draft, in one creative vision of his spirit, conceives a work."[312]

---

[312] Rudolf Steiner, Kosmogonie, (Dornach: RSV, 1970) 91, „Aber wir können uns zu einer anderen Bewußtseinsstufe erheben als diejenige ist, die nur die Verstandeserfahrungen reproduziert. Es gibt gewisse Zustände einer schöpferischen Aktivität, wo der menschliche Geist zum Schöpfer wird und Neues, noch niemals Gesehenes schaffen kann. Solcherart ist zum Beispiel der Seelenzustand des Bildhauers im Moment der Konzeption, wo er blitzartig vor seinem Geist die Form einer Statue sieht, deren Vorbild er

To experience through a higher faculty, if only for a moment, the essence of a new work of art is, for Steiner, a specific form of higher consciousness, wherein access to 'thought-forms', existent in Devachan, is attained. In *Die Pforte*, this creative power which results in an artwork, is shown as efficacious on participants, not just the artist, Johannes, himself. As the characters are discussing the portrait of Capesius, Strader, who is a technician, and the least inclined to spiritual development, becomes quite agitated,

> And these forms, which seem to be the colours' work, they speak about the weaving of the spirit; they speak of much which they themselves are not. Where can that be, of which they speak? It cannot be upon the canvas, for here are pigments, devoid of spirit. Then in Capesius? But why can I not see it in him?...This canvas – I would like to break it through, to find what I am seeking..." [313]

This incident becomes a decisive one for Strader, who is consequently impelled into an inner turmoil, it has the effect of accelerating his interest in esoteric enlightenment, a theme explored in Steiner's second Drama, *Die Prüfung der Seele*, (*The Testing of the Soul*). The underlying esoteric development process involved here, in which the Life-Spirit is seen as one of three aspects of the true self, is expressed by Maria, "In order to find oneself one has first to unfold the power which can penetrate into one's own being. The wise

---

niemals gesehen hat, sondern die er erschafft. Solcherart ist auch der Seelenzustand des Dichters, der in einem Entwurf, in einer schöpferischen Vision seines Geistes ein Werk konzipiert."

[313] Pforte, 130, „Und diese Formen, die als der Farbe Werk erscheinen, sie sprechen von dem Geistesweben, von vielem sprechen sie, was sie nicht selber sind. Wo ist, wovon sie sprechen? Nicht auf der Leinwand kann es sein; denn da sind geistentblößte Farben. So ist es in Capesius? Warum kann ich es nicht an ihm erschauen? ...Die Leinwand, ich möchte sie durchstoßen, zu finden, was ich suchen soll."

maxim says so truly, 'Develop yourself, to be able to behold your self.'"[314]

A further element in the structure of Die Pforte which reflects the cosmological worldview of Steiner is to be noted here. The first seven scenes are substantially larger than scenes 8 to 11; in total they occupy some 100 pages, averaging 14 pages per scene. The remaining scenes occupy only 25 pages, averaging only 6 pages each. In Steiner's worldview, the septenary phases are distinctly manifested in human life, every seven years a new element of the soul-life become efficacious. However, after the seventh phase, at age 63, this process fades away, there are no further manifestations of these seven year phases of life, as the past consists only of seven phases, not a higher number. The remaining years build upon the preceding, without any especial septenary dynamic at work.

---

[314] Pforte, 132, „Man muss, um sich zu finden, die Kraft entfalten erst, die in das eigene Wesen dringen kann. In Wahrheit sagt das Weisheitwort; entwickle dich, um dich zu schaun.

3k: Scene Nine

In this brief scene Johannes has a soliloquy, speaking of his success in attaining to higher consciousness. He ascribes this to the efficacy of the Delphic maxim, "Know yourself", which has now become "experience yourself". Throughout this entire scene, this maxim resounds repeatedly, as if uttered by the environment itself. The stage directions specify that it is the same setting as in Scene Two, when the environment likewise resonated the maxim. This is another instance of the cycle of seven phases being completed. Obviously in this scene, it is now incumbent upon the playwright to clearly present the fruits of the meditative path to initiation, which so intensely admonishes the acolyte to achieve self-knowledge. The quest for this has brought painful tribulations to Johannes.

Consequently, Johannes' words here are of considerable significance. He declares that for three years "I have sought for the power of soul, that has wings of courage, which gives the truth to these words, through which the human being, who frees himself, conquers – and conquering himself, can find freedom." [315] In this remark of Johannes we again see clear allusions to Steiner's interpretation of Goethe's attitude to spirituality. In the poem, *Die Geheimnisse*, considered earlier with regard to the Rosicrucian movement, a work often quoted by Steiner, Goethe writes, "Von der Gewalt, die alle Wesen bindet, befreit der Mensch sich, der sich überwindet (From the power which binds all being, that person frees himself, who overcomes himself.)[316] There is also a maxim to this effect, in Wilhelm Meisters Wanderjahre, namely, "Alles, was unsern Geist befreit, ohne uns die Herrschaft über uns selbst zu geben, ist verderblich (Everything which frees our spirit, without giving us the mastery over ourselves, is pernicious.)" [317]

---

[315] Pforte, 135, „Ich habe sie drei Jahre lang gesucht, die mutbeschwingte Seelenkraft, die Wahrheit gibt dem Worte, durch das der Mensch, sich selbst befreiend, siegen und sich besiegend, Freiheit finden kann."
[316] HA, Bd.2, op. cit.
[317] HA, Bd. 12, S. 520, Maxim 1119.

In equating spirituality with freedom, this speech is directly expressive of a primary concept in Steiner's pre-anthroposophical, epistemological writings, especially *Die Philosophie der Freiheit*. In this text, which we considered in Section 1A2, freedom is that state wherein true ethics arises when it is perceived within one's inner being, deriving from the human spirit, and not drawn from any external source. Steiner's comments on the Delphic maxim, given in his opening address at an international college course on anthroposophy in 1921, reveal how significant these words of Johannes are to his anthroposophy,

> But to me it appears that today even such an apparently rock-solid magic saying, can only have a continued existence, in our times of great changes, if, taking up the energies of our times, it itself undergoes a transformation. And so it seems to me that the primeval Delphic word today must resound to people in this way; "Human being, cognize yourself and become a free being!"....Why did Greek wisdom inscribe on the temple at Delphi the significant word: Know thyself? There shone towards this Greek culture, from primeval times, which historically has its beginnings in the mists of time, a primordial and venerated wisdom and knowledge. The origins of this knowledge goes back to the dimness of pre-historical times....
>
> The Greek stood as if at the shores of the past, taking in the treasures of wisdom of the past, with all its contents. We – and I believe that every unprejudiced person can feel this – stand at another shore. We are standing on the shore of an uncertain future, but a future, which humanity, in regards to the spirit, must create by itself. And we feel that we need a maxim, in order to contemplate, with full power of our humanity, what can exert an influence over into the uncertain future as a creative reality from our inner being. On the shore of the past the Greeks created the

maxim; Know your self! – on the shore of an uncertain future, we must create the maxim; Become a free being !"[318]

Johannes continues, praising the effectiveness of the words in this maxim, in securing his newly attained spiritual consciousness. This speech contains some further instances of the neologisms to which Steiner has recourse when he attempts to describe supra-sensible processes. Such texts present a challenge to the translator, in the task of rendering them in English. In Steiner's view the various verse metres had important supplementary contributions to make to a spoken text, indeed these quite substantially supported the meaning of the text. To Steiner, the iambic metre is important in Die Pforte because it was the correct metre for texts which spoke of the spiritual, "If one wants to lead directly over to the spiritual....if one wants to lead from the physical into the spiritual, then one has to form the text in a soothing language style, in fact the iambic style...."[319]

---

[318] Rudolf Steiner, Die befruchtende Wirking der Anthroposophie auf der Fachwissenschaften, (Dornach: RSV, 1977) 10, „Mir scheint aber, daß selbst ein solches, wie es schien, felsenfest in der Menschheitsentwickelung drinnenstehendes Zauberwort heute, in unseren Zeiten der großen Verwandlungen, nur mehr Bestand haben kann, wenn es, aufnehmend die Kräfte unserer Zeit, selbst eine Art Verwandlung durchmacht. Und so scheint mir, daß das uralte Delphwort heute also zu den Menschen klingen müsse: Mensch erkenne dich selbst und werde ein freies Wesen!....Warum schrieb griechische Weisheit auf den Temple zu Delphi das bedeutungsvolle Wort: Erkenne dich selbst? Zu diesem Griechentum leuchtete herauf, aus uralten, historisch ihrem Anfange nach unbestimmbaren Zeiten, eine uralte geheiligte Weisheit und Wissenschaft. Die Ursprung dieser Wissenschaft gehen in das Dunkel der vorgeschichtlichen Zeiten zurück....Der Grieche stand wie am Ufer der Vergangenheit, hereinnehmend mit ihrem vollen Inhalt der Vergangeheit Weisheitsschätze. Wir - und ich glaube, jeder Unbefangene kann das fühlen - stehen an einem anderen Ufer. We stehen an dem Ufer einer unbestimmen Zukunft, aber einer Zukunft, welche die Menschheit in geistiger Beziehung selbst schaffen muß. Und wir fühlen, wir brauchen eine neues Wahrwort, um uns mit voller menschlicher Kraft zu besinnen auf das, was aus unserem Innern als Schaffendes hinüberwirken kann in die unbestimmte Zukunft. Am Ufer der Vergangheit richtete der Grieche das Wahrwort auf: Erkenne dich selbst! - am Ufer einer unbestimmten Zukunft müssen wir das Wahrwort aufrichten: Werde ein freies Wesen!"

[319] Rudolf Steiner, Sprachgestaltung und Dramatische Kunst, (Dornach: VRSN, 1969) 353, „Will man direkt zum Spirituellen hinüberleiten...will man vom Physischen ins Geistige hineinführen, dann muß man in einer sanftgestalteten Sprache gerade aber jambisch gestalten."

Johannes has attained to some spiritual enlightenment, and he describes with delight, the feeling of how a spiritual influence is being seen and heard in a subtle sense, from the words of the old Delphic maxim, "Know yourself!" The German text and the relevant passage in the Pusch version is,

I feel them sounding in my soul,
Ich fühle – wie es tönt in meiner Seele,
rousing themselves to give me strength.
Sich regend kraftverleihend.
There lives in me the light,
Es lebt in mir das Licht,
there speaks around me brightness,
Es spricht um mich die Helligkeit,
there germinates in me the light of soul,
Es keimt in mir das Seelenlicht,
there works in me world-radiance:
Es schafft in mir die Weltenhelle:

This translation reveals another difficulty in assessing Steiner texts in English, namely the tendency in English anthroposophical literature towards a stultifying adherence to qualities of the German, in this case its prosody and word order. Steiner used the iambic metre in poetic passages in Die Pforte, and a translator may attempt to retain the metrical characteristics of the original, as in Pusch version above. But in published Steiner texts, this can be done at the expense of the clarity of understanding. The experiences which Johannes is undergoing, as he responds to the Delphic maxim, are not so clearly communicated in this rendering.

In our consideration of Scene Five (Section 3g) we noted that this passage in Die Pforte is intended to parallel an episode in the Goethean tale where the Green Snake has become more radiant, and hence she can both see, and hear speech from the statues of the kings. A conversation ensues, wherein the Golden King asks the Green Snake, "What is grander than gold?" She replies, "Light." The king then asks, "What is more quickening than light"? To which she replies, "Conversation". We also noted that in his commentary on this tale, Steiner maintains that the 'conversation' referred to here is that which occurs between divine beings in realms of light.

We need to note that firstly, that in terms of Steiner's model, in so far as Johannes is attaining to such an experience, it is because the Green Snake is now efficacious within him; his increased selflessness and readiness to sacrifice his egocentric attitudes, has opened up the higher faculties. Secondly, Johannes is now having some form of perception of spiritually audible realities, which are within the light. This is a separate, distinct form of spiritual experience and is an allusion to the second stage of higher consciousness, in Steiner's model of spiritual development. Experiences at this higher stage are accompanied by, or rather permeated by, a symphonic sea of celestial sounds. He gives a description of this stage in a public lecture in 1904,

> "…then a moment arrives which comes all at once for each person who has brought their soul to tranquillity and calmness. This is the moment when within their own soul begins to speak, where their own inner being begins to perceive the great eternal truths. Then suddenly the world around is radiant with colours, which he has not seen before. Something becomes audible for the meditant, which he has never before heard resounding. The new light and the new splendour come to him from spiritland."[320]

On another occasion when describing the higher stages of spiritual consciousness Steiner compared the harmony which

---

[320] Rudolf Steiner, Ursprung und Ziel des Menschen, (Dornach: RSV, 1981) 197, „….dann kommt ein Moment, der für jeden einmal eintritt, der in seiner Seele Ruhe und Stille hat zur Entwickelung kommen lassen. Das ist der Moment, wo die eigene Seele zu sprechen beginnt, wo das eigene Innere die großen ewigen Wahrheiten zu schauen beginnt. Dann ist plötzlich die Welt um ihn herum erleuchtet von Farben, die er vorher nicht gesehen hat. Es wird für ihn etwas hörbar, was er früher niemals hat ertönen hören. Dieses neue Licht und dieser Glanz leuchtet ihm aus dem Geisterlande."

prevails in the movements of celestial bodies, and in the human pulse, to the inner tranquillity which this second stage brings about. He then contrasted these to the chaotic soul state of human beings generally, characterizing this soul state with imagery drawn from Goethe's fairy tale, "Make the attempt sometime to contemplate the regularity of your pulse and your breath, and compare this with the irregularity of the thinking, feeling and will. It's like being lead astray by Will-o'-the-Wisps."[321]

Johannes has now far outstripped the uncertainty and egocentricity of Capesius and Strader. This scene in Die Pforte has affinity to the episode in Das Märchen where the Snake encompasses the Youth, who is unconscious, by encircling him, and taking her tail into her mouth, forming the symbol prominent in Gnosticism.

In Section 1B4, we noted that Mommsen assimilates this episode into the overall role of the Green Snake, making her into a symbol of friendship, based on a text in a letter written by Goethe. In Steiner's model, this Gnostic image refers to a significant event in spiritual development; the attainment of a spiritual state of being, wherein the ether-body is imbued with divine influences. He calls this state the Life-Spirit condition.[322] He maintains that this state confers a consciousness of the eternal realms, echoing the accepted meaning of the Gnostic symbol as one which infers eternal consciousness. It also confers a form of spiritual hearing, not only a seeing into the realm of the Idea.

In view of these conclusions of Steiner, a rendering of the above words of Johannes, which gives a clearer indication as to the intention of this speech would perhaps be,

---

[321] Rudolf Steiner, Die Welträtsel und die Anthroposophie, (Dornach: VRSN, 1966) 240, „Versuchen Sie einmal, an Ihrem Geiste vorbeizuziehen zu lassen das Regelmäßige Ihres Pulses und Ihres Atems, und vergleichen Sie es mit der Unregelmäßigkeit des Denkens, Fühlens und Wollens. Es ist ein Irrlichtelieren."
[322] Steiner, Goethes Geheime, 304.

I feel – how it resounds in my soul:
stirring, it is bestowing strength.
Light lives in me,
the radiance all around me is speaking,
soul light is germinating in me,
cosmic radiance is creating in me.

In the above rendering the iambic metre used in the original has not been retained, but the meaning emerges more clearly. The locus of the dialogue is a spiritual one, as the episode is taking place on a higher level of consciousness. Johannes can now experience this realm through the capacity of the Green Snake to be a bridging faculty across the River, that is, the barrier to the realm of the Idea.

We noted earlier (Section 2) that this scene ends with an allusion to the Platonic realm of Ideas, in that Johannes declares that his consciousness has now attained to the spiritual origins of thinking. But there two further significant themes in the final part of this scene, expressive of Steiner's view of spiritual attainment. Firstly, Johannes declares that with his enhanced consciousness, he now perceives a lofty spirit being, in higher radiant realms, and the ability to elevate himself up to this being, "From radiant heights a being illumines me, I feel wings to raise myself to it….I want to become like it in future times. The spirit in me shall free itself through you, lofty goal. I want to follow you."[323] Secondly, it is immediately after this episode that Maria comes on stage, and explains that "My soul lead me here. I could see your star. It shines in its full power."[324] Johannes affirms that he can feel the power of the 'star' in himself.

The first theme, that of the 'being' whom Johannes perceives, and to whom in reverence he exclaims that he will become

---

[323] Pforte, 137, „Aus lichten Höhen leuchtet mir ein Wesen, Ich fühle Schwingen, zu ihm mich zu erheben….Ich will ihm gleich in Zukunftzeiten werden. Der Geist in mir wird sich befrei'n durch dich, erhabnes Ziel. Ich will dir folgen."
[324] Pforte; 138, „Mich trieb meiner Seele hierher. Ich konnte deinen Stern erschauen. Er strahlt in voller Kraft."

similar in future times, is considered tentatively by the two translators of published versions of Die Pforte, to be a reference to Jesus Christ. Consequently, one translator capitalizes 'being'; the other capitalizes both 'being' and 'him' without any footnotes or further commentary.[325] However it is quite possible that the 'being' whom Johannes perceives, and the 'star' seen by Maria, both refer to the same entity, namely the higher self or spirit of Johannes. It is my conclusion that this star-like entity which Johannes sees, is not a reference to Christ, but to what Steiner views as the spirit of a human being. This 'spirit' is also referred to by Steiner, following theosophical terminology, as the eternal 'causal body'. This does not contradict the matter we have noted earlier, namely that it is a central tenet of anthroposophy that Christ has an intimate link to the human spirit.

To examine this text further, it is necessary to bear in mind that the experience which Johannes is having, is attainable to both the initiated and to those who have died. For it is axiomatic in Steiner's worldview that the processes which occur after death, when the soul is released from the body, form a direct parallel which those which the person encounters who is undergoing high spiritual development. The initiated person in meditation, anticipates the future, extra-corporeal state of him or herself, so to speak,

> When the human being inwardly experiences the spirit-soul element in this way – when he is body-free and yet still retains a life, and has reached the condition of having his own corporeality as an object outside of himself, as if it were any other external object, then he will come to an understanding as to why spiritual researchers of all ages have closely

---

[325] The Portal of Initiation, trans. Hans Pusch, (Toronto: Steiner Book Centre, 1973) 139-140, "From light-filled heights a Being shines on me, and wings I feel that lift me up to Him..." and The Portal of Initiation, trans. Adam Bitttleston, (Englewood: Rudolf Steiner Publications, 1961) 177, "Out of clear heights there shines on me a Being, and wings I feel to raise myself to Him..."

juxtaposed two experiences: the experience of so-called *initiation* and the experience of death. (Emphasis in the original)[326]

In his lectures on life after death, Steiner describes the state of the disembodied soul. The bulk of this material dates from 1904 to 1918. The point relevant to the above speech of Johannes is the account Steiner gives of how the recently disembodied soul experiences its own spirit. In early lectures on life after death to Theosophists, he describes how, shortly after death, during a short period of sleep, "…the causal body forms itself. It asserts itself as {an organism formed of} rays of light, which radiate out from the normal flame-like forms, passing into blue and indigo colours." [327]

When speaking of this radiant star eight years later, he refers to "this radiant cosmic wisdom…it gleams and shines on us, as if a fiery star." Steiner then comments that this star-radiance, referring to it as the fruit of our life, describing how it moves away from the disembodied soul, receding into the distance, so that one "has the feeling of oneself having remained behind at an earlier point of time…we must move on towards it", to be able to merge with it some time in the future.[328] It also becomes clear that in these two speeches of Johannes and Maria, the shining star is another example of an 'apparent' metaphor in Steiner's texts (in this case, for the human spirit). Since Steiner regards the human spirit as

---

[326] Rudolf Steiner, Geisteswissenschaft als Lebensgut, (Dornach: VRSN, 1959) 120, „Wenn der Mensch auf dieser Weise im Geistig-Seelischen innerlich erlebt, wenn er leibfrei noch ein Leben hat und dazu gekommen ist, sei eigenes Leibliches als ein Objekt wie einen äußeren Gegenstand außer sich zu haben, dann wird er gewahr, was es bei den Geisterforschern zu allen Zeiten bedeutet hat, daß sie zwei Erlebnisse nahe aneinandergerückt haben: das Erlebnis der sognenannten *Initiation* und das Erlebnis des Todes."

[327] Rudolf Steiner, Kosmogonie, (Dornach: RSV, 1979) 154, „…kurzer Schlafzustand, während dem sich der Kausalkörper herausbildet. Dieser selbst macht sich geltend als Strahlen, die aus den übrigen flammenartigen Gebilden herausstrahlen nach der blauen und Indigofarbe hin."

[328] Rudolf Steiner, Inneres Wesen des Menschen und Leben zwischen Tod und neuer Geburt, (Dornach: RSV, 1978) 146-147, „Diese erstrahlende kosmische Weisheit…das glimmt und glitzert uns entgegen wie von einem feurigen Stern…man hat das Bewußtsein, man ist an einem früheren Zeitpunkt verblieben, die Lebensfrucht zieht schnell fort,…und wir müssen ihr nachziehen… "

perceptible to higher clairvoyant faculties, this passage in this speech of Johannes, conveys Steiner's view that the human spirit is perceived as having this appearance, either after death or when experienced in the course of spiritual development.

3l: Scene Ten

As we noted earlier (section 2), in this scene Johannes, despite his success in Scene Nine, makes a major misinterpretation of an entity in the spirit realm. In his first triumphant experience of higher consciousness, he mistakes Benedictus for an evil being. Shortly before Johannes is subject to this error, he is addressed by the character Theodosius, an allegorical character representing love. His statements are especially enticing to Johannes, offering subtle praise. He tells Johannes that "In your self you can experience all worlds. Live from me, as cosmic power of love; a being who is illumined by me feels his own powers of existence enhanced when he offers himself for other beings' happiness." [329]

Clearly there was nothing sinister in the words of Theodosius, and Johannes is delighted to accept his urging, "Before my soul's eye you appear, bringer of happiness to worlds! Creative pleasure surges through my spirit's power when I see you as the fruit of self-experience …I will reveal your being in my deeds, through you they shall be a healing force."[330] As Johannes' response indicates, they are subtly appealing to an egotistical trait in him – and this is precisely the element which Lucifer represents to Steiner, as we have noted in Section 4f. Hence Theodosius here is representing a 'luciferically' influenced form of love, which is in effect, self-love.

Since Johannes is still subject to subtle ego-centric tendencies – finding delight and unwarranted self-affirmation in the words of Theodosius – the admonishing words of Benedictus fail to correct his inner attitude, and hence Theodosius reappears and in his speech subtly replaces Benedictus as the

---

[329] Pforte, 139, „In dir erleben kannst du alle Welten. So lebe mich als Weltenliebesmacht. Ein Wesen, das von mir durchleuchtet ist, fühlt eigne Daseinskraft erhöht, ergibt es sich beglückend andren Wesen. "

[330] Pforte, 139, „So trittst du, Weltbeglücker, vor mein Seelenauge! Es treibt mir Schaffenslust durch meine Geisteskraft, erblick' ich dich als Frucht des Selbsterlebens!…Ich will dein Wesen in meinen Taten offenbaren… "

spiritual source for Johannes' quest, by appealing to Johannes' conceit,

> You will free yourself from illusion, once you fill yourself with my forces. Benedictus was able to accompany you to me, but now your wisdom must lead you on. If you experience only what he has placed in you, then you can not experience yourself. In freedom strive towards the light-filled heights..."[331]

The role of Theodosius as Lucifer is strongly indicated here, as this speech closely parallels Steiner's view of the role of Lucifer in the Biblical Fall of Man. To Steiner, the story of the serpent in Genesis was an allegory for the fact that ancient humanity, who was not yet endowed with a sense of personal egohood, became subject to the influence of Lucifer and his hosts.[332] In connection with Scene Four, the dynamics associated with Lucifer were discussed. In particular that he inaugurates the sense of self, by diverting the human soul from the normal influences of deity.

That is, Lucifer obtains his goal of distancing humanity from God, by slandering the intentions and nature of deity, assuring Eve that it is not the case that humanity shall suffer rather, "You surely shall not die, for God knows that when you eat of it, your eyes will be opened, and you will be like God, knowing both good and evil."[333] In the same way, and with the same implication, Theodosius directly slanders Benedictus – Johannes' guide in the quest, and hence the primary representative of the divine worlds – by telling Johannes "If you experience only what he has placed in you, then you cannot experience yourself."

---

[331] Pforte, 142, „Du wirst vom Wahne dich befreien, wenn du mit meinen Kräften dich erfüllst. Es konnte Benedictus dich zu mir begleiten, doch muss dich jetzt die eigne Weisheit führen. Erlebst du nur, was er in dich gelegt, so kannst du nicht dich selbst erleben. "
[332] To Steiner, the story of the Serpent in Genesis was an allegory of the influence of Lucifer and his hosts upon ancient humanity.
[333] The Holy Bible, Genesis, 3:4. NIV Study Bible, 10th edition (Grand Rapids: Zondervan Publishing House, 1995)

So, at this stage of spiritual development, which is quite advanced in comparison with goals such as those which one could expect Estella to espouse, Johannes is still exposed to error. Indeed Johannes' error is a result of the recapitulation of the dynamics underlying primal error, the Fall, but now at the dawn of self-consciousness in supra-physical existence, rather than at the dawn of self-consciousness in physical, post-Paradisiacal existence for the human race. The ethical blindness in Johannes is then exposed as an even deeper error perception a few minutes later. He invokes the manifestation of his inner {selfless} love-nature, and declares that he can now feel it approaching manifestation. To his dismay, instead of a sanctified spiritual reality emerging, both Lucifer and Ahriman emerge, from inside his soul as it were. Lucifer speaks, repeating in this speech the first half of his speech from Scene Four,

> You have wrenched yourself away from spirit guidance, and you have fled into free earthly realms. You've sought your own being in Earth's confusion; to find yourself proved your reward, and proved your fate. You found me.

But now in this scene Lucifer proceeds to more subtly retain the attractiveness of his dynamics in the acolyte, "Maintain your self in spirit daring. You will find alien being in the wide regions of the heights. It will confine you to human fate."[334] Then Ahriman speaks, and like Lucifer, he repeats the first part of his earlier speech, "You have fled from spiritual darkness. You have found the light of Earth. So suck the power of truth from my solidity. I harden secure ground." Ahriman then proceeds, as did Lucifer, to maintain his power over the soul which is intent on finding its way into the spiritual, by cautioning against the higher realities. Ahriman cautions that ascent into the divine spiritual realms could lead to the disempowering of the acolyte, " You could lose it (the solid ground). In your vacillating you disperse the power of

---

[334] Pforte, 143, „Bewahr dich selbst im Geisteswagnis. Du findest fremdes Wesen im weiten Höhenreich; es wird dich bannen an Menschenlos."

your being. You can squander the power of spirits in radiance of the heights."[335]

Johannes is distraught about this second appearance of these two powers, from within his own soul depths. The scene ends with a chorus of spirit voices. Earlier – at the end of Scene 3, this chorus had earlier spoken these words,

> His thoughts are ascending into the foundations of the primeval world – a world of whose fullness people, in thinking, are merely dreaming in shadows, of whose fullness people, in seeing, are merely living in apparitions. What he thought as shadows, what he experiences as apparitions, now soars above the World of Forms.

But now, the chorus repeat the initial part of their earlier words, to which is added a new section, this expresses the current dynamic,

> His thoughts are ascending into the foundations of the primeval world – what has impelled you in soul illusion, what has held you in error, this appeared to you in spirit light. A light through whose fullness, people when beholding, in truth are thinking! A light of whose fullness, people, when striving, in love are living. [336]

Similarly to the initial chorus presented in Scene Three, the last section of this second chorus is especially obscure. The audience could scarcely be expected to discern a meaning here, without extensive prior study of the text. As we have earlier noted (Section 3f) regarding higher states of

---

[335] Pforte, 144, „Du kannst ihn auch verlieren. In deinem Schwanken zerstreuest du die Kraft des Seins. Du kannst vergeuden im Höhenlicht die Geisterkraft."

[336] Pforte, 144, „Es steigen deine Gedanken in Urweltgründe; was in Seelenwahn dich getrieben, was in Irrtum dich erhalten, erscheinet dir im Geisteslicht, durch dessen Fülle die Menschen schauend in Wahrheit denken! Durch dessen Fülle die Menschen strebend in Liebe leben."

consciousness, these occur as the meditant enters into a realm that illumines his consciousness. Hence his mind is permeated by radiant light, and what is perceived is also formed from such spiritual light. We have also noted that Steiner describes this higher perceiving as 'thinking'. This term is not restricted to logical thought processes.

The implication of this is that the higher illumined condition of Johannes is the same radiant condition in which 'spiritual' thinking occurs, spiritual thinking which brings truths to the human mind. However the chorus also extends this implication of the illumined condition into one which has an association with human volition, 'A light of whose fullness, people, when striving, in love are living.' In other words, the effect of attaining to these higher consciousness states is that the volitional aspect of the soul is rendered more spiritual; love arises in the sense of selfless compassion.

The chorus lets its cryptic words resound, and the curtain falls. Johannes has attained to higher faculties indeed, but he has also failed to pass the test of the temptation of Lucifer. It becomes clear that the attainment of esoteric spiritual faculties does not bestow an immediate, perfect enlightenment; there are still other stages of inner development that Johannes has to reach.

It is also important to note the last speech of Johannes, which provides a précis of the implications of the scene; "Oh, what was this; out of me Lucifer and following him, Ahriman! Am I experiencing only a new illusion, because I strongly desire the truth?"[337] In this speech we see a primary didactic device often used by Steiner in the drama, namely moving the inner events, which had been externalized on the stage, back into the inner self of his personae dramatis – in this way, he transfers these inner events into the mind of the spectator.

---

[337] Pforte, 144, „ O was war dies; aus mir der Lucifer und folgend ihm auch Ahriman! Erlebe ich nur neuen Wahn, da ich mir Wahrheit heiss erfleht?"

3m: Scene Eleven

Scene eleven is the last scene in the drama, the setting is a Mystery Temple dedicated to the Sun, and which is described as being "situated on the surface of the Earth". This curious description allows the scene to correspond with the latter part of Goethe's' tale, Das Märchen, wherein a previously subterranean temple – where the Green Snake encountered the kings – has risen up from subterranean depths, and come to rest on the surface of the Earth. In this temple the Youth unites with the fair Lily, a dynamic found in classical fairy tales.

Now, Johannes is seen to have succeeded in attaining to his higher spiritual state, and thus he has an ongoing comradeship with Maria affirmed, by Benedictus. He declares that, "Johannes' and Maria's souls have exterminated the darkness of error. They have opened the spiritual eye." Retardus laments that Johannes and Maria have wrestled themselves free of his influence, but he declares that the triumph of Johannes and Maria is in fact linked to the failure of Capesius and Strader to resist spiritualizing,

> "You two have brought severe distress to me. The task which I have given you, you have badly mismanaged…Capesius…I guided your activity to circles where you met Johannes and Maria. You should have driven out their inclination towards spiritual vision through the power which your words might have upon them….I opened for you, Strader, the path to scientific certainty. Your strength of thought should have destroyed the magic power of spiritual vision…My destiny is closely linked to what you do.[338]

---

[338] Pforte, 146, „Ihr habt mir bittre Not gebracht, das Amt, das euch von mir gegeben war, ihr habt es schlecht verwaltet….Capesius….ich lenkte deine Wirksamkeit in Kreise in denen du Johannes und Maria trafest. Du hättest ihre Neigung für das Geistesschauen verdrängen sollen durch die Kraft, die deine Worte hätten wirken sollen….Dir, Strader, öffnet' ich den Weg in

This speech reflects a similar dynamic in Das Märchen, where the Will-o'-the-Wisps are called upon to help the Youth to achieve entry to the temple. The Youth and other characters are on their way to the final great ritual wherein the Youth and the fair Lily are united. They find the doors to the temple bolted. The Will-o'-the-Wisps are asked to devour the metal bolts which were keeping the doors to the temple locked with their flames; this they do, and the procession can enter the sacred precincts. There the mixed king interacts sullenly with the two Wisps, trying to avoid their influence.

The Johannes and Maria commence a dialogue – representing the interaction between the Youth and the fair Lily in Das Märchen's final stages. Maria confirms Johannes' achievements, and thereby provides a quintessential definition of the aim of Steiner's Rosicrucian initiation path, "...you have won knowledge through me; to spiritual knowledge you shall add the soul's true being, when you can find your own soul, as you found mine." Shortly after this, she re-affirms this seeing of the higher self, but then points out the next step; the actual experiencing of the spirit, the attainment to the realm of the Platonic Idea, "Johannes, through my self, you have beheld your self in the spirit; you will experience your being as spirit, when cosmic light can behold itself in you."[339]

We have seen that the goal to Steiner is in effect conscious awareness of the realities to be found in the realm of the Platonic Idea. This includes the <u>beholding</u> of one's spirit, a stage which was portrayed in Scene Nine, where Johannes and Maria both see Johannes' higher self. However, there is also as a further stage of attainment, a <u>union</u> with one's spirit. In the last episodes of Das Märchen, the Youth awakens from

---

sich're Wissensbahnen. Du solltest durch das strenge Denken die Zauberkraft der Geistesschau zerstören...Es ist mein Schicksal euren Taten eng verbunden."

[339] Pforte, 151, „Johannes, du hast dich nun selber im Geist an meinem Selbst geschaut; du wirst als Geist dein Sein erleben, wenn Weltenlicht in dir sich schauen kann."

the traumatic state induced by his too vehement urge for the Lily; he can gaze at her and begin to approach her. Finally, he reaches the summit of the stairway and can embrace her. Similarly in *Die Pforte*, Maria tells Johannes in the above speech that he is to seek an experiential encounter with the spirit.

In these words of Maria's, Steiner's view of the Mysteries – expressed in his Das Christentum als Mystische Tatsache (Christianity as mystical fact) – is clearly reflected,

> The mystics (in the Mysteries) did not want to attain a mere *conviction* of the eternal nature of the kernel of human nature. From the viewpoint of the Mysteries such a conviction would have been devoid of any value. For according to this viewpoint the Eternal is not even livingly existent in the non-mystic. If such a person spoke of the Eternal, they spoke about a nothing. It was rather this Eternal itself, which the mystics sought. They had to firstly awaken it in themselves, and then they could speak about it.[340]

At the end of Scene Eleven, this theme of actually experiencing the spiritual is given further focus when Benedictus declares, "Capesius feels the light and shall gain the power to establish in his soul that which Felicia must bring about in him." Then Strader speaks despairingly of his chances of developing spirituality, "It seems that I alone am lost, I cannot banish doubt itself, and I surely shall never find again the path that leads to the temple."[341] To his despairing

---

[340] Rudolf Steiner, Das Christentum als mystische Tatsache und die Mysterien des Altertums, (Dornach: RSV, 1976) Tb, 24, „Nicht die bloße Überzeugung von der Ewigkeit des Lebenskerns wollen die Mysten gewinnen. Nach der Auffassung der Mysterien wäre eine solche Überzeugung ohne allen Wert. Denn nach einer solcher Auffassung ist in dem Nicht-Mysten das Ewige gar nicht lebendig vorhanden. Spräche er von eienem Ewigen, so spräche er von einem Nichts. Es ist vielmehr dieses Ewige selbst, was die Mysten suchen.Sie müssen in sich das Ewige erst erwecken; dann können sie davon sprechen."
[341] Pforte, 152, "Verloren scheine ich allein. Ich kann die Zweifel selbst nicht bannen, und wiederfinden werde ich doch sicher nicht den Weg, der zu dem Tempel führt.

remarks, Theodora then makes a response, which brings the drama to its end. Her words are also a prophecy, announcing that she sees a spectral form arising from Strader's heart, from which words are emanating,

> "And I hear this human image speaking. The words sound like this, 'I have now conquered for myself the power to reach the light.' My friend, trust yourself! For you yourself shall speak these words, when your time has been fulfilled."[342]

It is clear that Capesius and Strader have not remained as they were at the beginning of the drama; they too have undergone a developmental process. Consequently, these speeches presage the possibility of eventual success for Strader and Capesius in the future, and thus open the way for the next drama, *Die Prüfung der Seele*, to take up the destinies of these two men.

There is also another rhetorical element here to be noted, namely that from Strader's viewpoint, this scene is the beginning of his journey towards spiritual development. He is in a similar state of despondency to that of Johannes in Scene One. In Scene One, Theodora inaugurated the new spiritual phase for Johannes by her visionary powers, and now at the end of the drama – which is the beginning of the spiritual journey for Strader – in making this prophetic declaration of a success for Strader in the future, Theodora is again acting as the initializing catalyst for a new evolutionary cycle – this time for Strader. Theodora provided the catalyst by which Johannes progressed towards the spirit through her dramatic vision of the imminent reappearance of Jesus in Scene One. Now in scene eleven she has a vision of the future, spiritualized Strader, and thereby heralds the potential for Strader to succeed.

---

[342] Pforte, 152, "Sie klingen so: 'Ich habe mir errungen die Kraft, zum Licht zu kommen'. Mein Freund, vertraue dir! Du wirst die Worte selber sprechen, wenn deine Zeit erfüllt wird sein."

In addition, this indication of an intrinsically new beginning at the concluding moments of Die Pforte, allows a further development of the theme of reincarnation, which is a major departure from the Goethean tale. Just as Die Pforte includes an elucidation of a karmic basis to the personal relationship between Johannes and Maria, the next drama may now explore the karmic background to Capesius and Strader (and others). This is in fact what Steiner does in his second drama, *Die Prüfung der Seele* (*The Souls' Probation*), which is described as a "Szenisches Lebensbild als Nachspiel zur "Pforte der Einweihung" (A life-tableau in dramatic scenes as a sequel to "The Portal of Initiation").

Furthermore, Scene Ten had portrayed the failure of Johannes to meet the test of subtly egoistic spiritual aspirations, and since this problem is not overcome in scene eleven, it opens the opportunity for Steiner to continue the spiritual quest of Johannes in future dramas.

4: CONCLUSION
THE PRIMARY FEATURES OF STEINER'S ANTHROPOSOPHY EXPRESSED IN DIE PFORTE

4a: The dramatic elements of Das Märchen provide the template for Die Pforte, but these are adapted for didactic purposes, with regard to Steiner's esoteric worldview

Steiner's drama, Die Pforte, develops its characters by presenting their responses to the demands of the spiritual quest, and to the dynamics inherent by other characters. In Die Pforte, the dramatic action derives primarily responses to spiritual realities taking place within the characters minds, rather than from earthy occurrences. In this way, the path to spiritual development as elucidated by Steiner is presented in a personalized context. Although there is character delineation in Die Pforte, the use of allegorical characters remains important for the presentation of processes involved in spiritual development. These include characters who represent elements of consciousness, and characters who are spiritual beings, both good and evil.

All of these characters, and their experiences, serve to illustrate the typical range of problems and challenges and triumphs which a modern person – that is, a student of Steiner – may expect to undergo if they seek to develop their spirituality. The rhetoric of Die Pforte is designed to serve the purpose of character delineation as well as to integrate his message of spiritual development with his view of Goethe's fairy tale. To achieve this, Steiner has to devote attention to the prosody of the drama.

In considering the parallelism which exists between Das Märchen and Die Pforte in the preceding sections, we noted that this was specifically mentioned by Steiner in his original drafts for Die Pforte. This parallelism is to be seen in the duplication in Steiner's drama of all the characters of the Goethean tale. However, the parallelism is not a binding criterion for Steiner. He felt free to deviate from this, for example there are several characters in Die Pforte who are not in Das Märchen, among these are Ahriman and Lucifer, and the human representative of Lucifer, Helena, and also a character called 'the Earth-brain'. These additional characters serve to assist in Steiner's dramatization of the quest for union with the higher self. Ahriman and Lucifer are spiritual beings, whose influences are manifested by Capesius and Strader. It is clear that these two characters portray Steiner's anthroposophical view that unethical qualities or unwise attitudes, derive from not one, but two, powers of evil. One of these powers is not fully evil, it tends towards the exacerbating of unrealistic attitudes and conceit.

The two people in the Prelude and Interlude, Estella and Sophia, are additional to the characters in the Goethean tale. These two enable Steiner to delineate a cultural context and to thereby demonstrate his view of the societal significance of the esoteric-religious life. However, where characters in Die Pforte do represent Goethean counterparts, the similarity between these is strongly maintained in their allegorical function, as understood by Steiner. In this thesis, we have noted where necessary the similarity and dissimilarities of the characters in these two works. But a brief review of the degree of parallelism is needed before we consider the adaptation of the dramatic elements of the Goethean tale in Steiner's drama.

In Goethe's tale, the Will-o'-the-Wisps are creatures intrinsically disharmonious to the magical environment and its inhabitants; they strongly arouse the ire of the Ferryman, and deport themselves in a haughty manner before the Green Snake. In Die Pforte, as we have noted, they are represented by Capesius and Strader, who bring forth the same ire in the Spirit of the Elements in the magical elemental realm. They also spurn, and are puzzled by, the Other Maria (the Green Snake), just as the two Wisps were puzzled by the Green Snake, and also spurned its suggestion of a pathway to the realm of the Lily. The Spirit of the Elements is the representative of the Ferryman who, in the Steiner model, ferries the two Wisps into the realm of the Earth. The Spirit of the Elements likewise ferries souls into incarnation. He 'ferries' Capesius and Strader into his realm, and their incompatibility with the realm becomes evident.

The Other Maria is representative of the Green Snake, which Steiner sees as a quality of selflessness. In her first speech in Scene One, she refers to her devotion to other people, "An inner urge has guided me to dedicate the rest of my life to those whose destiny has brought them suffering and need."[343] As one of the persons who attend the esoteric lectures, she testifies to the empowering quality of anthroposophical truths as the vivifying source of her nature, "...I see their truth, when, full of life, they give me life....daily they create myself anew for me."[344] Here Steiner's dramatized adaptation of Goethe's tale allows the audience to learn that the source of the key soul quality needed for the spiritual quest, is to be found in the renewed Mystery wisdom, which is present in anthroposophical teachings.

The Other Maria also appears in a metamorphosed form, as a snake-like character in Scene Four, and thus becomes a direct parallel to the Green Snake. The Green Snake tells the Will-o'-the-Wisps of two pathways to the realm of the Lily, whereas the Other Maria points out to the two men that there are two ways to find their way to truth. This parallelism between the characters in both literary works is also reflected in the character of Johannes with respect the Youth. In the Goethean tale, the Youth is seeking union with the fair Lily, but he appears in a depressed state, "With bare feet he walked resignedly over the hot sand, and a deep pain appeared to

---

[343] Pforte, 46, „Mich hat ein innrer Trieb gelenkt; den Rest des Lebens, der mir noch zugeteilt, zu widmen jenen Menschen die des Geschickes Lauf gebracht in Elend und in Not..."
[344] Pforte, 47, „Ich schaue ihre Wahrheit, wenn lebend Leben sie mir spenden...und deutlich seh' ich jeden Tag,... täglich sie mich neu mir selber schaffen."

numb all external sense-impressions."[345] Similarly in *Die Pforte*, Johannes, as the human being in the discontented, early stages of the spiritual quest, states, "I feel as if the earlier soul-fire has disappeared, and my eyes gaze unmoved upon the splendour that the sunlight spreads over all things."[346] Meanwhile Maria, like the Lily is lamenting her fate, waiting a better time.

It is the unrequited yearnings of the Youth for the Lily which has brought him into this state, and the reader is informed that a worse fate would await the Youth if he attempted to touch her, for such an act would be almost fatal. In Scene One of *Die Pforte*, Johannes is shown as suffering from a despondent, disinterested condition, and Maria is distressed about this. This same dynamic in the Goethean tale is somewhat more dramatically portrayed than in Die Pforte. The Prince actually does vehemently rush forward, touching the fair Lily and consequently falls to the ground, as if dead, and The Lily is then deeply distressed: "…if thy touch kills, I will die at thy hand"…consciousness fled from him, and with a cry she stepped back, and the fair youth sank soulless from her arms to the ground."

The Lily is thereupon very distraught, "…the sweet Lily stood motionless and gazed numbly at the {apparently} soulless corpse. Her heart seemed to have stopped beating in her breast…"[347] As was noted earlier, Johannes' despondent condition is to some extent due to the impasse in his yearnings for a relationship with Maria. A major deviation from the parallelism occurs in Die Pforte here, because Johannes does not fall into a coma-like state. If *Die Pforte* is

---

[345] Das Märchen, 220, „Mit nackten Sohlen ging er gelassen über den heißen Sand hin, und ein tiefer Schmerz schien alle äußeren Eindrücke abzustumpfen. "

[346] Pforte, 22, „Ich fühle wie verschwunden der Seele früh'res Feuer und stumpf nur schaut mein Auge den Glanz der Dinge, den Sonnenlicht verbreitet über sie."

[347] Das Märchen, 228, „ "…wenn deine Berührung tötet, so will ich von deinen Händen sterben."...das Bewußtsein verließ ihn, und mit einem Schrei trat sie zurück, und der holde Jüngling sank entseelt aus ihrem Armen zur Erde. Die süße Lilie stand unbeweglich und blickte starr nach dem entseelten Leichnam. Das Herz schien ihr im Busen zu stocken... "

to illustrate in human terms, the responses to the trials in the way to spirituality, then Johannes must remain conscious, to be able to interact with others, and to thus progress on his quest.

The fair Lily's condition of 'searing the soul', so to speak, of the person who is too eager for higher attainment, and of having her own self tentatively impaired by the impact of the eager seeker, are two themes which are taken up in Die Pforte. The first theme is prominent, being reflected in the struggles which Johannes has to undergo, whereas the second theme is a minor theme, and feels somewhat artificial in *Die Pforte*. In Goethe's tale, the Lily's delicate canary is harmed by the Youth's impetuous hawk. In *Die Pforte*, Maria's adopted child has developed a negative attitude towards her, after Theodora prophesised in its presence, causing some mild trauma. The child remains a representation of the Goethean canary, being introduced only briefly in Scene Three, to maintain the parallelism with Das Märchen, and never appears again in the drama.

In the Goethean tale, The Old Man with the Lamp facilitates the search for the Lily, acting as a catalyst in the dialogue between the Green Snake and the three Kings. In *Die Pforte* he is represented by the wise Felix Balde, who supports Johannes by declaring that such yearnings for spirituality as Johannes is experiencing, is valuable for the spiritual beings who guide human evolution. Felix assists Johannes' quest by mediating in the conversation with the three hierophants in a subterranean temple. This correlates to the episode to the Goethean tale, wherein the Old Man's dialogue with the three Kings takes place in an underground cavern.

The correspondence of the three kings to the triune human spirit in Steiner's worldview has already been discussed. As we noted earlier, Benedictus correlates to the golden king, Theodosius and Romanus to the silver and brass kings. We have noted too, the correlation of the Mixed King to Retardus. Retardus is in effect, representative of negative spiritual influences active within the illusory personality, influences that derive from Lucifer and Ahriman. At the end of the Goethean tale, the mixed king collapses into a heap, whilst in close parallelism to Goethean tale, Retardus in Die Pforte loses his power over Johannes and Maria.

The character 'German' (Gairman or better, Tuetonus) in *Die Pforte*, as noted in Section 4h, is representative of the Giant in Goethe's tale, and in Steiner's view, is an allegory for atavistic, psychic faculties. Hence Gairman, like the Giant, has only an a minor role in the drama, giving two speeches, and serving to remind the audience that there is a negative element in human nature which is antagonistic to the conscious efforts towards spirituality. Similarly, the Giant appears twice in the Goethean tale, and opposes the efforts of other characters. Finally, the three serving maidens of the Lily are represented by the three women, Philia, Luna and Astrid, and they are active as intermediaries between the soul and the ether world.

Die Pforte is then a dramatized version, with some major adaptations, of the Goethean tale, itself conceived of by Steiner as an allegorical description of the Rosicrucian path to spiritual development. There are however, elements that Steiner has placed in *Die Pforte* which have no parallel in Das Märchen. We have noted the striking inclusion of a Christian eschatological element through Theodora, and also how there is a dynamic interaction encompassing all the various characters in *Die Pforte*. Their different actions and attitudes have a significant impact upon the possibilities for spiritual development by other characters. This was already introduced in Scene One, where we noted that Johannes found his depressive state triggered off by listening to the speeches of the others. This subtle interdependence of one person upon the inner life of others is strongly indicated in Scene Eleven. Here Retardus identifies the factors responsible for success of Johannes as the 'failure' of Capesius and Strader to remain in a Luciferic-Ahrimanic state.

In Scene Four, the representative of the subtle forces behind nature, the Spirit of the Elements, emphasizes repeatedly to Capesius and Strader how their mental life affects the very realm of the nature spirits. In *Die Pforte* nature spirits play a role, speaking or making dramatic noises behind the curtain. These dynamics follow closely Steiner's interpretation of the declaration by the Ferryman in Das Märchen, that the River would rise in anger, if the gold coins of the Will-o'-the-Wisps were to fall into it. That is, to Steiner, the River represents an intermediary elemental realm, to which the untruthful or unenlightened attitudes of the imperfect human soul are detrimental. There is, in Steiner's viewpoint here, an allusion to the Pauline statement, concerning the need felt in the spirit to bring about a spiritual renewal of human kind, "We know that all creation has been groaning as in the pains of childbirth right up to the present time." (Rom. 8:22) Steiner views this statement as a reference to the distress the elemental realm experiences due to the 'fallen' condition of the soul of humanity.[348]

However, the parallelism between the two literary works is significantly altered with regard to the Green Snake and her equivalent, the Other Maria. In *Das Märchen* the Green Snake has a pivotal role, and her actions are dramatic, especially towards the expositional phase, where her decision to become a bridge by self-sacrifice enables the union of the Youth and the Lily. In Steiner's view, Goethe's tale portrays the path to initiation or high spiritual attainment, in an allegorical form. The episodes that portray this process in *Das Märchen* flow in powerful, evocative imagery, and dramatic moments, in the usual sense of the term, are numerous. For example, at the commencement of the tale the angry admonitions of the ferryman to his two passengers is striking, "The boat is heeling, if you don't be still, it will capsize...!" Later on, the Green Snake's encounter with the statues of the kings, and their sudden breaking into dialogue is a gripping scene, which ends with a highly dramatic exiting

---

[348] Rudolf Steiner, Die geistigen Wesenheiten in den Himmelskörpern und Naturreichen, (Dornach: RSV, 1974), lect. 9.

of the Old Man and the Green Snake through the solid walls of the cavern. The following episodes in the tale all maintain the dramatic tension and magical ambience of the tale, culminating in the thunderous ascent of the underground temple to the Earth's surface. This dramatic quality is not present in *Die Pforte*.

The primary theme in the Goethean tale, as Steiner views it, is the quest for the higher self, but portrayed through allegory, hence no specific individual is involved. As noted earlier, in Steiner's interpretation, many of the characters in Das Märchen are aspects of the Youth; the Lily is his higher self, the Old Woman is his core soul qualities, the three kings are his triune spiritual qualities. The Mixed King is his hidden lower self, the Hawk is his premature egocentric eagerness for spirituality, the Green Snake is his innate potential for selflessness, the two Will-o'-the-Wisps represent his Luciferic and Ahrimanic tendencies.

In *Die Pforte*, the principal theme is still the quest for the higher self, exemplified in parallel with the Goethean portrayal. However in Steiner's drama the quest is portrayed as undertaken by several people, whose personalities are delineated, in order that the audience may learn about the emotive and intellectual issues which arise in the soul of a person who is seeking to rise above their current personality and assimilate eternal truths into their life, with the consequent changes in outlook that this will bring. The use of allegorical characters in *Die Pforte* is therefore minimal. *Die Pforte* follows the struggles of Johannes Thomasius, in particular, but the quest for the spirit by Capesius and Strader, is also present as a sub-plot; so too, are the final challenges for Maria.

There are some allegorical characters in *Die Pforte;* for example, Philia, Astrid and Luna, who represent aspects of Maria's soul. Additionally, we noted there is 'Gairman' who represents the mysterious 'spirit of the Earth-brain', a term, which in keeping with Steiner's intention to create a Mystery drama, with cryptic content, remains unexplained. However, since the primary theme is the struggle towards the spirit by people in a contemporary setting, the dramatic tension in *Die Pforte* is in effect limited to the inner struggles and experiences on the threshold between this world and the next, by Johannes, and to a lesser extent, by other souls.

In Goethe's tale, the dramatic tension and the crucial points in the narrative depend upon the Youth faithfully following his inner knowing of the Lily's existence, (this is seen by Steiner as arising from the memory of the spiritual realms, still vaguely present after birth). In addition, the sacrifice of the Green Snake is also a pivotal factor, although this is a less prominent element, until the actual moment arrives. The Youth can unite with the Lily once selflessness and the will to transformation of the personal egocentric ego has been born (the sacrifice of the Green Snake).

We noted in the preceding section that the role of the Other Maria, as the representative of the Green Snake, is diminished in *Die Pforte*. In Scene One, her speech embodies and discretely advocates humility, and in Scene Four her speech provides a contrast between the materialistic or humanistic attitudes to those of the esoteric-spiritual. She is then absent until Scene Eleven, where her speeches are merely affirmative of what Johannes and Maria have achieved. The reason for her lesser role is connected with the purpose of this drama, namely a didactic presentation of the demands made upon the person who in modern times seeks the Mysteries, or spiritual development. *Die Pforte* needs to portray the challenges met by a seeker in a personal manner, hence it is important that Johannes (and to a lesser extent Strader and Capesius) are seen to portray the personal struggle to become spiritualized and selfless. Their speeches and actions have to embody what the Other Maria represents. Hence in *Die Pforte*, Johannes, as a real individual, has to follow a complex and very personal path in which his triune mental qualities are constantly tested and refined. Firstly, his activities, and the success or failure of these, is linked to the actions of others, in particular, how much integrity these people have. Secondly, Johannes has to spiritualize his consciousness, his specific triune mental qualities, to attain to a functional state beyond the threshold. This process requires in the first instance, the absorption of the anthroposophical wisdom, namely, the lectures to which Johannes and his friends are going.

This need to demonstrate the personal, human element in the quest for spiritual development is made possible through the diminished role of the Other Maria. For example, in Das Märchen, the Green Snake becomes luminous and consequently is placed in a position of being able to perceive the three noble kings and the unpleasant mixed King. In *Die Pforte,* Johannes encounters firstly the ignoble 'double' of himself, and then later, the three great hierophants, only after he has developed a more enlightened, or 'illumined' quality, through his stimulated conscience. This leads to his acknowledgment of his lower self, finally resulting in an enhanced integrity.

In addition, Johannes has also attained to more integrity through his having garnered greater understanding of the spiritual realities through his more engaged approach to earthly life. But, as was noted in Section 3b and 3c, for this to occur, Johannes needs to have the efficacy of his conscience enhanced. However, for this he in turn requires, in a striking deviation from the Goethean tale, a remarkable process as a catalyst, to give an impetus towards his high ethical insights. As we noted earlier, this impetus is provided from the Risen Christ, whom Theodora announces.

The intention of Steiner to depict in *Die Pforte* in personal terms, the responses in the inner life of people to the challenges of the spiritual path, tones down the dramatic elements of *Das Märchen*, and creates a more introspective or covert dramatic element. The social milieu of Johannes is presented in Scene One, and he testifies to its effect on him, revealing that, " All former fire has disappeared from my soul." This is due to his problems concerning his relationship with Maria. Later in the scene, after Theodora has a vision of the Second Coming, his despondency deepens, "First came our leader's words, and then what all these people said – now I feel shattered to the core." The dramatic quality becomes a little more overt in Scene Two when he encounters his lower self, and also in Scene Three when Maria's body is used by a malignant being, this event is revealed to the audience through a very long speech by Benedictus.

In Scene Four where there could have been a strongly overt dramatic element, through the appearance of Lucifer and Ahriman, this is muted by these two beings declaring their essential nature, as if letting it resonate from them in a somewhat archetypal manner, rather than directly confronting Johannes. However the spiritual-epistemological or introspective dramatic tension here is quite powerful, in that Johannes identifies these two powers as intimately associated with earthly life, Lucifer being the tempter within, and Ahriman casting an illusion over sensory perception. These are the two main battlefields for the acolyte towards initiation, the soul nature, which needs spiritualizing, and the hollowed-out, material sense perceptible, 'behind' which reality, the Platonic Goethean Idea, is veiled.

In Scene Four the dialogue between the Spirit of the Elements and the two men includes some dramatic elements. The audience witnesses the lightning-like flashes, and the thunderous noises produced by the elemental forces, angered by the comments of Capesius and Strader. However, the following scenes – Scenes Five to Scene Nine – continue the inner development challenges of Johannes, without any dramatic episodes. The audience experiences much less dramatic content than a direct dramatization of *Das Märchen* would yield. The dramatic content in these scenes of the play is only to be found in becoming absorbed in the existential implication of esoteric truths for Johannes (and others), and in the subtle dynamics underlying spiritualization.

In Scene Ten Johannes' inability to distinguish truth from error in the use of higher faculties is the major theme. This episode is a matter of considerable subtle dramatic tension in terms of his struggle for spirituality. It is portrayed with some dramatic elements on stage. Scene Eleven is entirely a dialogue about the stages of spirituality attained by the main characters, without any surprising or dramatic incidents. Since the intention is to carefully portray the individual person's journey so far, the dramatic element is again only to be found in the consciousness processes elaborated in the various speeches.

A departure from the Goethean tale occurs in the last scene of *Die Pforte*, because although the primary emphasis is on the spiritual attainment of Johannes, a secondary emphasis falls on the future possibilities of Strader and Capesius, whose parallels in the Goethean tale are the two Will-o'-the-Wisps. In *Das Märchen*, these two characters fade out some time before the union of the Prince and the Fair Lily. Although at the end of the text, the narrator does make a suggestion that perhaps it is they who have caused some further gold pieces to clinker down into the new, reformed word, over which the now united Prince and Fair Lily rule.

The suggestion is that the dynamic which was encountered at the beginning of the tale – two negative characters as an essential element in the quest to cross the river – does continue on, perpetually, as an intrinsic and constant dynamic in the human world. But in *Die Pforte* the Will-o'-the-Wisps are not static characters, representing a constant factor in human consciousness, they have become specific individuals. They both are told that they may look forward to a future in which they will succeed on the path to spiritual renewal.

We have seen already in Section 1 and Section 2, that to Steiner the attainment of spiritual thinking, that is, conscious functioning in the Platonic realm of the Idea, is the height of spiritual attainment. In *Die Pforte* the primacy of the 'realm of Ideas' is reflected in its role as the goal of initiatory consciousness, and as the realm in which is found the source of all created, structured reality. The spirit chorus at the end of Scene Three affirms this perspective. Hence it can also be concluded that to Steiner the person who achieves this state has also developed a form of divine or selfless love. This virtue is traditionally associated in religious texts, with nearness to God. But, in *Die Pforte* there is only one direct mention of the supreme Deity – at least in the accustomed sense. But in an indirect and unorthodox manner, Deity is referred to, through the agency of the 'divine hierarchies'.

A prominent element in Steiner's anthroposophical worldview is the activity of divine spirits, referred to 'hierarchical beings'. Steiner describes the activity of nine ranks of these beings, and equates them with the nine ranks of such beings recorded in the Neo-Platonic texts of the pseudo-Dionysus.[349] It is also a central feature in Steiner's cosmology, that these beings in their creative activity are an expression of the will of God. These beings exert their efficacy through the sevenfold evolutionary cycles whose dynamics, as we saw earlier, are directly reflected in the structure of *Die Pforte*. Steiner has adapted the dramatic elements of *Das Märchen* to indicate that the realm of the Idea is closely associated with these 'divine-spiritual' beings. An additional feature of the seven evolutionary phases is that they are the direct expression of these hierarchical beings. They have brought the universe into being, and created humanity; but in doing this, are revealers or servers of the will of the primal God.[350]

The role of these beings is incorporated into Scene Five, where a variety of such beings are referred to, in a curiously discrete way. In *Das Märchen*, the Youth is united eventually to the fair Lily with the help of the three Kings. But in *Die Pforte*, Johannes, the representative of the Youth, becomes

---

[349] The primary Neo-platonic text concerning these hierarchies, listing their names, is The Mystical Theology and the Celestial Hierarchies of Dionysius the Areopagite, (Fintry, The Shrine of Wisdom, 1965).
[350] Rudolf Steiner, Die geistigen Hierarchien und ihre Widerspiegelung in der physischen Welt, lect. 5, (Dornach: RSV, 1991).

united to the spirit – that is accesses the realm of the Idea – through the help of the three hierophants (three Kings), who also need these hierarchical beings to ensure that Johannes is successful. When the three hierophants are gathered in the temple, Benedictus requests that Romanus invokes them, to bless the efforts of Johannes towards the goal of divine consciousness. Romanus acquiesces, saying that Johannes shall enter those spheres where spirits act creatively and,

> ....Der Weltenbildner Ziel,
> Sie werden ihn beleben;
> Und Urbeginne sollen durchgeistern ihn,
> Die Weltgewalten werden durchkraften ihn;
> Die Sphärenmächte durchleuchten ihn;
> Und Weltenherrscher befeuern ihn,[351]

This passage is a striking example of Steiner's neologistic metaphorical rhetoric, which in the process of describing the influence of these hierarchical spirits creates a somewhat awkward text. The difficulty of understanding such texts is exemplified in the Pusch translation,

> The cosmic builders' goals
> shall quicken him with life;
> divine primordial sources
> bespirit him;
> world-ruling powers
> grant strength to him;
> and lords of worlds
> befire him.

In an attempt to render the assumed meaning of the original, the translator has resorted to English verbal neologisms and vague phraseology. What is striking in the German original is that Steiner avoids using the specific names that he has coined for these beings in his own cosmological writings and lectures. He also used the Biblical terms at times, but he created names for these ranks of beings as well. These terms,

---

[351] Pforte, 91.

from the highest rank downwards are, in English translation, the spirits of love, the spirits of the harmonies, the spirits of will, the spirits of wisdom, the spirits of movement, the spirits of form, the spirits of personality, and finally, the archangels, the angels – he uses the Biblical terms for the these. Why he refrains from using his own standard terms which are well known to his students, and replaces them with analogous, but unfamiliar, terms is unclear. In Section 2a, however, we saw that some obscurity is a feature of Steiner's rhetoric, and its effect is to make the text less accessible.

In the above speech by Romanus, the 'Urbeginne' (Primal-Beginnings) refers to the spirits of personality, as these are also named in Steiner's writings as 'die Urbeginne'. The 'Weltgewalten' (Powers of the Cosmos) refers to the spirits of form, who are also known as 'die Gewalten'. The expression, 'die Sphärenmächte' (Mights of the Spheres) refers to the spirits of movement, as their alternate name is 'die Mächte.' The term, Weltenherrscher' (Rulers of Worlds) refers to the spirits of wisdom, as an alternate name Steiner uses for these is the German Biblical term, 'die Herrschaften', which in English is 'the Dominions'.

This leaves the first name mentioned in this passage, the 'Weltenbildner' (Sculptors of Worlds); this is presumably a reference to the archangels, since the list proceeds in order, from the lower to the higher ranks, and the archangels precede the "Urbeginne'. A clearer rendering into English of the passage would now be,

The goals of the Sculptors of Worlds, they shall quicken him;
And Primal-Beginnings shall permeate him with spirit.
The Powers of the Cosmos, they shall strengthen him,
The Mights of the Spheres illumine him;
And Rulers of Worlds enflame him.

Here, Steiner is merging the Platonic concept of the realm of Idea with a traditional Christian context, specifying the various deities involved, whereas according to Plato (in

Phaedrus) it is simply stated that 'the gods' exist in that realm. When one notes Steiner's view that these divine-spiritual beings express the intention of God, then the above passage is indicating that Johannes, in seeking to attain to initiation in the context of Steiner's anthroposophical model, shall in effect, be granted access to God.

That the role of God in *Die Pforte* is in effect a discrete one, in that the hierarchies are the revealers of deity, expresses two closely linked didactic intentions of the drama. These are firstly, to allude to the role of the hierarchies as indirectly manifesting God – a theme which is elucidated in many hundreds of his lectures. Secondly his intention is to allude to his conviction about Natural Theology, that is about the nature of God; and a corollary to this, the relationship of humanity to deity.

We have noted in various places that Steiner refers to (the realm of) the Spirit or (the realm of) God – seen as the origin of all creation – as the Weltengrund, that is, the "'foundational element' or 'ground' of the cosmos. Steiner maintained that God is the 'Weltengrund', literally, the 'ground of the cosmos', or more appropriately expressed in English, the substratum, or foundational element of the cosmos. This is an expression which is scarcely translatable directly into English. Some examples of Steiner's usage of this phrase includes, "…for in the process of thinking taking hold of the Idea, it merges into the primal foundations of cosmic existence" (Urgrunde des Weltendaseins); and, "All things in the world derive from a primal spiritual foundation of all creation (geistigen Urgrunde). The human being, too, initially has its origin from this primal source of all creation (geistigen Urgrunde)…"

His advice to theologians concerning the term, 'God' in the Lord's Prayer reflects his conclusion in this regard, "In the Lord's Prayer one should be thinking of the Foundation of the Cosmos (Weltengrund). In the Lord's Prayer, the first sentence does not actually refer to the later development, but to the beginning."[352] The impersonal and indefinable qualities which Steiner sees in God implies its own corollary, namely that specific hierarchical entities are needed to interact with a definable created cosmos, and to form a link to humanity. There is still a link in Steiner's worldview between the uncaused primal God – the foundational element of the cosmos – and human beings, but it is especially subtle. In his early epistemological text, *"Grundlinien einer Erkenntistheorie der Goetheschen Weltanschauung, mit besonderer Rücksicht auf Schiller.* (Outlines of a theory of epistemology of the Goethean worldview with especial reference to Schiller)" he writes,

> God (Weltengrund) has fully poured out Himself into the cosmos; He has not withdrawn from it in order to guide it from outside. Rather He impels it from within, He has not withheld Himself from it. The highest mode of His manifestation within the reality of normal existence is (human) thinking and through this factor, the human personality. Thus if God has goals, then they are identical with the goals that human beings set themselves, as He lives within these. But this does not occur through the human being trying to investigate one of other command of the Regent of the cosmos, and acting according to such a goal. It occurs through the human being acting from his or her own understanding. For within these is living this Regent of the cosmos. He does not exist as Will somewhere outside of the human being; for he has forgone such a will of his own, in order to make everything dependent upon the will of the human being.[353]

---

[352] Rudolf Steiner, Vorträge und Kurse über Christlich-Religiöses Wirken, (Dornach: RSV, 1993) 631, „Im Vaterunser hat man zu denken an den Weltengrund. Im Vaterunser bezieht eigentlich der erste Satz sich nun nicht auf das spätere Werden, sondern auf den Anfang, auf den Ursprung."
[353] *Grundlinien einer Erkenntistheorie*, in *Die menschliche Freiheit* (*Human freedom)*,124-129.

This conception of deity is close to panentheism, in which God has some of the attributes of pantheism, as well as some of those of theism. The 'foundation of the cosmos' exerts its efficacy discretely in the evolving consciousness of human beings. This quasi-panentheistic viewpoint is affirmed in *Die Pforte* by Maria, "…der Geist, der uns beseelt, verbindet innig sich mit allem, was in den Lebensgründen des Menschen Schicksal spinnt (the spirit who en-souls us, unites itself intimately with all that which, in the foundations of human life, spins human fate.") [354]

Steiner's conception of Deity here obviously exposes the ongoing evolutionary future of human destiny to the vagaries of human consciousness processes.[355] However, it is the case in the above text, that any such dependency is linked to the human volitional power, not the intellect as such. To Steiner the will or volition is an element of the soul-life of human beings that has a deeper, more vital link to deity than the intellect, even though much of the will is seen to lie in the unconscious sphere of the human mind. This subject will be considered in more detail in Section 4d.

Steiner's view of God in effect refutes the concept of God as 'almighty'. In various cosmological writings and lectures Rudolf Steiner describes the process of creation as deriving from this God, but in fact, expressed through these nine ranks of spiritual beings. As he writes in his *Die Geheimwissenschaft*, as this process gets underway via the sevenfold evolutionary cycle, the primal evolutionary dynamics therein become the sole arbiter; if a group of beings falls behind in their own evolutionary potential, then from that condition, evil arises.

---

[354] Pforte, 48, the reference to 'spinning fate' refers to the mythological image of a spindle, upon which the threads of destiny are interwoven by the three Norns or three Fates, an image often used by Steiner to describe karma.

[355] John McQueren, In search of deity: an essay in dialectical theism, (London: SCM Press, 1984) 54, "The champions of panentheism hold - rightly, I think - that deism and pantheism are over-simplifications. The being of God, they claim, is both transcendent and immanent, both impassible and passive, both eternal and temporal…".

The leaders of the two main groups of such entities are Lucifer and Ahriman. Steiner, in clarifying his teachings, and as a partial explanation of the enigma of evil, maintains strongly the implications of his approach to Natural Theology, namely that God does not have absolute power. In short, to Steiner, God is not "all-mighty". In a lecture given in 1912, Steiner elucidates three great virtues, associated with deity, namely wisdom, power and love. He explains to his audience that God cannot be all-wise as that would prevent humanity attaining to true freedom, because God can only know all things, if the decisions that are as yet unborn in the human soul were also known in advance.[356]

In *Die Pforte* many substantial adaptations from the Goethean tale are made to accommodate the above view on deity. Lucifer and Ahriman exert a strong influence on both Capesius and Strader, whilst Johannes has to struggle to free himself from their power. Just how they shall perform in the face of such trials is not known in advance to the audience, the power of the divine has to be sought by Johannes and also actively mediated to him, at the request of the three hierophants, via the hierarchies.

The presence of God in the challenges and triumphs of Johannes is fully in the background, externally, that is in terms of his encountering sacred spiritual realities; he sees his higher self, he feels the higher spiritual realms and so on, but he doesn't mention a drawing near to God. However, the presence of God in Johannes's quest, internally, that is in terms of his perception of his spiritualizing inner being, is prominently and precisely defined – if one knows the quasi-panentheistic Natural Theology of Steiner. For in terms of the immanent presence or subtle efficacy of God, arising in the free, that is, independent, soul-life of Johannes, the imprint of God is very clear in a speech he makes in Chapter Nine.

---

[356] Rudolf Steiner, Erfahrungen des Übersinnlichen, (Dornach: VRSN, 1970) 208.

Johannes is now rejoicing in the success of his meditation work, sensing the spiritual spheres around him. He declares that when the power of the Delphic maxim – in an adapted version – becomes efficacious, then, "The entire cosmic-being lives in the soul's being, when such power is established in the spirit as to give these words their power; O human being, experience yourself!" He continues on a little later in the speech with this theme of the 'Weltengrund', as subtly active in the human being, declaring that these same wise words,

> ... place me close to lofty Godly-intentions; and blissfully I feel the Creator-power of these high intentions in my weak earthly humanity. And out of myself there shall be revealed the reason why the germinal seed-bud is concealed within me. I want to give myself to the world, through the life of my own being.[357]

The implication here is that 'Urgrund' of the cosmos, having long ago placed itself into the depths of human being – in this case, Johannes – is now being cognized by its previously unaware bearer, and consequently is also being enabled to proceed in a more empowered manner within this same bearer. God is then mentioned, but as part of a complex noun, which focuses upon the will of Deity.

It is clear that Steiner has adapted and dramatized the entire Goethean fairy tale in a didactic manner for the purpose of elucidating many elements of his anthroposophy. I conclude that there are many passages in *Die Pforte* which show that Steiner regards the Goethean fairy tale as a text appropriate to the task of elucidating his view of the process of esoteric

---

[357] Pforte, 136-37, „Es lebt das ganze Weltenwesen in dem Seelensein, / wenn solche Kraft im Geiste wurzelt, Die Wahrheit gibt dem Worte: O Mensch, erlebe dich!" / ....Und stellst mich neben hohe Gottesziele; /Und selig fühle ich / Des hohen Zieles Schöpfermacht/ In meinem schwachen Erdenmenschen. / Und offenbaren soll sich aus mir selbst, / Wozu der Keim in mir geborgen ist. / Ich will der Welt mich geben / Durch Leben meines eignen Wesens."

spiritual development, and the nature of the spiritual realities, and human dynamics which are encountered in this process. It is also emerging that a primary characteristic of Steiner's commentary on Goethe's works in general, is that he sees them as particularly assimilable to his anthroposophical understanding of spiritual realities.

4b: Steiner's view of the spirituality portrayed in Die Pforte, is quintessentially expressed by his interpretation of Goethe

We have seen how Steiner has adopted and adapted Goethe's Märchen, as a vehicle to communicate his view of how esoteric initiatory spirituality is achieved. In the course of his elucidation of Goethe's *Märchen*, Steiner comments on a particular Goethean text which he finds very assimilable to his understanding of the spiritual goal of Johannes. The text in question is Goethe's deeply passionate love poem, from 1823, *Elegie*, in which he is grieving over the loss of the relationship with a young woman, Ulrike von Levetzow. In this poem Goethe reflects on many subtle aspects of love, loss and romantic yearning.

However, in a lecture on Goethe's *Märchen*, from April 1904, Steiner quotes an extract of this poem, and points out to his audience how in this section of the poem the theme is sensing the approach of the divine. He comments that this occurs as one's higher self becomes empowered, and earthly desires fall away. This interpretation, so far, is in agreement with scholarship, this passage concerns the urge to become united to the divine. To Steiner, it reflects Goethe's conviction that precisely such a sublime state of divine love is possible, as that represented by the fair Lily in *Das Märchen*, in Steiner's interpretation. In *Die Pforte* this is reflected in the figure of Maria, as she is the representative of the fair Lily. The German text – the two stanzas which Steiner quotes – is as follows,

> ...In unsers Busens Reine wogt ein Streben,
> Sich einem Höhern, Reinern, Unbekannten
> Aus Dankbarkeit freiwillig hinzugeben,
> Enträtselnd sich den ewig Ungenannten;
> Wir heißen's: fromm sein ! –
> Solcher seligen Höhe fühl' ich mich teilhaft,
> Wenn ich vor ihr stehe.

> Vor ihrem Blick, wie vor der Sonne Walten,
> Vor ihrem Atem, wie vor Frühlingslüften,
> Zerschmilzt, so längst sich eisig starr gehalten,
> Der Selbstsinn tief in winterlichen Grüften;
> Kein Eigennutzt, kein Eigenwille dauert,
> Vor ihrem Kommen sind sie weggeschauert...

This concept of encountering the divine, is clearly expressed in lines 1 to 4, that is,

> "In the purity of our heart, there surges a striving, born of gratitude, to freely surrender oneself to a higher, purer, Unknown [Power]; thus resolving the enigma to oneself of the Eternally Un-named; we call this – being pious!"

This is agreed to by scholars in general, and by Steiner. However, Goethe then proceeds to say that he experiences this mood of piety, in the broader, mystical sense implied here, whenever he is in the presence 'ihr', which is a feminine or neuter pronoun, meaning either 'it' or 'her'. This word is normally thought of as feminine, and scholars agree that it refers to the object of Goethe's love, the young woman, Ulrike. This pronoun occurs three more times, and in each of these cases it is also thought of as 'her', and as referring to Ulrike. Consequently, the passage is translated in published texts, along the following lines; this pronoun is in bold font,

> 1 …… in the purity of our heart, there surges a striving, born of gratitude,
> 2 to freely surrender oneself to a higher, purer, Unknown [Power];
> 3 thus resolving the enigma to oneself of the Eternally Un-named;
> 4 we call this – being pious!
> 5 Of such blessed heights I feel
> 6 myself partake, when I stand before **her** –

259

7 before **her** gaze, just like before the power of the Sun,
8 beneath **her** breath, just like beneath springtime breezes,
9 melts away what long has lasted in chasms, in icy rigidity,
10 self-centredness that has persisted so long deep in wintry tomb;
11 No egoism or self-will lasts,
12 before **her** advent they have fled.[358]

It is clear from the above, that the section of the poem comprising lines 6 – 12, is understood to refer to Ulrike and is thus a testimonial to how powerfully Goethe was inspired by his feelings. That is, the piety mentioned earlier (lines 1-4) arises in his heart whenever he imagines he is in her presence, being seen by her, or feeling her breath, by which he may mean her ambience. Consequently, the triune forms of egocentric attitudes, in lines 10 and 11, are conquered as this woman (or the thought of her) draws near. As such, this interpretation is on particularly solid grounds, as Goethe was famously inspired in his artistic endeavours through his enflamed love affairs, and the entire poem is a powerful testimonial to his passionate love of Ulrike, and grief over her loss. The poet is moving from expressions of an utmost personal, romantic love, to a passage about the experience of divine love, though triggered by the contemplation of romantic love.

The stanza in *Elegie*, prior to the two that are under consideration here, reinforces this view, as Goethe writes of comparing the peace of God with the happy peace felt in romantic love. He also writes of feeling Ulrike's presence, and wanting to belong to her,

---

[358] The normal view that all of the lines here refer to Goethe's sweetheart, can be found -addition to Trunz's commentary "ein Liebender klagt (a person in love mourns)" - for example in, The Eternal Feminine: selected poems of Goethe, trans. Frederick Ungar, (New York: F. Ungar Publishing Co. 1980) 163, and in Goethe: Selected Poems, ed. Christopher Middleton, *Elegie*, trans. John F.Nims, (Boston: Suhrkamp/Insel, 1983), 250.

The peace of God, which, as we read,
Blesses us here below more than reason,
I would indeed compare with Love's happy peace,
When in the presence of the dearest one.
There the heart rests, and nothing can disturb
the deepest intention: the thought of being hers.

In a lecture on *Das Märchen* Steiner comments that in this passage of Goethe's *Elegie* the symbol of the lily as used here was also used by Spinoza in the same way, namely to designate a condition of wisdom which also bestows the condition of (inner) freedom,

> One designates as the 'lily' what Spinoza …expresses in his 'Ethics' when he designates that which the human being, when he arises into higher spheres of being…designates as the realm of divine love within the human soul; that realm where the human being is no longer compelled {to action}, but rather where everything which is the sphere of human knowledge and development occurs through freedom and devotion, and full of love…Goethe has designated such love as the highest state of freedom, as the freedom from all desires and wishes of daily life…[359]

Steiner then quotes these twelve lines from *Elegie*, referring to, "this Spinoza-like love of God, which Goethe wants to attain through spiritual alchemy…"[360] But in Steiner's interpretation of this verse, the verse concerns the dynamic in

---

[359] Steiner, Goethes Geheime, 152-153, „Als Lilie bezeichnet man gleichzeitig dasjenige, was Spinoza…ausdrückt, wenn er dasjenige, was der Mensch, der hinaufgestiegen ist in die höheren Sphären des Seins…bezeichnet als das Reich der göttliche Liebe in der Menschenseele; das Reich, wo der Mensch zu nichts mehr gezwungen wird, sondern wo alles dasjenige, was im Bereich der menschlichen Erkenntnis und Entwickelung liegt, aus Freiheit und Hingebung, aus voller Liebe geschieht…Goethe hat jene Liebe bezeichnet als das höchste Freisein, als das Freisein von allen Begierden und Wünschen des alltäglichen Lebens."
[360] Steiner, Goethes geheime, 152, „Diese Spinozistische Gottesliebe, die erreichen will durch spirituelle Alchimie…wo jeder Zwang, jede Willkür verwandelt wird durch spirituelle Alchemie, wo alles Handeln einfließt in das Gebiet der Freiheit."

the human soul, wherein our most spiritual, most purified desire, can impel us on to a sense of the divine. There is no reference to a woman in Steiner's comments. In the above lecture, he quotes the two stanzas without indicating that they are preceded by, and followed by, stanzas in which the theme of romantic love is central. Hence in this interpretation, the pronoun 'her' in line 6, "feel myself partake, when I stand before **her**" – the entity that has caused him to feel a nearness to the divine – would now refer to the purity of the heart.

This becomes the factor which is stimulating Goethe to feel the uplifting mystical presence of the divine. Furthermore, in the way that Steiner quotes the text, the referent of the entire section remains that of purity, from the phrase in line 1. Hence all of the references to this divine spiritual reality, expressed in lines 7–12, derive from feeling a nearness to the divine, not to Ulrike.

Consequently, in the way that Steiner uses this verse, the pronouns, the references to 'her' in the usual translation, from line six to twelve, all refer to the purity of the heart. These have to been rendered as 'it' in English, although it can still be read as 'her' in German, as 'purity' is a feminine noun. Additionally, a few phrases need to be adjusted as to their nuances, so that the translation would read accordingly as follows,

1 ……in the purity of our heart, there surges a striving, born of gratitude,
2 to freely surrender oneself to a higher, purer, Unknown [Power];
3 thus resolving the enigma to oneself of the Eternally Un-named;
4 we call this – being pious!
5 In such blessed heights I feel
6 myself partake, when I am in its presence –
7 before its gaze, as if facing the power of the Sun,
8 before its breath, as if before springtime breezes,
9 melts away what has lasted so long in icy rigidity –

262

10   self-centredness, deep in wintry tombs;
11   No self-interest, no self-will, lasts;
12   before its dawning presence they have shuddered away.

In this form, the passage accommodates Steiner's interpretation that the element which is bringing about this condition in Goethe is not his beloved, but 'the heart's purity', because now the yearning is to achieve union with the divine. There are two major differences between the accepted meaning of this section of the poem, and Steiner's interpretation. Firstly, to Steiner, that Goethe, impelled by his yearning for the woman, has now moved to the theme that, amongst the emotional drives in human heart, there is a particularly spiritualized, purified urge, namely to seek union with the divine. But, now Goethe feels this urge when he senses the efficacy of this purity, and not the presence of his sweetheart. Secondly, to Steiner, whenever Goethe senses this purity exerting its influence upon him, and thus feels a divine presence is approaching, and removing his egocentric urges, this is due to the nearness of 'the heart's purity', not his beloved woman.

Thus in line 6, "myself partake, when I am in its presence –" the intended image, in Steiner's view, is not that of physically standing before another physical person, nor a visionary view of the beloved woman. Rather the image is one of cognizing that oneself is within the immediate and activated ambit of something, namely the highest urges in the heart. The German phrase used here, and usually rendered "when I stand before it", is based on a well-established German idiom, which can be so understood, and then directly transferred into English. But it also has a nuance of being in the ambit of something, and, in terms of Steiner's interpretation, line 6 would be understood as 'when I am in the presence of', and not 'when I stand before'.

It is with other phrases in the poem that Steiner's interpretation of this Goethean text reveals how he can view the verse as affirmative of his esoteric-spiritual worldview. The major divergence in Steiner's interpretation is that the experiences in this passage are descriptive of a universal mystical experience, and no longer a personal experience of Goethe's, deriving from romantic love. On this basis, line 7, which is usually, "before her gaze, just like before the power of the Sun" now has to read, "before <u>its</u> gaze, as if facing the power of the Sun".

This now implies that it is the heart's purity which is encountered, and <u>this</u> has the effect mentioned later, that selfishness melts away. Thus to Steiner the experience is one in which one's own highest spiritual urges – enveloped in a divine milieu – are encountered, <u>as an external reality</u>, radiantly illumining (with spiritual light) one's sentiency. This stands in strong contrast to the accepted view, of Goethe himself seeing his beloved, either physically, or in a visionary sense.

Furthermore, line 8 which is usually, "beneath her breath, just like beneath springtime breezes," now is viewed as indicating the presence of a sacred spiritual reality, and has to read, "before <u>its</u> breath, as if before springtime breezes." This interpretation views the encountering of the purity of the heart, the highest spiritual drives active in the soul-body, as similar to sensing quickening springtime breezes. This contrasts to the normal interpretation of this line, namely that the effects of perceiving the breath-stream (or subtle ambience?) of a deeply beloved person is causing selfishness to melt away. The usual rendering here may possibly allow that the term, 'her breath' is metaphorical for Ulrike's ambience, rather than her breath as such. However, the expression, 'her gaze', in the previous line, does not appear to be metaphorical.

Finally, the last three lines in Steiner's interpretation bring into yet sharper focus his differing interpretation and consequent utilisation of Goethe's text. These lines become an attestation to the spiritual path for any acolyte; it is no longer a personal experience of Goethe's. It thusly concerns the powerful effect of the impinging upon 'Everyman's' normal consciousness of his most spiritual urges – rather than a sensing by Goethe himself of his beloved's presence. These three lines are usually,

10 self-centredness (that has persisted so long) in deep wintry tombs;
11 No egoism or self-will lasts,
12 before her advent they have fled.

But they now become, to accommodate Steiner's use of this text,

10   self-centredness, deep in wintry tombs;
11   No self-interest, no self-will, lasts;
12   before its dawning presence they have shuddered away

Consequently all three negative attributes, self-centredness, self-interest and self-will, 'shudder away' as the heart's purity manifests. The image created by this interpretation, accords with Steiner's view of the outcome of attaining to a high state of spirituality (piety). It allows Steiner to affirm his anthroposophical perspective that precisely the polar opposite to the condition of piety – self-centredness – is eradicated from one's attitudinal qualities and emotive responses through the condition of attaining to spirituality, or at least of sensing its approach. With regard to line 12, to accommodate Steiner's interpretation here, a more suitably nuanced rendering of Vor ihrem Kommen ('before its advent'), has been necessary, 'before its dawning presence'.

This same way of interpreting Goethe was evinced some 16 years earlier, when Steiner was still working on Goethe's scientific writings, for inclusion in the Kürschners National Literatur series. In his editorial comments, in 1888, he writes,

> ...Goethe has the need to sense something higher {in all things} and works his way up to this. Everything frivolous, thoughtless, was stripped away and love becomes piousness for Goethe. This basic characteristic of his nature is most beautifully expressed in these words of his, '...In unsers Busens Reine wogt ein Streben, sich einem Höhern, Reinern, Unbekannten aus Dankbarkeit freiwillig hinzugeben, Enträtselnd sich den ewig Ungenannten; Wir heißen's: fromm sein![361]

So here too, in the pre-anthroposophical phase of his life, Steiner views this same verse in a similar way to that which he expresses in 1904, quoting only the section which does not refer to Ulrike. Just whether Goethe intended any such nuance in Goethe's in this slightly ambiguous passage in *Elegie*, is unknown, for, as Trunz points out, Goethe kept the verse as a special, sacred work, which was shown to only a few privileged people.[362]

In his above comments on this passage from *Elegie*, Steiner describes the state of spirituality in terms of his holistic epistemology; the condition of spirituality which manifests as love for God, is also a condition of true freedom. That is, in true freedom, all actions are carried out from an inherent ethical quality, which has now been attained. Hence these actions occur in the realm of divine love in the human soul,

> ...the realm where the human being is no longer compelled to any deed, rather where everything, which lies in the realm of human knowledge and development, happens through freedom and devotion, from deep love...where every compulsion, every arbitrary act, becomes transformed through a spiritual alchemy, where all actions flow into the realm of freedom.[363]

---
[361] Kürschners Nat. Lit. Goethes Werke, Bd. 115, liv.
[362] Goethes Werke, HA Bd.1, S. 586.
[363] Rudolf Steiner, Goethes geheime, 152, „...das Reich wo der Mensch zu nichts mehr gezwungen wird, sondern wo alles dasjenige, was im Berich der

To Steiner the condition of freedom is an ethical state, the final goal of spirituality, and is crucial both for the fulfilment of the human potential as well as for the future of civilisation. This condition is one in which a person has the above qualities of a spontaneously ethical nature as an inherent quality. It is also to Steiner a state of exceptional spirituality, because to him 'freedom' is not simply a condition bestowed upon the human being, rather as a condition which, developed through specific arduous esoteric soul-exercises, is the truest manifestation of the human spirit. To Steiner, 'love' is primarily a capacity developed in the volitional powers of the soul; in effect, 'good will'.

Further, the attainment of such spirituality is seen by Steiner as the fulfilling of the actual intention underlying the creation of humanity, that is humanity has the mission to be the bearers of (spiritual, selfless) love. He elucidates his theory in lectures on the Gospel of St. John, where he maintains that Christ is the Being of spiritual love, or good-will in the finest sense. He concludes that the result of the Incarnation of Christ, fulfilled through the Passion and Resurrection is that human souls have the very real potential to achieve this state of freedom, or ethical intuitiveness.[364]

It is also this condition of inherent volitional morality, which he writes about in his pre-anthroposophical phase, in his Philosophie der Freiheit, referring to it as the 'standpoint of free (or independent) morality', which does not declare,[365]

---

menschlichen Erkenntnis und Entwickelung liegt, aus Freiheit und Hingebung, aus voller Liebe geschieht...wo jeder Zwang, jede Willkür verwandelt wird durch spirituelle Alchemie, wo alles Handeln einfließt in das Gebiet der Freiheit."
[364] Rudolf Steiner, Das Johannes Evangelium, (Dornach: RSV, 1981) Lect. 3
[365] Steiner, Philosophie, 134-135, „...nicht, daß der freie Geist die einzige Gestalt ist, in der ein Mensch existieren kann. Sie sieht in der freien Geistigkeit nur das letzte Entwickelungsstadium des Menschen....Wenn Kant von der Pflicht sagt: „ Pflicht! du erhabener, großer Name, der du nichts Beliebtes, was Einschmeichelung bei sich führt, in dir fasst, sondern Unterwerfung verlangst, der du kein Gesetz aufstellst..., vor dem allem alle Neigungen verstummen, wenn sie gleich in Geheim ihm entgegenwirken", so erwidert der Mensch aus dem Bewußtsein des freien Geistes: „Freiheit! du freundlicher, menschlicher Name, der du alles sittlich Beliebte, was mein Menschentum am meisten würdigt, in dir fassest, und mich zu niemandes

>...the free spirit to be the only form in which a person can exist. It sees the free spirit just the final stage of development of the human being...When Kant says, " 'Duty! You exalted and mighty name, you who comprise nothing loving nor ingratiating, but demands submission, you that 'sets up a law'...before which all inclinations are silent, even though they secretly work against it..." then, out of the consciousness of the free spirit, the human being replies, " 'Freedom!, you friendly, human name, who encompasses all that is morally most lovable, all that my manhood most values, and makes me a servant of no-one, you who sets up no mere law, but rather waits what my moral love itself will recognize as a law, because in the face of every merely imposed law, it feels itself unfree.'

This perspective is closely echoed in Steiner's lecture on the Goethean tale in which he quoted from *Elegie*, he comments that "Goethe {in his Elegy} has designated this love as the highest state of freedom, as a freedom from all desires and wishes of the every-day mundane world.[366]

However, central to this entire process of achieving divine illumination in Goethe's tale, are the actions of the Green Snake, it is her actions in sacrificing herself, which make possible the resolution of the dilemma facing the Youth. The character of the Green Snake was regarded by Steiner as an expression of a profound insight by Goethe. To him, as we have seen, it is the representative of the ability slumbering within the human being to selflessly engage itself in life, to rid oneself of egocentric drives; it is therefore the key to

---

Diener macht, der du nicht bloß ein Gesetz aufstellst, sondern abwartest, was meine sittliche Liebe selbst als Gesetz erkennen wird, weil sie jedem nur auferzwungenen Gesetze gegenüber sich unfrei fühlt."

[366] Rudolf Steiner, <u>Goethes geheime Offenbarung</u>, (Dornach: RSV, 1982) 152, „Das Höchste, was der Mensch anstreben kann, das Höchste, in was sich der Mensch verwandeln sollte, das bezeichnet Goethe mit dem Symbol der Lilie. Es ist gleichbedeutend mit dem was wir die höchste Weisheit nennen." Goethe hat jene Liebe bezeichnet als das höchste Freisein, als das Freisein von allen Begierden und Wünschen des alltäglichen Lebens.

initiation.[367] As such, to Steiner the Green Snake must also represent subtly the result of the Incarnation and consequent sacrifice of Christ, however, this is not brought to expression in *Die Pforte*. However, Steiner's differing interpretations of the pronouns in these lines of the poem supports his view of the Green Snake, and its pivotal role in allowing access to the fair Lily.

I conclude that Steiner's view of spirituality is quintessentially expressed by his interpretation of this section of Goethe's *Elegie*. His interpretation of Goethe's *Märchen* in general, expresses his view of how to attain to this state. Hence, the 'shuddering away of self-will' occurs through the 'dawning presence' of one's approaching spiritual-self; which he sees expressed in the *Elegie*. And this process is the result of attaining to the selfless 'harvesting' of life's experiences, which the Green Snake represents. The Goethean metaphor of the Lily has become to Steiner descriptive of the attainment of selfless love; the bridge over to this condition is the capacity which bestows an urge to harvest wisdom from life's experiences.

---

[367] Rudolf Steiner, Goethes Geheime Offenbarung In Seinem Märchen von der grünen Schlange und der schönen Lilie, (Dornach: RSV 1982) 158-9.

4c: The concepts of reincarnation and karma are seen as compatible to Christianity, and are understood to have a rational basis

We have seen how the concepts of karma and of reincarnation are an integral part of the thematic elements of *Die Pforte*. The past lives of Maria, Johannes and the child are revealed. The inclusion of this episode, quite new to the thematic elements of the Goethean tale, brings the concept of pre-existence and past lives to the fore, and reveals the importance Steiner places on emphasizing the concept of repeated earth-lives.

In the early scenes of the play, Johannes is undergoing what Steiner would term, 'karmic awareness'. This episode portrays the concepts of karma and of reincarnation as a reality, and as providing insightful understanding of the feelings that arise between people. So Johannes needs firstly, to gain the knowledge of the past life – which Theodora provides – and then he can become aware of subtle spiritual forces at work in his consciousness processes, and of how these have their origin in his past lives upon the Earth.

These concepts also provide an explanation for people becoming associated with other people in a future lifetime. That Steiner included these themes in *Die Pforte* is indicative of their considerable importance in his anthroposophical worldview. This is indicated strongly in regard to the past life of the child; this child was, as Theodora reveals, the one member of the forest tribe who felt hatred for the missionary (Maria), and vowed revenge. As we noted in Section 3d, the child is a representative of the canary in *das* Märchen.

This is a minor theme in Goethe's tale, and the child does not reappear in Steiner's drama after Scene Three, even though in Goethe's tale it does appear in later episodes. Steiner has reduced the role of the canary (the child) in terms of its allegorical meaning in Goethe's tale, but utilizes it to present further aspects to his view of karma, namely, that if a person conceives hate for another, it will be drawn into the destiny of that person, in a future life. Furthermore, it is clear that Maria was a loving foster-mother, despite the child's antipathy, and despite the fact that through her spiritual enlightenment she knew of the child's past-life of hatred towards her. The implication here is that the person who is the victim, or target of the hate, will be faced – through the dynamics of 'karma' - with the Christian challenge of 'loving those who are one's enemies'.

Hence this dynamic appears to be an allusion to the words of Christ expressed in Matthew's Gospel, 5:43, "But I say to you, love your enemies and pray for those who persecute you." The implication is also there that this will be the case whether one has knowledge of the dynamics through attaining to karmic awareness, or whether one simply has the other person brought into one's life by destiny, since Maria did not have this knowledge of karma at first, she attained it after some years.

However, it is also significant that the actual theme within the sequence of lives of Johannes and Maria is Christianity, indicating to the audience that these two themes are not mutually contradictory. Maria as a male was then a Christian missionary, and quite skilled at representing Christ, and even though at first the tribes-people are angered, he is able to calm them, "…But still the man speaks calmly on. He tells about the God who descending to Earth as man, who thus has conquered death. He speaks of Christ. And as he goes on speaking, their souls grow gentler…"[368] An additional conclusion which can be drawn here, is that this speech informs the audience that today's representatives of the Christian religion are themselves a constituent part of the web of karma of humanity, whether they accept the concept or not.

---

[368] Pforte, 114, „Es spricht der Mann gelassen weiter. Er redet von dem Menschengotte, der zu der Erde niederstieg, und der den Tod besiegte, Von Christus redet er. Und wie er weiterspricht, da sänftigen sich die Seelen…"

Steiner spoke on numerous occasions to refute concern that the concept of reincarnation stands in conflict with central doctrines of Christianity, in particular, those of Redemption and vicarious Atonement. Steiner's Christology and general theological tenets and exegesis of Christian texts, cannot be examined this thesis, but it is necessary to briefly note his position on this matter. In an early lecture cycle, he maintained that it is possible to reconcile the apparent incompatibilities between these two attitudes by considering that karma posits that a person influences the karma of another, by a good or evil deed. Further, a karmic deed can be one in which someone helps (or harms) a thousand people; likewise the deed of Christ in the Crucifixion and Resurrection – the deeds which brought about Redemption and Atonement – assisted mightily the destiny of many millions, of all humanity. Hence, Steiner argues, in this sense it is an instance of a deed which has wrought an immense karmic consequence.[369]

However, we noted in Section A4 his concern that his anthroposophical worldview, or 'spiritual science', be considered a worthy adjunct to the emerging rational, scientific approach to life. Consequently, Steiner sought to place such convictions as that of repeated earth lives on a rational basis. In his early text, *'Theosophy: an introduction to the Supra-sensible Knowledge of the World and the Destination of Man'*, Steiner argues that a phenomenological approach to the human soul-life can result in conclusions which are supportive of the concept of 'karma'. He starts his argument by referring to cognitive dynamics, and after elucidating them briefly, he returns to these same dynamics, and draws further conclusions from them.

His exposition begins by pointing out that one would have to repeatedly see a sense-object, for example, a rose, in order to recall its colour, if one did not possess the faculty of memory. Through this capacity, he concludes, we have made a transient object into an ongoing object ('enduring', if not

---

[369] Steiner, Theosophie des Rosenkreutzers, 78-79.

eternal'). This is the outcome of our ability to form an image of the rose, and to recall this image. The soul can subsequently recall such images at will in the years ahead, or they manifest in consciousness when some external inducement stimulates this recall. Thus the soul-life has become an ongoing result of a transient cause, the fleeting sense-impression.

But, he also points out; action receives permanence, once it becomes fully acted out, that is, once a deed is stamped onto the outer world. By performing a deed, such as closing a factory, or cutting down a tree, or helping an injured person, something has happened which completely changes the course of events in the world. He then argues that what one has done externally as a deed, which was also transient, taking only perhaps a few minutes, has now become ongoing, enduring. He then points out that normally we do not form a clear, specific concept of this "ongoing-ness" of a deed. That is, we don't have a concept for this, which is parallel – but polar – to the concept of 'memory', wherein a transient external stimulus becomes ongoing within human consciousness.

Nevertheless, his argument continues in Theosophie, what I have done today endures into tomorrow (and beyond), just as my impressions of yesterday have become permanent through the faculty of remembrance. Steiner then points out that the ego of the human being is linked to, and changed by, the various transient sense-stimuli. That is to say, we assess and respond to sense impressions differently, according to what our reservoir of sense impressions contains. If this is the case, he asks, "Will not the self of a person be just as much linked to the alterations in the world, which result from his deeds, as it is to a memory, resulting from a sense impression?"[370]

Steiner draws a conclusion at this point, namely that we assess new sense impressions differently, according to what

---

[370] Rudolf Steiner, Theosophie: Einführung in übersinnliche Welterkenntnis und Menschen- bestimmung, (London: Rudolf Steiner Press, 1975) 89.

we have as sensory memories. That is, the world has a different relationship to us, to our inner life, as a result of what we taken into ourselves, and which have become mental images, capable of being recalled. He then argues for the polar opposite of this dynamic, concluding that so too, the human being, considered as an ego, has entered into a different relationship to the world, as a result of the (transient) deeds that we imprinted into the world (and which are ongoing). Steiner also points out in Theosophie, that the human will is in effect embodied in actions that we undertake, a deed is an expression of intention. He then concludes his argument by asking,

> If one really thinks out what is here being considered, the question must arise as to whether the results of a deed on which the ego has stamped its own nature might not retain a tendency to return to the ego, just as a sense-impression, preserved in the memory, revives in response to some external inducement? What is preserved in the memory waits for such an inducement. Could not that which has retained the imprint of the ego in the external world also wait, so as to approach the human soul *from without*, just as memory, in response to a given inducement, approaches *from within*?[371]

It becomes clear from this argument that the concept he is attempting to logically validate is that of 'karma', understood as the deeds invoked into one's life experience, once they are given the appropriate inducement, that is, opportunity. He further concludes it is clear that, for this concept we do not have a specific word – that is, a term in a European language

---

[371] Rudolf Steiner, Theosophie 89-92, „Man wird, wenn man das hier in Betracht Kommende wirklich durchdenkt, zu der Frage kommen, könnte es nicht sein, daß die Folge einer vollbrachten Tat, denen ihr Wesen durch das „Ich" aufgeprägt ist, eine Tendenz erhalten, zu dem Ich wieder hinzuzutreten, wie ein im Gedächtnis bewahrter Eindrück wieder auflebt, wenn sich dazu eine äußere Veranlassung ergibt? Das im Gedächtnis Bewahrte wartet auf eine solche Veranlassung. Könnte nicht das in der Außenwelt mit dem Ich-Charakter Bewahrte ebenso warten, um so von *außen* an die Menschenseele heranzutreten, wie die Erinnerung von innen an diese Seele bei gegebener Veranlassung herantritt?"

that has arisen from the thoughts and life-experience of European thinkers. Both the European and English peoples only have the term borrowed from Sanskrit for this, because the terms, 'destiny' and 'fate' do not specifically denote multiple lives in normal conversation.

Steiner is aware in the argument, that he has not yet refuted the theory of pre-destination, which asserts that the differing life experiences and abilities of humankind have been determined before birth by God. Again, when arguing for the validity of karma, Steiner attempts by logical argument to affirm, if not prove, that pre-destination is incorrect. He does this by deducing that the human soul further develops its aptitudes, and strengthens it abilities, whilst in the spiritual realms, between life times.

His attempt in *Theosophie* to logically demonstrate the validity of such a spiritual concept, is one of the most difficult passages in all of his works. His argument is based on defining the characteristic formative dynamics implicit in those influences efficacious on the human being in the earthly environs, in contrast to those active when the disembodied soul is within a spiritual environment. In a section of the book that examines the concept of repeated earth-lives, he seeks to refute the alternative argument, namely that the soul attains its abilities through acquiring them whilst in Heaven, before birth. So, in this scenario, the different qualities in human beings are the result of a differing time in the spiritual realm, prior to the one life-time upon the Earth,

> The first thinkable alternative would be this, that I owe the form of the content of my life-history to a spiritual life only prior to birth, that is, prior to conception. But one would only be entitled to hold this perception only if one were willing to assume that what acts upon the human soul from its physical surroundings is of the same nature as what the soul

receives from a purely spiritual realm. But such an assumption contradicts really exact observation.[372]

This next passage is a difficult text, which illustrates his approach to establish a logical argument for spiritual concepts, and it is appropriate here that the German text accompanies my translation,

> For, what is determinative in this physical environment for the human soul is of this nature – its efficacy is similar to the effect that an earlier experience – in physical life – has upon another experience, of the same kind. In order to correctly observe this relationship, one has to learn to perceive how there are influences efficacious in human life, which effect the aptitudes of the soul as if one were placed before a deed which has yet to be done, in contrast to that which one has already practised. Except that such influences though not indeed, encountering something already practised in this life {abilities} – encounter soul-aptitudes which do allow themselves to be influenced in the same way, as do talents which are acquired through practise.[373]

The initial statement "For, what is determinative in this physical environment for the human soul is of this nature – its

---

[372] Steiner, Theosophie, 104, „Der andere *zunächst* denkbare Fall wäre der, daß ich die Ausgestaltung dessen, was Inhalt meiner Biographie ist, *nur* einem geistigen Leben *vor* der Geburt, (beziehungsweise der Empfängnis) verdanke. Zu dieser Vorstellung hätte man aber nur Berechtigung, wenn man annehmen wollte, daß, was auf die Menschenseele aus dem physischen Umkreis herein wirkt, gleichartig sei mit dem, was die Seele aus einer von geistigen Welt hat. Eine solche Annahme widerspricht der wirklich genaue Beobachtung."

[373] „Denn was aus dieser physischen Umgebung bestimmend für die Menschenseele ist, das ist so, daß es wirkt wie ein später im physischen Leben Erfahrenes auf ein in gleicher Art früher Erfahrenes. Um diese Verhältnisse richtig zubeobachten, muß man sich den Blick dafür aneignen, wie es im Menschenleben wirksame Eindrücke gibt, die so auf die Anlagen der Seele wirken, wie das Stehen vor einer zu verrichtenden Tat gegenüber dem, was man im physischen Leben schon geübt hat; nur daß solche Eindrücke eben nicht auf ein in diesem unmittelbaren Leben schon Geübtes auftreffen, sondern auf Seelenanlagen die sich so beeindrucken lassen wie die durch Übung erworbenen Fähigkeiten." Theosophie, 104.

efficacy is similar to the effect that an earlier experience – in physical life – has upon another experience, of the same kind" is to be seen in the context of abilities and aptitudes. It means that, with regard to life on the Earth, a later, repeated, experience reinforces one's existential understanding of the challenges involved, and hence leads to greater skill in that ability.

His next statement in the above extract, points out that there is also a different kind of repetitious influence to which we can be subject. This influence is different in two ways; firstly, it encounters solely aptitudes, not abilities. Aptitudes are of course, abilities which are still only potential, so the aptitude has not as yet actually become manifested in a practical activity. Secondly, the aptitude actually does allow itself to be influenced by these (repeated) influences, in a dynamic similar to that which causes an ability to become enhanced through repeated exposure.

An analysis of this passage is greatly assisted by reference to his lectures concerning the existence of the soul in the realm of the Idea, the spiritual realms, between lifetimes. In these texts, Steiner maintains that in the spiritual realm the soul is exposed to influences that are attracted to, and flow into, their corresponding qualities within that soul, "Just as the human being here is continually under the influence of the external atmosphere, likewise in Devachan; and there the 'atmosphere' is formed all the sum total of the soul-life {prevalent in that realm}. He explains to his audience that all this is constantly exerting its efficacy upon the soul, and in this way the disembodied soul gathers new forces for its approaching new life.[374]

This passage clarifies the extract from Theosophie namely; the result of this ambient activity on the soul in the spiritual

---

[374] Rudolf Steiner, Menschheitsentwickelung und Christus-Erkenntnis, (Dornach: VRSN, 1967) 60, „Wie nämlich hier auf Erden der Mensch dauernd unter den Einflüßen der äußeren Atmosphären steht, so auch im Devachan, und dort ist die Atmosphäre ja gebildet aus allem Seelenleben...All dies Seelenleben wirkt dauernd auf den Menschen ein..."

realm of the Idea is that the milieu of that realm strengthens any tendency towards any given talent, until it becomes an incipient aptitude. This <u>incipient</u> aptitude then manifests as an aptitude, once the soul is reborn. Here Steiner is not concerned with a specific ability, rather with the concept of how a person on the Earth can become equipped with a talent for something, such as being a composer of classical music. He is arguing that any slight tendency towards a certain gift, which exists in the soul between lifetimes, becomes strengthened as a potential, as an incipient aptitude, as a result of the environment in the spiritual realms.

On Earth, that aptitude may never be given an opportunity to be developed, and hence may never proceed further to become an ability. In any event, that aptitude can be come a talent only through earthly activity; it is the repeated practising of an activity by a person that develops their aptitude into an ability, and consequently allows the ability to become ever more enhanced.

In the above quote extracted from Theosophie, Steiner is implying that it is the constant exposure to spiritual influences that gradually incubates an aptitude; and this, in turn, is only possible because the soul does actually respond to these influences. He is further implying that only on the Earth, in physical life, can an ability be enhanced, whereas in a spiritual sphere the most that can be achieved with regard to a person's capability, is to incubate an aptitude, and to strengthen any aptitude that already exists. But the presence of an ability, a tangible talent, can only arise through the experience of using those skills on the Earth.

Hence Steiner concludes that the differing talents of people can only have their origin in a past life. To illustrate his point, he refers to an exceptional case, that of Wolfgang Amadeus Mozart, who could write down the entire score of a long musical composition, which he heard as school child. He concludes that this talent, in accordance with his viewpoint here, must have been repeatedly exercised in prior lives, perhaps several lives of musical activity. That is, Mozart would have had a mere aptitude, several lifetimes ago, which, in the times he passed in the spiritual realm, was able to gradually develop into a fully developed talent.[375]

Steiner then argues against 'materialists', by which he means those to whom there can be no existence before conception or after the body has died. He points out that this viewpoint is against 'miracles', these are not permitted to the materialist. But those who support this viewpoint ascribe the phenomenal memory capacity of Mozart to heredity. This is an argument which, Steiner argues, is another form of superstition. He argues that just as a frog cannot have its origin in mud – as was thought in mediaeval times – so too, it can not be argued that Mozart's talent has arisen out of nothing. Steiner maintains that if the materialist wishes to ascribe this memory to heredity – but wherein no such musical genius has existed – then this is a form of 'reversed superstition'. Steiner's conclusion here is based on the view that, as a consciousness capacity, such a talent of genius must have a cause which derives from consciousness processes occurring in someone, and thus it has to be derived from the repeated development of an ability over several lives,

> Those who, in accordance with a materialistic viewpoint accept that such a perfect memory as that of the young Mozart can arise out of nothing, should draw the consequences of their viewpoint, and accept that, for example, frogs arise out of mud, which, as is well known, science had accepted, before Francesco Redi.[376]

---

[375] Rudolf Steiner, Menschheitsentwickelung, 51.
[376] Steiner, Menschheitsentwickelung 52, „Und diejenigen, die nach materialistischer Anschauungsweise annehme, daß ein so vollkommenes Gedächtnis wie das des jungen Mozart aus dem Nichts entstehen kann, die sollen auch die Konsequenz aus ihrer Anschauungsweise ziehen und annehmen, daß zum Beispiel Frösche sich ohne weiteres aus dem Schlamm entwickeln, wie es ja die Naturwissenschaft bekanntlich vor Francesco Redi angenommen hat."

Francesco Redi (1626-1698) was an early Italian scientist who established by experiments, that the concept of spontaneous generation was invalid; that is, living creatures can only be produced by other living creatures, that inanimate material cannot produce life. He carried out experiments with flies, disproving the doctrine, ascribed to Aristotle, that they arise spontaneously from rotting flesh.[377]

The insertion into *Die Pforte* of the episode in which Theodora perceives the past life personalities of Johannes and Maria reflects the didactic purpose of Steiner, to present this central theme in his anthroposophy as a reality in human existence. Maria is declared by Theodora to have been a noble soul in a past life, for she was a skilled missionary for Christ, and this generated the karma that she was reborn as someone capable of having interest and ability in anthroposophical spiritual teachings. However, the past lives episode in Chapter Seven is also a reflection of another didactic intention in this regard. It is Steiner's understanding that the outcome of a lifetime's experience is absorbed into the eternal spirit of each human being, enriching and consolidating this transcendent aspect of the human being.

Within the human spirit, whose locus is the spiritual realm, indeed the realm of the Platonic Idea, are preserved the memories of events in each past life. He taught that the eternal 'causal-body' exists in the Platonic realm of Ideas, and also that which some mystics refer to as 'the memory of nature' occurs here.[378] Steiner, using theosophical terminology, refers to this record as the 'Akashic Record'; this means a realm consisting of a substance, or rather energy, known as 'akasha' in Theosophical terminology. This energy has the capacity to receive an imprint of all events which occur as history unfolds on the Earth. Steiner taught that it contains the scenes of all persons' prior lives.

---

[377] Encyclopaedia Brittanica, ed. Warren E. Preece, (Chicago: William Benton, 1971) vol. 8, *Entolomology*, 610.
[378] Rudolf Steiner, Die Theosophie des Rosenkreuzers, (Dornach: RSV, 1979) 44.

Consequently, it is clear that this episode in Scene Seven is intended to point to the concept of karma as a reality, and to portray an experience of this archetypal realm, thereby illustrating that the nature of the higher consciousness which Johannes' initiation makes possible access to the Platonic realm of the Idea. I also conclude that it is Steiner's wish to point out, by including the past-lives episode in *Die Pforte*, that in order to attain to a consciousness which embraces the eternal higher ego, the meditant must attain to this realm.

4d: Steiner's earlier holistic epistemology is based on a proto-type of the 'ether-body' postulate

A perspective underlying Steiner's philosophical writings, prior to 1900, is that human consciousness is not body-derived, but rather the human being has a soul, in which (undefined) spiritual forces are also active. The structure and dynamics in this model of this soul-spiritual human being are presented in *Die Pforte*, but this was never elucidated in his earlier phase. We noted in Section One that his philosophical writings merely imply that the omission of some unidentified 'holistic' factor has resulted in an erroneous purely mechanistic, materialistic view of the human being and its consciousness processes. To Steiner, the term' objective' is extended to mean a valid existence, not only in the material molecular realm, but also in the ether energies. In his Theosophie, this subtle body is said to be responsible for the maintenance of our life-processes.

It is the function of the life-force organism, Steiner's 'ether-body', to mediate thoughts, feelings and will, as well as sensory objects, to consciousness. Furthermore, and significantly, in terms of his epistemology, hallucinations and visionary experiences are also regarded as being objectively perceived contents of the soul-life of the person. The categorizing of these latter as deceptive or inherently non-existent, in terms of cognitive processes, is regarded by Steiner as just as epistemologically invalid as the same conclusion regarding sense impressions. Because in his view, whether a human being registers the presence of a sensory stimulus or an element of their soul-life, or a spiritual being, these are experienced via the mediating function of the ether-body.

The ether-body registers an intuitive idea, a flowering bush, a flash of anger or a non-physical (spirit) entity; these are considered objective experiences, because he views them as images formed in the ether-body, and mediated to consciousness by this 'body'. Perception of them is underpinned by the function of the life-force organism or ether-body. That is, not only is the sensory registering of a sense object carried through to consciousness by this energetic organism, but so too is perception of consciousness dynamics.

Furthermore, hallucinatory images (sounds, odours) are considered to be objectively perceived, whether induced by schizophrenia, drug addiction or psychic practises. Steiner does not dispute that when a disturbed mental dynamic conjures forth a normal sense-world image or sound, (where it cannot actually be present), or a fantastical creature, this is a deceptive product of consciousness. But with regard to hallucinatory imagery, Steiner maintains that the ether-body brings both these images, arising in the soul, to consciousness.

An hallucination has validity in so far as it is an image manifesting unhealthily in the network of energies which constitutes the life-force body, and there it is cognised by the soul. With regard to hallucinations, Steiner maintained on one occasion that a bodily illness can result in these if the ether process extends beyond its limits into the corporeal, because of the fact that the body, through its ill-health can not provide the appropriate resistance, then that arises which one calls an hallucination." [379]

The implication here is that perception of images, whether of a recalled memory, or an 'hallucination' is, by definition, a perceived image and therefore must have its locus in this life-force organism. No image or sound or amorphous coloured psychic 'form', etc can be perceived without it being present in the life-force organism. Steiner views the question as to its reality in terms of its origin in that organism. Naturally if the 'hallucinatory' object is not physically present, then the

---

[379] Steiner Geist, 172, „Wenn der Äthervorgang seine Grenze überschreitet nach dem Leiblichen hin, dadurch daß der Leib ihm durch seine Krankhaftigkeit nicht den richtigen Widerstand entgegensetzt, dann entsteht das, was man eine Hallucination nennt."

respective image is existent only in the ether-body and the soul.

But Steiner also gives a role to the soul in cognition. The implications of his argument in Theosophie is that the ether-body mediates the images of sense impressions, detected by the sense organs in the ambient environment, and conducts these further into the corporeality. When this reaches the brain, the soul, which interpenetrates the body, and is especially linked to the brain, does the registering or perceiving of the sensory impression (or indeed, spiritual reality). Hence instead of concluding that sense impressions (or spiritual dynamics in the inner life) have no objective existence or no existence outside of an observer, Steiner concludes that their existence is indeed valid, but that they can not have any existence in chemical or nerve processes.

In the 1880's in the course of his work as editor of Goethe's scientific writings, in the first volume of this material for Kürschner's *National Literature*, Steiner writes of Goethe's opposition to a 'mechanisation' of the world, and humanity's perception thereof, and quotes in this regard, Goethe's verse from Faust (Part One, 1936-1939), "Whoever seeks to recognize and describe a living thing, firstly seeks to drive out the spirit; then he has parts in his hand, but the spiritual link is missing, alas!"[380] Then, some years later, in volume four, in his comments on Goethe's theory of colour, Steiner reveals his conviction that the registration of sense impressions is due to an holistic factor,

> It is impossible to build a 'living bridge' from the fact – at this point in space there exist certain movements of colourless material – to the other fact; the human being sees at this place the colour red. Only movement can be derived from movement. And from the fact that a movement becomes efficacious upon a

---

[380] Deutsche National Literatur, 114. Band, heraus. J. Kürschner, Goethes Werke, dreiunddreißigster Teil, Naturwissenschaftliche Schriften, erster Band, heraus. von Rudolf Steiner (Berlin: Verlag von W. Spemann), *Begriff des Lebens*, XX1.

sense organ and thereby upon the brain, it can only follow – from the mathematical and mechanical method – that the brain will be induced by the external world to make certain movements; and not that it perceives certain tones, colours, sensations of warmth, etc.[381]

Already in these conclusions, it is clear that to Steiner sense impressions must be carried within a living medium, a life-force medium, and from thence to the soul. In the following lecture extract, from his later, anthroposophical phase, Steiner elucidates his theory, and is concerned with the supra-sensible aspects. The scientific details about the reception of light inside the eye is not his concern, these are not relevant to his theory, as it does not include the physical processes,

> You can never seek the sense perceptions in the sense-organs themselves. What happens when the light of a flame meets my eye? This light exists within external space; the so-called ether waves are in motion from the source of light into my eye, these penetrate my eye, there they bring about certain chemical processes in the rear wall of my eyeball, they transform the so-called visual crimson, and these chemical changes continue on in my brain. My brain perceives the flame, it receives the impression of light. If another person could observe the processes which occur in my brain, what would he see? He would see nothing else than physical processes; he would see that which occurs within space and time; but in these physical processes occurring within my

---

[381] Kürschners Nat. Lit., Goethes Werke Bd. 36, xii „Es ist unmöglich, eine <lebendige Brücke> zu schlagen von der Tatsache: An diesem Orte des Raumes herrscht ein bestimmter Bewegungsvorgang der farblosen Materie,- und der andern Tatsache: der Mensch sieht an diesem Orte Rot. Aus Bewegung kann nur Bewegung abgeleitet werden. Und aus der Tatsache, daß eine Bewegung auf ein Sinnesorgan und dadurch auf das Gehirn wirkt, folgt - nach mathematischer und mechanischer Methode - nur, daß das Gehirn von der Außenwelt zu gewissen Bewegungsvorgängen veranlaßt wird, nicht aber daß es die konkreten Töne, Farben, Wärmeerscheinungen usw. wahrnimmt."

brain he could not see the light impression {*the image of the flame*}.

This light impression is something other than a physical impression, which is the basis of the above processes. For the light impression, the image, which I must first create, in order to be able to perceive the flame, is a process within my astral body. Those who possess an organ for seeing such astral processes, see exactly how the physical phenomenon {mediated by the ether forces} in the brain, is transformed within the astral body, into the image of the flame, which we {then} register....A sensory impression of light is thereby made possible, because as I have already said, ether vibrations enter into my eye, and these are transformed by my soul organism into an image of the light, and one cognises this light-image; it is in this way that I become aware of this light-image.[382]

---

[382] Rudolf Steiner, Spirituelle Seelenlehre, 257, „Sie können niemals die sinnlichen Wahrnehmungen in den Sinnesorganen selbst suchen. Was geschieht, wenn das Licht von einer Flamme mein Auge trifft? Dieses Licht besteht ja im äußerlichen Raume darin: die sogenannten Ätherwellen bewegen sich von der Lichtquelle in mein Auge, sie dringen in mein Auge ein, sie bewirken gewisse chemische Vorgänge in der Hinterwand meines Augapfels, sie verwandeln den sogenannten Sehpurpur, und dann pflanzen sich diese chemischen Vorgänge in mein Gehirn fort. Mein Gehirn nimmt die Flamme wahr, es bekommt den Lichteindruck. Könnte ein anderer diejenigen Vorgänge, die sich in meinem Gehirn abspielen, sehen, was würde er wahrnehmen? Er würde nichts anderes wahrnehmen als physikalische Vorgänge; er würde etwas wahrnehmen, was sich in Raum und Zeit abspielt; nicht könnte er innerhalb der physikalischen Vorgänge in meinem Gehirn meinen Lichteindruck wahrnehmen. Dieser Lichteindruck ist etwas anderes als ein physikalischer Eindruck, der diesen Vorgängen zugrunde liegt. Der Lichteindruck, das Bild, das ich mir erst schaffen muß, um die Flamme wahrnehmen zu können, ist ein Vorgang innerhalb meines astralischen Körpers. Derjenige, welcher ein Sehorgan hat, um einen solchen astralischen Vorgang wahrnehmen zu können, sieht ganz genau, wie sich die physikalischen Erscheinungen innerhalb des Gehirns in dem astralischen Körper umwandeln in das Bild der Flamme, das wir empfinden. Ein Lichteindruck wird dadurch bewirkt, wie ich schon gesagt habe, daß Ätherschwingungen in mein Auge kommen, daß sie durch den Astralkörper umgewandelt werden in ein Lichtbild, und daß man dieses Lichtbild als Vorstellung auffaßt; dadurch werde ich mir dieses Lichtbildes bewußt."

That is, he maintains that the ether-body bears the sense stimuli into the soul-permeated corporeality, where the soul-body cognises these. The following lecture extract, presents Steiner's view, with regards to spiritual vision, that any ideas which are glimpsed by the meditant as flashes of insight, without any tangible form or logical structure, are actually existing as images in one's 'ether-body',

> This first stage of knowledge of the supra-sensible may be called 'Imaginative knowledge'....then the person finally arrives at the point of...developing a image-consciousness, not dreaming in images, rather being able to think in images...this image-thinking does not descend into the corporeality, rather it is free and separate from one's corporeality...then one can say from inner experience...I experience myself as a person not only in a physical body, I experience myself as a person in an etheric body...[383]

This reference to the ether-body is of great significance for the question of resolving Steiner's insistence on the validity of perception; both for the sense-world and of the spiritual world. Hence, the spiritual images, which the seer experiences are deemed to have an objective origin in spiritual realities. Nevertheless, Steiner does not maintain that this process is free of error; in the rhetoric of *Die Pforte* becomes clear that the acolyte is cautioned to treat initial higher experiences as possibly self-created. Accordingly, Johannes is unsure whether some of his experiences are 'genuine',

---

[383] Rudolf Steiner, <u>Was wollte das Goetheanum und was soll die Anthroposophie?</u> (Dornach: VRSN, 1961) 274, „Diese erste Stufe der Erkenntnis des Übersinnlichen sei genannt die Imaginative Erkenntnis....dann kommt der Mensch endlich dazu....ein Bilderbewußtsein zu entwickeln, in Bildern nicht träumen, sondern denken zu können....dieses Bilddenken taucht nicht unter in die Körperlichkeit, ist frei und unabhängig von der Körperlichkeit...man kann dann aus innerer Erfahrung....heraus sagen: Ich erlebe mich als Mensch nicht nur im physischen Leibe, ich erlebe mich als Mensch in einem ätherischen Leibe... "

> And much more have I seen with my organs of spirit, than what the senses first revealed to me in their narrow way. And the light of clarifying discernment shone in my new world. But whether a dream was dawning within me, or whether spiritual reality already encompassed me, I could not yet distinguish. And whether my spiritual vision encountered other things or whether I had only widened myself into a world, I could not tell.[384]

As noted in the Introduction, Steiner was quite clear that if his 'spiritual research' were to be acceptable in the modern context, then the epistemological objections to any type of 'higher' cognitional experiences, such as those portrayed in *Die Pforte* would need to be answered. Hence he undertook to explain his approach to harmonizing epistemology to the experience of spiritual vision, in the course of his lecturing on spiritual subjects, as we have seen.

In *Die Pforte* however, although many themes are presented in complex speeches, he does not introduce epistemological argument. The only exception is a brief reference in Scene One where the character 'Strader', who is an agnostic scientist, declares that the limits to cognition are unsurmountable;

> Though this admission can be very hard for him who would so eagerly learn things which are not knowable – at every glance, the limits to knowledge with their huge power do meet the thinker's soul, whether he is looking out at the world, or into himself. [385]

---

[384] Pforte, 112, „Und vieles hab' ich noch gesehn mit meinen Geistorganen, was erst die Sinne mir gezeigt auf ihre enge (sic!) Art. Und klärend Urteilslicht erstrahlte in meiner neuen Welt. Doch ob ein Traum mir dämmerte, ob Geisteswirklichkeit mich schon umgab ich konnte es noch nicht entscheiden. Ob meine Geistesschau berührt von andern Dingen ward, ob ich das eigne Selbst mir nur zu einer Welt erweitert, ich wusst' es nicht."
[385] Pforte, 30, „Wenn solch Bekenntnis auch recht hart der Seele wird, die allzugern ergründen möchte, was jenseits allen Wissens liegt: der Denkerseele drängt ein jeder Blick,ob er nach außen sich bemüht, ob man ins Innre ihn gerichtet hält."

Apart from inserting this speech by Strader in *Die Pforte*, Steiner does not take up the question as to the epistemological validity of spiritual vision any further, in terms of rational debate. Instead, he follows this theme through with Strader, who by Scene Nine has started to acknowledge, reluctantly, the validity of Johannes' perceptions – as they come to indirect expression in his artwork. So, again, the validity and value of art on the path to spirituality is affirmed.

In his anthroposophical teachings, Steiner provides the answer to the question of the modus operandi whereby an accurate reliable perceiving of sense objects – or of intuitive thoughts and spiritual realities – by positing the efficacy of an ether-body. Steiner sees the solution to the epistemological conundrum regarding the validity of sense stimuli in the efficacy of the ether body. And consequently, spiritual perceptions are validated, because, as the above quotations indicate, the meditant, in experiencing a spiritual reality, in the first (and later) stages of higher consciousness, is functioning in his or her ether-body. The entire drama, *Die Pforte*, not only presupposes this, but it demonstrates that the ether body is essential to registering perceptions, and that the soul-body then becomes the actual recipient of these.

There is an additional significance to the ether-body in regard to the role of art in Steiner's worldview. We noted in the preceding Section, that in Steiner's view, part of the triune human spirit is the life-spirit, and that this in effect, is the 'transformed' ether-body. The concept of life-spirit bears a logical consistency to his view of the role of art in human life. It is the result of a 'spiritualization' process of the ether-body, but in Steiner's holistic epistemological theory, the ether-body is the bearer of sensory impressions, including of course, artistic sensory stimuli. It follows from these postulates that the exposure to art as a spectator will 'refine' the ether-body; no doubt, this process is more potent, for those who are artists. Similarly, exposure to ugly or discordant sensory impressions will coarsen it. A passage from an early lecture affirms these conclusions, and integrates them into the postulate of repeated earth lives,

> An artistically formed musical composition, or a painting, is directly efficacious on the ether-body. A virtue is efficacious on the astral-body. Many fine people, returning {to an incarnation} from Devachan, encounter an ether-body which is not compatible to their advanced astral-body, because they have done nothing {in their previous lifetime}, in the sense of beauty, towards an activity which improves the nature of their ether-body.[386]

To see the fuller implication of the above words, it is necessary to bear in mind that Steiner affirmed the ancient concept of the four temperaments. He maintained that the choleric, sanguine, phlegmatic and melancholic temperaments are valid and significant features of the human being's inner life.[387] These derive from specific energies in the ether-body. In view of Steiner's exposition of the ether-body as the bearer of the temperament of a person, this lecture extract has an additional implication, namely that the temperament or predisposition of the person returning to Earth will be coarser.

I conclude that Steiner's epistemological conclusions, evinced in his editorial comments on Goethe, that humanity possesses an inherently valid perceptual ability – both with respect to the sensory and to the spiritual realities – is based on a privately held postulate of the ether-body, or some form of proto-type of this. Further, I conclude that Steiner sees the value of art as relevant for this ether-body. In addition to the ability to convey a message in ways differing to, and

---

[386] Rudolf Steiner, Grundelemente der Esoterik, (Dornach: RSV, 1972) 163, „Ein künstlerisch gestaltetes Tongebilde oder ein Gemälde wirkt unmittelbar auf den Ätherkörper. Manche edle Menschen, die aus dem Devachan zurückkommen, treffen, weil sie gar nichts getan haben zu einer im Sinne Schönheit organisierenden Tätigkeit, einen Ätherkörper an, der gar nicht zu ihrem fortgeschrittenen Astralkörper paßt."
[387] Rudolf Steiner, Vor dem Tore der Theosophie, lect. 6, (Dornach: RSV, 1978).

enriching of, the conceptual medium, it also exerts a refining effect upon the ether-body, thereby assisting in the development of part of the triune human spirit. Additionally, as a corollary to this, as a preparatory phase of this refining of the ether-body, artistic experience refines the temperament or pre-dispositional qualities of the person.

I further conclude that it is highly likely that Steiner in his earlier years, whilst writing on epistemology, was already persuaded as to the existence and efficacy of this ether-body postulate. It was very likely his concern about the fate of his academic work that prevented him for integrating a general 'theosophical' element into his dissertations at that time.

4e: Steiner's holistic epistemological conviction that the limits to knowledge may be extended, is reflected in Die Pforte's portrayal of the efficacy of meditation

As we have seen in the earlier section of the thesis, Steiner's philosophical writings sought to argue two primary postulates. One is that sense perception is valid and reliable, despite the acknowledged fact that sensory stimuli become physiological substances and electrical nerve energy inside the body. The second postulate is that the human mind has the ability to perceive the Idea of a perceived object, existent in a spiritual ream. This postulate defies the general conclusion in philosophical circles, as to the existence of 'limits to knowledge'.

It may be concluded that once Steiner took up the task of speaking on esoteric-spiritual subjects, in his new career with the Theosophical Society, he was open to the charge of forsaking or contradicting his earlier philosophical convictions. In 1903, Steiner began to produce his first articles for a Theosophical magazine, on various esoteric themes, including the theme, "Knowledge of the Higher Worlds, how is it attained". In October of that same year, however, he announced a series of three lectures on 'Die erkenntnistheoretischen Grundlagen der Theosophie' (The epistemological bases of Theosophy).

In these lectures, he sets out to give his audience an overview of the main issues in epistemology in order to then demonstrate that an extension to consciousness is possible. He begins by commenting that many of the audience have probably had their theosophical interests treated with some ridicule by friends and associates, who view it as dilettante, at best. He says his intention is to equip his listeners with the requisite philosophical skill, which their academically oriented contemporaries have acquired. Steiner comments that a contemporary philosopher would object to theosophical statements about beings and objects in spiritual realms (termed 'the astral plane') as being 'quite real'. He tells his audience that, such a person would tell Theosophists that they are making a mistake in believing that this is a true reality, saying, 'Don't you know that that, which we call our experience, is nothing other than our own mental image' (Vorstellung)?' On this subject in his Die Philosophie, Steiner had quoted Eduard von Hartmann that perception is entirely subjective, "What the subject perceives are thus always only modifications of his own psychological conditions, and nothing else." [388]

It is his task in these three lectures to equip his audience with the means by which they can defend themselves from this position. The understanding of the term, 'mental image' and associated terms in Steiner's works, need to be noted here. These are explained in Die Philosophie and Wahrheit und Wissenschaft. To Steiner, the act of cognition commences with an inherently reliable perceiving of a sense object, which results in a person experiencing a 'percept'. This forms into a Vorstellungen ('mental image') by itself. In the course of repeated formation of such images of the same object, the beholder may, and usually does, gradually form a 'concept'.

The 'concept' differs from a 'mental image' in that it encompasses an understanding of the inner nature of the perceived object, that is, the natural laws or properties operative within it have been discovered. Whereas a mere mental image enables only recognition of the fact that has seen such an object previously. A mere mental-image differs thusly from a concept, and there is a third step, for the concept can be laboriously formulated into a complex 'idea'.

We have earlier considered Steiner's view that a cognizing person can experience intuitively the 'Idea' which relates to a perceived thing; and that these are also given – or rather <u>can</u> be given – in the moment of perception. However, the above process describes the gradual formation of a concept, which in a fuller version of itself becomes an 'idea'. This does not

---

[388] Steiner, Philosophie, 59.

stand in contradiction to his postulate of the (Platonic) Idea being received as the 'other half' of reality, the first part of it being the perceived object. In the instance where an Idea is perceived, a different process is active, wherein the concept is perceived directly, intuitively, and not logically formulated. Such intuitive access to concepts occurs in regard to higher, more transcendent realities, such as a spiritual being, or a religious-philosophical-spiritual tenet, as well as the holistic factor of a sensory object (for example the healing life-forces of a plant). So we are subject to the formulation of an 'idea' or the reception, intuitively, of an 'Idea'. In Section 2a, the question of language with regard to supra-sensible themes, and the difficulty of translating Steiner's terms were considered.

In these three lectures of 1903, Steiner then recounts briefly much of the ground covered in Die Philosophie concerning sense perceptions that we have noted above, in order to refute prevailing concepts. He cautions however, that the Theosophist can never take the attitude of 'various philosophers', namely that his or her specific worldview is the correct one. Instead, Steiner told his listeners that the Theosophist sees some truth in all religions, and in all the philosophical systems. However he makes it clear to the Theosophists, that one may trust in the validity of perception, and the idea that the perceived word-content is one's own mental image is an error. At this early stage in his esoteric-spiritual career he does not provide the holistic-esoteric basis for this conclusion. He then comments that nevertheless the world around about them is an illusion, in some respects, an attitude with which his listeners would be familiar from the traditional Oriental wisdom that had found a strong reception amongst the Society based in Adyar, India.

At this point in the lectures, Steiner has to resolve the looming problem of inconsistencies in his message, namely that the world is to some extent, an illusion – as many in his audience would have accepted that the real, the true, realm of being lies beyond the material level of being – and yet he was affirming that a deeply true reality was accessible to humanity. His solution is to clarify the underlying implication his earlier philosophical works, namely that the human being, especially in moments of higher insights, can perceive the truth of a material reality through this process wherein the two halves of reality (or 'the world-content') are perceived. This process, he tells his audience, includes a phenomenological dynamic in which the spiritual Idea of the object leaves its 'signature' on it.

Steiner refers to the philosophical concept of the 'thing-in-itself' in a general sense, that is, the Kantian postulate which as we noted earlier, effectively denies any bridging over to reality. He then provides an alternative perspective, using a simile of a sealing-wax stamp. He points out to his audience that the 'thing-in-itself' postulate creates a reality in which perceiving is like the process of stamping a seal into hot wax. The 'thing-in-itself' is the seal, and the mental image is simply its impression made in the wax, "Indeed everything remains outside of the substance of the seal, which has taken up only the impression of the seal."[389] The implication here that nothing of the real (Idea) of an object may be in a mental image is then argued against.

Steiner then introduces a concept which he sees as a well known, general mystical perspective, namely that although the barrier to perceiving objects truly is formidable, human beings perhaps have never left the objects, that is, they could be *in* the objects. He points out that this a pivotal thought of Theosophy, namely that our ego does not belong to us, it is not enclosed within our physical organism, but rather, our individual humanity is in fact a manifestation of the divine Self of the cosmos. He then elaborates this general mystical concept by saying that "within our thinking is something which extends beyond our ego…the capacity of thinking derives from the primal foundation, the Spirit." This term,

---

[389] Rudolf Steiner, Spirituelle Seelenlehre und Weltbetrachtung, (Dornach: RSV, 1972) 128, „Vom Siegel bleibt alles außerhalb des Substanz, die den Siegelabdruck aufnimmt."

'primal foundation' occurs in *Die Pforte* in Scene Four, as we noted in Section 3f, "What a strange being!...from what primal foundation of the cosmos do such beings come into being?" ("...welch sonderbares Wesen! ...aus welchem Weltengrund erstehen solche Wesen?). It has the general connotation of the realm of the spiritual, in effect of the Platonic Idea, as we saw in our consideration of Steiner's *Credo*.

On the basis of these considerations, Steiner then returns to his simile of the wax stamp, concluding that although nothing of the substance of the true object may be in the wax impression, it does bear however, the person's name. Similarly, he argues, the Idea endows the perceived object with its imprint, namely the associated Idea. Steiner then emphasizes that the spiritually striving Theosophist can attain to this deeper and more empowered form of thinking through a meditative process. This activity activates a spiritual consciousness which is able to discern the fuller primal reality indicated by the impression of the seal. He tells his audience that subjective elements are overcome in this process, and objective reality can be discerned by such empowered thinking, derived from the Spirit. Therefore, he concludes, it is not correct that all truths which one obtains in this way are subjective products, derived from the personal ego,

> "Nothing in the field of wisdom is associated with your ego. Because you can raise yourselves to an objective thinking which is enclosed within itself, you can also form objective judgements about the world....in our {intuitive} thinking is something which is above our ego."[390]

---

[390] Rudolf Steiner, Spirituelle Seelenlehre, 133, „Nichts im Felde der Weisheit hat mit ihrem Ich zu tun. Weil Sie sich zu einem objektiven, in sich geschlossenen Denken erheben können, können Sie auch objektiv über die Welt urteilen... Denn innerhalb unseres Denkens ist etwas, das über unserem Ich liegt."

Steiner finishes his lectures on the subject by concluding that "The right way is <u>the way itself</u>; above all, it is that which had been placed over the door to the Greek temples, 'Know yourself'. We are one with the universal spirit."[391] We have seen how this ancient Greek inscription is used as a very prominent device in several scenes of *Die Pforte*. This maxim resounds repeatedly as a chorus, in several scenes as Johannes, the main character in the drama, seeks to attain to higher consciousness through a meditative state.

A few months after he gave his lectures on a theosophical approach to epistemology, Steiner published his basic manual on extending cognitional faculties through meditative techniques, referred to above. This is his book, "Wie erlangt man Erkenntnisse der höheren Welten? ('Knowledge of higher worlds, how is it attained?'). This text does not enter into the questions concerning the inherent reliability of perception, in the philosophical sense, but proceeds on the basis of the accuracy of perception, including that of a spiritual visionary nature. The following year, Steiner published two further volumes which elaborated in more detail the soul exercises, such as Die Stufen der Höheren Erkenntnis (The stages of higher knowledge), Ein Weg zur Selbsterkenntnis des Menschen, (A way to self knowledge of the human being).

A decade later, 1914, Steiner published another philosophical work, Die Rätsel der Philosophie (The Riddles of Philosophy). This is a large volume that surveys historically philosophical perspectives from the ancient Greek times through to early twentieth century.[392] In the last chapter Steiner presents his anthroposophical approach. Again the audience will be primarily theosophists, owing to the new direction that his life has taken since 1900. In this last chapter he is concerned with the problem of the epistemological validity of his anthroposophy. He quotes a passage from his

---

[391] Steiner, <u>Spirituelle Seelenlehre,</u> 137, „Der Rechte Weg is der Weg selbst, vor allen Dingen derjenige, der über den griechischen Tempeln gestand hatte; Erkenne dich selbst. Wir sind eines Wesens mit dem Weltengeist."
[392] Rudolf Steiner, <u>Die Rätsel der Philosophie</u> (Dornach; VRSN, 1961)

Die Philosophie where the divide between observer and the world-content is bridged through experiencing insights,

> What is perceived is that part of the reality which is objectively given, the concept is that which is subjectively given...The one factor appears to perception, the other to intuition. Only the connection between these two, the perception appropriately membered into the universe, is the full reality. The mere perception is no reality, rather a disconnected chaos...the abstract concept does not possess reality – but contemplative observation certainly does, which does not consider one-sidedly the concept, nor the perception, but rather the connection of these two.... Whoever can make their own the points of view indicated here, wins the possibility, with his soul-life, to conceive of the self-conscious ego united with the fertile reality. This is the view towards which philosophy through history has striven since the Greek age, and which shows its first discernible traces in the worldview of Goethe.[393]

In connection with the enhanced consciousness modality needed for direct cognition of supra-sensible realities, Steiner refers to Goethe's declaration that just such a new form of perceiving has to be developed which he refers to as an 'perceptive discernment', in order to behold such non-molecular aspects to creation. Steiner maintained that it is this kind of perceiving that he used in undertaking his research, and he quoted from Goethe's well-known essay, "Anschauliche Beobachtung" ('perceptive discernment'),

---

[393]Steiner, Die Rätsel, 600-601, „Wer die hier angedeuteten Gesichtspunkte zu den seinigen machen kann, gewinnt die Möglichkeit, mit seinem Seelenleben in dem selbstbewußten Ich die fruchtbare Wirklichkeit verbunden zu denken. Das ist die Anschauung, zu welcher die philosophische Entwickelung seit dem griechen Zeitalter hinstrebt und die in der Weltanschauung Goethes ihre ersten deutlich erkennbaren Spuren gezeigt hat."

> In his beautiful essay about 'Perceptive Power of Discernment', Goethe has pointed out that the human being, when it seeks to attain knowledge that is supportive of spiritual reality, must arrive at the point where he does not simply passively assimilate the external material world, but empowers himself inwardly, in order to be able to comprehend inwardly this spiritual reality, just as one from outside comprehends the external world through the senses.[394]

In the concluding pages of his book, Steiner emphasizes that the capacity for such a condition of being able to experience the archetypal Idea inhering to the perceived object, requires an extended consciousness. He refers to soul exercises, similar to those in Knowledge of the higher worlds, how is it attained? through which the soul develops special organs (in the aura or soul-body) for perceiving in the spiritual. It is through such inner exercises that meditation becomes effective, because the meditant attains the ability to contemplate deeper themes in a higher state of consciousness. In *Die Pforte* a good description of how Steiner views this process is given in the spirit voice of Scene Three, a passage which we examined in Section 2a,

> His thoughts descend into the foundations of the primeval world – a realm of whose fullness, people, in thinking, are merely dreaming in shadows, of whose fullness, people, in seeing, are merely living in apparitions. What he thought as shadows, what he experiences as apparitions, now soars above the world of Forms.

---

[394] Rudolf Steiner, Geist und Stoff, Leben und Tod, 28, „In seinem schönen Aufsatz über „anschauende Urteilskraft" hat er hingewiesen darauf, wie der Mensch, wenn er zu einer das Geistige stützenden Erkenntnis streben will, dazu kommen muß, nicht bloß passiv die äußere stoffliche Welt aufzunehmen, sondern sich innerlich so zu erfassen, um erkenntnismäßig dieses Geistige innerlich so zu fassen, wie man von außen her die äußere sinnliche Welt durch die Sinne erfaßt."

Steiner instituted a schooling process in meditation for Theosophists (Anthroposophists) in 1904 which ran until 1914, when World War One brought this activity to an end. He taught his approximately 1,000 students that a text or symbol for meditation must be something that proclaims actual 'spiritual' reality that is, a reality that transcends the sense-world. The actual component-ideas in the verse may be readily understood, and these of necessity would have to contain words which also refer to earthly concepts. Terms such as 'light', 'heart', 'wisdom', 'pure' could be in such a text.

The implication of Steiner's teachings on this theme is that to him, although the component words are understandable in themselves, the over-all 'statement' that the verse or symbol is conveying nevertheless must transcend logic. It must be ineffable, that is inaccessible, to the logical rational intellect. This he maintains is the essential point; our intellect's logical ability must not be able to completely comprehend and analyse the meaning of the material used for meditating. It is not a question of Steiner teaching something that is ineffable, nor communicating such to the student's mind, since by definition that is not possible.

Rather, the concept which Steiner is advocating is here is that an initiated person, an enlightened spiritual teacher, attains to the state of consciousness which confers the ability to comprehend truths which are transcendent. Secondly this person has the ability to compose a text, the words of which en-clothe or perhaps 'encrypt' such truths. This concept as such is not alien to the mystical traditions of humanity, in that texts in Scripture are regarded as having such a quality, these 'divinely inspired' texts are thought of as inspired by God. The difference with Steiner is that such texts can be composed by an initiated person, however, as we have seen, such a person has access to the Platonic realm of the Idea, and as such, through the office of the hierarchies, this person is in effect, in communion with God. This concept is expressed in *Die Pforte* at the end of Scene Three, in the episode where Maria leaves her body, and Ahriman speaks through it. Johannes perceives that this is what has happened. Benedictus affirms his perspicacity and gives him a meditation text, commenting that it will give him the key to the Heights.,

> The light's weaving Being, it shines through widths of space, to fill the world with Being. Love's blessing, it en-warms the cycles of time, invoking revelation of all worlds. And spirit messengers, they unite the light's weaving Being with soul-revelation: and when the human being can unite its own self with both, it living in spiritual heights.[395]

The meaning of such texts, Steiner maintains, can gradually be discovered by the meditant through accessing the power of intuitive insight; this is achieved by gaining access to the ether-body. It is here that the cosmic thoughts, or divine truths are reflected. The accessing of such a level of thinking requires the meditant to use the higher consciousness states to which Steiner refers in his book, *Knowledge of Higher Worlds, how is it attained*? In this regard, Steiner considered the first fourteen verses of the Prologue to the Gospel of St. John to be a good example of a text suitable for meditation. This text contains such phrases as, "In the beginning was the word, "the word was with God", and "the word was God".

It is immediately obvious here that although logical thinking can analyse the component-ideas in these verses, the full significance of the statements is not comprehensible to the logical mind. For the referent of ideas that these words are proclaiming is in a spiritual sphere, their meaning derives from higher realms and dynamics than those of the mundane world. This is even more so with the following words in this

---

[395] Pforte, 75, „Des Lichtes webend Wesen, es erstrahlet durch Raumesweiten, zu füllen die Welt mit Sein. Der Liebe Segen, er erwärmet die Zeitenfolgen, zu rufen aller Welten Offenbarung. Und Geistesboten, sie vermählen des Lichtes webend Wesen mit Seelenoffenbarung; und wenn vermählen kann mit beiden der Mensch sein eigen Selbst, ist er in Geisteshöhen lebend."

same text, "In him was life, and that life was the light of human beings." The separate nouns used are comprehensible in themselves, but the overall implication of the sentence as a coherent entity is not comprehensible, not fully explicable. According to Steiner, it is precisely this quality of eluding the deductive thought process, whilst conveying – or attempting to convey – a meaning which deals with spiritual beings and realities, which enables these verses to be a meditative text.

In public lectures given in 1921, Steiner takes up the task of presenting the higher consciousness, or higher thinking, which leads to spiritual wisdom. Steiner elucidates the nature of this anthroposophical enhanced perceptiveness in terms of enhanced thinking, which one achieves by the soul exercises. He describes it as 'morphological thinking',

> "...then usual thinking is a combinational type, a type which brings into association the separated objects. We need this type of thinking for normal, healthy living, we also need it for healthy normal science. But that kind of thinking which is required in addition, for knowledge of higher worlds, and which one attains through such exercises; that is a thinking which I would like to call morphological thinking, thinking in forms. This thinking does not stay in space, this thinking is indeed the kind which lives in the medium of time, in the same way that the other thinking lives in the medium of space.
>
> This kind of thinking does not join one concept to another, this thinking places before the soul something like a conceptual organism...it is so inwardly mobile that continuously brings forth one form out of the other. It is this morphological thinking which has to be added to the other, and to which one can attain through such meditation exercises, I have indicated these in principle, these make the thinking stronger, more intensive. With this morphological thinking, one attains to the first stage of supra-

sensible knowledge, namely that kind that I have designated as 'Imaginative knowledge' in my books.[396]

A little later in this lecture from 1921, Steiner describes the kind of extended cognitional capacity which is implied in *Die Pforte* in more detail;

... {a kind of} inside-out thinking, supra-morphological thinking... a thinking that has its own inner life...a thinking which has its own {morphological} growth, wherever one concept arises from its predecessor.....that which lives in the spirit can not be comprehended by mere combinational thinking, it has to be apprehended by an inwardly vivified thinking. A thinking which lives not only in thought-forms which metamorphose, but a thinking which also has the ability to turn the formation of the interior inside out and to thereby change its form....I remember in this connection, that Goethe saw a metamorphosis, a transformation, of the vertebra of the spinal column in the individual skull bones....One enters into a reality which exists beyond time and space.[397]

---

[396] Rudolf Steiner, Die Wirklichkeit der höheren Welten (Dornach: VRSN, 1962) 48, „....das gewöhnliche Denken ein kombinierendes ist, ein solches, das auseinanderliegende Gebilde zusammenfaßt. Dieses Denken brauchen wir für das gesunde gewöhnliche Leben, brauchen wir auch für die gesunde gewöhnliche Wissenschaft. Dasjenige Denken aber, das zum Behufe der Erkenntnis höherer Welten hinzukommen muß, und das man durch solche Übungen erringt, das ist ein Denken, welches ich nennen möchte das morphologische Denken, das Denken in Gestalten. Dieses Denken bleibt nicht im Raume stehen, dieses Denken ist durchaus ein solches, welches im Medium der Zeit so lebt, wie das andere Denken im Medium des Raumes. Dieses Denken gliedert nicht einen Begriff an den anderen, dieses Denken stellt vor die Seele etwas wie einen Begriffsorganismus....es ist so innerlich beweglich daß es eine Gestalt aus der anderen hervorruft, fortwährend wächst. Dieses morphologische Denken, das ist es, das zum anderen Denken hinzukommen muß, und das man durch solche Meditationsübungen erlangen kann, wie ich sie im Prinzip angedeutet habe und die das Denken verstärken, intensiver machen. Mit diesem morphologischen Denken, mit diesem Denken, das in Gestalten, in Bildern verläuft, errinqt man die erste Stufe der Erkenntnis übersinnlicher Welten, namentlich dasjenige, was ich in meinen Schriften die imaginative Erkenntnis genannt habe."
[397] Rudolf Steiner, Die Wirklichkeit, 56-59, „...umgestülptes Denken, übermorphologisches Denken...ein innerlich lebendiges Denken..ein Denken das ein eigenes Wachstum hat, wo immer ein Begriff, ein Gedanke aus dem

In effect, Steiner's approval of the Goethean Platonic Idea stems from his conviction that Goethe was somehow inherently able to attain to this supra-morphological state of thinking, and thereby bridge the gap (the River) to the Idea. Steiner explains the role of this bridging intuitive faculty as follows,

> The development of the powers and capacities which are slumbering in humanity, namely {the capabilities effective in} meditative thinking, which lead into the spiritual world, rests on nothing other than the lively following through of the inner metamorphoses of the powers of the soul. .... the person who wishes to become a spiritual researcher attempts to so arrange his perceiving, that he can repeatedly guide the will – which usually *slumbers* within perceiving and mental picturing – into his perceiving and mental picturing in such a way that he can voluntarily invoke the presence of these. As a result, what is usually merely weak thinking or imposed perceiving, can be transformed into Imagination, into pictorial beholding. For the spiritual can only be beheld in a pictorial form. The will and the feeling, which normally can be pictured mentally, but not apprehended in their actual true nature, are metamorphosed through the meditative life itself, so that they become mental-imaging life, perceiving life."[398]

---

anderen hervorwächst. Dasjenige was lebt aus dem Geiste heraus, kann man nicht erfassen mit der bloße kombinierende Denken, das muß erfaßt werden durch ein innerlich lebendiges Denken. Ein Denken, das nicht nur in sich verändernden Gestalten lebt, sondern ein Denken der in der Lage ist, die Gestaltung des Inneren nach außen zu kehren und dabei die Form zu verändern....Ich erinnere daran, daß Goethe ...hat eine Metamorphose, eine Umgestaltung der Rückgratswirbel in den einzelnen Kopfknochen gesehen....man kommt in eine Wirklichkeit, die jenseits von Raum und Zeit liegt."

[398] Rudolf Steiner, <u>Das Ewige in der Menschenseele</u> (Dornach: VRSN, 1962) 93, „Die Ausbildung der in dem Menschen schlummernden Kräfte und Fähigkeiten, des meditativen Denkens, das in die geistige Welt hineinführt, das beruht auf nichts anderem als auf dem lebendigen Verfolgen der inneren Metamorphosen der Seelenkräfte. Auf der einen Seite versucht derjenige, der Geistesforscher werden will, sein Vorstellen, sein

However, Steiner did not advocate one indefinable state of higher spiritual awareness which bridged over the gap between this physical realm and the spiritual. He taught his students that there are three modes of spiritual perceiving; he termed them, Imagination, Inspiration and Intuition. At the first stage, that of "Imagination', the meditant develops some psychic tendencies, and may experience visions, the primary attainment is that of holistic insights being detected, even if only faintly, on the periphery of consciousness. The term 'Imagination' is prone to misunderstanding when read in an English text, since it commonly has a meaning associated with fantasy. In the English context, a more appropriate term for what Steiner wishes to convey would perhaps be Psychic Image Consciousness, because this is the term associated with the faculty of experiencing images, and the concomitant 'insightful' thinking that such a consciousness type exhibits.

These may not be able to be logically formulated, and may be quite tenuous, however, they convey deeper understanding of supra-sensible realities than one is normally able to have of life through logical thinking. But as consciousness becomes more enhanced, the second stage, Inspiration, is attained. This next stage, wherein thinking begins to merge with a cosmic spiritual 'thinking' which is understood to underlie creation, is termed *Inspiration* because, as Steiner explains, the way in which this stage of consciousness perceives the actual spiritual realm is akin to an infusion, absorption or inhaling process, one also breathes in the spiritual wisdom, so to speak. But again the term 'inspirational' whilst acceptable in German, is ambiguous in English; it appears that in

---

Wahrnehmen so auszugestalten, daß er den Willen, der sonst nur schlummert im Wahrnehmen und Vorstellen, in dieses Wahrnehmen and Vorstellen immer wiederum so hineinführt, daß er dasjenige, was als unwillkürliche Vorstellung auftritt, willkürlich sich vor die Seele ruft. Dadurch verwandelt sich dasjenige, was sonst als blasses Denken oder aufgezwungenes Wahrnehmen ist, in die Imagination, in das bildhafte Schauen. Denn das Geistige kann nur bildhaft geschaut werden. Das Wollen und das Fühlen, die sonst zwar vorgestellt werden können, aber nicht in ihrer eigentlichen Wesenheit erkannt werden, die werden durch das meditativen Leben selber umgewandelt, so daß sie vorstellendes Leben, wahrnehmendes Leben werden".

English such a phrase as *Ideal-Spiritual consciousness* more clearly expresses the concept Steiner wishes to express.

At this second stage, the acolyte can begin to experience the archetypal thoughts more directly, and in this sense, the spirit is beginning to suffuse the soul with its radiance. That the result of Johannes' quest for spirituality will be in effect, an inner illumination, as a necessary concomitant of attaining 'higher thinking' is indicated in many places in Steiner works, for example, "...cosmic thoughts are that according to which divine powers have created the world...they pervade the cosmos as rays of energy", and, "cosmic thinking is that true thinking which pervades the cosmos like rays of energy in it."[399] Steiner identifies these cosmic thoughts as the Platonic Idea, they are described as "having created the physical body over ages, thus in the body cosmic wisdom is slumbering."[400]

In this second stage of higher consciousness, 'Inspiration', instead of experiencing a psychic vision, Steiner explains that the meditant becomes directly aware of spiritual realities in the Platonic realm of Ideas. This second stage brings an enhanced experience in which the visual radiance and colours are maintained, but in addition, an audible element is added. He maintains that a new splendour shines from the soul world, and the new tones are heard which derive from spiritland. The implication here is that hearing of cosmic resonances occurs, so what was previously 'only' a supernal radiance, now becomes an auditory experience, and in indeed in two ways. Firstly, there is the sense of specifically resonated tones, in particular, the famous 'music of the spheres'. The meditant may now attain to perceiving the 'tones' that resonate from the celestial orbs.

Secondly, when an entity perceived in the spiritual realm, it is also now perceived in a deeper sense, in a (spiritually)

---

[399] R. Steiner: G/A 93, 204 & G/A 84, 78-83.
[400] R. Steiner G/A 96, 302, „Der Weltengedanke hat durch unzählige Zeitenläufe gewirkt, er hat in der Natur gewirkt, um zuletzt die Krone all seines Schaffens zu bilden: den menschlichen Leib...in dem menschlichen Leibe schlummert nun die Weltenweisheit..."

audible sense, as if its inner nature is speaking to one. Steiner comments in a lecture from 1907,

> "in the consciousness{state} of Inspiration, the human being will see deep, deep into the nature of the beings, when he is in this consciousness…the human being does not only perceive in coloured imagery and forms, but also hears the essential nature of the other {entity} resounding and ringing."[401]

An actual experience of the higher kind is presented in Scene Nine, where Johannes can behold in spiritual realms, and there perceives as a star above him, his own higher self,

> I feel how my thinking penetrates into deep foundation of cosmic existence; and how, radiant, it shines through it. Thus is the efficacy of these words, O man, experience yourself! From radiant heights a being shines upon me, and I feel as if I have wings to raise myself up to him, I will to free myself, as does every being that conquers itself.[402]

It is significant that in the first level of enhanced consciousness, Johannes sees (not with physical eyes, but via his ether-body) images and beings, whereas at the higher level, he begins to sense that his thinking is entering into the source of thought itself. In this developmental process Steiner's above view of spiritual encounters is didactically portrayed.

The first stage of higher consciousness – that depicted in Scene Two, has given Johannes the power to behold other

---

[401] Rudolf Steiner, <u>Die Theosophie des Rosenkreutzers</u>, (Dornach: RSV, 1979) 91, „Tief, tief hineinsehen wird der Mensch in die Natur der Wesenheiten wenn er in diesem Bewußtsein lebt, dem Bewußtsein der Inspiration…Der Mensch wird nicht nur wahrnehmen in Farbildern und Formen, er wird die Wesenheit des andern tönen und klingen hören."

[402] Pforte, 137, „Ich fühle, wie mein Denken dringt in tief verborgne Weltengründe; und wie es leuchtend sie durchstrahlt. So wirkt die Keimkraft dieses Wortes: O Mensch, erlebe dich! Aus lichten Höhen leuchtet mir ein Wesen. Ich fühle Schwingen, zu ihm mich zu erheben. Ich will mich selbst befrei'n wie alle Wesen, die sich selbst besiegt (sic!)."

beings, and also his lower self. It is immediately after the encounter with Theodosius that Johannes mistakes Benedictus, (who is approaching, but not yet discernible), for an evil spirit. The implication of this is that if the soul of Johannes were more purified, then his perceiving would be more accurate, it could have perceived on the level of Inspiration, and not have been deceived at all.

The third stage of higher consciousness is termed "Intuition" in Steiner's system and he describes that with this faculty, it is as if one enters into the other being or whatever is being perceived, becoming one with it, that is, one intuits the core of the perceived object. And then, from within it, the meditant gazes outwards, almost as if one has become that being. As Steiner explains of the meditant who reaches this stage, "In (the stage of) Inspiration he is aware that he becomes one with the deeds of a being, with the manifestations of their will, but only in Intuition does he merge with the beings themselves, beings which are self-contained."[403] Again, the Latin term, 'Intuition' is ambiguous in English, and perhaps an expression such as, 'initiatory oneness consciousness' may indicate more clearly his intentions.

I conclude that *The Portal of Initiation*, through its portrayal of the roles of Philia, Astrid and Luna in regard to Johannes' spiritual striving, expresses didactically the following primary element in his anthroposophy:

That the limits to knowledge may be extended through meditation, in a triune manner; in this the dynamics of the soul become transformed through the influence of the spirit. This process in turn invokes the help of the divine hierarchies, whose activities are an expression of the Deity. These beings enable the meditant to attain consciousness in the Platonic realm of the Idea, and thus consequently, the

---

[403] Rudolf Steiner, Die Stufen der Höheren Erkenntnis, (Dornach: RSV, 1979) 79, „In der Inspiration wird er sich bewußt, daß er eins wird mit den Taten solcher Wesen, mit den Offenbarungen ihres Willens; erst in der Intuition verschmiltzt er mit Wesen, die in sich selbst geschlossen sind."

divided world-content – of perceived thing and originating Idea – is finally united.

The portrayal in *Die Pforte* of the efficacy of meditation provides Steiner's students with the requisite validation of his early holistic epistemological conviction, that the limits to knowledge may be extended.

4f: A major element in Steiner's anthroposophy is an esoteric-mystical Christian perspective, in which a connection between conscience and the Second Coming – as understood by Steiner – has a discrete role.

Die Pforte *does not make extensive reference to Christianity; h*ence a detailed consideration of Steiner's Christology is inappropriate here. However, it should be briefly noted that Steiner advocates, from his own spiritual experiences, a form of Christianity in which Jesus and 'Christ' are two separate beings – although as a result of the Passion events, the two became united as one. To Steiner, the term 'Christ' is one which refers to a deity, whilst 'Jesus' refers to a human being, albeit the most sacred of all human beings. He views the beginning of the union of these two entities as occurring at the Baptism in the Jordan. Steiner's Christology is complex, and only a bare outline is given here. Steiner's conclusions that there is a deity and a human being involved, forming a kind of composite figure, is not new. This composite view of the Christian Saviour was present in various forms in the first Christian centuries, and became rejected under the general term 'Subordinationism'. [404]

One motivation for the inclusion of the Theodora episode is that Rudolf Steiner maintained that in the 1930's the Second Coming of Christ would occur. But as we noted in Section 3b, he understood it to be a discrete, ethereal phenomenon. He maintained that the process was one in which Jesus, who had become united to the 'cosmic Christ' since the Resurrection, would become perceptible to humanity, although not physically, rather in a form of higher seeing. Since to Steiner, Jesus was is permeated by the deity, Christ, any cognizance of him would also imply in some subtle form, an encounter of the cosmic Christ, as well as of Jesus.

Steiner consequently argued that the perception involved was not physical, and yet neither was it spiritual, in the sense of

---

[404] The New International Dictionary of the Christian Church, ed. J. D. Douglas, (Exeter: Paternoster Press, 1974) *Subordinationism,* 938.

traditional visionary experiences of Christian saints. Steiner understood these visions to be the result of clairvoyant visions in the traditional sense. Whereas he taught that visionary perceiving of the returned Saviour would be an ethereal phenomenon. These would be appear almost as tangible as a physical perception, and yet their locus would be an energy field, in which Christ-Jesus will assume an ethereal form.

This conviction is put into the mouth of Theodora, in Scene One, where she makes the proclamation of the imminent reappearing of the Saviour. Theodora speaks here in a grammatically clumsy and complex manner, this is presumably to reflect her special condition. She has been transported into a visionary state, and is attempting to communicate back to what has become an alien, removed sphere, that of the earthly. Perhaps also the magnitude of the mystery of what she is beholding, is a factor as well,

> He has united with the spiritual part of the Earth. But not able were human beings yet Him to behold, in a form of existence such as he reveals Himself, because eyes of spirit lacked to their being, which shall only be theirs in the future. But near is the future…[405]

Steiner's position with regard to his exegesis of Scripture was that if the full range of nuances of meaning of the Greek text of the New Testament were carefully considered, his interpretation would not be conflict with the Biblical texts. His lectures included quotations from the Greek, sometimes several sentences in length.[406]

In his theological lectures on Biblical prophecies concerning the Reappearing of Christ, given after he wrote *Die Pforte*, he

---

[405] 37, „Er hat sich mit der Erde Geistesteil vereint. Die Menschen konnten schauen ihn noch nicht, wie er in solcher Daseinsform sich zeigt, weil Geistesaugen ihrem Wesen fehlten, die sich erst künftig zeigen sollen. Doch nahe ist die Zukunft…"
[406] For example in his lectures on <u>Exkurse in das Gebiet des Markus-Evangeliums</u>, pages 74, 79, 110 etc) and on <u>Das Matthäus-Evangelium</u>, pages 208, 211, etc).

refers directly to the inclusion of the Theodora scene, indicating that he wanted to express the perspective that this event would have similarities to the Damascus encounter of St. Paul.[407] In this lecture, he proceeds to quote from the 'little apocalypse' of St. Mark, "And if any man shall say to you, 'Lo, here is Christ or lo, he is there', believe him not. For false Christs and false prophets shall rise and shall show signs and wonders..." This text also states, "Take heed, that no person deceives you, for many shall come in my name, saying, 'I am He'...take heed and watch", (Mk: 13:5 & 33,37).

Steiner then emphasizes in his exegesis of this text that Christ is not to return as a physical person. In other words, Steiner is arguing that the above text removes all persons as the possible returned saviour – the term 'persons' implying a human being with a physical corporeality. Steiner explains to his audience that, "It is important that we realize that it is our duty to comprehend Christ <u>in the spirit</u>...and the attempt was made to explain this duty at the place in the Portal of Initiation where words are placed in the mouth of the seeress Theodora."[408] (emphasis mine)

It was Steiner's practise to refer to the Christian Saviour as 'the Christ' or 'the Christ-impulse', to emphasize the cosmic divine aspect of the Christian Saviour as the primary element of the composite being, Christ Jesus. In another lecture, after referring to the phenomenon of false Christs, he elaborated the possibility of the Reappearing not being recognized,

> It is still to be seen whether humanity has developed sufficiently to be able to recognize the Christ in his

---

[407] Steiner, <u>Exkurse</u> 165 and <u>Matthäus</u> 199.
[408] Steiner, <u>Exkurse</u> 165, „Wichtig ist es, daß wir einsehen, daß es unsere Aufgabe ist, den Christus im Geiste zu begreifen, daß wir begreifen müssen, wie sich für die verschiedenen Zeitpunkte in die Zukunft hinein der Christus offenbaren wird.Für unsere Zeit wurde versucht, diese Aufgabe anzugeben in den Stellen des Rosenkreuzermysteriums „Die Pforte der Einweihung" in den Worten, die der Seherin Theodora in den Mund gelegt werden."

full significance, precisely because he is revealing himself as spiritual. This will be the greatest test and trial for humanity, that the greatest impulse of our Earth is to reveal itself and say to them, you can only recognize Me if you do not simply talk about the spiritual, but know that the spiritual is more real, more actual, more valuable than the mere carnal material reality.[409]

In his exegesis of passages in Matthew's Gospel concerning the Reappearing, quoting from Matthew 24:43, "...coming like a thief in the night", Steiner concludes that this verse infers a process of human consciousness 'growing into the spiritual world'. Therefore, Steiner argues, in referring to false prophets in this context, Christ wished to point out that a material conception of this process is decidedly wrong.[410] We have earlier noted that Steiner sees the effect of Christ as vivifying the conscience, and that it was only after the Theodora episode in Scene One that Johannes has his conscience stimulated, an event which at first plunges him into despondency, as he realizes his earlier moral errors.

In Section 3b we noted that in addition to the three Kings (three hierophants) and the three hand-maidens of the fair lily (Philia, Astrid and Luna) another triune set of beings is implicit in *Die Pforte*. This additional set of three beings, to whom there is a subtle allusion, is composed of Lucifer, Ahriman and Christ. It is indicated in Scene Four by the fact that Johannes only encounters Lucifer and Ahriman <u>after</u> his conscience has been vivified, by the Theodora episode. Since Steiner sees the conscience as such a manifestation of Christ in the soul, and its quickening as the increased efficacy of Christ in the soul, then just as Helena is a representative of

---

[409] Steiner, Das Ereignis, 72, „Zeigen wird es sich müssen, ob die Menschen so weit sein werden, den Christus in seiner ganzen Bedeutung wieder zu erkennen, gerade weil er sich ihnen als Geistiges zeigt. Das wird die größte Prüfung und Probe für die Menschen sein, daß sich ihnen der größte Impuls unserer Erde zeigt und ihnen sagen wird : Erkennen könnt ihr mich nur, wenn ihr nicht bloß redet vom Geistigen, sondern wißt, daß das Geistige realer, wirklicher, wertvoller ist als das bloß fleischlich Materielle."

[410] Rudolf Steiner, Das Matthäus-Evangelium (Dornach: RSV, 1978) 203-4.

Lucifer, so too, can Johannes, in his newly enhanced condition of moral integrity, be a representative of Christ. Hence when Lucifer and Ahriman appear to Johannes, the new triune set of characters is created.

The dramatic element of *Die Pforte* then becomes that of Johannes struggling with the challenges posed by the twofold opposing forces, but with the Christ influence subtly efficacious within Johannes. In view of the fact that *Die Pforte* also incorporates through its structure, allusions to Steiner's cosmology, it is also significant that this trinity of influences is present in Scene Four, as it is in this pivotal fourth scene of the seven scenes that the new element emerges, which carries the evolution power onwards.

It is a central theme in Steiner's anthroposophy that the struggle of the spirit, represented by the Christ presence in the human soul, against Lucifer and Ahriman constitutes the primary spiritual dynamic of earthly life. And it is from the outcome of this conscious ethical struggle that the new 'leaven' for the next phase develops; hence the occurrence of these thematic elements in Scene Four, the pivotal scene of the first seven scenes.

It is didactically very significant that this episode occurs just prior to Johannes becoming acutely aware of the voice of his conscience. The implication of this episode is that the awakening of Johannes' conscience is subtly stimulated by this revelation from the seeress, which has resulted in an enhanced efficacy of influences from Christ Jesus. In this sequence of events is the further didactic statement of a direct connection between the enlivening of the conscience and spiritual development, and hence of a link between Christ and the human conscience.

In various lectures Steiner maintains that the conscience is able to be vivified, and eventually transform, becoming the faculty of directly perceiving spiritual realities.[411] By the seventh scene, Johannes, as we saw, does succeed in attaining to the realm of the Platonic Idea. I therefore conclude that these rhetorical elements of *Die Pforte* are specifically didactic, expressing quintessentially Steiner's Christological convictions in regard to the relationship of the reappearing, ethereally, of Christ Jesus to contemporary spirituality, to the conscience, and the role of the vivified conscience in attaining to awareness of the realm of the Idea.

I conclude further that the appearance of Theodora in Scene Seven may be seen as alluding to an additional element in Steiner's view of cosmic evolution. In Steiner's cosmology, that same spiritual influence which acts as the initial catalyst at the commencement of each aeon, becomes active again in its last phase, consolidating which has been achieved.[412] It is now clear, that through Theodora's actions, Johannes' conscience is vivified, and that Steiner sees the conscience as a faculty which can become enhanced and transform into spiritual vision. Thus, in the seventh scene, Theodora, by confirming the attainment by Johannes to powers of spiritual vision, is in effect affirming and consolidating that which she prophesied, and catalytically assisted to emerge, in Scene One.

---

[411] Rudolf Steiner, Der Christus-Impuls und die Entwickelung des Ich-Bewu˜tseins, (Dornach: VRSN 1961).
[412] Geheimwissenschaft, *Die Weltentwickelung und der Mensch*, 137-299.

4g: The spiritual development process underlying Die Pforte is derived from the view of the human being as an interrelated septenary organism of body, ether-body, soul, self and a triune spirit

In his Theosophie, Steiner elucidates a model of human nature as sevenfold. To the physical body, Steiner adds an ether-body, which as noted in Section 1B2, maintains the life of the physical body. The third element enumerated is the soul, and it is a major postulate of Rudolf Steiner's view of the soul or human consciousness, that it is triune. As we have noted in earlier sections, commenting on Philia, Astrid and Luna, Steiner sees the soul as possessing three primary strands or elements, namely thinking, emotions, and volition. These three capacities form the basis of human consciousness, and exist in their own right, independent of the physical body. The structure of the body enables the soul to manifest and cognize them. The human being is then, an 'embodied soul', whose three primary dynamics are not produced by the body, but made manifest in it, precisely by means of its specifically designed, complex neurological and physiological processes.

Steiner uses the term 'thinking' to mean logical, rational, deductive intelligence, but this term is also used of higher modalities of cognising, modalities that transcend logic. He termed this soul, the intellectual soul (die Verstandesseele). Logical thought is considered by Steiner to be a somewhat hollowed-out or silhouetted form of what thinking is in its real nature. So 'thinking' itself in Steiner worldview has three aspects to it. It can manifest as logical thought, or as the process of forming mental images, , and thirdly, as a higher 'spiritual' thinking, which is in effect, the apprehending of the content of the Platonic realm of Ideas.

Another one of the three souls is the 'sentient-soul' (die Empfindungsseele), Steiner defines this term by differentiating 'emotion' from 'feeling' in its meaning of perceiving. Emotions are such qualities as happiness, sadness, jealousy, revenge, yearning, grief, delight, and so on. He acknowledges that these can also be defined as 'feelings', that is, the term 'felt' in normal use of language, can also refer to sense impressions. Elaborating on this, in order to establish his terminology precisely, he differentiates between *emotion* as an expression of the human being's consciousness, and *feeling* as the registration of a stimulus by that consciousness.[413] So 'feeling' is cognate with sensing, but 'emotion' with wishes and desires, etc. Sense perceptions however can be felt from without – that is from the physical environs via the body's sense system – or from within, through the registering of one's own emotion or thought, or volitional impulse. Hence one 'feels' an emotion, or a cold draught; one 'senses' a spiteful thought or the swaying of a tall building.

The third element of human consciousness is volition, which is understood as an expression of an intuitive faculty. That is, when a person makes a decision to act, the consciousness processes involved need not have emotional nor logical components. An act of will need not arise from an emotive or deductive process. It is however difficult to define the actual processes that underlie an act of will or volition, the process can in fact times occur within a fraction of a second. Steiner defines this impelling force as 'intuition', and termed this soul, 'die Bewußtseinseele' (the consciousness soul). To Steiner these three faculties of human consciousness have ontological integrity, they exist as separate entities in their own right. We noted earlier, that Luna is the representative in *Die Pforte* of the will, and therefore she is representative of the 'consciousness-soul'.

The fourth element of the human organism is the 'ego' or 'self', this is defined in Theosophie, as the name which we give to ourselves, a name which indicates awareness of oneself as a separate reality from the milieu in which one lives, and from other human beings. He maintains that it arises into being in the third year of life, and its presence is

---

[413] Rudolf Steiner, Theosophie (Dornach: VRSN, 1974) 39-41.

indicated by the use of the personal pronoun, "I", as from that time. Steiner views the sense of self as deriving from the reciprocally interrelated dynamics of one's personal way of thinking, of experiencing emotion and will. He sees the awareness of this selfhood as gradually awakening during infancy, through the infant experiencing a contrast between itself and the environs, by the impact of external stimuli. Prior to that, he maintains, the infant has awareness, but not self-awareness.

Consequently, the personal pronoun becomes an important indicator to Steiner, in his Theosophie he argues that every person can call a table 'a table', a chair 'a chair'. But with the designation "I", with this personal pronoun, this is not the case. No person can use this word to designate another person; each can only call himself "I". So, never can we hear the name "I" being used towards oneself, or of oneself, by another person. Through the fact that the human being designates itself as "I", one must within oneself be giving a name to oneself. He views the personal pronoun as a name for the sense of self, which arises from within this sense of self. Steiner then maintains that,

> "The 'I' as the essential being of man remains entirely invisible….and this 'I' is the human being itself. This justifies the human being in regarding this 'I' as his true being. He may therefore describe his body and his soul as the sheaths or veils within which he lives; and he may designate them as bodily conditions through which he exerts his efficacy…"[414]

In these words another aspect of the ego is implied, a spiritual core element that transcends his personality. Steiner emphasizes that there is another aspect to the ego, an aspect

---

[414] Steiner, Theosophie, 66, „Das Ich bleibt als die eigentliche Wesenheit des Menschen ganz unsichtbar…Denn mit seinem Ich ist der Mensch ganz allein. Und dieses Ich ist der Mensch selbst. Das berechtigt ihn, dieses Ich als seine wahre Wesenheit anzusehen. Er darf deshalb seinen Leib und seine Seele als die Hüllen bezeichnen, innerhalb deren er lebt; und er darf sie als leibliche Bedingungen bezeichnen, durch die er wirkt."

which also implies the presence, or at least indirect influence of, a transcendent spiritual element in human consciousness, this is the eternal self. Consequently, Steiner regarded the ego as not simply encompassed by the amalgamation of the above psychological dynamics, but as dualistic, comprising the conscious everyday sense of selfhood, and yet also susceptible continuously to the efficacy of the higher or eternal ego.

In a lecture on education, he gives a succinct explanation of the important role in the spiritual development of the person by the ego, in which it is a dualistic reality, "It is indeed precisely the task of this fourth member to refine and spiritualize the other three sheaths or members of the human being."[415] In a lecture on the nature of eternity and the human soul, Steiner takes up this theme, and opposes the traditional view of the human ego found in Buddhism. He is referring to the 'anatta' doctrine, in which the ego is really only the result of deeds done in a previous incarnation, and has no inner reality. In his lecture he doesn't refer to any specific doctrine or text, but the Buddhist principle of non-being (anatta) with regard to the ego is a primary theme in Buddhism,[416]

> What Buddhism allows to play over into the present life, from the earlier one, that is only the deeds of the earlier life, the karma. According to Buddhism, it is the manner in which the deeds group themselves together, which invokes in each new life an illusory ego. Thus, in our new life, not an ego, only the deeds, only the karma, comes into play....However this ego is a mere illusory centre-point. Therefore I should extinguish that which comes into life with the karma. Spiritual science says the reverse of this; the ego which appears there is the concentrating deed of the

---

[415] Rudolf Steiner, "Die Erziehung des Kindes vom Gesichtspunkte des Geistes" (Dornach; VRSN, 1981).
[416] Already in the Dhammapada the anatta concept is mentioned (verse 279), and it became elaborated in many Buddhist sacred texts, such as the *Mahayana Shraddhotpada Shastra* section 2, and the *Lankavatara* text, chpt. 4; both in A Buddhist Bible, ed. Dwight Goddard, (London: George Harrap, 1956).

karma. And whilst all other deeds are temporal and are also balanced out in time, that deed of karma, which has lead the human being into ego-consciousness is not a temporal one. Consequently, with the ego consciousness something appears which we can only characterize in the way which have now, that is, that it constantly intensifies its own existence, and that we, when we appear again in existence, appear grouped around the ego.

Thus the Buddhist extinguishes the ego and only allows karma to have a validity, which works over from one life into the next, and creates there an illusory ego. Whereas the follower of spiritual science, for whom karma and ego are not the same, says; my ego departs from my present earthly stage with an inner intensification and will reappear in this new state in my next life, and it will then unite itself with the deeds of this next life. When I as ego have done something, then it remains united with the central point and proceeds with the deeds from life to life.[417]

---

[417] Rudolf Steiner, <u>Menschengeschichte im Lichte der Geistesforschung</u>, (Dornach: VRSN, 1962) 474, „Was der Buddhismus aus dem früheren ins gegenwärtige Erdenleben herüberspielen läßt, das sind nur die Taten des früheren Lebens, das Karma. Wie sich die Taten zusammengruppieren, das ruft nach dem Buddhism in jeden neuen Leben ein Schein-Ich hervor, so daß in unser neues Leben kein Ich, sondern nur die Taten, nur das Karma hinüberspielt....Jedes Ich ist aber ein bloßer Schein-Mittelpunkt. Daher muß ich auslöschen, was mit dem Karma in das Leben hereingestellt ist. Umgekehrt sagt die Geistesswissenschaft: das Ich, welches da auftritt, ist die konzentrierende Tat des Karma. Und während alle anderen Taten zeitliche sind und auch in der Zeit wieder ausgeglichen werden, ist jene Tat des Karma, die den Menschen zum Ich-Bewußtsein geführt hat, keine zeitliche, so daß mit dem Ich-Bewußtsein etwas auftritt, was wir nur so charakterisieren können, wie wir es heute getan haben, das heißt, daß es sein Dasein steigert und steigert, und daß wir, wenn wir wieder ins Dasein treten, um das Ich gruppiert wieder auftreten.
So löscht der Buddhist das Ich aus und läßt nur das Karma gelten, das von dem einen Leben in das nächste hinüberwirkt und dort ein Schein-Ich schafft. Während der Bekenner der modernen Geisteswissenschaft, für den Karma und Ich nicht eins sind, sich sagt: aus meiner jetzigen Erdenstufe geht mein Ich mit einer Lebenssteigerung hervor und wird als solches wieder erscheinen in meinem nächsten Erdendasein und sich dann mit den Taten dieses nächsten Lebens verbinden. Wenn ich als Ich etwas getan habe,

In this text itself, Steiner is already using the term, 'ego' to designate an intrinsically dualistic entity. For if the ego is a form of Buddhist illusory entity, then it cannot retain any formative link to its previous deeds, as ontologically, it doesn't have any validity, it will fade out at death. The ego which has effected influences on the Earth, is an earthly personality, but if it retains a link to those deeds, in such a way that the next lifetime brings an organic development from the past life, then such an 'ego' has to be an ontologically substantive entity. In effect, to Steiner the ego of every human being is at once a somewhat illusory personality and also an eternal spiritual reality; it is a composite being. The Youth in Goethe's tale is seen by Steiner as representative of the everyday ego, and yet also of the higher ego.

An interesting detail in Scene Seven indicates that this is in fact Steiner's viewpoint, and that he sees this same esoteric conclusion in Goethe's tale, which he wishes to maintain in *Die Pforte*. In this scene, Theodora reveals the past incarnations of Maria and Johannes, and the audience learns that Johannes, as a 'heathen' woman, was once in love with 'Maria', and this implies that he was able to be in proximity to her (who was then a male), at least in his own mind. Thus Johannes, as this tribal woman, experienced a comforting and sustained romantic mood during the infatuation.

In Das Märchen, a very curious passage – inviting of an esoteric interpretation – indicates, discretely but definitely, that the Youth was once "thrice happy", because he had actually been snugly embraced by the fair Lily, at some undisclosed time in the past. This passage occurs when the Youth and the Old Woman are first approaching the Lily, and the Old Woman calls out, respectfully to her, describing the blessed circumstances of the harp, that the Lily is in effect caressing and playing, and then says, "Dreifach glücklicher

---

so bleibt es mit dem Mittelpunkt verbunden und geht mit den Taten von Verkörperung zu Verkörperung."

Jüngling, der du ihren Platz einnehmen konntest!"[418] This sentence means, "Thrice happy youth, you were able to take its place!" The verb here is in the imperfect, not the subjunctive case, so it is not a wish for the Youth to be with the Lily sometime soon, but a statement that he was once with her, and there was a triune blessedness condition.

The implication here is plainly that there was once a condition when the Youth was united with the Lily, and indeed he tells the Old Woman, when they first met, that he was really a Prince, but he had since fallen into a distressed state. This correlates closely to Steiner's view that once the ego was united with the spirit, it was not subject to evil. He refers to this as the condition of the human self, prior to the Biblical Fall of Mankind. This condition prevailed in a evolutionary cycle prior to the time when Lucifer and Ahriman became active in human evolution.[419]

The self and its (germinal) triune soul, at that pre-Fall of Man stage, were also able to be in the lap of the gods. It appears then, that this past life of Johannes in *Die Pforte*, as a person previously bonded in love to Maria, portrays not only the principle of reincarnation, but – similarly to the introduction of the child – it also serves to maintain the parallelism with the impersonal-allegorical thematic message of the *Märchen*, as seen by Steiner.

Returning now to the septenary human being, the fifth, sixth and seventh members of the septenary human organism in Steiner's writings constitute the triune human spirit. We noted earlier that in his Theosophie he maintains that these three members, existing in a germinal form, are separate from the 'human soul'. *Die Pforte* incorporates a significant element in his anthroposophical worldview, with regard to the septenary human nature. In his advice on the subject of spiritual development, Steiner emphasizes that much

---
[418] Goethe, HA Bd. 6, S. 223.
[419] Steiner, Geheimwissenschaft *Die Weltentwickelung und der Mensch*

preparation has to be undergone by an aspirant to higher consciousness.

If this is omitted, then severe problems arise for such a person, and in any event, as *Die Pforte* portrays, there will be challenging times for the acolyte. In particular, Steiner emphasized that the attainment of genuine higher consciousness (and perceptions) demands a substantial ethical development before any enhanced cognitional capacities in the spiritual dimension of existence is attempted. In his book for aspirants seeking such developmental processes, "Knowledge of Higher Worlds, how is it attained?" he reiterates the following precept as the primary rule "When you attempt to take one step forward in knowledge of hidden truths, take three steps forward in the ethical improvement of your character."[420]

The reason for the stipulation of three steps in ethical development, rather than another quantity, say, two or four, was not explained by Steiner. It seems clear that, given Steiner's view of human consciousness as triune, that this rule affirms that the spiritualization process which enables initiation to occur, is based on the concept of spiritualizing the three primary dynamics in human consciousness. That is, thinking, emotion and will need to be ethically ennobled and attuned to the spiritual, if higher consciousnesses is to be attained. The triune spirit will emerge from its lower aspect,

---

[420] Rudolf Steiner, Wie erlangt man Erkenntnisse der Höheren Welten? (Dornach: RSV 1982) 67.

the triune soul. As we saw in Section 4e, in Steiner's model of the sevenfold human being, the dynamic underlying the three souls – thinking, feeling and volition – can be subject to a spiritualizing process.

This process gradually brings the triune human spirit into being. In his lectures and writings on meditation and higher consciousness, Steiner maintains that it is the spiritualizing of these three consciousness dynamics – thinking, emotion and will – which leads to the development of Imagination, Inspiration and Intuition. That is, that within the dynamics of logical thought, emotional capacity and the capability for will, respectively, the potential for these three higher faculties are present.[421] This conclusion is supported by the role of the three women, Luna, Astrid and Philia in *Die Pforte*, for they have to undertake activity without which Johannes cannot attain to spiritual consciousness, to the realm of the Spirit, the Idea.

In summary, underlying *Die Pforte*'s rhetoric is Steiner's view of the human being as a body-soul-spirit entelechy, which has in total seven elements to its constitution, providing the ego is counted as a single entity with dualistic qualities, not as two separate entities. In addition to the physical body, there is secondly, an energy organism that maintains the physical body, and sustains consciousness processes within the soul, to the extent that these are interlinked with the physical body. He designates this entelechy as the life force body or ether-body.

Thirdly there is a soul, with its three consciousness dynamics. Fourthly, there is also an 'ego' or sense of selfhood, within which the eternal ego is active. Furthermore, the human being also possesses a triune spiritual element that is generally only present as a potentiality; these constitute the fifth, sixth and seventh members of human nature. This spiritual element is

---

[421] Rudolf Steiner, *Das Seelenleben des Menschen und seine Entwickelung zur Imagination, Inspiration und Intuition,* in Was wollte das Goetheanum und was soll die Anthroposophie? (Dornach: VRSN, 1961) 67- 90.

commonly unsuspected, and is therefore usually undeveloped; it requires specific inner effort to awaken this. The emergence of the spiritual aspects of the human being occurs as effort is made to spiritualize the triune soul.

FINAL CONCLUSIONS

Firstly, it is clear then that the adoption of, and dramatic adaptation of, Goethe's *Märchen* by Steiner, for his drama, *Die Pforte der Einweihung* has its origin in the convictions of Steiner that,

1: Goethe's view of spirituality is closely related to the anthroposophical worldview, and both are allied to the Rosicrucian movement of the late Middle Ages and the Renaissance.

2: That spiritual perception, like sensory perceiving, is inherently viable because it derives from the efficacy of the postulated ether-body, and this enables viable spiritual enlightenment.

Secondly, it is clear that the rhetoric of *Die Pforte* is intended to didactically communicate, in an artistic medium, the following esoteric convictions which are central to Steiner's anthroposophy:

A: That reincarnation and karma are real dynamics affecting human life, and offer a rational and accurate explanation for the differing destinies and abilities in human life.

B: That the philosophically assumed limits to knowledge are not valid, because human cognitional power can be extended beyond their present boundaries through meditation, which gives access to higher consciousness states.

C: That human life unfolds on Earth as a microcosmic reflection of a sevenfold macrocosmic evolutionary template.

D: That the attainment of spiritual consciousness is linked to the ethical refinement of the human being, especially the conscience, and this is linked to a subtle influence from within the ethers, of Christ Jesus.

E: That the Earth is a living being, possessing subtle spiritual levels of Being to which humanity is subtly linked, and that the continuance of unethical activity and attitudes in humanity is harmful to this realm.

F: That in the quest for spiritual development, the triune human soul must resist the influences of a twofold source of unethical tendencies. The soul must seek to allow a transformation of its triune qualities into a triune spiritual entity.

G: That artistic media offer a valuable method for the instruction of people into spiritual themes, and also that artistic experience is a valuable assistance in attaining to spirituality.

The overall perspective of Steiner's on the need for a spiritual holistic attitude, and the value of his own life's work in providing this, is conveyed, in an artistic manner, in a poem written in 1920,

The world without the spirit is
For the human being like a book
Written in a language
Yet of which he knows its content
determines life itself.
And spiritual science wants to strive
Towards the art of reading;
It believes itself to be necessary
Because it must believe
That it is demanded
By life itself
Into which humanity,
Through the forces of development
Of the present has entered.

The German text of the poem on the preceding page:

Die Welt ist ohne den Geist
Für den Menschen wie ein Buch,
Abgefaßt in einer Sprache,
Die er nicht lesen kann,
Doch von dem er weiß
Daß sein Inhalt lebenbestimmend ist.
Und Geisteswissenschaft will
Erstreben die Kunst des Lesens;
Sie hält sich für notwendig,
Weil sie glauben muß,
Daß sie von dem Leben
Selbst gefordert wird,
In das die Menschheit
Durch die Entwickelungskräfte
Der Gegenwart eingetreten ist.

6 BIBLIOGRAPHY

Note: Of the approximately 360 volumes that comprise Rudolf Steiner's Complete Works, approximately 320 of these are the transcripts of his lectures. The remaining 40 volumes comprise his written works, of these, 28 volumes expound his anthroposophical teachings, including his four dramas, and the rest comprise his correspondence, collected articles on literary subjects, comments on contemporary events and philosophical writings.

Books:

A: General literature

Apuleius, The Golden Ass, trans. Robert Graves, Harmondsworth: Penguin, 1956.
Bulwer-Lytton, E. Zanoni. Blauvelt: Rudolf Steiner Publications, 1971.
Besant, Annie. The Herald of the Star. Madras: The Theosophist office, 1912.
Blavatsky, H.P. The Secret Doctrine. Los Angeles: The Theosophy Company, 1925.
Cosmopoulos, Michael B. Greek mysteries; the archaeology and ritual of Greek sacred cults. London: Routledge, 2003.
Goethe, The Fairy Tale of the Green Snake and the Beautiful Lily. transl. Thomas Carlyle, New York: Steiner Books, 1979.
Goethes Werke. Hamburger Ausgabe (HA), Trunz, Erich. ed. Hamburg: Christian Wegner Verlag, 1955.
Goethes Briefe, ed. Erich Trunz, Vol 1, Hamburg: Christian Wegner Verlag, 1962.
Grassi, Ernesto. Rhetoric as Philosophy. University Park: Pennsylvania State University Press, 1908.
Kant, Immanuel. Kritik der reinen Vernunft. Berlin: Bruno Cassirer Verlag, 1913.

King, Charles William. The Gnostics and their remains. San Diego: Wizards Bookshelf, 1982.
McQueren, John. In search of deity; an essay in dialectical theism. London: SCM Press, 1984.
Maund, Barry. Perception. Chesham: Acumen Publishing, 2003.
Melas, Evi. ed. Temples and Sanctuaries of Ancient Greece. London: Thames and Hudson, 1973.
Middleton, Christopher. ed. Goethe: Selected Poems. Boston: Suhrkamp/Insel 1983.
Mommsen, Katharina. Goethe Märchen. Frankfurt: Insel Verlag, 1984.
Plato, The Republic, trans. Paul Shorey. London: Heinemann, 1963.
Parrini, Paolo. ed. Kant and Contemporary Epistemology. Dordrecht: KluwerAcademic Publishers, 1994.
Rhys, Ernest, ed. Five dialogues of Plato bearing on poetic inspiration. London: Dutton & Co, 1927.
Roberts, Marie. Gothic Immortals. London: Routledge, 1990.
Samuel, Richard. ed. Novalis Werke, Tagebücher und Briefe Friedrich von Hardenbergs, Bd. 1 München: Carl Hanser Verlag, 1978.
Schiller, Friedrich. Schillers Werke, Nationalausgabe , Bd 1, ed. Julius Petersen and Friedrich Reißner. Weimar: Hermann Böhlaus Nachfolger, 1943.

B: Rudolf Steiner texts

Steiner, Rudolf. Anthroposophie als Kosmosophie. Dornach: RSV, 1972.
Stener, Rudolf. Bewußtsein, Leben, Form. Dornach: RSV, 2001.
Steiner, Rudolf. Briefe 1 1881-1890. Dornach: RSV, 1985.
Steiner, Rudolf. Das Christentum als Mystische Tatsache. Dornach: RSV, 1976.
Steiner, Rudolf. Das Ereignis der Christus-Erscheinung in der ätherischen Welt. Dornach: VRSN, 1965.

Steiner, Rudolf. Das Ewige in der Menschenseele. Dornach: VRSN, 1962.

Steiner, Rudolf. Das Johannes Evangelium. Dornach: RSV, 1981.

Steiner Rudolf. Das Johannes Evangelium im Verhältnis zu den drei anderenEvangelien. Dornach: RSV, 1975.

Steiner, Rudolf. Das Wesen der Ewigkeit und die Natur der Menschenseele im Lichte der Geisteswissenschaft. PAV, 1912.

Steiner, Rudolf. Der Christus-Impuls und die Entwickelung des Ich-Bewußtseins.Dornach: VRSN, 1961.

Steiner, Rudolf. Der Jahreskreislauf als Atmungsvorgang der Erde und die vier großen Festezeiten. Dornach: RSV, 1980.

Steiner, Rudolf. Der Münchner Kongress Pfingsten 1907. Dornach: RSV, 1977.

Steiner, Rudolf. Der Orient im Lichte des Okzidents. Dornach: VRSN, 1960.

Steiner, Rudolf. Die befruchtende Wirking der Anthroposophie auf der Fachwissenschaften. Dornach: RSV, 1977.

Steiner, Rudolf. Die Brücke zwischen der Weltgeistigkeit und dem Physischen des Menschen. Dornach: VRSN, 1970.

Steiner, Rudolf. Die Ergänzung heutiger Wissenschaften durch Anthroposophie. Dornach: RSV, 1973.

Steiner, Rudolf. Die Erziehung des Kindes vom Gesichtspunkte der Geistes. Dornach; VRSN, 1981.

Steiner, Rudolf. Die geistige Hierarchien und ihre Widerspiegelung in der physischen Welt. Dornach: RSV, 1991.

Steiner, Rudolf. Die geistigen Wesenheiten in den Himmelskörpern und Naturreichen. Dornach: RSV, 1974.

Steiner, Rudolf. Die Geheimnisse – ein Weihnachts– und Ostergedicht von Goethe. Dornach: RSV, 1977.

Steiner, Rudolf. Die Geheimwissenschaft im Umriss. Dornach: RSV, 1977.

Steiner, Rudolf. Die geistige Vereinigung der Menschheit durch den Christus-Impuls. Dornach: VRSN, 1968.

Steiner, Rudolf. Die Mission der neuen Geistesoffenbarung. Dornach: RSV, 1975.

Steiner, Rudolf. Die neue Geistigekit und das Christus-Erlebnis des zwanzigsten Jahrhunderts. Dornach: VRSN, 1970.

Steiner, Rudolf. Die pädagogische Praxis vom Gesuchtspunkte geisteswissenschaftlicher Menschenerkenntnis. Dornach: RSV, 1982.

Steiner, Rudolf. Die Philosophie der Freiheit. Dornach: RSV, 1973.

Steiner, Rudolf. Die Rätsel der Philosophie. Dornach; VRSN, 1961.

Steiner, Rudolf. Die Theosophie des Rosenkreuzers. Dornach: RSV, 1979.

Steiner, Rudolf. Die Weihnachtstagung zur Begründung der Allgemeinen Anthroposophischen Gesellschaft, 1924-1224. Dornach: VRSN,1963.

Steiner, Rudolf. Die Welt der Sinne und die Welt des Geistes. Dornach: VRSN, 1959.

Steiner, Rudolf. Die Welträsel und die Anthroposophie. Dornach: VRSN, 1966.

Steiner, Rudolf. Die Wirklichkeit der höheren Welten. Dornach: VRSN, 1962.

Steiner, Rudolf. Entsprechungen zwischen Mikrokosmos und Makrokosmos, Der Mensch – eine Hieroglyphe des Weltenall. Dornach: RSV, 1987.

Steiner, Rudolf. Entwürfe, Fragmente und Paralipomena zu den vier MysterienDramen. Dornach: VRSN, I969.

Steiner, Rudolf. Erfahrungen des Übersinnlichen. Dornach: VRSN, 1970.

Steiner, Rudolf. Ergebnissse der Geistesforschung. Dornach: VRSN, 1960.

Steiner, Rudolf. Esoterische Betrachtungen: karmisher Zusammenhänge Bd. 5,Dornach: RSV, 1975.

Steiner, Rudolf. Geist und Stoff, Leben und Tod. Dornach: VRSN, I961.

Steiner, Rudolf. Geisteswissenschaft als Lebensgut. VRSN, 1959.

Steiner, Rudolf. Geisteswissenschaftliche Menschenkunde. Dornach: RSV, 1973.

Steiner, Rudolf. Das Johannes Evangelium. Dornach: RSV 1981.
Steiner, Rudolf. Geistige Wesenheiten und ihre Widerspiegelung in der physischen Welt. Dornach: RSV, 1972.
Steiner, Rudolf. Gesammelte Aufsätze zur Dramaturgie. Dornach: VRSN, 1960.
Steiner, Rudolf. Gesammelte Aufsätze zur Literatur. Dornach: RSV, 1971.
Steiner, Rudolf. Goethes Geheime Offenbarung In Seinem Märchen von der Grünen Schlange und der Schonen Lilien. Dornach: RSV, 1982.
Steiner, Rudolf. Goethes Naturwissenschaftliches Schriften. Dornach: RSV, 1973.
Steiner, Rudolf. Goethes Weltanschauung. Dornach: RSV, 1979.
Steiner, Rudolf. Heilfaktoren für den sozialen Organismus. Dornach: VRSN, 1969.
Steiner, Rudolf. Individuelle Geistwesen und ihr Wirken in der Seele des Menschen. Dornach: RSV 1974.
Steiner, Rudolf. Innere Entwicklungsimpulse der Menschheit. Dornach: VRSN, 1964.
Steiner, Rudolf. Inneres Wesen des Menschen und Leben zwischen Tod und neuer Geburt, Dornach: RSV, 1978.
Steiner, Rudolf. Kosmogonie. Dornach: RSV, 1970.
Steiner, Rudolf. Lecture, Berlin 30th Oct 1904, archive manuscript.
Steiner, Rudolf. Lecture 28th Dec 1905, archive manuscript.
Steiner, Rudolf. Luzifer Gnosis. Dornach: VRSN, 1960.
Steiner, Rudolf. Meditative Betrachtungen und Anleitungen zur Vertiefung der Heilkunst. Dornach: VRSN, 1967.
Steiner, Rudolf. Mein Lebensgang. Stuttgart: Verlag Freies Geistesleben, 1975.
Steiner, Rudolf. Menschengeschichte im Lichte der Geistesforschung. Dornach: VRSN, 1962.
Steiner, Rudolf. Menschheitsentwickelung und Christus-Erkenntnis. Dornach: VRSN, 1967.
Steiner, Rudolf. Menschenschicksale und Völkerschicksale. Dornach: VRSN, 1981

Steiner, Rudolf. Menschenwerden, Weltenseele und Weltengeist. Dornach: VRSN, 1967.
Steiner, Rudolf. Metamorphosen des Seelenlebens. Dornach: RSV, 1972.
Steiner, Rudolf. Mysterienwahrheiten und Weihnachtsimpulse. Dornach: VRSN,1966.
Steiner, Rudolf. Philosophie und Anthroposophie: 1904-1918. Dornach: VRSN 1965.
Steiner, Rudolf. Seelenübungen mit Wort- und Sinnbild Meditationen. Dornach: RSV,1997.
Steiner, Rudolf. Spirituelle Seelenlehre und Weltbetrachtung. Dornach: RSV, 1972.
Steiner, Rudolf. Sprachgestaltung und Dramatische Kunst. Dornach: VRSN, 1969.
Steiner, Rudolf. Theosophie. Dornach: R St Vlg, 1975.
Steiner, Rudolf. Über die Astrale Welt und die Devachan. Dornach: RSV, 1999.
Steiner, Rudolf. Über Philosophie, Geschichte und Literatur. Dornach: RSV, 1983.
Steiner, Rudolf. archive lecture, date unknown, ca. 1914.
Steiner, Rudolf. Ursprung und Ziel der Menschen. Dornach: RSV, 1981.
Steiner, Rudolf. Vom Leben des Menschen und der Erde. Dornach: RSV, 1980.
Steiner, Rudolf. Vor dem Tore der Theosophie, Dornach: RSV, 1978
Steiner, Rudolf. Vorträge und Kurse über Christlich-Religiöse Wirken. Dornach: RSV,1993.
Steiner, Rudolf. Wahrheit und Wissenschaft: Vorspiel einer Philosophie der Freiheit. Dornach: RSV, 1980.
Steiner, Rudolf. Wahrspruchworte. Dornach: RSV, 1969.
Steiner, Rudolf. Was wollte daß Goetheanum und was soll die Anthroposophie? Dornach: VRSN, I961.
Steiner, Rudolf. Wege und Ziele des geistigen Menschen. Dornach: RSV, 1973.
Steiner, Rudolf. Wie Erlangt man Erkenntnisse der Höheren Welten? Dornach: RSV, 1982.
Steiner, Rudolf. Welt, Erde und Mensch. Dornach: RSV, 1974.

Steiner, Rudolf. Wo und wie findet man den Geist? Dornach: VRSN, 1961.
Szondi, Peter. Das lyrische Drama des Fin de Siècle. Frankfurt am Main: Suhrkamp Verlag, 1975.
Ungar, Frederick. Trans., The Eternal Feminine: selected poems of Goethe, New York: F. Ungar Publishing Co. 1980.
Vince, Ronald W. Ancient and Medieval Theatre London: Greenwood press 1984.
Yates, Frances A. The Rosicrucian Enlightenment. London: Routledge, 1972.
The Zend-Avesta, part 2, The Sirozahs, Yasts und Nyayis; trans. James Darmesteter. Delhi: Motilal Banarsidass, 1884, repr. 1981.

C: Literature on Steiner

Wieberger, Hella. ed. Rudolf Steiner und die Tempellegende. Dornach: RSV, 1979.
Rittelmeyer, Friedrich. Rudolf Steiner enters my life. London: The Christian Community Press, 1931.
Rittelmeyer, Friedrich. The Lord's Prayer. London: The Christian Community Press, 1931.
Mann, William and Liselotte. The Calendar of the Soul. transl. Stroud: Hawthorn Press, 1990.
Lindenberg, Christoph. Rudolf Steiner; eine Biographie. Stuttgart: Verlag Freies Geistesleben, 1997.
Hoffmann, David Marc. ed. Dokumente zur "Philosophie der Freiheit". Dornach: RSV, 1994.
Bettle, Erika and Vlerl, Kurt. Eds. Erinnerungen an Rudolf Steiner. Stuttgart: Verlag Freies Geistesleben, 1979.
The Portal of Initiation, trans. Adam Bittleston. Englewood: Rudolf Steiner Publications, 1961.

Journals and periodicals:

Beiträge zur Rudolf Steiner Gesamtausgabe, ed. Walter Kugler. Nr. 121.
Blätter für Anthroposophie, ed. H. E.Lauer, Nov.1966.

Mensch und Welt 3, ed. Gerhard Wehr, 1968.
Mitteilungen für die Mitglieder der Anthroposophischen Gesellschaft -Theosophischen Gesellschaft. ed. Mathilde Scholl, April 1913, No.1
Mitteilungen für die Mitglieder der Deutschen Sektion der Theosophischen Gesellschaft ed. Mathilde Scholl. January 1913, 15.
Philosophy and Rhetoric, ed. Donald Philip Verene, Vol 17, No. 4
The herald of the Star. July 1912. Vol. 1, No.3
World Theosophy, centenary issue, Aug. 1931, Vol 1, No. 8
Zeitschrift für Religions- und Geistesgeschichte, 48th annual edition,Ed. H. Julius. 1966.

Reference works:

A Latin-English Dictionary. eds. Rev. John. T. White and Rev. J.E. Riddle, London: Longman, 1862.
Dictionary of Word Origins. ed. J.T. Shipley, Totowa: Littlefield Adams, 1967.
Encyclopaedia Brittanica, ed. Warren E. Preece. Chicago: William Benton, 1971 vol. 8.
Kindlers Literature Lexikon im dtv, ed. Gert Woerner, Rolf Geisler and Rudolf Radler, 1970.
Historisches Wörterbuch der Philosophie, ed. Joachim Ritter. Darmstadt: Wissenschaftliche Buchgesellschaft, 1971-1998.
Deutsche National Literatur, Goethes Werke, vols. 33,36, Naturwissenschaftliche Schriften, ed. Rudolf Steiner, Berlin: Verlag von W. Spemann.
Lexikon der Platonischen Begriffe. ed. H. Peris, Bern: Francke Verlag, 1973.
The New International Dictionary of the Christian Church. Exeter: ed. J.D. Douglas,The Paternoster Press, 1974.
The Legends of the Jews, Louis Ginzberg, Vol. V. Philadelphia: Jewish Public.Soc. of America, 1968.
The New International Dictionary of the Christian Church, ed. J.D. Douglas, Exeter: Paternoster Press, 1974.

The Oxford Classical Dictionary, ed. N. G. L. Hammond, 2nd edit. Oxford: Clarendon Press, 1970.
The Oxford Dictionary of Christian Names. ed. E.G.Withycombe, London: OUP, 1950.
The Oxford Dictionary of English Etymology. ed. C. T. Onions, Oxford: OUP, 1966.
The Penguin Dictionary of Philosophy. ed Thomas Mautner. London: Penguin, 1997.
Theosophical Glossary, ed. H. P.Blavatsky, London: Theosophical Publishing Co, 1892.

Note to the 2018 issue of this thesis.

Dr.Anderson is the author of many other books, as well as numerous articles. These writings present, and comment on, various aspects of Rudolf Steiner's anthroposophy, or associated themes.

The reader can find these further works listed on his website:

www.rudolfsteinerstudies.com

www.ingramcontent.com/pod-product-compliance
Lightning Source LLC
Chambersburg PA
CBHW020330240426
43665CB00043B/197